INFORMATION TECHNOLOGY AND ORGANIZATIONS

Challenges of New Technologies

Mehdi Khosrowpour

IDEA GROUP PUBLISHING
Harrisburg, U.S.A. • London, U.K.

Senior Editor:	Mehdi Khosrowpour
Managing Editor:	Jan Travers
Printed at:	BookCrafters

Published in the United States of America by
Idea Group Publishing
Olde Liberty Square
4811 Jonestown Road, Suite 230
Harrisburg, PA 17109
Tel: 717-541-9150
Fax: 717-541-9159

and in the United Kingdom by
Idea Group Publishing
3 Henrietta Street
Covent Garden
London WC2E 8LU
Tel: 071-240 0856
Fax: 071-379 0609

British Cataloguing in Publication Data
A Cataloguing in Publication record for this book is available from the British Library

ISBN 1-878289-18-7

Other IDEA GROUP Publishing Books

Table of Contents

Part I: Information Technology and Organizational Issues 1

CHAPTER 1
Improving Organization Absorption of Emerging Technologies: A Socio-Technical Approach 3
Godwin Udo, *Tennessee Technological University*
Tor Guimaraes, *Tennessee Technology University*

CHAPTER 2
Designing Architectures for Emerging Information Technologies: A Multiple Methodology Approach 31
Robert A. Stegwee, *University of Groningen*
Enno J. Ebels, *American Power Conversion Europe, SA*

CHAPTER 3
Evaluating IS Effectiveness: A Survey of Business Practice and Implications for Emerging Information Technologies 61
Edward J. Szewczak, *Canisius College*

CHAPTER 4
IThe Challenge of Implementing SIS Across the The Value Chain: A Case Study of Negative IT Consequences in a Supplier Firm 81
C.R. Sndograss, *Canisius College*
G. Rosenfelder, *Canisius College*
E.J. Szewczak, *Canisius College*

Part II: Emerging Technologies in the 1990s 101

CHAPTER 5
Emerging Applications of Computer Graphics in Support of Managerial Decision Making 103
Jerry A. Van Os, *Westminster College of Salt Lake City*

CHAPTER 6
Communication Challenge in Designing, Teaching and Using Emerging Information Technologies 131
Karen J. Pettingell, University of Texas, El Paso

CHAPTER 7
Expert Systems to Support Managerial Diagnosis and Evaluation 154
Nancy Green Hall, *Kennesaw State College*
P. Mohan Rao, *Salisbury State University*

CHAPTER 8
Example-Based Information Systems for Expert Managerial Decision Support 174
Aaron Patula, *Memphis State University*

CHAPTER 9
Expert Systems Development Issues Confronting Organizations in the Evolving Global Marketplace 203
Brenda L. Killingsworth, *East Carolina University*
Michael E. McLeod, *East Carolina University*

Part III: Strategies for Emerging Technologies ... 225

CHAPTER 10
Strategies for Information Resources Management: Developing Corporate-Wide Information Systems ... 226
Richard M. Kesner, *Babson College*

CHAPTER 11
Symbiosis: A Theoretical Foundation for the Development of Strategic Information Systems Alliances 250
Gregory B. Turner, *Mississippi State University*
Mark A. Mitchell, *Mississippi State University*
Ronald L. Berry, *Mississippi State University*

CHAPTER 12
Issues in Teaching Globalization in Information Systems 262
Mathew Klempa, *Cal State University-Dominguez Hills*

Part IV: Emerging Technologies Decisions 315

CHAPTER 13
Technology Choice and User Training: 316
A Tradeoff Perspective
Nancy C. Weida, *Bucknell University*

CHAPTER 14
An Overview of the Outsourcing Decision..................331
Karen Ketler, *Eastern Illinois University*
John Walstrom, *Eastern Illinois University*
Jennifer L. Wagner, *Roosevelt University*

CHAPTER 15
Implementing Decision Support Systems: Lessons 359
Learned From Implementing a Danish Regional
Computerized Economic-Demographic Model
Kim V. Andersen, *University of Copenhagen*

CHAPTER 16
CASE Tools as Work Redesign 386
Systems: Toward a Global View
Dwight A. Haworth, *University of Nebraska at Omaha*
Leah R. Pietron, *University of Nebraska at Omaha*

Glossary 407
Authors' Biographies 412
Index 416

ACKNOWLEDGMENT

Editing a book of this magnitude requires tremendous cooperation from everyone. Many thanks to all the authors of the chapters for their significant contribution to this book. Special thanks to Dr. Girish Subramanian at Penn State Harrisburg and Dr. Mohammad Dadashzadeh at Wichita State University for their valuable assistance in reviewing chapters for this book. I would also like to thank Dr. Krishna Dhir, Director of the School of Business Administration, Dr. Howard Sachs, Associate Dean of Research and Graduate Studies, and Dr. Ernie Dishner, Associate Provost and Dean of Faculty, all at Penn State Harrisburg for their support for my initiatives. Finally, I would like to thank Jan Travers at Idea Group Publishing for her hard work and devotion toward this book.

Mehdi Khosrowpour
Harrisburg, PA
September 1993

Part I

Information Technology and Organizational Issues

CHAPTER 1

IMPROVING ORGANIZATION ABSORPTION OF EMERGING TECHNOLOGIES: A SOCIO-TECHNICAL APPROACH

Godwin Udo and Tor Guimaraes
Tennessee Technological University

Business organizations are increasingly dependent on emerging Information Technology (IT) for their survival and growth. They can no longer afford a laissez faire attitude toward emerging technologies without incurring great risks. Given the increasing importance of emerging technologies to corporate health, a systematic process to identify, evaluate, acquire and implement available IT is proposed. The approach uses the basic project selection process to balance the need for organization innovativeness against the need for control over resources use and return on investment. Further, the project selection process follows the socio-technical framework for reducing commonly encountered problems and balancing the major components of the emerging IT adoption phenomenon: new technology, various stakeholders and the different tasks involved.

The importance and magnitude of information technology (IT) applications in business have increased greatly since their inception in the mid 1950s. The initial efforts used to be focused on transforming existing manual procedures into accounting applications such as accounts payable, accounts receivable, and payroll systems. Systems development at this stage consisted primarily of program coding and system developers were mostly concerned with the technical aspects of the projects. This limited view of IT system development has since given way to one with a much broader perspective where customers, suppliers, and a wide variety of end-users play important roles. Also, over the years, the technical aspects of IT systems development have assumed a secondary role with the primary concerns being with system quality, user satisfaction, intangible benefits, organizational relevance and project management considerations.

Today, business organizations are extremely dependent on emerging IT for their survival and growth. For several reasons, they can no longer neglect emerging IT absorption without incurring great risks due to several reasons. First, IT applications are increasingly becoming integrated parts of a corporate-wide IT infrastructure which many times directly connects the company to customers and suppliers, as well as connects the various organization sub-units. In such environment, many of the new applications tend to be quite large and expensive. The unsuccessful implementation of such applications is extremely wasteful of company resources and in many cases may financially bankrupt the organization.

Second, IT systems are increasingly being used by firms to gain competitive advantage in the form of cost savings, product/service quality improvement and/or differentiation, and overall customer satisfaction (Ives & Learmonth, 1984; Keen, 1981). Organizations are increasingly suffering major consequences from competitors getting ahead in the use of IT if they lag in the identification, selection, development and successful implementation of strategically important applications.

Third, the importance of effectively using emerging IT to gain strategic advantage is exacerbated by a steady increase in business competition which manifests itself through the shortened life cycle of products and services, the steady increase in global competition, the relentless need for cost control and the major emphasis being put on speed to market management.

Fourth, the number and sophistication of newly emerging technologies continue to increase as their potential market grows beyond mainframes to include departmental machines, personal computers and workstations, LANs, and different configurations of client-server technology with the power to run sophisticated applications with obvious business benefits. The number of relatively new technologies being widely deployed in industry include LANs, client-servers, various expert systems development approaches (methodologies and shells), imaging systems, CASE tools, etc. Few organizations have established a systematic approach to handle the number and diversity of emerging IT in an effective fashion. What we have today is piece meal experimentation with a particular technology or tool depending on whether or not someone in a particular company is aware of the technology, is willing and able to "sponsor" the particular technology or tool, and is attempting the application amidst his/her organization's operational/political jungle.

While much of what is being proposed here is applicable to "older" IT as well, the increasing pace of new IT introduction into the market place, the increasing company dependency on emerging IT for survival and growth, the increasing complexity of new IT absorption due to greater integration of systems and various stakeholders' perspectives, exacerbates the need for organizations to effectively manage the absorption of new IT applications. A systematic process to identify, evaluate, acquire and implement recently available IT must be established. The purpose of this paper is to propose a practical approach to improve organization absorption of emerging technologies by: (1) using the basic project selection process to balance the need for organization innovativeness versus control over resources use and return on the investment; (2) using a socio-technical approach in project selection for reducing commonly encountered problems and ensuring a proper balance between the major components of the emerging technology adoption phenomenon: new technology, different groups of people and business tasks involved. The next section discusses the conceptual framework underlying our proposal.

EFFECTIVE ORGANIZATION ABSORPTION OF EMERGING IT

Effective absorption of emerging IT requires that organization managers understand and provide capabilities for five major sub-functions: (1) technology forecasting and evaluation, (2) pro-active information requirements definition, (3) pro-active business process re-engineering, (4) business process integration, and (5) appropriate project selection and implementation.

As discussed in the introduction, the increase in business competitiveness and importance of IT as a competitive weapon has created considerable pressure for organizations to carefully select, acquire and implement IT applications. Emerging technologies, if properly deployed, have the potential to shift competitive advantage. Therefore, organizations must establish a technology forecasting function to identify and follow promising technologies from research lab ideas to field test, commercial availability and cost/effective application tools. Many large organizations have created technology forecasting groups, but smaller organizations can also implement this function by buying commercially available reports on specific technologies.

Concurrently with technology forecasting, organizations must proactively attempt to define information requirements important to accomplish its goals and objectives. Methodologies helpful in this area are widely available: Critical Success Factors, Business Systems Planning, etc. Similarly, organizations cannot afford to allow their "bread and butter" business systems to decay and/or grow obsolete. Methodologies similar to the above can be used to re-design business processes to keep up or gain advantage over competitors. What can be done to develop new applications or re-engineer existing ones is many times directly dependent on the technology available, and on the proper matching of cost/effective technologies to the business processes involved. The latter is most critical and can only be accomplished by an effective project selection, development and implementation process. This process is key to ensure that only useful, cost/effective technologies will be acquired to maximize the organization's investment in IT applications.

Last, effective new technology absorption must take into consideration that a major corporate application is likely to be linked to many others in the organization, and increasingly is likely to affect various departments, and in many cases customers and suppliers. The interests and opinions of the different groups of people affected by a new or changing application must be taken into consideration. Emerging technologies are likely to be poorly understood and can have strong impact on the social/political structure of the organization. The project selection, development and implementation mechanism must provide an opportunity for the different parties to express their views, thus minimizing the risk of disfunctional behavior later on in the implementation process.

While all five sub-functions enumerated above are important, project selection is where most of the problems occur today because it is by far the most complex one to perform effectively, given its requirement to balance new technology with established people's interests and aspirations, and with existing organization goals and objectives. Thus, the focus of this article is on project selection to effectively manage emerging IT absorption. The next section discusses the many problems associated with project selection today.

IT PROJECT SELECTION PROBLEMS

As we have learned over the years, an effective evaluation and selection process can do much to increase the likelihood of a system's success. A careless project evaluation can lead to improper system selection which in turn can lead to an ineffective system or abandoned project as is often the case with many firms. Based on a survey study, McFarlan (1981) attributes IT project failures to lack of assessment of individual project risks and the after effects of the risk on a portfolio of projects. White (1984) concludes that IT project failures are caused by how participants interact with each other and how they perceive work-related issues. In their recent study, Ewusi-Mensah and Przasnyski (1991) found information system projects failing mainly because of issues that relate to organizational behavior and politics. Allowing technically oriented personnel to introduce new technologies into the organization without carefully considering its behavioral and business impact is an invitation to disaster.

System projects selection typically take place in a highly political environment (Hirschheim & Smithson, 1987; Ginzberg, 1979; Melone & Wharton, 1984; Guimaraes & McKeen, 1988). In most organizations, the criteria and the mechanisms for measuring them seem to assume away the obvious presence of organizational bias. Most of the project and evaluation/selection criteria and mechanisms used in practice operate under the pretention that project selection is an objective technical/economic business exercise, whereas the information systems to be developed have both technical and social components, and the organization where the project will be implemented is comprised of people who are subjective and interest-seeking. Some authors (Hirschheim & Smithson, 1987) have stressed the importance of a comprehensive project evaluation method which has to incorporate both subjective and objective evaluation criteria. Turner (1982) has warned that if organizations fail to adequately address the political and behavioral problems with project selection, or if all the different interest groups are not satisfied with a project, project failure rate will continue to be high. Bostrom and Heinen (1977) demonstrated how the socio-technical approach could be adopted for solving systems design problems.

IS project failure is a common experience to most corporations (Bienkowski, 1989). But since no one is willing to discuss the issue openly, organizations often assume the experience to be particular to them. Determining the causes of project failures continues to be a difficult challenge for both academicians and practitioners. Pinto and Mantel (1990) have identified the following three reasons that make the task of determining causes of project failure difficult. First, the concept of project failure is nebulous; different people have different definitions and cases to exemplify project failure, which suggests a lack of consensus on some of the important issues involved. Second, most of the research studies on the topic are not based on practical experience and as such, are limited in their usefulness. A third reason is based on the fact that causes of project failure are contingent upon the characteristics of project in question, and no two projects are exactly alike. Causes of project failure also depend on the phase of the project life cycle.

There is a growing body of literature on the subject of project selection and implementation failure. One group of studies deals with classifying and quantifying project benefits (Keen, 1981; King & Schrems, 1978; Knutsen & Nolan, 1974); this led to the development of tools for modeling and assessment of benefits to support project selection process. A second group of studies attempts to investigate the causes of project failure and suggest methods to reduce the problem by eliminating or reducing the causes (Bienkowski, 1989; Pinto & Mantel, 1990; Pinto & Slevin, 1987; McFarlan, 1981; Keider, 1984). A third group of studies deals with ways to more systematically and objectively identify projects that need to be abandoned to avoid unnecessary future expenses associated with project failure Ewusi-Mensah & Przasnyski, 1991; Staw & Ross, 1987; Balanchadra & Raelin, 1980). The last group of studies focuses on project selection mechanisms rather than techniques (Doll & Mesbah, 1984; Grindlay, 1981; Guimaraes & McKeen, 1989); this has led to a realization that the project selection process plays a critical role in project success or failure.

Before going on to discuss the socio-technical approach and what it can do to help improve the project selection process, the remainder of this section addresses specific reasons why projects fail and groups project selection problems into ten major categories which can be remedied by a socio-technical approach to the selection process. Bienkowski (1989) has given 10 reasons for IS project failures: (1) The project is a solution in search of a problem and as such its objectives are not clear. (2) Only the project team is interested in the end result, end-user participation is not considered. (3) No one has the overall responsibility of the project execution. (4) The structure of the project plans are poorly defined. (5) The project plans lack sufficient details that can lead to oversight of important variables. (6) The cost of the project is underestimated because of lack of foresight for the total project picture. (7) Top management is not committed to the project and as a result insufficient non-financial support is provided to the project. (8) There is no feedback to compare the progress to the actual plans of the project, which often leads to gradual departure from its original plans. (9) The project team members are not communicating enough among themselves. (10) The project is redirected from its original goals.

Keider (1984) studied the responses of 100 IS professionals and concluded that lack of knowledge of project management is the main cause of IS project failures. Some project teams know very little about existing project management tools or how to use them effectively. How well a project is managed depends to a large extent on the types of tools used (Mason & Swanson, 1981). McFarlan (1981) attributes project failures to lack of proper assessment of risks involved with individual projects and the ripple effects of such risks on an organization's project portfolios. Carroll (1988) identifies schedule and cost overruns as one of the frequent causes of project failure. These overruns are based on original estimates, which might have been underestimations of the total time and budget to complete the projects, but just as likely they result from a long series of small set backs (Brooks, 1975). A project may also fail because of the rapidly changing technological base and the external environment of the project. A project can become obsolete before its completion due to quick and unexpected changes in technology (Brooks, 1975).

In their recent attempt to identify causes for information system project abandonment, Ewusi-Mensah and Przasnyski (1991) found that all types of projects are subject to abandonment, not just high risk, complex, or unstructured projects. They concluded that the explanation for information system project abandonments are multidimensional and complex. A more comprehensive technique is required to identify and deal with the causes of IS project failures, most of which emanate from the selection stage. It is possible to manage IS project failures like any other business situation (Devaney, 1991). A technique capable of fostering project selection based on factual, user-oriented criteria should be advocated.

As mentioned earlier, poor system design is another source of IS project failures. Where the IS design does not match the attributes of the users, the tasks, or organizations, the project has a high probability to fail. Bostrom and Heinen (1977) believe that poor system design is caused by faulty system designers perception (or frame of reference) of their organizations, end-users, and the business tasks involved. This can also be true of project selection teams, where the team does not have a full knowledge and appreciation of the users' needs, nature of their business tasks, and organizational goals and objectives.

Organizational bias has been identified as a major hindrance to successful IS project selection and implementation. Several studies (Hirschheim & Smithson, 1987; Ginzberg, 1979; Melone & Wharton,

1984) have dealt with the effects of organizational bias on some phases of IS development project. Guimaraes and McKeen (1988) evaluated the process of IS projects selection in order to assess the nature and extent of organizational bias implicit in the use of certain selection mechanisms, namely: top management, steering committee, user department, and IS department. Their results indicated a substantial degree of selection bias.

The significant biasing effect by each of the different project selection mechanisms suggests that each of the various interest groups (stakeholders) in an organization uses different cues when selecting systems projects. In other words, certain selection criteria are more important to one group than another. Much of the bias is due to differences in perspective such as department managers being solely interested in projects which directly benefit their own departments without considering the project's impact on other departments and the organization as a whole. A project evaluation/selection approach capable of preventing or reducing these problems should provide: (1) a broader evaluation perspective which includes technical/operational project evaluation criteria as well as factors which address the impact of the system on the organization as a whole and on the different groups interested in the project; (2) allowance for the inclusion of tangible and intangible benefits in the evaluation process; and (3) a vehicle to combine the objective technical/economical considerations and the people oriented subjective evaluation criteria which are extremely important for effective project selection.

For simplicity, we have consolidated the IT absorption problems discussed above into ten broad categories: (1) lack of knowledge and skills on IT management; (2) system design problems which represent a lack of "fit" between the technology and the people, tasks, and organization structure; (3) lack of IT specific objectives or non adherence to original IT goals; (4) misalignment of IT objectives with organizational and business unit goals; (5) poor IT planning; (6) isolated view of IT by different interest groups; (7) lack of support from top management and participation/commitment by users; (8) poor communication and feedback between the IT management committee and the other units in the organization; (9) inappropriate or insufficient IT evaluation tools; (10) poor Change Management Tools. Table 1 provides the literature sources for the specific problems under each category.

The main objective of this paper is to demonstrate how a socio-technical approach can be used in selecting IT projects to eliminate or minimize these ten categories of selection problems. Because new IT is not as well understood as more mature technology, project

Problem Category	Problems and References
• Lack of knowledge/skills on IT management	No Project director with full responsibility Bienkowski) Project plan poorly designed (Bienkowski) Insufficient training & knowledge (Tom) No experience with project management tools (Keider) Insufficient project risk analysis (McFarlan)
• System design problems	Faulty system designers' perception (Bostrom) Lack of reference to users' needs (Bostrom) Lack of "fit" between the technology and people (Bostrom) Only the project team is interested in the project (Bienkowski)
• Lack of IT specific objectives	Project is a solution in search of a problem (Bienkowski) Insufficient project risk analysis (McFarlan) Project is redirected from its original goals (Bienkowski) Project become obsolete soon after completion (Brooks)
• Misalignment of IT objectives with organizational goals	Top management lack interest and offer no support (Bienkowski) IT lacks Operational alignment (Walton) IT lacks strategic alignment (Burn) Users are not committed to IT (Bienkowski)
• Poor IT planning	Time over run (Carroll) Cost over run (Carroll) Overload due to lack of resources (Tom) Structure of the project plans are poorly defined (Bienkowski)
• Isolated view of IT	Organizational bias exists (Guimaraes & McKeen) IT does not operate optimally (Bostrom) Lack of balance in IT portfolio (Guimaraes & McKeen) IT is underutilize (Tom)
• Lack of support from management and participation/commitment by users	Lack of financial support (Bienkowski) Users are dissatisfied with IT (Tom) IT lacks official approval (Tom)
• Poor communication and feedback	No feedback to compare progress to actual plans (Bienkowski) Overreliance on the system for remote

Table 1: Summary of Emerging IT Project Selection Problems

Problem Category	Problems and References
	communication (Tom) Disappointing results of system use (Tom)
• Inappropriate or insufficient IT evaluation tools	Rewards that emphasize operational efficiency only (Tom) Repeated mistakes in future IT projects A false conclusion on IT success or failure
• Poor Change Management Tools	Low employee morale (Tom) Opposite effects of what was expected from IT (Walton) Disaster in management and control of business operations (Jaikumar) Political and power conflicts (Tom)

Table 1: Contd.

selection and implementation mistakes are more likely. Further, new IT is increasingly being brought in as part of an organization's IT infrastructure, it must integrate well among other systems, user communities and other stakeholders (development groups, vendors, suppliers, management groups, etc). Thus, our proposal is particularly applicable to emerging IT.

FUNDAMENTALS OF SOCIO-TECHNICAL PHILOSOPHY

The concept of socio-technical systems was first advocated in the early 1950's by a team at the Tavistock Institute of Human Relations, London, England (Trist & Bamforth, 1951). It is the concept which explains the interactions in a work place between machines/tools and people, their tasks, and organizational structure. In this concept, every organization is made of two subsystems: the technical and the social, which are so closely related that changes in one affect the performance of the other. The technical subsystem is concerned with the procedure, technology, and operations needed to provide the products or services the organization is designed for. The social subsystem is about human behavior—how people perceive, value, and react to situations and effects. According to the socio-technical concept, the close relationships between the subsystems make it counterproductive to draw a boundary between people and technology since they are integral parts of the same system (Vaill, 1967).

The concept is based on the simple fact that machines/tools

place limits on the type of task structure while the task structure, in turn, has its own social and psychological requirements. Pictorially, the concept of socio-technical system shows the relationships or interactions in a diamond form as illustrated in Figure 1. The goal of the socio-technical system is to make a decision that lies with the ideal center point X, which is where all parts of the system are equitably satisfied. In essence, the different parts of a socio-technical system are so closely connected that if the link breaks between any two parts, the whole system is significantly affected. For the best results to be achieved, the effects of each part on the other parts of the system have to be considered jointly at any point in time of the system's life span. The approach is based on the assumption that people are willing to contribute to the overall goals of the organization, use their skills to the fullest, eager to learn and adapt to a changing condition, and able to master new skill requirements. These philosophical underpinnings of the socio-technical approach can help IS designers develop a better frame of reference toward end-users, which in turn, can lead to improved system design (Bostrom & Heinen, 1977). We propose that the same approach is useful for increasing project selection effectiveness.

The goal of a socio-technical approach is to minimize the friction caused by the differences in individual and departmental goals within an organization. These differences cause a boundary to arise

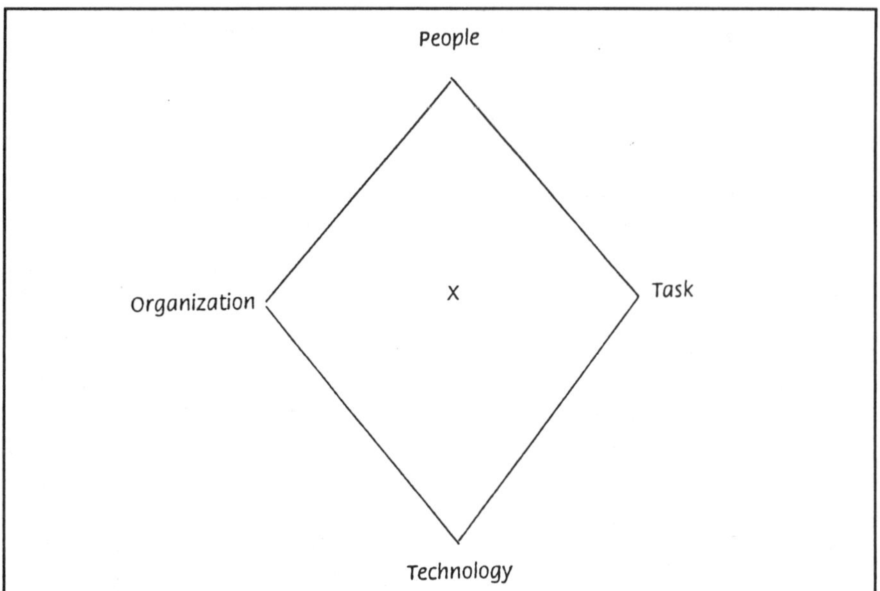

Figure 1: S-T Approach to Technologies Absorption

between them, thus making the system or process less effective. A socio-technical system attempts to set goals relevant to all the parties involved. According to Bostrom and Heinen (1977), the goal of socio-technical systems is "to optimize the uniqueness of the organization's technical requirements along with the needs and values of its individual members into a productive organization with a high quality of working life." This is increasingly important as new technology is to be integrated with existing systems affecting end-users throughout the organization. Optimizing several opposing goals of different parts of a system is referred to as joint or dual optimization. It does not imply a system that is both socially and technically optimal since some compromise between the social and technical subsystems has to be made. Rather, it implies a system that is wholly optimal. To design a system that satisfies the goals of the individual parts is difficult (Sharma, Conrath & Dilts, 1991), but several research efforts have been directed toward this end (Peters & Waterman, 1982). Another goal of a socio-technical approach which makes it specially suitable for managing the absorption of fast changing emerging technologies is that of producing a work system capable of adapting to a changing environment, adding flexibility and learning capability to a work system by providing effective feedback between the different groups and other components of the system. The feedback provides information on changes in technologies, organization structure, task requirements, and people's needs.

In the past, several authors (Bostrom & Heimen, 1977; Argyris, 1970; Mumford, Mercer, Mills & Weir, 1972; Tomeski, 1975; Hirschheim & Smithson, 1987) have suggested that information system problems be resolved using the socio-technical concept. Different information technologies can be viewed as socio-technical systems that involve the interactions of technology, organization and people which continually undergo mutual adjustments and discoveries (Laudon & Laudon, 1991). The socio-technical philosophy contends that a new information system should not be installed without considering the people who are part of it, the business processes re-engineering caused by the system, how the organizational structure will be affected, and how unplanned interactive effects may affect other subsystems within the organization.

The features of the socio-technical approach make it a powerful tool for addressing a wide variety of problems by enhancing the clarity of the interaction among people and the emerging IT being used, thus improving communication and control within the organization. Many specific advantages are associated with using the socio-technical approach for managing the absorption of emerging IT through the project selection process:

(1) More effective and sustained feedback which keeps the project evaluation and selection team on its original goals and helps identify problems in a timely fashion.
(2) A better understanding of the interaction among all parts of the system.
(3) More participation in decision making by all parties affected by the project.
(4) Increased sharing of responsibility for the evaluation and results from project selection.
(5) Increased task identity and work variety in the jobs related to the project as a result of project completion and system implementation.
(6) Increased system flexibility and organizational ability to learn and adapt to future changes.
(7) A greater feeling of participation and empowerment to individuals related to and affected by the project.
(8) Increased communication and reduced conflict between individuals and groups related to the project.
(9) Enhanced skills and knowledge about the project, the implemented system and the business tasks performed.

USING THE SOCIO-TECHNICAL APPROACH FOR IT ABSORPTION

Figure 2 demonstrates the step-by-step socio-technical approach for managing IT absorption through the project selection process, which if properly implemented can drastically reduce or prevent the five categories of problems listed earlier and deliver the benefits enumerated above. The proposed approach could be thought of as an evaluation process, which although formal and technical on the surface, can capture the essence of the social and political variables via an informal channel underneath. Such evaluation method would have to reflect a socio-technical equilibrium in its evaluation mechanisms. The proposed process comprises of seven steps:

(1) IT committee selection,
(2) objective formulation,
(3) criteria formulation,
(4) system evaluation/selection,
(5) formulating plans and implementation procedures,

(6) system introduction,
(7) post-implementation audit.

Though the steps have to be followed in the sequence shown in Figure 2, any step can be repeated at any time during the process. The next step should not be initiated unless the previous step passes a "delphi test". To demonstrate how the proposed method can be used, consider a firm whose top managers are faced with the task of deciding whether or not the firm should acquire the technology necessary to implement an institutional decision support system (IDSS) which by definition means a system used by several people throughout the organization. This hypothetical system is of great interest to several groups in the organization. The IS department would like to adapt a system alternative which uses the latest technology, has standardized procedures and interfaces well with existing systems. Top management would like to see a system alternative with moderate price tag but whose functions rate very favorably in terms of training time, ease of use, strategic support, and a short payback period. The accounting department would like a system with excellent capabilities for accounting tasks. The marketing, production department, human resources, and so forth, would wish to have a system alternative of their own, able to support their departmental requirements. The challenge then becomes to select and implement a system that combines the requirements and desires of all parties involved while at the same time achieving overall organizational goals. Table 2 shows the problems addressed by each phase (step) of the socio-technical approach thus providing an IT absorption process that accomplishes the best possible overall results.

Step 1: Selection of The IT Committee

The first step of socio-technical approach to IT absorption management is that of selecting the permanent steering committee members. The committee has to have proportional representation of all the relevant groups in the organization. The committee members can be selected in a number of democratic ways. For example, everyone in each participating department can be requested to nominate one or more persons they wish to represent their department in the selection team. The most nominated persons would then be selected. Or department heads can nominate a few representatives and ask the department members for approval. Appointment to a steering committee should be seen as an official assignment and

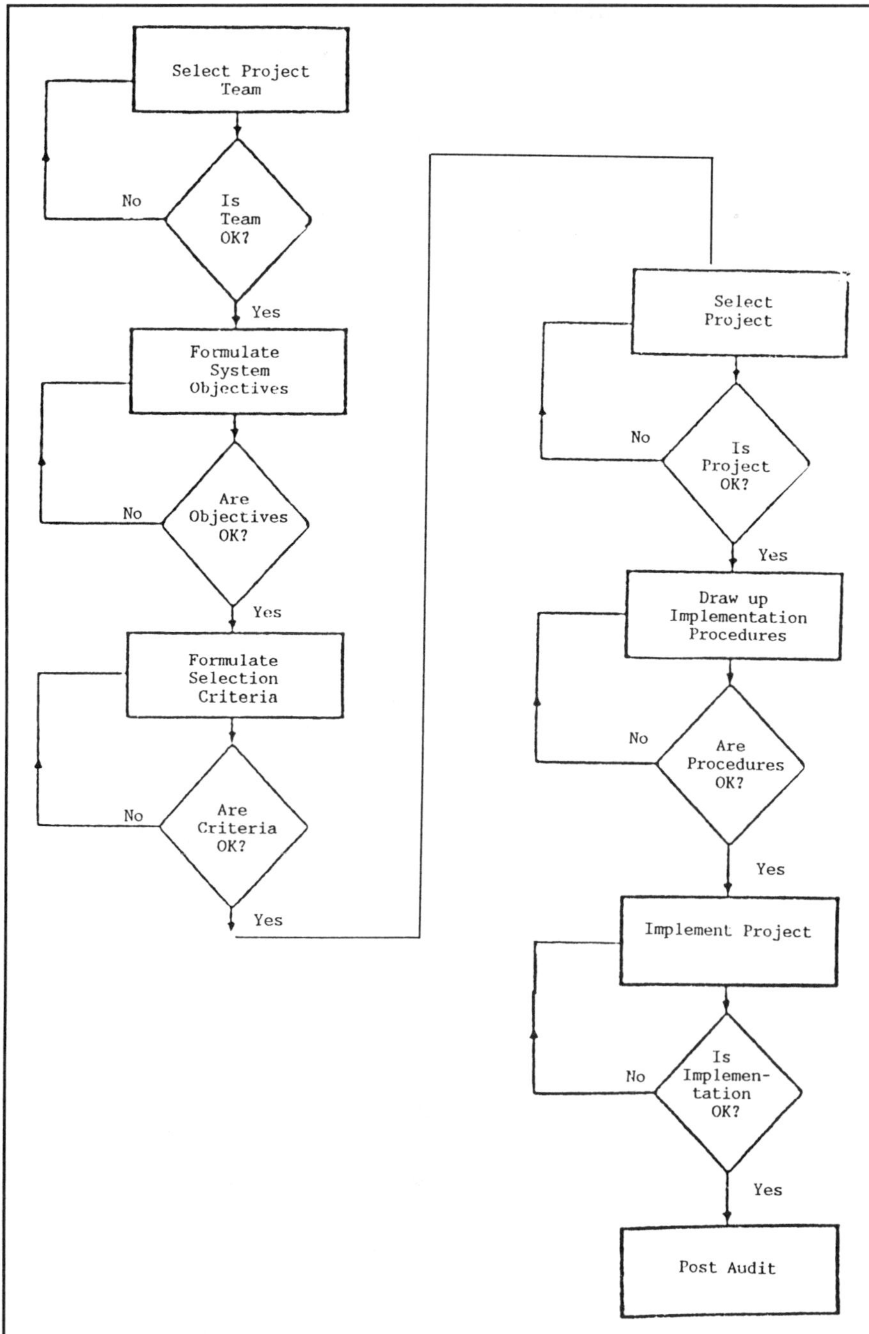

Figure 2: S-T Apporach to Technologies Absorption

not one of those ad hoc activities that must take place after official hours. By having the opportunity to participate in the decision of who represents individual units or interest groups, users can develop a sense of responsibility and identification with the potential information system which is likely to create a positive attitude and commitment to the new technology and the system.

Tom (1991, p. 163) provides the following nine functions of the IT steering committee:

- determining the appropriate level of expenditure and capability for the IT based on the organization's strategic and tactical plans;
- evaluating and approving specific proposals for the acquisition of major hardware and software;
- approving long- and short-term IT plans;
- determining which specific IT projects are to be undertaken, on the basis of a given set of criteria;
- setting IT project priorities;
- reviewing and updating IT cost allocation procedures;

Phases	Problems Addressed
Steering Committee Selection	Poor Planning, Goals Misalignment, Isolated Views, Lack of Support and Participation, Poor Communication and Feedback.
Objective Formulation	Lack of IT Objectives, Poor Planning, Goals Misalignment.
Criteria Formulation	Poor Planning, Isolated View, Inappropriate Evaluation Tool.
System Evaluation/ Selection	Poor Planning, Isolated View, Lack of Participation/Commitment.
Formulating Plans and Implementation Procedures	Lack of IT Management Knowledge, Poor Planning, Participation/Commitment.
System Introduction	Poor Change management Tool, Poor Planning, Lack of Participation/ Commitment.
Post-Implementation Audit	Inappropriate Evaluation Tool, Poor Change Management Tool, Lack of IT Management Knowledge.

Table 2: Relationship of Socio-Technical Phases and IT Absorption Problems Addressed

- monitoring and enhancing IT project progress;
- deciding which IT projects should be continued or abandoned at specific times and conditions; and
- managing territorial and political conflicts arising from the impact of new IT.

The functions of the IT steering committee will vary both in scope and number from one organization to another. No matter the scope and size of functions, successful IT implementation is greatly influenced by the composition, motive, and competence of the steering committee. According to Tom (1991, p. 165), the factors that impact the effectiveness of the steering committee are: (1) maintaining a business focus and staying on course; (2) having executives play active roles as committee members; (3) preplanning the meetings and conducting the meetings effectively and professionally; (4) ensuring that committee members understand and agree to the business objectives; and (5) running a committee that is action- and result-oriented.

As a general rule of thumb, two groups of people—the IS professionals and top managers—must be part of any IT steering committee to provide the necessary technical and financial support, respectively. The rest of the team members have to be selected based on how they will affect or be affected by the potential system. Selecting IT committee members in the manner described above can neutralize the impact of organizational bias, increase participation and personal commitment. It can boost top management support while increasing a sense of shared responsibility. The project team would have a better frame of reference about users's needs, organizational structure, the tasks to be performed with the new system, and the technology requirements. An appropriate frame of reference is mandatory for effective IT implementation. When the selection committee is democratically selected and approved by all parts, the next step can then be initiated.

Step 2: Formulation of System Objectives

Effective IT absorption demands that specific system objectives be spelled out and more importantly that these objectives be aligned with the goals of the company. As indicated by the survey conducted by Herber and Harton (1986), the most important IT issue facing organizations today is its alignment with the goals of the business. To accomplish that, necessary data has to be collected and used in projections and forecasting concerning the strategic and tactical goals and objectives of the whole organization and those of its individual departments. Determining system objectives also requires a thorough understanding of the organizational goals as well as those of the business units because system objectives have to be in harmony with them. With a traditional approach to IT management, IS departments single-handedly set system objectives independent of organizational and business unit goals. IS departments often hope to "work" the new IT into organizational goals once the new system is up and running. The main reason for this awkward practice is: IS departments may not fully understand the organizational and business unit goals or may not be committed to them. This situation often leads to a new system whose objectives are out of phase with the goals of the organization and that of the individual business units they are meant to serve. This problem is eliminated in a socio-technical approach. First, it requires that representatives from different sections of the organization who are both knowledgeable and committed to their unit's goals be involved in the implementation process. Second, the approach requires that IT objectives be spelled out before any commitment or investment be made. This requirement helps identify, at the early stage, systems whose objectives conflict with the firm's goals. It also helps eliminate systems which do not support the general interest of the individual groups involved.

By formulating system objectives with the socio-technical approach, the steering committee is made to address the hard questions regarding the proposed system. Answers to the following questions have to be provided at this step:

- Why is the proposed system necessary?
- What will the system be used for?
- What present problems will the system help solve?
- What is the expected capacity/scope of the proposed system?
- How does the purpose of the system enhance goal attaintment at organizational and business unit levels?
- How compatible are the system's goals and objectives with organizational and business unit goals and objectives?
- What are the expectations from the proposed system? What can and cannot the proposed system do, given the particular business situation?

As is to be expected, IS departments cannot answer these questions without help from knowledgeable individuals across the organization. Effective participation by representatives selected in step one is required to answer these questions. By answering the questions in a participative manner, the steering committee can formulate system objectives capable of meeting the needs of different groups of individuals in the organization. As mentioned earlier, Bienkowski (1989) observed that most IT implementation projects fail because they are solutions in search of problems. This is particularly important in the case of emerging IT which tends to be less understood than older IT and are more likely to be used as status symbols, new toys, etc.

This phase of the socio-technical approach is very similar to the first phase of Walton's (1989, p. 2) framework, which proposes that management first aligns business, organization, and IT strategies before the development of the system is undertaken. The task of aligning a specific IT system with organization and business unit goals is not as easy as it may sound. Several factors can make the task extremely complex. Tom (1991, p. 426) identified some of the problems encountered in coordinating IT and company's strategies: (1) Individual user or user groups setting the priorities for system development. (2) "Bootleg" development shops spring up inside various business units. (3) Too many complaints about slow delivery of new systems, high cost, and chargebacks. (4) Business divisions or senior management are pressing for systems that will deliver competitive advantage. (5) Information systems and user departments are in conflict over areas of responsibility and control.

By formulating system objectives which match the whole organization's interest as well as individual business units, potential conflict and resistance can be minimized and system effectiveness can be enhanced. Communications among project team members and within the whole organization become easier and clearer since everyone knows what to expect and what others expect from the implementation process. The problem of business managers over expectation, which is increasingly common to IT projects, can also be overcome by this approach since specific system objectives are formulated and agreed upon by all parties before the system is implemented. Formulating system objectives before implementing it will eliminate the problems of non adherence to system original goals, goals misalignment, and poor system planning. With clearly defined system objectives, the committee can then proceed to define project evaluation and selection criteria.

Step 3: Formulation of Evaluation/Selection Criteria

No one can measure what is not properly defined and no one can determine how well a system will do without first defining performance measures. Establishing evaluation criteria for systems requiring new technology is probably the single most important factor to ensure that both the objective and subjective evaluation/selection processes effectively address the important system characteristics across the different interest groups involved: top management, IS department, project team, and users groups. A comprehensive and well-defined set of criteria can ensure the acquisition of useful technology through a more effective evaluation and selection of projects of potentially greater value to the company. These are also more likely to be successful. The criteria have to originate from all parties concerned and represent fairly the interests of the organization as a whole, the IS department, and the other groups involved. If the criteria unfairly discriminate against one or more groups in the organization, the evaluation/selection process may lead to disaster.

A representative list of criteria can be developed by asking members of the different groups to make a list of items on which they believe the project selection should be based. A consolidated list of evaluation criteria can then be produced by the steering committee and presented to other interested persons for remarks before final approval. The steering committee members at this step act as facilitators and liaisons to their respective units. A delphi method is used at this step to produce a list of criteria that is a true representation of the different groups' needs and wants. In most cases there has to be some form of compromise and consensus if the set of criteria are to be of any practical use. For example, top management may want the IT to be evaluated based on an unrealistic payback period. The steering committee would have to educate top management on why the criterion is unreasonably high for the particular IT and a more practical payoff criterion can be negotiated.

In general, the basic IT performance parameters which have to be included among the criteria fall into three major groups: organizational relevance, system quality requirements, and project management. Organizational relevance criteria should address how compatible the new technology and system are with the goals and objectives of the organization. It should not address specific system capabilities. System quality criteria should define requirements for flexibility, functionality, and ease of maintenance. Project management criteria should enable a mechanism to determine if the project was completed on time, within budget, and the degree of user's involvement in the system development process. If criteria are properly determined at this step, it would greatly simplify the task of post auditing discussed later.

Formulating selection criteria in an interactive and representative manner as described here would bring the advantages of the Delphi method to bear on the selection process. It would minimize the impact of organizational bias in that no one group can dominate under this method. With well defined criteria, the IT selection and implementation process can not easily deviate from its original goals. Given the excellent feedback system inherent in this approach, communication between the steering committee and user groups and also among the committee members would be enhanced. Commitment and support from top management and end-users would also be enhanced. Since criteria from every group are represented, the approach will maximize goal attaintment. In essence, the problems of inappropriate or insufficient evaluation tools for emerging IT and isolated perception of IT by the different user groups will be minimized by criteria formulation phase.

Step 4: IS Project Evaluation and Selection

When a representative and realistic list of criteria is approved by all parties, the next step in a socio-technical approach is to select an appropriate version (e.g. specific product, method) of the new technology from among a group of possible alternatives which matches the requirements of the business problem/opportunity at hand. Several project evaluation and selection methods have been discussed in the literature and all have been shown to have some strengths and weaknesses. Some of the popular methods include: cost/benefit analysis, value analysis, multi-attribute utility value approach, and the analytic hierarchy process methods (Toraskar & Joglekar, 1990; Keen, 1981; Huber, 1974; Saaty, 1977). Depending on the choice of method, the results from the project selection process can be quite different.

The cost/benefit method is simple to use but is not suitable for evaluating the intangible benefits which can dominate the analysis of benefits for projects with long-term and strategic implications. Its equations are concerned primarily with the quantitative and not the qualitative measures of system projects. Value analysis is simple, intuitive and relatively easy to do. It involves the sequential steps of listing the likely benefits; determining the cost threshold which is the maximum cost for the benefits; developing a prototype system; and then assessing the actual benefits and costs of the project. Value analysis allows users to define the qualitative benefits of the project in more specific terms but organization wide objectives are many times overlooked.

The multi-attribute utility value approach measures the users' perception of the overall value of the project. There are many types of models in existence and the selection of the most appropriate model depends upon the characteristics of the project in question. This approach is strong in incorporating multiple viewpoints and qualitative criteria but very weak in incorporating costs with the quantitative benefits. The analytic hierarchy process method captures complex, multi-criteria, multi-evaluator, and multi-period evaluation process into a hierarchical structure. The components at the higher levels of the structure represent general issues, for example, overall goals of the project. The lower level components represent the detailed issues, such as specific criteria for the project.

As said earlier, each evaluation method is more suitable than others depending on the nature of the project being evaluated and what the evaluators hope to measure. However, no one method is suitable for handling all the subjective and objective criteria for complex emerging IT projects. For effective evaluation in this case, we suggest an approach that combines more than one of the evaluation methods briefly discussed here in a way that they complement each other. For example, the cost/benefit method could be used to account for the quantitative measures while multi-attribute utility value method could be used to account for the subjective, qualitative measures. This hybrid approach can be more helpful to minimize organizational biasing than any of the individual methods used alone and seems quite suitable to the objectives underlying the socio-technical approach.

Whatever evaluation technique(s) is adopted, the socio-technical approach will ensure that individual group preference, interest, or bias is canceled out since the averages of scores from all the group representatives are considered. For example, the high weights on technical criteria from the IS professional will be dampened by the low weights from the user groups. The same is true of financial and social criteria. This type of scoring system can result in sound overall selection decision with a higher probability of success than that of a non-sociotechnical method. Although the evaluation/selection technique recommended is not new, the representative evaluation enforced by the socio-technical approach has the potential of overcoming the inherent IT project selection problems discussed earlier. In particular, the system evaluation and selection phase will help reduce the problems of poor planning and lack of user participation and commitment, in addition to integrating the perception and interests of the different groups in the organization.

Step 5: Formulating Plans and Implementation Procedures

This is an aspect of IT management often overlooked by companies. If the planning of implementation procedures for a new system is overlooked or left in the hands of a few people, a number of things can go wrong, which in turn can significantly reduce the overall implementation effectiveness. It is logical that the people who will be affected or affect the project implementation process should play a part in the planning process. For instance, if the process of installing and testing a new expert system in the accounting department will require that the office be closed down for a few hours, people in the department should be consulted for approval and necessary rescheduling of work.

At this point, the steering committee has already selected the most attractive alternative IT configuration based on the criteria derived at step 3 and the method chosen in step 4. The challenge of the present phase is to draw up a master plan on how the system would be implemented. The procedures, sequence of events, and general time table accepted by all parties are laid out at this milestone. A mutually approved procedure is necessary to prevent cost and schedule over runs. As much as possible, the procedures have to be specific and comprehensive enough to ensure a successful completion of the project. A tight project schedule that does not leave room for uncertainties can unnecessarily increase the project cost or lead to a sub-optimal job. Equally, a drawn out schedule can result in loss of users' interest, increased overhead cost, loss of business opportunities, or even project abandonment. All significant possible constraints and uncertainties have to be considered in order to come up with a realistic and effective implementation procedure and schedule that will act as a credible yardstick during project implementation. By formulating implementation procedures and introducing the new IT as described by the socio-technical approach, the problems of poor planning, lack of participation and commitment, and poor change management will be reduced.

Step 6: IT Implementation

At this phase the IT application is put into operation and the required changes are made. Implementation using a socio-technical approach is more likely to succeed than with the traditional approach because the new system has a much broader base of support from the different parties in the organization. The implementation task in this case becomes simply following the "blue print" drawn earlier, with the end product more likely to stay on course in terms of time and cost, and more likely to meet the overall organization's objectives and needs. In case of unforeseen events, any of the previous steps can be repeated before completing this phase. For example, if for any reason some or all of the procedures derived in step five are no longer feasible, the steering committee would have to meet and repeat step five before proceeding with step six. Or if for some reason, some of the team members leave the company, step one would have to be repeated to fill the vacancies.

This phase requires a careful execution of the master plan, bearing in mind the system objectives and the evaluation criteria already established. A socio-technical approach ensures a relatively smooth introduction of emerging IT since it requires that the previous steps be taken prior to this step, thus providing a strong framework for the organization to experiment with new, high impact technology. At this step, the committee has a workable implementation timetable for every procedure needed for the new system to be up and running.

Since nothing except change is constant, the steering committee should not be hesitant to revise its game plan at any stage. However, revision should be done only when it is absolutely necessary since it could be expensive both in time and financially. The key socio-technical requirement in this phase is that, unless absolutely necessary, the plan execution should stick to the game plan. Communications among committee members is crucial and has to be very frequent. For some systems where prototyping is not possible, the steering committee, which is a representative of all the interest groups in the company, has to provide the much needed feedback at each step of the implementation phase. But where prototyping is possible, feedback should be obtained directly from as many users as possible.

The implementation phase starts with the acquisition, development and testing of the new technology to be used, in the form of procedures, data, hardware, software, and personnel requirements. It ends with the effective management of the organizational changes resulting from the new system. It is the act of taking a well-designed system and making it a useful working system.

Literature abounds on the topic of change management that could be applied to changes resulting from IT implementation (Ashmore, 1989; Jaikumar, 1986; Rochart & Short, 1989; Burn & Caldwell, 1990; Zuboff, 1988). Increasingly, emerging IT implementation is reflecting business trends to globalization; and affecting organization internal structure (in terms of new roles, power shifts, changes in the hierarchy structure, etc.); organizational borders (by interconnecting the company electronically with suppliers, customers, and competitors); business processes are re-engineered; and products and/or services are added or improved with emerging IT. Through the type of training required in the introduction phase, IT management skills and user motivation to accept and use the system would be enhanced.

Step 7: Post-Implementation Audit

Most organizations use formal methods which are incapable of capturing the social aspects of new IT implementation. As discussed earlier, these provide an inappropriate evaluation for applications of emerging technologies and allow organizations to suffer the detrimental effects of organizational bias. The socio-technical approach during project selection is likely to improve things substantially. Beyond that, organizations should establish a sound post-implementation audit program to identify and correct possible problems which may have escaped the selection process.

Post-implementation audit is a particularly important phase of the implementation process for new and poorly understood technologies. Yet, in most companies it is omitted or much neglected because it is one of the most difficult phases of the whole process. Given the increasing importance of emerging IT, the required budget sizes and organization impact, conducting post-implementation audits is probably worthwhile. Many companies approach the post audit with a judgmental mindset, instead of thinking of it as a learning process which could add great value to company assets as well as improve the absorption of new technology. The importance of post-implementation audit is mainly that of playing back the whole system development process in order to identify areas where the IT project selection and implementation process can be improved for future projects. It provides an opportunity to systematically study the application of a new technology, its strengths and limitations, as well as correcting its implementation problems.

Several studies have suggested different tools and techniques for IT post-implementation audit. It has been said that how system evaluation is done depends to a large extent on the tools and techniques used (King & Schrems, 1978). Most of the evaluation tools and techniques currently available are decidedly technical, quantitative and rational in nature. These are more suitable for physical sciences but not for emerging IT applications which have significant social implications thus requiring alternative methods. Many discussions for and against formal and informal evaluations exist in the literature (King & Schrems, 1978; Guimaraes & McKeen, 1988). Both the formal and the informal evaluation methods can effectively be used to supplement each other, resulting in a more meaningful post audit program than what is presently done in some organizations.

An effective post-implementation audit has to reflect the dual nature of IT applications and should incorporate both formal and informal methods, which reflect both objective and subjective criteria. A socio-technical approach to evaluation has a great potential to account for or to reduce the effect of the obvious presence of organizational bias on the IT post-implementation audit. To help keep the organizational biasing effects at minimum, an appropriate and realizable time frame has to be set in advance for project evaluation. The new system has to settle down before any reasonable evaluation can be done. Also, some evaluation criteria may require a certain amount of time to be properly measured, after or before which the measurement may not be accurate. Setting the post audit time frame too early or too late may lead to invalid conclusions about the value of the new system and/or the value of the new technology for future applications. The most appropriate waiting period before evaluation is project specific and should be established by the project team during Phase 5, the formulation of plans and implementation procedures.

CONCLUSION

Emerging IT are increasingly being used to enhance company operations and decision making. New systems are continuously brought in to the fabric of IT applications. Many of these systems must be carefully integrated into increasingly complex business environments.

Effective absorption of emerging IT by large, sophisticated organizations requires two major ingredients. First, as company dependency on new IT, the degree of system integration, and the company-wide impact of new IT grow, the absorption process must account for the interests of many different groups within the organization. Second, proper balance between the technical aspects of a new and untried technology, and its impact on the organization's business tasks and social fabric, must be struck. The most appropriate time and mechanism to ensure that these requirements are met is the project evaluation and selection process.

The socio-technical (S-T) approach proposed here for evaluating and selecting projects is particularly useful in the case of new IT, which increasingly affects the organization as a whole and is often used for business process re-engineering. The process will account for the different interests and perspectives from the various groups related to a project, and will enable an appropriate balance between the social and the technical aspects of the new system. While the seven-step process proposed here may seem elaborate to some people, it is likely to be quite useful in the case of large projects using new and unfamiliar technology which involve different units in the organization.

REFERENCES

Ashmore, G.M. (1989). A New Approach for Managing Information Technology. *Journal of Business Strategy, 10*(1), 57-59.

Argyris, C. (1970). Management Information Systems: The Challenge to Rationality and Emotionality. *Management Science, 17*(6), B275-B292.

Balanchadra, R. and Raelin, J. A. (1980). How to Decide When to Abandon a Project. *Research Management, 23*, 24-29.

Bienkowski, D. (1989). Ten Causes of Project Busts, *Computerworld, 23*(6), 99, 102.

Bostrom, R. P. and Heinen, J. S. (1977, September). MIS Problems and Failures: A Socio-Technical Perspective, Part 1: The Causes. *MIS Quarterly*, 17-32.

Brooks, F. P. Jr. (1975). The Mythical Man-Month. Reading, MA: Addision-Wesley.

Burn, J. and Caldwell, E. (1990). *Management of Information Systems Technology*, Oxfordshine, UK: Alfred Waller Ltd., 56.

Carroll, P. B. (1988, January). Computer Glitch. The Wall Street Journal, 1, 12.

Devaney, M. (1991). Risk, Commitment, and Project Abandonment. *Journal of Business Ethics, 10*(2), 157-159.

Doll, W. J. and Mesbah, A. (1984). Tradeoffs in Selecting an Executive Steering Committee. *Journal of Systems Management, 35*(1), 6-11.

Ewusi-Mensah, K. and Przasnyski, Z. H. (1991). On Information Systems Project Abandonment: An Exploratory Study of Organizational Practices. *MIS Quarterly, 15*(1), 67-85.

Ginzberg, M. J. (1979). Improving MIS Project Selection. *Omega, 7*(6), 39-51.

Grindlay, A. (1981). Steering Committees. *Business Quarterly, 46*(4), 10-14.

Guimaraes, T. and McKeen, J. D. (1988). Organizational Bias in the Selection of MIS Projects. *Omega, 16*(4), 297-307.

Guimaraes, T. and McKeen, J. D. (1989, Summer). The Process of Selecting Information System Projects. *Data Base*, 18-24. Herber, M. and Harton, C. (1986, December). MIS Rates The Issues. *Datamation*.

Hirschheim, R. and Smithson, S. (1987). Information Systems Evaluation: Myth and Reality. In R. Galliers (Ed.), Information Analysis Selected Readings (pp. 367-380). Sydney, Australia: Addison-Wesley Publishing Company.

Huber, G. P. (1974). Multi-attribute Utility Models: A Review of Field and Field-like Studies. *Management Science, 20*(10), 1393-1402.

Ives B. and Learmonth, G. P. (1984). The Information System as a Competitive Weapon. *Communications of the ACM, 27*(12), 1193-1201.

Jaikumar, R. (1986, November-December). Post-Industrial Manufacturing. *Harvard Business Review*, 69-76.

Keen, P. G. W. (1981). Value Analysis: Justifying Decision Support Systems. *MIS Quarterly, 5*(1), 1-16.

Keider, S. P. (1984). Why Systems Development Projects Fail. *Journal of Information Systems Management, 1*(3), 33-38.

King, J. L. and Schrems, E. L. (1978). Cost-Benefit Analysis in Information System Development and Operation. *Computing Surveys, 10*(1), 19-34.

Knutsen, K. E. and Nolan, R. L. (1974). On Cost-Benefit of Computer-Based Systems. In R. L. Nolan (Ed.), *Managing the Data Resource Functions.* St. Paul: West Publishing Co.

Laudon, K. C. and Laudon, J. P. (1991). *Management Information Systems: A Contemporary Perspective.* New York: MacMillian Publishing Company.

Mason, R. and Swanson, E. (1981). *Measurement for Management Decision.* Reading, MA: Addison-Wesley.

McFarlan, F. W. (1981, September-October). Portfolio Approach to Information Systems. *Harvard Business Review*, 142-150.

Melone, N. P. and Wharton, T. J. (1984). Strategies for MIS Project Selection. Journal of Systems Management, 35(2), 26-33.

Mumford, E., Mercer, D., Mills, S. and Weir, M. (1972). The Human Problems of Computer Introduction. *Management Decision, 10*(1), 6-17.

Peters, T. J. and Waterman, R. H. (1982). *In Search of Excellence.* New York: Harper and Row.

Pinto, J. K. and Mantel, S. J. (1990). The Causes of Project Failure. *IEEE Transactions on Engineering Management, 37*(4), 269-276.

Pinto, J. K. and Slevin, D. P. (1987). Critical Factors in Successful Project Implementation. *IEEE Transactions on Engineering Management, 34*(1), 22-27.

Rochart, J.F. and Short, J.E. (1989). IT in the 1990's: Emerging Organizational Interdependence. *Sloan Management Review, 30*(2), 7-17.

Saaty, T. L. (1977). A Scaling Method for Priorities in Hierarchical Structures. *J. Math. Psychology, 15*(3), 234-245.

Sharma, R. S., Conrath, D. W. and Dilts, D. M. (1991). A Socio-Technical Model for Deploying Expert Systems—Part I: The General Theory. *IEEE Transactions on Engineering Management, 38*(1), 14-23.

Staw, B. M. and Ross, J. (1987, March-April). Knowing When to Pull the Plug. *Harvard Business Review*, 68-74.

Tom, P.L. (1991). *Managing Information As a Corporate Resource.* New York: Harper Collins Publishers, Inc.

Tomeski, E. A. (1975). Building Human Factors into Computer Applications: The Computer Profession Must Overcome a 'Jackass Fallacy'! *Management Datamatics, 4*(4), 115-120.

Toraskar, K. V. and Joglekar, P. N. (1990). Comments on "Price and Value of Decision Support Systems. *MIS Quarterly, 14*(1), 7-12.

Trist, E. L. and Bamforth, K. W. (1951). Some Social and Psychological Consequences of the Longwall Method of Coal-getting. *Human Relations, 4*, 3-38.

Turner, J. A. (1982). Observations on the Use of Behavioral Models in Information Systems Research and Practice. *Information and Management, 5*(4,5), 207-213.

Vaill, P. B. (1967). Industrial Engineering and Socio-technical Systems. *Journal of Industrial Engineering, 16*(9), 530-538.

Walton, R.E. (1989). *Up and Running: Integrating Information Technology and the Organization.* Boston: Harvard Business School Press.

White, K. B. (1984). A Diverse, Balanced Team Approach Generates Vital Management Strategy. *Data Management, 22*(9), 31-41.

Zuboff, S. (1988). *The Age of The Smart Machine.* New York: Basic Books, Inc.

CHAPTER 2

DESIGNING ARCHITECTURES FOR EMERGING INFORMATION TECHNOLOGIES: A MULTIPLE METHODOLOGY APPROACH

Robert A. Stegwee
University of Groningen

Enno J. Ebels
American Power Conversion Europe SA

Emerging information technologies confront the management with a set of challenges in the field of information and organization. Traditionally information management has relied on structured methods for information planning, leading to the specification of information architectures which strive for manageability, stability, and integration of information systems within the organization. Nowadays, information architectures designed along these lines are no longer sufficient. Information technology has developed to a point where questions have to be asked with respect to strategic use of information technology and business redesign. Methods for information architecture specification should evolve accordingly. In this chapter we describe a new way of thinking about information architecture specification, backed by a decision support system, which relies on the specification of radically different information architectures and the evaluation of alternatives. We start out by providing some background in the area of traditional information planning and information architecture specification. From the challenges of new information technology, we elaborate our case for a new approach toward the specification of these architectures. We describe our multiple methodology approach toward information architecture specification and establish the foundation of the GOSSIP system, to be used in conjunction with this new approach. A case description illustrates the use of both method and tool. In the concluding paragraphs we look onward to a future in which flexibility dominates the design of organization and information systems. We argue that our multiple methodology approach toward information architecture specification contributes toward such flexibility, and thus toward coping with the challenges of new technology.

The impact information technology (IT) has on organizations is increasing as the capabilities of IT are boosted. Emerging information technologies confront today's organizations with both technological and organizational issues, such as:

- downsizing and decentralization,
- electronic data interchange and vertical integration, and
- networking and globalization.

Organizations try to cope with these challenges through processes of information policy formulation and information planning. Both information policy and plan are aimed at focussing the attention of IT application on those areas that are essential for survival and strategic success of the organization. Without them, the development of IT applications for the organization can become haphazard, with the inevitable outcome of excessive expenses, incompatible systems, and angry users, but most of all: a diminished performance of the organization.

Architectures are a principal means of planning the development of information systems support and the application of information technology through-out an organization. In a recent study, Van Waes provides an extensive treatment of the role of architectures in information management. She concludes (Van Waes, 1991, p. 205) "[...] that architectures can be very effective tools in information management, e.g. by providing:

- an effective means of controlling IT expenditures;
- a flexible platform for integration of IT applications;
- a roadmap for the development of future IT applications and
- a basis for re-designing business and IT structures."

Information planning methods have kindled this enthusiasm for architectures by providing guidelines on how to develop an integral set of architectures that will meet the needs of an organization. One of these architectures is the so-called information architecture, which displays the boundaries and the dependencies of information systems to be developed for an organization. However, the methods employed for information planning today have been developed during the last two decades. As such, they provide answers to the issues of that time. Emerging information technologies pose new challenges for business and information management. Therefore, enhancements to current methods are needed to resolve the issues facing information management today (see e.g. Stegwee & Van Waes, 1990).

This chapter outlines a new approach toward the design of information architectures. In order to provide some background, we discuss current methods for information planning and the objectives of an information architecture. Then, we will argue that these objectives, as put forward by the current methods, are insufficient to cope with tomorrow's challenges. As the objectives change, the employed methods should be altered as well. It is our opinion that these alterations can well be met by means of a multiple methodology approach, as suggested by Earl (1989). However, for such an approach to be feasible, tools are needed to facilitate the employment of a multiple methodology. We have developed such a tool specifically for information architecture specification. The *Solutions and Recommendations* section outlines this decision support system, and an example of its application is given.

BACKGROUND

It is well known that the use of information technology (IT) within organizations has increased during the last decades. This increase has led to a need for controllability and manageability of the use of IT, resulting in policy and planning in the field of IT. Information planning can be seen as a process leading toward the definition of an information plan to be used as the basis for the development of the information systems described in it. The information planning process and the ensuing IS development projects are led by a directive framework, called the information policy (Boersma, 1989).

Several methods for information planning can be distinguished (see e.g. Davis & Olson, 1985, Theeuwes, 1988). Davis and Olson distinguish five different approaches for, as they call it, the determination of information requirements at the organizational level. These, as we call them, different classes of methods for information planning are (Davis & Olson, 1985, p. 483):

1. Normative Analysis
2. Strategy Set Transformation
3. Critical Factors Analysis
4. Process Analysis
5. Ends-means Analysis

Normative Analysis is based upon the idea that standard software areas should be recognized within the organization. After these areas have been recognized, the necessary adaptations can be specified to make the areas fit specific organizational aspects. *Strategy Set Transformation* and *Critical Factors Analysis* are examples of a top down approach. Their respective starting points for the determination of information requirements are Business Goals and Critical Factors (such as Critical Success Factors). In this way strategic or critical information systems can be given priority in further systems development. *Ends-means Analysis* is a systems analysis approach that defines the information requirements in terms of input and output of the different areas that can be recognized.

Process Analysis is the approach in which organizational processes are arranged in groups according to functional areas within the organization. Each functional area can be divided into one or more business functions. This division can be continued up to the level of the business processes. An overview of these divisions and the assignment of business processes to business functions is called a functional decomposition. A prime representative of this class of methods is Business Systems Planning (BSP) as described in (International Business Machines [IBM], 1984). Other BSP-oriented methods for information planning, such as ISP (to be discussed), also fall within this class.

In the following description of information planning, and information architecture in particular, we will focus on the BSP-oriented process analysis methods. These methods are widely used and well described. Over the years they have incorporated some of the characteristics of other approaches as well, but, with respect to information architecture specification, they have remained unchanged. In the description of a multiple methodology approach, to overcome the perceived problems with the design of an information architecture, we will return to the other types of information planning methods.

The Information Planning Process

In general, summarizing the multitude of methods, one can view information planning methods as proceeding along the lines indicated in figure 1 (see also Stegwee & Van Waes, 1990). The information planning process has to take into account forces coming from two sides: the business needs, as specified by business strategies and plans, and trends and opportunities with respect to information technology. Methods for IP stress the alignment of the information plan, i.e. the outcome of an information planning process, with overall business goals. In order to establish this linkage, an analysis is made of business strategic material, such as mission statements, strategic plans, and critical success factors. Trends and opportunities in the field of information technology (IT) are analyzed in order to identify new application areas and alternatives for the technical infrastructure. This IT analysis can also give rise to the identification

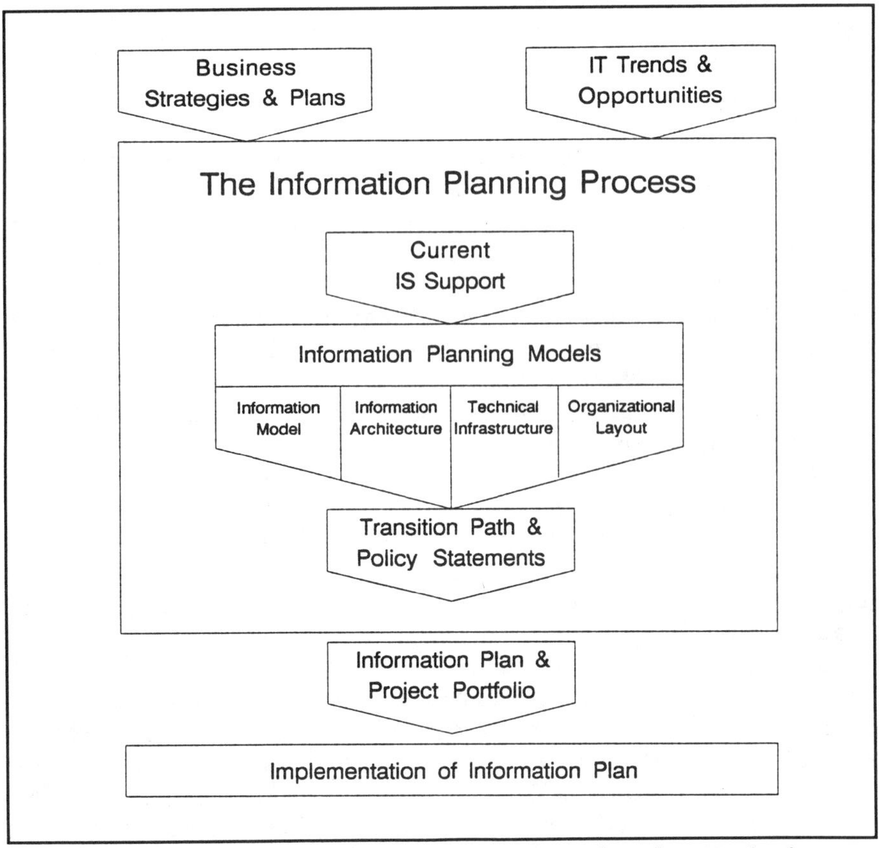

Figure 1: Structure of an Information Planning Method

of strategic information systems, which provide a competitive edge for the organization, or which prevent the organization from lagging behind its competitors.

Another force influencing the information planning process, falling within the category of business needs, comes from the current situation with respect to information systems support, both in a technical sense, and in terms of user satisfaction with the information systems provided. Comparison of the current situation and alternative designs for information systems support limits the number of feasible alternatives. Some alternatives differ so much from the current situation that the cost of lost investments or the effort needed to bring about the new situation is prohibiting.

Information Planning Models

The set of information planning models, to be developed as a blueprint for the future information systems support, contains four models, each focussing on a different area of interest. The information model provides a view of business activity and the resulting information flows. The information architecture specifies information systems areas, which are relatively autonomous, such as to enable manageable information systems analysis and design projects. The technical infrastructure defines the hardware and systems software needed to support the information architecture specified. The organizational layout gives an impression of the roles and responsibilities to be fulfilled by parts of the organization, with respect to information resource management, including planning, development, operation, and maintenance of information systems. Each of these models will be discussed in more detail below.

Information Model. An information model is built upon a process model of business activity and a data model of business related data. The process model usually contains a functional decomposition of business activity, distinguishing between primary functions and support functions, detailed to a certain level, at which basic business processes are defined. This functional decomposition forms a tree-structure, with the business processes at the leaves. An example of such a process model is given in figure 2. The data model consists of entity types and relationships between them, at a fairly high level of abstraction. By no means are the data in this model in some sort of normalized form. A common way to represent this data model is by means of an entity-relationship diagram, an example of which is shown in figure 3. Each relationship in this diagram has two names, one for each direction. For example, Research is carried out by Staff, is one direction, while Staff carries out Research represents

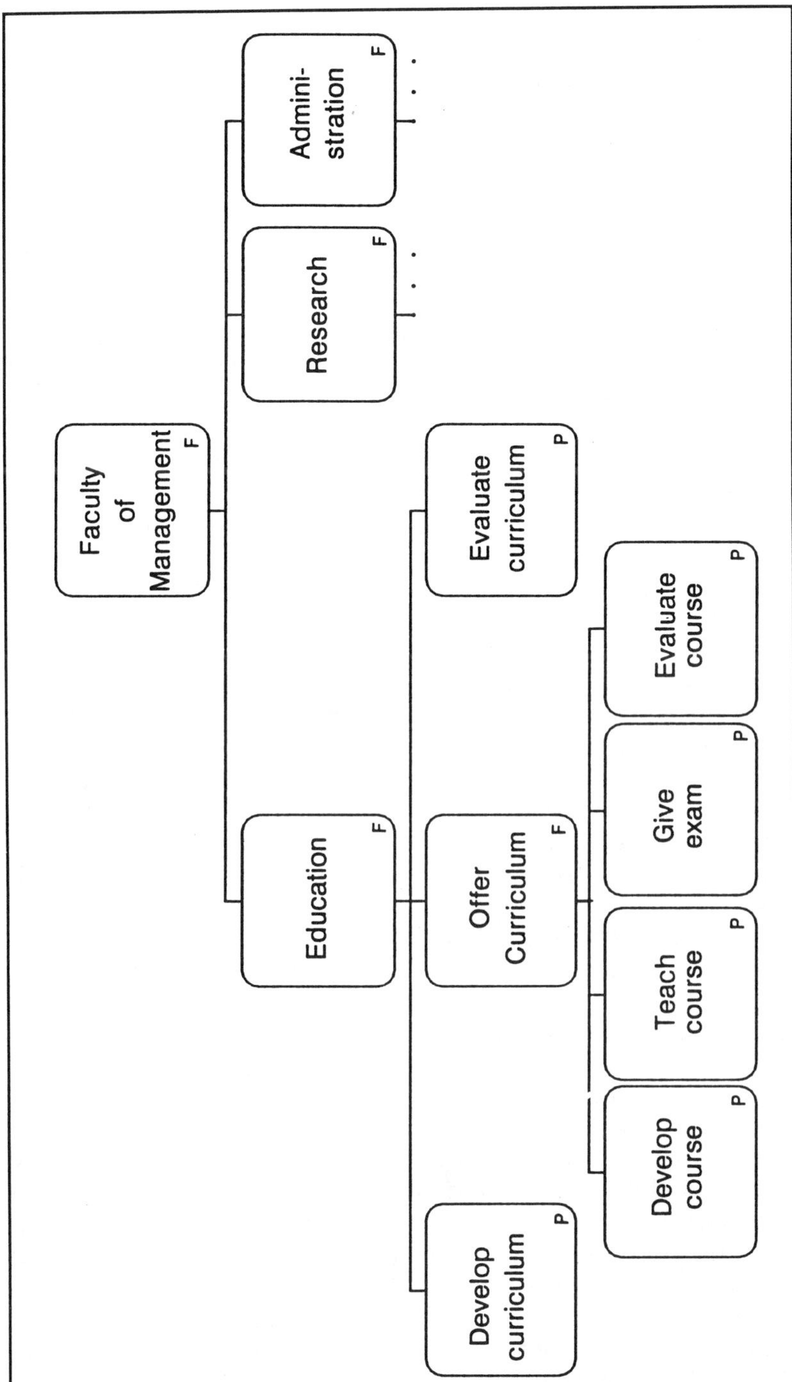

Fgure 2: Example of a Functional Decomposition of Business Activity, into Functions and Processes

the other.

The information model specifies the interaction between business processes and entity types. This interaction can be established by means of an input-process-output analysis of each business process. One usually distinguishes two different types of interaction: if data on an entity type is part of the input of a business process, then the interaction is labelled U, for 'process uses data on an entity type'; in case the output of the business process contains the entity type specified, the interaction is labelled C, for 'process creates data on an entity type'. Other labelling schemes have been proposed, such as Create, Retrieve, Update, and Delete (KnowledgeWare, 1989), or Create, Modify, and Use (Beaupain, 1989). The information model usually takes the form of a two-dimensional matrix, as depicted in figure 4.

Information Architecture. An information architecture (see figure 5) contains a demarcation of information systems areas (the shaded regions) within the information model. In addition, the information architecture also shows the interrelationships between the information systems areas (the arrows). These information systems areas are meant to provide an appropriate limitation of scope for an information systems analysis project. Such an information systems analysis project is also called Business Area Analysis in Information Engineering (Martin, 1986), or Business Analysis (Olle, et al., 1988). A discussion of the objectives and ingredients of an information architecture will be given in the section *Objectives of an Information Architecture.*

Technical Infrastructure. In relation to the proposed information architecture, a technical infrastructure has to be developed, specifying the hardware and systems software components to be used. In addition, communications facilities have to be specified. As an integral part of the technical infrastructure, standards can be adopted for different types of hardware, systems software, and communications facilities.

Organizational Layout. With respect to the planning, development, operation, and maintenance of information systems support throughout the organization, a number of functions can be specified. Choices have to be made about where these functions have to be performed, and the responsibilities have to be assigned. This includes the design of an information management organization, responsible for the design and development aspects of information systems support, and the structuring of an EDP function, responsible for the actual operations. It should be stressed that responsibilities in both areas are not necessarily limited to separate organizational units. Especially information management is a function that

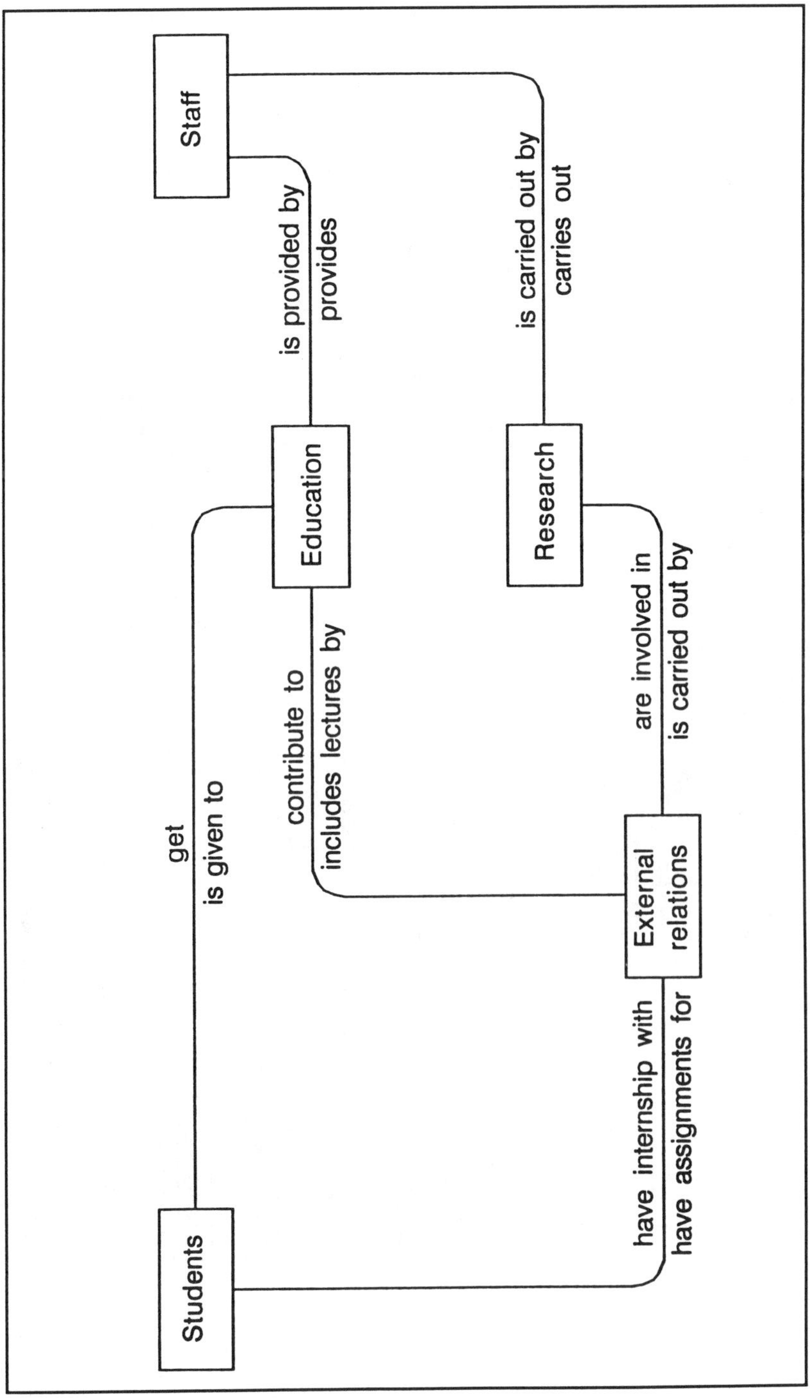

Figure 3: Example of an Entity-Relationship Model, as a Representation of the Data Model

	Course	External organisation	External relation	Final Project	Grade	Publication	Research program	Research project	Specialization	Student
Develop curriculum	U								CU	
Develop course	CU									
Teach course		CU	CU	C						U
Give exam					C					U
Evaluate course					U					
Evaluate curriculum	U			U	U				U	
Develop research program							CU			
Develop research proposal		CU	CU				U	CU		
Carry out research								CU		
Report research findings		U	U			C	U	U		
Evaluate research project						U		U		
Evaluate research program						U	U			

Figure 4: Part of an Information Model, Showing the Interaction Between Business Processes and Entity Types

	Specialization	Course	Final Project	Student	Grade	External organisation	External relation	Research program	Research project	Publication	General Ledger	Supporting Staff	Scientific Staff	Computer	Office
Develop curriculum	CU	U											U		
Develop course		CU													
Teach course			C	U		CU	CU								
Give exam				U	C										
Evaluate course					U										
Evaluate curriculum	U	U	U		U								U		
Develop research program								CU					U		
Develop research proposal						CU	CU	U	CU						
Carry out research									CU						
Report research findings						U	U	U	U	C					
Evaluate research project									U	U					
Evaluate research program								U		U					
Financial Planning											U				
Personnel Planning								U					U		
Financial Administration											CU				
Personnel Administration												CU	CU		
Facilities Management														CU	CU

Figure 5: Part of an Information Architecture, Showing Information Systems Areas and Their Interrelationships

has to be carried out in cooperation with user departments, which might actually be made responsible for parts of these tasks. Common examples of user responsibility are data and application ownership. User departments are thus made responsible to approve changes in either data model or applications. Apart from choices with respect to the responsibility structure, the organizational layout may include rules and regulations governing the actual development, operation, and maintenance of information systems support.

Objectives of an Information Architecture

As the focus of this chapter is on the design of an information architecture, we will refrain from discussing the technical infrastructure and the organizational layout in more detail. An information architecture serves as "a map or blueprint to plan development and anticipate requirements of computing, communications and data" (Earl, 1989, p. 100). Frielink makes the more or less obvious comment that "information systems support for (part of) an organization can be viewed as one whole information system. However, not everything can be done at the same time, hence prioritization is needed between subsystems." (Frielink, 1987, p. 91). BSP lists this also as the first reason for specifying an information architecture: "a total information system to support the entire business unit's needs is too big to build in any single project" (IBM, 1984, p. 8). These objectives of an information architecture are very obvious and lie at the heart of information planning methods. Complexity reducing measures, in terms of the specification of (smaller) information systems areas, have to be applied in order to arrive at feasible solutions. Information systems areas are described in such a way that information systems development can commence based upon this description (Aarts & Janssen, 1989, p. 85). Reduction of complexity can also be seen in the light of the *manageability* of the ensuing systems development projects. The Arthur Young Planning method uses the information systems areas for the definition of projects, defined as manageable units which can be independently analyzed, designed, and constructed (Arthur Young, 1988, p. xxi).

However, reduction of complexity is not the only objective. As is implied by the top-down planning and bottom-up design philosophy (the foundation of the BSP method), bottom-up design on its own incorporates several difficulties. Greveling, among others, therefore mentions the integration of separate information systems as one of the major aims of an information architecture (Greveling, 1990, p. 176). The ISMOD manual for the Information Systems Study method describes it as follows: "[...] the architect must understand the total information system, to better understand the interfaces to the other subsystems during the detailed design and implementation phase" (IBM, 1986, p. 2). The objective here is to arrive at integrated, shared-data systems. It should be noted that it is not the intention to physically integrate the separate information systems into one giant system. Rather, the separate information systems should operate in a coordinated fashion, such as to appear to its users as an integrated system.

Given the planning horizon of a typical information planning study, stability can be given as another objective of an information architecture. Stability in this context means that a changing environment has little influence on an information architecture over a prolonged period of time. Stability can also be seen as a measure to increase the manageability of information systems development and maintenance processes. Theeuwes mentions with respect to stability that an information architecture is based upon patterns of communication and data characteristics within the organization. Should the demarcation of information systems areas be based upon, for example, output specifications or the structure of programs, then the slightest change in information needs or application programs (caused e.g. by a change in hardware) would influence the architecture (Theeuwes, 1988, pp. 84-85).

Summarizing, the three main objectives of an information architecture are:

- manageability,
- integration, and
- stability.

It remains to be seen whether these objectives satisfy the needs of information planners today. Many issues arise when an organization is confronted with emerging information technologies. Some of these issues will not be resolved through the design of an information architecture that strives for the objectives mentioned above. However, before going into these issues in the next section, a description is provided of some of the methods for information architecture specification.

Information Architecture Specification

The most common method of specifying information systems areas within an information model is given by BSP (IBM, 1984, pp. 39-45). Recall that an information model consists of a matrix listing business processes versus entity types and the interaction between them.

- Business processes are arranged according to their business resource life cycle, separately listing management control processes (as these are specified separately during a BSP study).
- Entity types are then rearranged, causing the C's in the matrix (business process creates data on an entity type) to appear along the diagonal.
- Groups of business processes are identified which have similar patterns of data usage.
- For each group, all the entity types created by the processes in that group are identified.

As such, information systems areas completely cover the information model, and thus the functional decomposition and the data model. The information architecture shows the data controlled by information systems areas and the business processes supported by information systems areas.

The Arthur Young Planning method describes a similar procedure, with the exception of the first step, in which business processes are ordered according to their appearance in the functional decomposition. These two orderings might coincide, depending on the rules applied to obtain the functional decomposition. For the third step, the grouping of processes, an additional guideline is given, stating that information systems areas should not cross functional boundaries.

Information Systems Study, as supported by the ISMOD tool, takes a slightly different view to the definition of information systems areas. Here business processes are grouped together solely on the basis of the interaction of data (IBM, 1986, p. 42). The ISMOD tool uses set of algorithms to determine the amount of coupling between business processes, based on their common usage of data. Highly coupled processes are supposed to form an information systems area, together with the data they create and use. However, the numbering scheme employed for business processes and the way this is handled in forming information systems areas leads, again, to a demarcation which follows the functional decomposition.

MAIN THRUST

Issues, Controversies, Problems

From the description above, a definition of information architecture is given as follows: An information architecture describes information systems areas in terms of

- the business processes they support,
- the (data on) entity types which they control, and
- the relationships they have with other information systems areas.

As such, an information architecture is a demarcation of information systems areas within an information model, as an information model specifies business processes (structured according to either a business resource life cycle or a functional decomposition), entity types, and the relationships between the two. The information systems areas are disjoint with respect to the business processes they support and the entity types on which they control the data.

Procedures for the design of an information architecture, as given by methods for information planning, only take into account the information model. Quite mistakenly, several authors suggest information systems areas are specified such as to minimize the exchange of data between them (see e.g. Theeuwes, 1988, p. 108; Argelo, 1987, p. 100). They seem to neglect the fact that prior to grouping processes on the basis of similar data usage, the business processes are arranged in either a business resource life cycle order or in the way they appear in the functional decomposition. Only if the functional decomposition (or business resource life cycle) gives rise to a minimization of data exchange will this minimization be the predominant feature of the information architecture. Subject databases, combined with modern database management systems, do not require the minimization of data exchange.

An information architecture which specifies information systems areas along the boundaries of business functions or business resources only partially satisfies the objectives of stability, integration, and manageability, as covered in the previous paragraph. Especially the objective of stability should be met through the specification of a functional decomposition of business activity which is independent of the organizational form chosen. Whether this independence can be realized has to be doubted. When an organization is seen as an information processing system, the design parameters of the organization can be used to regulate the information flows through the system (Galbraith, 1973). Therefore, the information systems support has to reflect in some way the structure of the organization. Moreover, as business processes indicate a certain division of labor, it gives rise to a complementary set of coordinating processes (Mintzberg, 1979). These coordinating process do not remain unchanged as the structure of the organization changes.

Beside stability, integration, and manageability, additional objectives are given by practitioners of information planning. Maintainability, the use of package software, and alignment with business objectives are some of the issues that come up in discussions about this subject. Emerging information technologies also provide new insights on the ways in which effective architectures can be established. Object oriented technology, distributed databases, open systems, and cooperative processing all provide new opportunities for information systems development. The specifics of these technologies have to be reflected in an information architecture. Also, the influence emerging information technologies have on the business environment have to be taken into account. Downsizing, electronic data interchange, and networking pose challenges to the organization that can only be dealt with in organizational terms. How the information architecture should reflect these organizational challenges is not taken into account in current methods for information planning. In general, one can conclude that current procedures for information architecture specification do not address organizational issues.

Most methods for information planning define the specification of an information architecture in such a way that no other focus than the prescribed one is allowed for specification. Moreover, due to the complicated procedures to be carried out by hand, it is hardly feasible to apply more than one method for IA specification, or to develop alternative information architectures from different viewpoints within one method. For this reason, there is a need for an approach which supports more than one view on information planning and hence on information architecture specification, based on the multiple methodology approach toward information planning, which will be described next. This approach needs to provide possibilities to specify alternative information architectures and to evaluate the differences between them. The way in which these possibilities can be implemented in a decision support system is the subject of section *Alternative designs and evaluation.* The section *Application Within a CASE Organization,* will show the application of this new approach.

Solutions and Recommendations

A Multiple Methodology Approach. Although several methods for information planning can be distinguished (see e.g. Davis and Olson, 1985, Theeuwes, 1988) a choice for the use of just one method must be judged not preferable. Earl concludes that using just one single IS strategy formulation methodology (his terminology for information planning method) will not work (Earl, 1989). He also states that the choice for a methodology depends on aspects like the sector in which the organization operates. Furthermore, the success of the use of a methodology depends on the experiences of the past.

In order to operate in a more flexible and more effective way, Earl suggests a multiple methodology approach, as an approach that better fits a changing organizational view upon information planning. Depending on the organizational starting point for information planning, a combination of approaches can be chosen. This view is supported by Welke, who proposes the concept of 'methodology engineering', i.e. the adaptation of methods to the specifics of an organizational setting (Welke, Kumar & Van Dissel, 1991). This calls for a large degree of flexibility in both methods for information planning and their supporting tools (Stegwee & Van Waes, 1991).

Earl's multiple methodology approach relies upon three so called 'legs' (see figure 6). The first leg is the top-down leg, in which information policy (and consequently, the specification of an information architecture) can be seen as derived from top management aspects like critical success factors, strategic opportunities, business goals, etc. A formulation of top management's ideas on these aspects should lead to the specification of (future) information systems. Generally, the top-down leg is an analytical process during which the business needs and strategy should be formulated in terms of IT. The processes that support a business goal or a critical factor become basis for the demarcation of an information system. *Strategy Set Transformation* and *Critical Success Factors Analysis* are examples of this approach.

The second leg is the bottom-up leg. This leg concerns the present situation as starting point for information planning. The present situation can be the organization's processes or present information systems. The current use of IT should be evaluated by the users in terms of available entity types and supported business processes. The information obtained as a result of the evaluation of the present situation can be used to (re)define information systems. (Re)definition can be done either in terms of standard software, or in terms of groups of processes or entity types. The *Normative Analysis* method is an example in this area.

The third leg Earl distinguishes — the inside-out one — considers methods for information planning that involve think-tanks, Delphi methods, etc. These methods are used as a support in the determination of opportunities offered by IT in general. After an investigation of these opportunities, the opportunities can be 'translated' into terms according to one of the approaches described above. For example, the opportunities can be translated into new processes, or new organizational goals. So after the translation of the opportunities into terms, they form an input to either the top-down or the

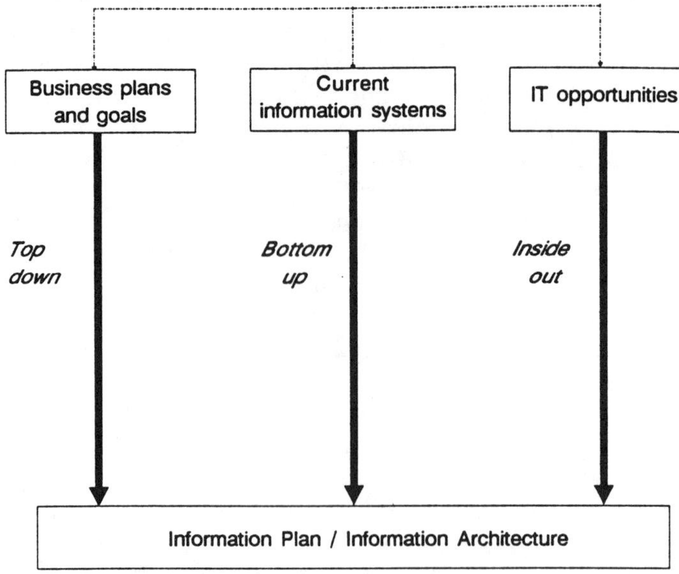

Adaptation of Earl, 1989, p. 71.

Figure 6: The Multiple Methodology Approach

bottom-up leg. *End-means Analysis* is most likely to fit into this area.

The methods mentioned can be seen as complementary to each other. However, each of them influences the information systems in place in their own specific way. The major problem is to integrate the results of the various methods into one direction. This can be realized by the specification of an information architecture that coordinates, integrates and leads these influences into the same direction. Such an information architecture results from the careful analysis and evaluation of alternative designs, as provided by the application of different strategies for information architecture specification, stemming from different information planning methods.

Alternative designs and evaluation. Recall the definition given previously: An information architecture describes information systems areas in terms of

- the business processes they support,
- the (data on) entity types which they control, and
- the relationships they have with other information systems areas.

In order to design an information architecture, groups of business processes and entity types have to be established. Each group, being a set of business processes and entity types, will be the basis for further information systems development. The relationships between processes and entity types within one group give an impression of the activities to be carried out by the (future) information system. The relationships between different groups indicate the necessary interfaces between (future) information systems. In principle, there are many ways in which groups of processes and entity types can be specified. The key to applying a multiple methodology approach toward information architecture specification is to apply several different strategies, each leading to a possible information architecture, and to analyze and evaluate the differences between them. This analysis will give rise to the modification of one or more of the alternative architectures, in order to incorporate as many of the desired characteristics as possible. Such a process should continue until an integrated information architecture has been specified which meets the objectives as well as possible. However, as information architecture specification is quite a cumbersome task, this approach is only feasible when supported by a computer based tool. We have developed such a tool, called the Groningen On-line Simulation Support for Information Planning (GOSSIP) system, the essence of which will be described below. This description serves to demonstrate how to apply a multiple methodology approach toward information architecture specification. A full description of the GOSSIP system and its theoretical foundations can be found in (Stegwee, 1992).

In general, the groups within an information architecture are specified by investigating the interdependencies between either entity types or business processes or both. For example, one can think of the specification of different groups of entity types according to the geographical locations at which they are stored. However, many other aspects can be taken into account, depending on the information gathered prior to IA specification. Cluster analysis[1] is used in the GOSSIP system to determine coherent groups of processes and entity types, according to a certain definition of coherence. Historically, such coherence is called similarity in cluster analysis. Similarity can be defined in several ways, such as in terms of locations as mentioned above. Through the application of different definitions of similarity, different information architectures can be obtained. The question that has to be solved now is: which information architecture to choose as the final one, from a set of alternatives?[2]

The choice between different information architectures is situation specific, depending on e.g. existing infrastructure, procedures, and culture. Therefore, this choice has to be taken by information planners themselves, rather than by the GOSSIP system. A DSS should support this choice, by means of ranking alternatives on certain criteria. In the GOSSIP system, such criteria can be developed on the basis of information gathered during information planning.[3] This information has been used already for obtaining groups of processes, by the use of cluster analysis, as described above. However, it can also be used for determining cluster validity (see Kiewiet & Stegwee, 1991b).

Cluster validity investigates the coherence of groups of processes, according to a predefined criterion. Taking several information architectures as an input it is possible, e.g. to investigate the quality of the architectures according to the coherence of the groups with respect to different geographical locations within the organization. In other words: do the various groups within the architectures take place at different locations? The use of cluster validity results in a list of scores for different architectures on the criterion. Other criteria, like 'coherent according to the different departments of the organization' can be applied too, as well as the way organizational goals or Critical Success Factors are supported by the different groups within the architectures. Which criteria can be applied in a specific situation depends on the information available from the preceding phases in the information planning process. This in turn depends on the employed method for information planning. It is clear that more information becomes available when a multiple methodology is used.

We now return to the classification of information planning methods, in order to show that the GOSSIP system is able to deal with all recognized approaches. For each category we indicate how cluster analysis can be used to achieve the desired result.

Normative Analysis is based upon the idea that standard software areas should be recognized within the organization. After these areas have been recognized, the necessary adaptations can be specified to make the areas fit specific organizational aspects. Normative Analysis can be applied within the DSS by definition of groups of processes and entities according to standard software available. After these standard software groups have been defined, the remaining entities and processes can be clustered according to any of the other approaches. These remaining entity types and processes can each be assigned to one of the standard software groups, which implies a modification to the standard software.

Clustering the business processes on the business goals they support or the critical factors they are involved with, the GOSSIP system can make use of the data necessary for Strategy Set Transformation and Critical Factors Analysis. Cluster validity can establish the fit of information systems with individual goals or critical factors. In this way strategic or critical information systems can be given priority in further systems development.

Process Analysis is the approach in which organizational processes are arranged in groups according to functional areas within the organization. The basis for a division of processes and entity types into groups in this case can clearly be found in the functional decomposition. Clustering business processes according to the functional decomposition implements the Process Analysis Approach in the GOSSIP system.

Ends-means Analysis is a systems analysis approach that defines the information requirements in terms of input and output of the different areas that can be recognized. A clustering of entity types can be based on the relationships that exist between these entity types, in terms of the business processes that use (as input) or create (as output) data on these entity types. This will result in a clustering that strives for a minimization of data exchange, which seems analogous to Ends-means Analysis.

The possibilities the GOSSIP system offers, assure a better usage of the data gathered during the information planning process and result in different architectures. The cluster validity techniques implemented in the DSS support the choice making process, that should result in a final architecture. One example may help to demonstrate the value of the GOSSIP system. As described above, during Normative Analysis entity types and business processes may remain unassigned to any group, due to the fact that they are not included in standard software. The assignment of these entity types and processes to the standard software groups can be done in several different ways. The cluster validity techniques can support the assignment, as different assignments result in different information architectures. Computing the scores of these architectures on any of the criteria will support the information planner in finding a relatively good assignment.

In summation, the use of the DSS enables the specification of several different possible information architectures. The choice among them is supported as well, and we therefore may conclude that the value of the DSS is the fact that no choice among the approaches for determination has to be made before information planning starts. Therefore, no longer a choice between approaches, but a choice between concrete plans has to be made. This leads to the capability of the tool to support a multiple methodology approach. The next section will show the potentials of the DSS when applied to a case organization. As we were not in the position to carry out a multiple methodology information planning study, this description focusses on the support the system can give in a Bottom Up approach, in this case Process Analysis.

Application within a case organization

Case description. The CBR (Central Bureau for certificates of driving proficiency) is the national institution in The Netherlands responsible for administering exams and for providing medical statements, both with respect to driving proficiency. The exams can be divided into theoretical exams and practical exams.

Theoretical exams can be taken in 28 Theoretical Examination Centers (TEC's), including one mobile center, which are spread over the country. These exams are administered using slide presentations of traffic situations which are accompanied by true/false questions. Practical exams are usually administered in cooperation with the driving schools. The examiner of the CBR judges the candidate while (s)he is driving the driving school's car. The exam starts at one of the Practical Examination Centers (PEC's). These PEC's can coincide with a TEC or other location of the CBR, but sometimes a PEC is not more than an agreement with a local restaurant. A practical exam has to be applied for at the CBR. This is usually done by the driving school.

The third main activity of the CBR is providing medical statements with respect to driving proficiency. On the basis of a Personal Statement a medic will judge the (medical) ability of a person to drive. In special cases, after consulting a general physician or the Common Medical Service, a conditional medical statement will be provided. In this case the candidate is only regarded medically fit to drive vehicles with specified adaptations.

Finally the CBR has a special organizational unit to handle appeals, the Bureau of Further Investigation (BFI). The procedures followed for this bureau are roughly the same as for the 'normal' theoretical and practical examinations. In total, approximately 900 people work for the CBR, of which 300 for the internal service. The internal service is responsible for the administrative work regarding the exams. Taken into account a yearly number of 600,000 practical examinations, 480,000 theoretical examinations and 800,000 Personal Statements (1987 data), one can imagine the vastness of the administrative task.

Information Architecture specification at CBR. The replacement of the central hardware and systems software, as well as the oncoming reorganization of the CBR, were reasons for the CBR management to carry out an information planning study. For this purpose, Moret Ernst & Young Management Consultants were brought in to help, which also meant a choice for the proprietary method, Arthur Young Information Engineering / Computer Systems Methodology - Planning, in short called Information Systems

Planning (ISP). Based upon this (BSP-oriented) method, several models have been specified for both the current situation and the desired situation with respect to information systems services. The Information Engineering Workbench (KnowledgeWare, 1989) has been used to store and manipulate these models.

The information architecture initially specified for the CBR was the one partly shown in figure 7. It has been specified by means of the Process Analysis approach, as prescribed by the ISP method. Manual manipulation of the information model has lead to a specification of groups which coincide with the business functions in the functional decomposition. The same result can be obtained by applying the Process Analysis approach within GOSSIP.

The challenges of emerging information technologies. The EDP-center at the CBR has always been a mainframe shop. However, in times of technological development, one has to wonder whether this, historically established, situation is still to continue. The advent of new information technology has provided us with the following capabilities, relevant to the CBR situation:

- on-line transaction processing is feasible on low-cost minicomputers;
- distribution of data is possible, using the state-of-the-art telecommunications infrastructure in the Netherlands;
- distributed databases provide access to distributed data, irrespective of their location of storage.

These new technologies have prompted the CBR, together with developments within the organization toward a more customer-oriented approach, to explore the possibilities of deconcentration of EDP facilities and decentralization of the organization. For this purpose, another Information Architecture has been obtained through the use of GOSSIP. Taking a decentralized organizational form as input, GOSSIP has been applied to specify an information architecture that distinguishes between departmental and interdepartmental information systems. In this way departmental information systems can be built under the sole responsibility of the specific department. The result of the application of GOSSIP in this sense was a different information architecture, parts of which are shown in figure 8.

Discussion of alternative architectures. As was discussed above, the GOSSIP system also offers support to compare different architectures, through the use of cluster validity. Figure 9 gives an indication of the results of the application of cluster validity to the two architectures described above. In these cases, cluster validity determination results in the conclusion that the first architecture

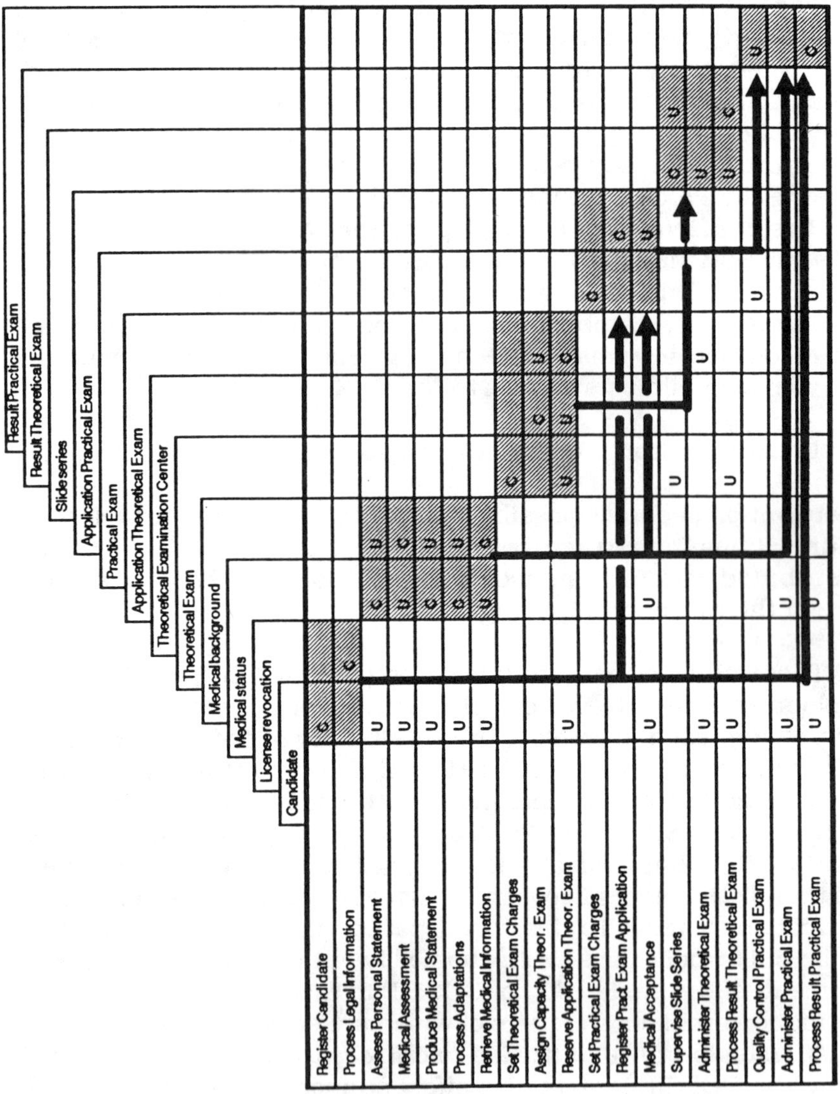

Figure 7: Part of the Original Information Architecture Specified for the CBR

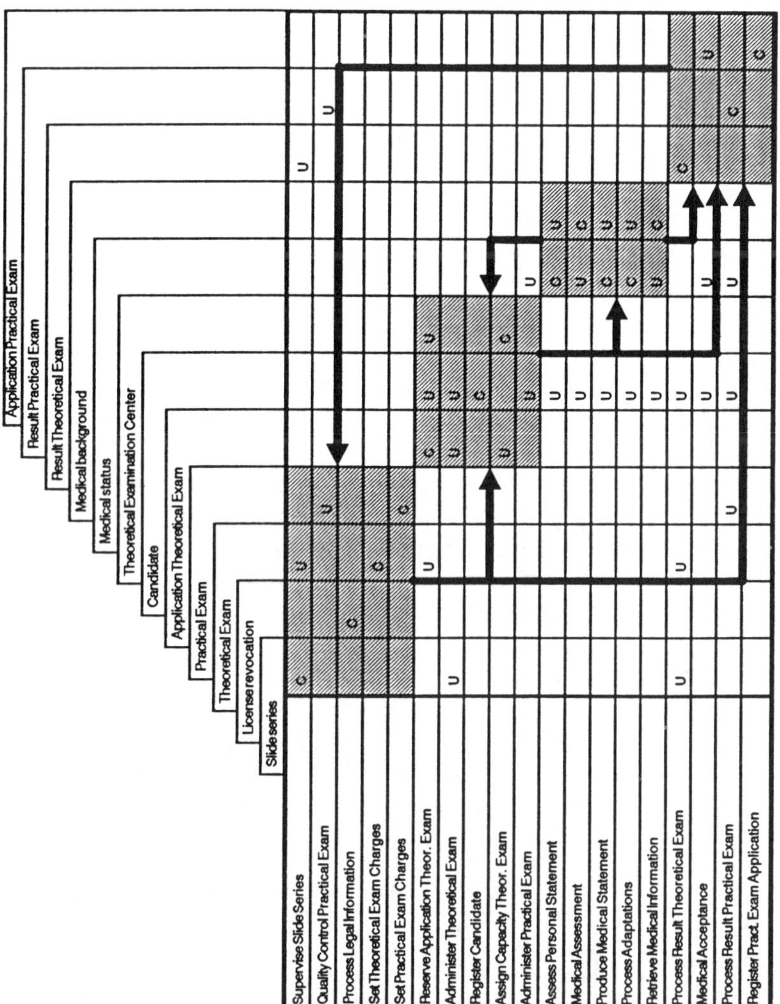

Figure 8: Part of an Information Architecture: a Process-Entity matrix arranged according to organizational responsibility

should be considered better than the second with respect to

- the fit with the functional decomposition and
- the number of interfaces necessary because of usage of data on an entity type by several information systems.

This is hardly surprising, as these are the exact objectives that a BSP-like method would strive for. However, the second architecture is rated better than the first when we look at

- the distribution of information systems over locations and
- the fit with the decentralized structure of the organization.

As you can see, the GOSSIP system enables you to incorporate the specific opportunities that new information technologies offer into the information architecture for your organization. In this case, deconcentration of hardware and systems software, together with a decentralization and deconcentration of the organization, renders a truly different information architecture, better equipped to take advantage of these new developments than the original ISP architecture developed at CBR.

An overall judgment of these two information architectures can not be given by the system, as it is not known whether these criteria cover all criteria deemed important by the user. Even in the unlikely event that these criteria were complete, their respective weights would have to be established in order to reach a final ranking.

FUTURE TRENDS

The ever increasing pace of changes in organizational goals and directions will lead to continuous changes in both business and/or IT structures. To handle new business issues like globalization, an

	location	**functions**	**entity**	**organizational unit**
Information Architecture partly shown in figure 7.		better	better	
Information Architecture partly shown in figure 8.	better			better

Figure 9: Ranking Two Different Information Architectures

increased customer orientation and vertical integration, new approaches will be added to the information planning approaches that already exist. For example, techniques for business modelling and business process redesign will be developed further. Such issues lead to an increased importance of top-down approaches to information planning, such as Strategy Set Transformation. On the other hand, we also find that the changes in IT-opportunities with high business relevance is subject to changes in an increasing pace. Also from this side, new claims are put forward. New approaches are developed for the analysis of IT opportunities (IT-Assessment methods). In addition, the information systems in place will become more and more a factor of importance. The investments in this field are becoming relatively high. As such, they determine the space and direction for new activities. This means that the bottom up approach increases in importance. Also in this area new approaches and techniques will be invented.

Summarizing, we can state that as a reaction to business and IT changes, the number and the character of the methods for information planning will also change the coming years. Depending on the organizational setting, a mix of approaches is needed to combine top-down and bottom-up characteristics. This requirement can be met through the application of a multiple methodology approach. This, in turn, means that in the future the need for flexible information architectures that coordinate and integrate these multiple viewpoints will be even more important. Accordingly, the need for a tool that supports the evaluation of various alternative information architecture solutions will increase.

The field of tool support, itself, is also changing nowadays. In the entire field of information systems development, starting with business changes up to the implementation of new systems, supporting tools are used. These tools will be further developed in the direction of an integral CASE-tool environment (CASE = Computer Aided Systems Engineering). This environment will have the following characteristics:

- covering all phases from new business demands to new information systems,
- more and more of the activities will be completely automated, and
- supporting various types of methods and techniques.

Integration of GOSSIP within such an integral CASE environment gives rise to new challenges. Two of these challenges will be elaborated here.

How can all the data, gathered in preceding phases of informa-

tion planning, be captured in the GOSSIP system?

In the prototype GOSSIP system only limited use has been made of the available data. For the sake of containing the complexity of the problem, relationships between elements have been limited to binary relations. However, current tools for information planning gather more than just binary data. For example, the Information Engineering Workbench permits the user to enter frequencies for the creation and use of data on entity types. The way in which such information is to be captured by GOSSIP and its influence on the specification of information architectures should provide an exciting research area. This issue does not of course stem directly from the integration of GOSSIP with CASE tools, but such an integration makes the issue more prominent.

Which data has to be available in order to apply the desired strategies and evaluation criteria?

Interaction between the phases of information architecture specification and business and information modelling, as carried out in the preceding phases of information planning, can lead to the determination of missing elements in the business and information models. The need or desire to apply certain strategies for information architecture specification or specific evaluation criteria can be rendered impossible due to a lack of data in the models specified. Notions of these desired strategies or evaluation criteria can hence give rise to the incorporation of new elements in the business and information models.

CONCLUSIONS

In this chapter we have argued that current methods for information planning do not address the issues facing management, when confronted with emerging information technologies. We advocate the usage of a multiple methodology approach to information planning in order to deal with these issues more satisfactorily. Key to the multiple methodology approach is the ability to develop and evaluate several alternative solutions to a problem, each focussing on a different set of objectives and constraints. In order to apply this multiple methodology approach toward the design of an information architecture, we have constructed the decision support system GOSSIP. Depending upon the information gathered during the phases prior to information architecture specification, the GOSSIP system is able to generate and evaluate several information architectures from radically different points of view. Thus, a multiple methodology approach toward information architecture specification has become feasible. Although the results of the experiments done with the prototype and the theories implemented clearly indicate that the DSS can be a good support during the information planning process, more research and practical experience with the DSS have to prove the real value of the DSS. The results up till now are however encouraging. Furthermore, the GOSSIP system provides a vehicle for studying the effects of a multiple methodology approach toward information planning. So far it seems empirical studies on the application of a multiple methodology approach are lacking.

ENDNOTES

[1] See e.g. Jain and Dubes (1988) for more about cluster analysis. See Kiewiet and Stegwee (1991a) and Kiewiet and Stegwee (1991b) for more about cluster analysis in the field of information planning.

[2] cf the choice among alternatives made during a decision making process, as described in Simon (1960). The availability of alternatives allows the information planner to make a real choice, instead of considering only one alternative as is the case in most (singular) methods for information planning.

[3] As the information necessary for a specific criterion may not have been gathered during the information planning process, not all desirable criteria can be applied. This, however, leads to questions about what informatin has to be gathered during the information planning process, which will not be addressed in this chapter. We have explicitly limited ourselves to the information available. See *Future Trends* section for a more eleaborate discussion.

REFERENCES

Aarts, A. F. H., & Janssen, P. M. C. (Eds.). (1989). *Handboek Informatieplanning* [Information Planning Manual]. 's Gravenhage, The Netherlands: Department of Defense.

Argelo, S. M. (1987). De aansluiting van informatieplanning op de ontwikkeling van informatiesystemen: praktijkbeschouwing [The connection of information planning to the development of information systems: a view from practice]. In R. Maes, J. M. van Oorschot, A. H. M. Schrama, D. G. van Til, & L. C. van Zutphen (Eds.) *Informatiebeleid en Informatieplanning: visies vanuit wetenschap en praktijk* (pp. 96-102). 's Gravenhage, The Netherlands: VUGA.

Arthur Young (1988). *Computer Systems Methodology: Information Engineering, Planning.* (Unpublished Proprietary Material, Arthur Young International).

Boersma, S. K. Th. (1989). *Beslissingsondersteunende Systemen: een praktijkgerichte ontwikkelingsmethode* [Decision Support Systems: a practice based development method]. Schoonhoven, The Netherlands: Academic Service.

Beaupain, D. (1989, October). SPIRIT. In *Informatieplanning: Voorsprong van nu, noodzaak van morgen* [Information Planning: Advantage of today, necessity of tomorrow]. Conference conducted by NOVI, Maarssen.

Davis, G. B., & Olson, M. H. (1985). *Management Information Systems: Conceptual Foundations, Structure, and Development* (2nd ed.). New York: McGraw Hill Book Company.

Earl, M. J. (1989). *Management strategies for information technology.* Englewood Cliffs, NJ: Prentice Hall.

Frielink, A. B. (1987). De aansluiting van informatieplanning op de ontwikkeling van informatiesystemen: theoriebeschouwing [The connection of information planning to the development of information systems: a view from theory]. In R. Maes, J. M. van Oorschot, A. H. M. Schrama, D. G. van Til, & L. C. van Zutphen (Eds.) *Informatiebeleid en Informatieplanning: visies vanuit wetenschap en praktijk* (pp. 87-95). 's Gravenhage, The Netherlands: VUGA.

Galbraith, J. R. (1973). *Designing Complex Organizations.* Reading, MA: Addison Wesley.

Greveling, N. J. W. (1990). *Informatieplanstudie: Model voor Informatiestrategie en Informatieplan* [Information Plan Study: Model for Information Strategy and Information Plan]. Schoonhoven, The Netherlands: Academic Service.

International Business Machines (1984). *Business Systems Planning: Information Systems Planning guide* (4th ed.). (Publication No. GE20-0527-4) Atlanta, GA: International Business Machines Corporation.

International Business Machines (1986). *Information System Model and Architecture Generator: Operation Guide* (2nd ed.). (Publication No. SB11-5989) Atlanta, GA: International Business Machines Corporation.

Jain, A. K., & Dubes, R. C. (1988). *Algorithms for clustering data.* Englewood Cliffs, NJ: Prentice Hall.

Kiewiet, D. J., & Stegwee, R. A. (1991a). Conceptual Modelling and Cluster Analysis: Design Strategies for Information Architectures. In J. I. DeGross, I. Benbasat, G. DeSanctis, & C. M. Beath (Eds.), *Proceedings of the Twelfth Annual International Conference on Information Systems* (pp. 315-326). Baltimore, MD: ACM.

Kiewiet, D. J., & Stegwee, R. A. (1991b, March), The use of cluster analysis in a decision support system. (Research Report 1991-02) Groningen, The Netherlands: University of Groningen, Faculty of Management and Organization. Paper presented at the First IFORS Specialized Conference on Decision Support Systems, Bruges (B).

KnowledgeWare (1989). *Information Engineering Workbench: Planning Workstation.* Atlanta, GA: Knowledgware, Inc.

Martin, J. (1986). *Information Engineering: The Key to Success in MIS.* Lancashire, United Kingdom: Savant Research Studies.

Mintzberg, H. (1979). *The Structuring of Organizations: A Synthesis of the Research.* Englewood Cliffs, NJ: Prentice Hall.

Olle, T. W., Hagelstein, J., Macdonald, I. G., Rolland, C., Sol, H. G., Van Assche, F. J. M., & Verrijn-Stuart, A. A. (1988). *Information Systems Methodologies: A Framework for Understanding.* Workingham, United Kingdom: Addison Wesley Publishing Company.

Simon, H. A. (1960). *The new science of management decision.* New York, NY: Harper & Brothers.

Stegwee, R. A. (1992). *Division for Conquest: Decision Support for Information Architecture Specification.* Groningen, The Netherlands: Wolters Noordhoff.

Stegwee, R. A. & Van Waes, R. M. C. (1990). The Development of Information Systems Planning towards a Mature Management Tool. *Information Resources Management Journal, 3*(3), 8-21.

Stegwee, R. A., & Van Waes, R. M. C. (1991). Flexible CASE Tools for Information Systems Planning. In M. Khosrowpour (Ed.), Managing Information Technology in a Global Society: *Proceedings of the 1991 Information Resources Management Association International Conference* (pp. 214-229). Harrisburg, PA: Idea Group Publishing.

Theeuwes, J. A. M. (1988). *Informatieplanning* [Information Planning]. Deventer, The Netherlands: Kluwer.

Van Waes, R. M. C. (1991). *Architectures for Information Management: A Pragmatic Approach on Architectural Concepts and their Application in Dynamic Environments.* Amsterdam, The Netherlands: Thesis Publishers.

Welke, R. J., Kumar, K., & Van Dissel, H. G. (1991). Methodology engineering: een voorstel om te komen tot situationeel specifieke methode-ontwikkeling [Methodology engineering: a proposal to establish situation specific method development]. *Informatie*, 33, 322-328.

CHAPTER 3

EVALUATING IS EFFECTIVENESS: A SURVEY OF BUSINESS PRACTICE AND IMPLICATIONS FOR EMERGING INFORMATION TECHNOLOGIES*

Edward J. Szewczak
Canisius College

This chapter discusses the issue of evaluating information system (IS) effectiveness with a view toward understanding the evaluation of emerging information technology (IT). In light of the large amounts involved in investing in IT that forms the basis for modern IS, it is reasonable to inquire into business practices with regard to existing and anticipated IS. The results of a mail survey of New York State companies are presented which provide some empirical evidence for actual business practice in the area of IS evaluation. The results indicate that most firms evaluate IS for effectiveness and utilize various evaluation approaches. Cost/benefit analysis and informal analysis are the two most frequently adopted evaluation approaches, while user satisfaction is the preferred measure of IS effectiveness. Two reasons in particular were cited as reasons for not evaluating IS effectiveness: a lack of time for conducting the evaluation, and a shortage of qualified personnel for conducting the evaluation. The value of existing approaches and measures is examined in light of recent developments in IT, in particular, strategic IT investments.

* This chapter is based on earlier papers presented at annual conferences of the Information Resources Management Association held in Memphis, TN and Charleston, SC. The comments and suggestions of discussants and session attendees which led to improvements in the paper are gratefully acknowledged.

This chapter examines the fundamentally important issue of the evaluation of IS effectiveness. It has three primary purposes: (1) to review the issues and approaches central to IS effectiveness evaluation; (2) to report on the results of a mail survey which collected data on current business practice relating to IS effectiveness evaluation; and (3) to consider how these results relate to the challenge of evaluating the effectiveness of emerging information technologies (IT).

Information technology (IT) is an integral part of many organizational systems addressing a wide range of business activities. Huff & Munro (1985, p. 327) characterize IT as referring to "the broad range of technologies involved in information processing and handling, such as computer hardware, software, telecommunications and office information." Weill & Olson (1989, p. 13) suggest that a broad definition of IT be adopted as the first step in managing IT investment, "including all hardware, software, people, communications (phone, telex, facsimile, satellite etc.), overhead, training and maintenance."

Organizations may have many reasons for making further investment in IT, including increased information processing demands on the organization and the threat of industry competition.

The decision to invest further in IT may be, in part, the output of an organization's strategic plan for its IS, perhaps to increase competitive advantage over the long-term, or to improve management decision making over the medium-term (Weill & Olson, 1989). The decision to invest in emerging IT can have broad operational and strategic consequences for a firm. The data indicate that firms generally perceive the importance of evaluating some or all IS for effectiveness. Various internal and external constraints serve to inhibit the conducting of IS effectiveness evaluation, yet the data suggest that firms regard the results of IS effectiveness evaluation to be useful in justifying further investment in IT. The rationale behind this attitude seems reasonable: If past investment in IT has been evaluated as successful, then the organizational mechanisms for ensuring that further investment in IT will be successful may continue to work favorably to limit the risks associated with the investment. Firms that consider investing in emerging IT without considering the effectiveness of their existing IS may be neglecting the value of their own experience in the name of gaining some business advantage (say, getting a jump on the competition). Such an approach to evaluating emerging IT may prove to be both premature and costly.

BACKGROUND

IS evaluation has generally been considered an integral part of systems development (King & Rodriguez, 1978; Keen, 1981; Davis & Olson, 1985). The large investment in hardware, software, data and personnel which organizations must make to develop and maintain various systems, as well as in the organizational mechanisms required to manage them, dictates the need to assess whether the systems are actually doing the jobs for which they were designed. Not surprisingly, this need is particularly felt during economic hard times, when cost-cutting and belt-tightening compel organizations to closely evaluate the worth of projects requiring large capital outlays (King, 1975). However, the need to evaluate systems effectiveness may be felt keenly even in favorable economic conditions. The effectiveness evaluation issue is becoming of ever increasing importance as firms are faced with the large risks of investing in strategic information technology necessary to compete successfully in today's business world (Clemons & Weber, 1990). Firms may look to assess the effectiveness of their current investment in information technology as embedded in existing organizational systems for reasons to justify investing in new information technology. Measuring IS effectiveness has been identified as one of the top ten issues for IS managers (Brancheau & Wetherbe, 1987).

The classification of various IS is difficult in light of the continuing evolution of the IS concept (Davis & Olson, 1985). For our purposes, a MIS was defined as an integrated, user-machine system for providing information to support operations, management, analysis and decision-making functions in an organization. A DSS is a kind of MIS which is used in planning, analyzing alternatives, and trial and error search for solutions, and is usually operated through terminal-based interactive dialogs with users (Davis & Olson, 1985).

Systems are said to be "effective" if they produce the desired result for which they were developed. Being effective implies doing the "right" thing. This differs from systems "efficiency" which refers to the use of systems resources to achieve the desired results. Being efficient implies the systems are operating the "right" way (Davis & Olson, 1985). This paper is concerned only with issues related to IS effectiveness. For a recent discussion of issues related to measuring IS efficiency, see Banker, Kauffman & Morey (1990).

Evaluating systems is a fundamental issue in the management of IS. Dickson & Wetherbe (1985, p. 164) identified six reasons for evaluating systems:

(1) Senior executives want to evaluate systems because organizations devote a large amount of resources to this activity.
(2) In many organizations there is a vague feeling that the benefits received from systems are not worth the level of expenditure for the systems.
(3) Usually the systems function has not been subjected to the same standards that have been applied to other organizational units, and it is time to attempt a formal measurement of the systems function.
(4) Senior management may feel that the organization is at risk should the computing function experience failure such as computer crime or misuse of computer resources.
(5) Management needs a basis for comparing the performance of systems over time in order to perform corrective action to improve the systems.
(6) It is very useful to accurately assess the current state of systems before embarking on new systems planning activity.

The literature on systems evaluation has suggested nine approaches to evaluating systems effectiveness:

Cost/benefit analysis involves the identification of factors contributing to system costs and benefits, and measuring, calculating, and comparing cost/benefit values. Usually two or more system alternatives are analyzed. Various quantitative methods are employed in the calculation of cost/benefit values, such as payback, net present value and internal rate of return. However, measuring costs and benefits often presents different kinds of problems. Costs may be categorized and quantified without excessive trouble (King & Schrems, 1978). However, benefits are classified into three categories: tangible monetary benefits, tangible nonmonetary benefits, and intangible benefits (Ahituv & Neumann, 1982). Whereas costs can be compared directly to tangible monetary benefits, they can be compared only indirectly to tangible nonmonetary benefits (for example, improving the chances of saving a life). Intangible benefits defy quantification, generally speaking, and so comparison to costs becomes problematic. This problem directly impacts the evaluation of systems effectiveness, since many of the benefits avowed to result from systems are intangible, such as improved decision making (Chervany & Dickson, 1970) and improved organizational communication (Montgomery & Benbasat, 1983).

Multiattribute analysis evaluates systems by identifying and combining various system attribute values into some overall effectiveness measure. Methods of combination vary and may include additive, multiplicative, or more complex forms of multiattribute value functions (Dyer & Sarin, 1979). Linear valuation models are employed where the weights represent the relative importance of the attribute values. The attribute values vary for different systems, and may be objective as in the case of utility functions (Ahituv, 1980) or subjective as in the case of user reported satisfaction (King & Epstein, 1983). (Strictly speaking, cost/benefit analysis is a kind of multiattribute analysis since the utility of a system may be measured in terms of system costs and system benefits.) Multilinear valuation models may also be employed (Kleijnen, 1980). Where linear valuation models are not possible or impractical, lexicographical ordering, the efficient frontier, and statistical analysis may be used (Ahituv & Neumann, 1982).

The variety of methods of measurement used and the general lack of consistent results with respect to systems evaluation has led to the development of a proposed standard instrument to measure "user information satisfaction" (Ives, Olson & Baroudi, 1983). Based on the work of Bailey & Pearson (1983), and reportedly developed according to accepted psychometric theory, the user information satisfaction instrument is intended to measure MIS effectiveness through the collection and analysis of system user subjective responses to questions about system attributes using the semantic differential technique. Both a long-form measure and a short-form measure have been developed (Ives, Olson & Baroudi, 1983; Baroudi & Orlikowski, 1988). The user information satisfaction instrument has been used to evaluate large-scale transaction processing systems, but has not been tested in a DSS environment (Baroudi & Orlikowski, 1988). However, the reliability of the instrument has been challenged recently (Galletta & Lederer, 1989).

Value analysis is an alternative to traditional cost/benefit analysis which emphasizes the value of a DSS project rather than its cost, focuses on identifying and interpreting intangible benefits, and is usually applicable to a single investment proposal (Money, Tromp & Wegner, 1988). Experience with developing DSS suggests that there is no common cost/benefit recipe that can be applied successfully to all DSS, since the degree to which supported decisions are structured, the level of managerial activity, the level of uncertainty, and the source of information used are factors which have differing impacts during the phases of the decision making process (Pieptea & Anderson, 1987). It has been suggested that decision support and office automation systems be evaluated in the aggregate, rather than individually, in terms of overall productivity improvements attributable to a portfolio of systems (Gremillion & Pyburn, 1985).

Simulation is a method of representing the general characteristics of systems within a dynamic model of a firm, and of evaluating systems in terms of the economic benefits of improved total performance attributable to better information provided by systems (Bonini, 1963; Boyd & Krasnow, 1963). The approach assumes that the intangible benefits of MIS are linked to the tangible economic benefits of performance, and that the provision of improved information will translate into improved performance (e.g. writing more accurate purchase orders based on current inventory figures). This approach has been criticized as being too general to be useful to MIS development specialists (Chervany & Dickson, 1970).

Goal programming, a mathematical programming algorithm from the operations research/management science literature, has been proposed as a technique for evaluating MIS by establishing a causal relationship between user multiple goal attainment and system activity, and iteratively examining different sets of targets in light of a set of constraints (Chandler, 1982). The approach assumes that all goals are quantifiable for purposes of comparison.

The *critical success factors* (CSF) method was proposed by Rockart (1979) as a way of assisting managers to define their significant information needs. It has been used as a methodology in MIS planning and control (Munro & Wheeler, 1980; Shank, Boynton & Zmud, 1985) and in determining the information needs of top MIS managers (Martin, 1983). The CSF method usually involves two basic steps: interview the manager, and review the results. Questionnaires may also assist the data collection effort. The CSF method has been used to perform the evaluation of the information function of MIS by comparing the information needs of a management team involved in planning and control to assess the usefulness and availability of critical information (Bergeron & Begin, 1989).

Various *attitudinal* approaches to systems evaluation have been reviewed in Ives, Olson & Baroudi (1983) and Goodhue (1988). Attitudinal approaches generally stress the futility of trying to evaluate systems using objective measures, and the need to examine the subjective attitudinal responses of users in assessing the value of their systems. These responses may be influenced by the social group to which an individual belongs which may affect how the systems are interpreted and used (Robertson, 1989). Data may be analyzed about user attitudes toward the effect of the system on a manager's job performance, on interpersonal relations and communication, on changes in organizational structures, etc. (King & Rodriguez, 1978).

Utilization was identified as a general effectiveness measure in Table 2. However, it has been observed that both actual usage measures and perceived effectiveness measures (user satisfaction) must be considered together when evaluating systems effectiveness, since neither measure category alone is sufficient (Srinivasan, 1985). It has been argued that utilization should be viewed as a factor affecting system performance rather than as an indicator of performance itself (Trice & Treacy, 1988). Utilization analysis can indicate flaws in system design (such as requiring users to expend more time than necessary on a task, or having features which prompt users to utilize the system in nonproductive ways) as well as design successes (such as improving the decision making process by decreasing the length of time required to make decisions) (Hamilton & Chervany, 1981a; Trice & Treacy, 1988).

Informal approaches to systems evaluation may also be used, such as talking to users during the normal work day (Halbrecht, 1977; Hamilton & Chervany, 1981a). Informal approaches may be used alone or in conjunction with the more formal approaches discussed above.

These various approaches have been available to organizations for nearly a decade and longer. Yet though the importance of evaluating systems effectiveness has been stressed in the literature, little empirical research has been reported except for personal observation of evaluation practice. (One notable exception is the study reported in Kumar (1990) on the role of evaluation in the post-implementation of systems.)

Evaluation is conducted during the systems development life cycle (SDLC), which may be broken up into distinguishable phases. For example, Powers, Adams & Mills (1984) distinguish five SDLC phases — investigation, analysis and general design, detailed design and implementation, installation, and review. Each of these phases may be characterized by various representative activities, as follows:

- Investigation - Initial investigation, feasibility study.
- Analysis and General Design - Existing system review, new system requirements, new system design, implementation and installation planning.
- Detailed Design and Implementation - Technical design, test specifications and planning, programming and testing, user training, system test.
- Installation - File conversion, system installation.
- Review - Development recap, post-implementation review.

Systems evaluation may occur in any of these phases. One approach to comparing systems over time is to evaluate systems feasibility during the investigation phase and then systems use during the review phase (Davis & Olson, 1985). King & Rodriguez (1978) recommend evaluating systems after each major phase of development to ensure that quality systems are the outcome of systems development efforts. Each organization must choose its own approach based on its consideration of the quality of systems desired and the costs associated with evaluation activities.

In addition, various effectiveness measures may be used with the evaluation approaches. General effectiveness measures have been identified as decision effectiveness/quality (Dickson, Senn & Chervany, 1977; King & Rodriguez, 1978; Zmud, 1979; Ives & Olson, 1984); utilization (Dickson, Senn & Chervany, 1977; King & Rodriguez, 1978; Zmud, 1979; Ives & Olson, 1984; Trice & Treacy, 1988), user satisfaction (King & Rodriguez, 1978; Zmud, 1979; Hamilton & Chervany, 1981a; Ives, Olson & Baroudi, 1983; Ives & Olson, 1984), changes in user behavior/attitudes (King & Rodriguez, 1978; Ives & Olson, 1984), and organization performance (Hamilton & Chervany, 1981a).

SURVEY METHODOLOGY AND RESULTS

A survey of New York State companies was conducted which addressed the broad issue of evaluating IS effectiveness in an attempt to begin closing the gap between normative thinking on the subject and actual business practice. Though the results of the survey must be considered exploratory at best, they provide some important insights which may be used to improve the state-of-the-art of business practice with regard to evaluating systems effectiveness.

A pilot study was conducted involving managers and systems development personnel from six firms in the Western NY area to determine an acceptable format for the survey questionnaire. Once finalized, the questionnaire was mailed to the President's office of 882 firms in New York State. Firms in the survey were selected at random from *MacRAE's New York State Industrial Directory* and from *COMPACT DISCLOSURE*, a CD-ROM database of U.S. firms. The cover letter asked that the questionnaire be forwarded to the individual in the firm who was most familiar with systems effectiveness evaluation. Eighty-eight questionnaires were returned (response rate = 10%), of which 62 were useable for purposes of statistical analysis. The response rate may be considered typical for a mail survey which attempted to be as unbiased as possible. No efforts were made to increase the response rate in advance (such as telephoning potential respondents to secure their cooperation, or appealing to mailing lists of potential respondents with a likely interest in the subject or in the researcher's affiliation).

The representativeness of the survey results may be judged in four ways. First, all areas of New York State were adequately represented, with 56% of the responses coming from Western and up-state New York, and 44% coming from the metropolitan New York City area. Second, both manufacturing and service sectors of the economy were adequately represented with manufacturing firms comprising 58%, and service firms comprising 42%, of the responses. The industries represented by the manufacturing firms included aeronautics, agricultural products, chemicals, consumer goods, energy, electronics equipment, industrial products, steel, and wood products. The industries represented by the services firms included advertising, banking, broadcasting, distribution, insurance, retailing, transportation, and utilities. Third, the size of the firms involved in the survey ranged from small (number of employees = 12) to large (number of employees = 116881). Fourth, 49% of the respondents identified themselves as systems development personnel (with titles such as "MIS Director", "Data Processing Manager", and "Technical Specialist"), while the remaining 51% of the respondents identified themselves as involved in some aspect of management not directly related to systems development (with titles such as "President", "Vice President - Strategic Technology and Research", and "Controller"). Almost half of the respondents (49%) reported having been involved in more than 15 systems effectiveness evaluation efforts.

Respondents were asked to report the percent of systems evaluated in their firms (Table 1). More than 88% reported that their

	Percentage of Firms	Cumulative Percent
76 - 100%	16.7	16.7
51 - 75%	30.0	46.7
26 - 50%	20.0	66.7
1 - 25%	21.7	88.3
0%	11.7	100.0

Note: Percentages are rounded to one significant decimal.

Table 1: Percent of Systems Evaluated

firms evaluated systems for effectiveness. Nearly 47% reported that their firms evaluated 50% or more of systems for effectiveness. Over 11% reported that their firms did not evaluate systems effectiveness at all.

A series of questionnaire items (based on Kumar (1990)) inquired about possible reasons why firms do not evaluate the effectiveness of some or all of their systems (Table 2). Respondents circled a number on a five-point scale, where 1 = Not at all Important and 5 = Extremely Important. Lack of time and a shortage of qualified personnel were reported to be the most important reasons for not conducting system effectiveness evaluation. No agreement on a set of criteria and measurement used for effectiveness evaluation was also reported as an important reason. It should be noted that these results are consistent with the findings reported in Kumar (1990), even though Kumar's study focused on only post implementation evaluations (i.e., "evaluations performed just before installation, just after installation, and considerably after installation after the system has a chance to settle down" — p. 203).

For those firms which evaluate systems effectiveness, respondents were asked to identify up to four evaluation approaches that

	Mean	(Std Dev)
Management does not perceive adequate benefits from systems effectiveness evaluation	2.89	(1.08)
Project personnel reassigned — not available for systems effectiveness evaluation	2.73	(1.42)
Lack of time for conducting systems effectiveness evaluation	3.66	(1.22)
Shortage of qualified personnel for conducting systems effectiveness evaluation	3.55	(1.35)
No useful approaches for determining systems effectiveness	2.71	(1.08)
Pace of technological change prohibits careful systems effectiveness evaluation	2.26	(1.16)
No agreement on set of criteria and measurement used for systems effectiveness evaluation	3.31	(1.15)
Feeling that effectiveness evaluation will unearth problems better left undisturbed	1.70	(1.04)

Table 2: Reasons for Not Evaluating Systems Effectiveness

Types of Analysis	Number of Firms A1	A2	A3	A4	Use Total	Percent	Cumulative Percent
Cost/benefit	22	6	4	0	32	26.7	26.7
Multiattribute	7	1	1	1	10	8.3	35.0
Value	7	5	2	0	14	11.7	46.7
Simulation	0	2	1	2	5	4.2	50.9
Goal Programming	0	0	0	0	0	0.0	50.9
Critical Success Factors	1	5	5	2	13	10.8	61.7
Attitudes	1	0	3	0	4	3.3	65.0
Utilization	5	3	3	4	15	12.5	77.5
Informal	6	16	3	2	27	22.5	100.0

(Note: A1 = Most frequently used approach
A2 = Next most frequently used approach etc.)

Note: Percentages are rounded to one significant decimal.

Table 3: Evaluation Approaches Adopted

were adopted in the order of frequency of use. (This number of approaches was determined to be adequate from the pilot study results.)

Firms reported using 2.4 evaluation approaches on average (standard deviation = 1.1). Table 3 presents descriptions of the approaches provided to respondents, and a summary of evaluation approaches adopted in terms of frequency of use. (Brief descriptions of the approaches provided to the respondents are given in the Appendix.) The most frequently used approaches are cost/benefit analysis and informal analysis. No firms reported adopting goal programming analysis.

In addition the questionnaire inquired about the phases of systems development in which the various evaluation approaches were adopted and the effectiveness measures used with an approach in each phase. The respondents were presented with a matrix in which it was possible to indicate which effectiveness measures were used in a given development phase by checking cells of the matrix. (See Figure 1 for an example of completing the matrix for multiattribute analysis.) Respondents were asked to complete one matrix for each evaluation approach adopted.

Table 4 presents a listing of evaluation approaches, the number of firms adopting an approach in a given phase of systems development, and the degree of satisfaction reported with an approach. (Results for simulation analysis, attitudes analysis, and goal programming analysis are not shown since only limited data were

DEVELOPMENT PHASE IN WHICH USED	EFFECTIVENESS MEASURES USED WITH APPROACH A = Decision Effectiveness B = Utilization C = User Satisfaction D = User Behavior Changes E = Organization Performance					SATISFACTION				
	A	B	C	D	E	Very Dissatisfied				Very Satisfied
Investigation			X			1	2	3	4	(5)
Analysis & General Design						1	2	3	4	5
Detailed Design & Implementation						1	2	3	4	5
Installation						1	2	3	4	5
Review			X			1	(2)	3	4	5

This example has been completed for an organization which has used Multiattribute Analysis during the Investigation Phase and the Review Phase, employing the User Satisfaction effectiveness measure in each of the two phases. The organization is very satisfied with the approach during the Investigation Phase but is relatively dissatisfied with it during the Review Phase. An additional matrix would be completed for each evaluation approach used.

Figure 1: Questionnaire Matrix of Development Phases, Effectiveness Measures

reported on these approaches.)

Two observations appear warranted in light of these results. First, systems effectiveness evaluation takes place throughout the systems development life cycle. Firms reported that evaluation was conducted in 4.0 phases on average (standard deviation = 1.1). There is more emphasis on effectiveness evaluation in the investigation phase and in the review phase than in the other phases, though clearly evaluation takes place in the other phases as well. Second, for the satisfaction item, respondents circled a number on a five-point scale, where 1 = Very Dissatisfied and 5 = Very Satisfied. The highest reported satisfaction was with multiattribute analysis and value analysis, though it should be noted that all of the approaches (with the exception of critical success factors analysis) fared nearly as well. Of course, this observation is based on a computed average of reported satisfaction in all phases, and does not consider that an approach may be highly useful in a given phase. Finally, the reader is cautioned that no assumptions about the effectiveness of applying the approaches should be made with regard to self-reported satisfaction.

Table 5 presents a summary of effectiveness measure use for the

Types of Analysis	Phase-	Number of Firms		Satisfaction (Mean	(Std Dev))
Cost/benefit	P1 -	26		3.48	(1.01)
	P2 -	19		3.53	(1.02)
	P3 -	12		3.58	(0.79)
	P4 -	8		3.50	(0.54)
	P5 -	22		3.62	(0.87)
			Average	3.54	(0.85)
Multiattribute	P1 -	9		3.78	(0.67)
	P2 -	8		4.17	(0.41)
	P3 -	7		4.00	(0.63)
	P4 -	7		3.50	(1.38)
	P5 -	7		3.38	(0.74)
			Average	3.77	(0.77)
Value	P1 -	12		3.75	(0.87)
	P2 -	6		3.67	(0.52)
	P3 -	6		3.83	(1.17)
	P4 -	5		3.80	(0.45)
	P5 -	10		3.80	(0.42)
			Average	3.77	(0.67)
Critical Success Factors	P1 -	10		3.38	(0.92)
	P2 -	8		3.29	(0.95)
	P3 -	3		2.50	(0.71)
	P4 -	2		2.00	(0.00)
	P5 -	7		3.60	(1.52)
			Average	2.95	(1.03)
Utilization	P1 -	7		3.38	(0.92)
	P2 -	4		3.00	(1.41)
	P3 -	4		3.25	(0.50)
	P4 -	4		4.25	(0.96)
	P5 -	14		3.71	(0.99)
			Average	3.52	(0.96)
Informal	P1 -	16		3.67	(1.11)
	P2 -	14		3.50	(1.16)
	P3 -	12		3.42	(1.44)
	P4 -	11		3.46	(1.29)
	P5 -	22		3.18	(1.22)
			Average	3.45	(1.24)

(Note: P1 = Investigation Phase
P2 = Analysis and General Design Phase
P3 = Detailed Design and Implementation Phase
P4 = Installation Phase
P5 = Review Phase)

Table 4: Evaluation Approaches, Phase of Adoption, and Satisfaction with Approach

six approaches. (Brief descriptions of the effectiveness measures provided to the respondents are given in the Appendix). Note that a firm may choose to use more than one effectiveness measure in any phase. Clearly, user satisfaction is the most frequently used effectiveness measure, with decision effectiveness and organization effectiveness occupying the next discernable level of preference.

DISCUSSION

The primary value of this survey is that it has yielded some limited empirical data on actual business practice of systems effectiveness evaluation. The fact that over 88% of firms reported evaluating some percentage of their systems for effectiveness indicates that the importance of systems evaluation is appreciated by most firms.

The most frequently adopted evaluation approaches —cost/benefit analysis and informal analysis— are, in a sense, complementary and well-known, having been championed in the IS literature (Chervany & Dickson, 1970; Halbrecht, 1977; Hamilton & Chervany, 1981a). Cost/benefit analysis is a formal approach to systems evaluation which tends to emphasize tangible (quantifiable) costs and benefits, though intangible costs and benefits may also be entertained. Informal analysis is, of course, less formal and tends to emphasize user satisfaction with the systems as its primary effec-

This table summarizes the number of times a given effectiveness measure was cited as being used with a given analysis type in all phases of systems development combined.

	D	U	S	B	O
Cost/benefit	32	17	35	4	24
Multiattribute	19	5	20	12	17
Value	14	10	15	6	10
Critical Success Factor	15	5	18	5	15
Utilization	5	11	12	7	5
Informal	13	10	58	15	14
	98	58	158	49	85

(Note: D = Decision Effectiveness
U = Utilization
S = User Satisfaction
B = User Behavior Changes
O = Organization Performance)

Table 5: Evaluation Approaches and Effectiveness Measures

tiveness measure. It is interesting that firms report using roughly two evaluation approaches on average. This result corroborates the findings of Singleton, McLean & Altman (1988) that firms generally use more than one evaluation approach, and suggests that firms perceive a need to approach systems evaluation from different perspectives utilizing different effectiveness measures.

The fact that some evaluation approaches are used less frequently, or not at all, may be attributable to the fact that the approaches are not well-publicized in the IS literature, or that they are not easily operationalized (for example, simulation — Chervany & Dickson, 1970), or that the skill requirements for adopting them are too prohibitive for the average systems evaluator (for example, goal programming analysis).

The data suggest that there may be different "levels of preference" with regard to which effectiveness measure systems evaluators adopt for use with the various approaches. The most preferred effectiveness measure is user satisfaction, while the least preferred measures are utilization and user behavior changes. However, before any definite conclusions about the adoption of effectiveness measures can be drawn, further research is needed to determine the role of "evaluator viewpoints" (Hamilton & Chervany, 1981b) in the choice of effectiveness measures to be used with the different evaluation approaches. It appears that the different approaches allow for the consideration of both tangible and intangible aspects of system use, and that system evaluators may adopt different effectiveness measures according to their interpretation of what "works" with a given approach. The fact that not all firms evaluate systems for effectiveness (or that even firms which evaluate systems for effectiveness do not evaluate all systems) is attributable to two basic reasons which can be dealt with through management education directed at changing skill levels and attitudes toward the importance of systems evaluation. It may be argued that all systems development personnel (and perhaps managers, too) should be versed in systems evaluation. The shortage of qualified personnel for conducting systems evaluation may be addressed in management development seminars or in college/university level IS program courses which focus on approaches and techniques of systems evaluation.

The reported lack of time for conducting systems evaluation is a somewhat tougher issue to deal with. Since survey respondents generally believed that management perceives adequate benefits from systems effectiveness evaluation, making time to perform systems evaluation will result only if management chooses to shift resources away from other organizational activities toward performing systems evaluation. The creation of an organizational policy emphasizing systems evaluation is a possible course of action, but this assumes a change of attitude on the part of management toward the relative importance of systems evaluation. Conducting management development seminars on the benefits of systems evaluation and the need for organizational policy is one approach toward this end.

FUTURE TRENDS

Among the factors which inhibit IS effectiveness evaluation are (1) the perception that there are no useful approaches for determining systems effectiveness, and (2) the lack of agreement on a set of criteria and measurement tools used for systems effectiveness evaluation. These factors are especially critical in the evaluation of emerging IT. For example, it has been argued that return on investment (ROI) calculations and other capital budgeting techniques do not apply to many IT investments, especially strategic IT investments (Weill & Olson, 1989; Clemons & Weber, 1990). It may well be that firms appeal to more informal approaches to systems evaluation than formal capital budgeting techniques to justify further investment in IT. Weill & Olson (1989) observe that many IT investments are made on "gut feelings," especially strategic IT investments.

It appears that an important topic for future research must be the development of approaches for determining systems effectiveness which are convincing enough to management to allow the results of systems effectiveness evaluation to be useful in supporting the IT investment decision. Where existing approaches are perceived to be inadequate to the task of systems effectiveness evaluation, attempts must be made to adapt the existing approaches themselves or to combine them in some fashion with other approaches. Also, effectiveness measures and performance measures must be carefully identified and examined to insure that they are relevant to the emerging IT being evaluated. These are continuing challenges for IS professionals, since future developments in IT can be expected to result in new and creative solutions to business problems.

CONCLUSION

The evaluation of systems effectiveness may be viewed as proceeding along lines suggested in the IS literature. Generally speaking, firms are using various systems evaluation approaches throughout the systems development process. Factors working against systems effectiveness evaluation include a lack of time for conducting the evaluation as well as a shortage of qualified personnel for performing the evaluation. These negative factors may be managed through additional management and IS personnel education directed toward developing the requisite skills for systems evaluation as well as changing the attitudes of top management about the worth of systems evaluation as a regular organizational activity.

Emerging IT make the challenge of evaluating systems for effectiveness all the more pressing and important. New approaches may have to be developed to adequately address emerging IT to insure that the value of these IT are fully understood and appreciated.

APPENDIX

Brief Descriptions of Evaluation Approaches

Cost/benefit Analysis identifies and summarizes the benefits to be expected from the system, the expected cost, and expected savings, if any. Tangible costs and benefits are usually quantified, whereas intangible costs and benefits (e.g. improved employee morale) usually defy quantification. Compare with Multiattribute Analysis below.

Multiattribute Analysis identifies, weights, and combines various system attributes into some overall effectiveness measure. Common approaches include linear and nonlinear mathematical models combining system attribute values, the rank ordering and comparing of system attributes, and statistical analysis. Since cost/benefit analysis is a kind of multiattribute analysis, choose this approach if system attributes other than costs and benefits are involved (such as the relevance of output information to its intended function, user perceptions that the system will be a success, etc.).

Value Analysis is an alternative to traditional cost/benefit analysis which emphasizes the value of a DSS project rather than a systematic analysis of its cost, and focuses on identifying and interpreting intangible benefits (such as improved decision-making).

Simulation Analysis is a method of representing the general characteristics of a system within a dynamic model of a firm and of evaluating the system in terms of the economic benefits of improved total performance attributable to better information provided by the system (e.g. greater profitability attributable to writing more accurate purchase orders based on current inventory figures).

Goal Programming Analysis uses a mathematical programming algorithm from the operations research/management science literature to establish a causal relationship between user multiple goal attainment and system activity, and to iteratively examine different sets of targets in light of a set of constraints.

Critical Success Factors Analysis is a two step process of eliciting the critical factors for operating and managing an organization and then deriving information requirements (e.g. of managers involved in planning and control activities). The information requirements so derived are instrumental in assessing the usefulness and availability of critical information.

Attitudes Analysis examines various subjective attitudinal responses of users to the system. Data may be analyzed about user attitudes toward the effect of the system on a manager's job performance, on interpersonal relations and communication, on changes in organizational structures, etc.

Utilization Analysis examines patterns of systems use to indicate flaws in system design (such as requiring users to expend more time than necessary on a task) as well as design successes (such as improving the decision-making process by decreasing the length of time required to make decisions).

Informal Analysis may be used alone or in conjunction with more formal evaluation approaches. Talking to users during the course of the normal work day or listening for "screams in the hall" are examples of informal analysis.

Effectiveness Measures (and Selected Performance Measures)

Decision Effectiveness - Quality of decision-making including lower costs, higher profits, decreased decision time, greater decision confidence.

Utilization - System logs permit measures of system use; users estimate their use of the system.

User Satisfaction - Satisfaction with accuracy, timeliness and format of output; confidence in the system; degree to which information needs are met.

User Behavior Changes - Changes in user resistance to system; in ways of doing things; in felt need for information; in effort levels; in new work patterns.

Organizational Performance - Achievement of financial objectives, customer objectives, organizational development

REFERENCES

Ahituv, N. (1980). A systematic approach toward assessing the value of an information system. *MIS Quarterly, 4*(4), December, 61-75.

Ahituv, N., & Neumann, S. (1982). *Principles of information systems for management.* Dubuque, IA: Brown.

Bailey, J.E., & Pearson, S.W. (1983). Development of a tool for measuring and analyzing computer user satisfaction. *Management Science, 29*(5), May, 530-545.

Banker, R.D., Kauffman, R.J., & Morey, R.C. (1990). Measuring gains in efficiency from IT. *Journal of MIS, 7*(2), 29-54.

Baroudi, J.J., & Orlikowski, W.J. (1988). A short-form measure of user information satisfaction: A psychometric evaluation and notes on use. *Journal of Management Information Systems, 4*(4), Spring, 44-59.

Bergeron, F., & Begin, C. (1989). The use of critical success factors in evaluation of information systems. *Journal of Management Information Systems, 5*(4), Spring, 111-1 24.

Bonini, C.P. (1963). *Simulation of information and decision systems in the firm.* Englewood Cliffs, NJ: Prentice-Hall.

Boyd, D.F., & Krasnow, H.S. (1963). Economic evaluation of management information systems. *IBM Systems Journal, 2*(1), March, 2-23.

Brancheau, J.C., & Wetherbe, J.C. (1987). Key issues in information systems management. *MIS Quarterly, 11*(1), 22-45.

Chandler, J.S. (1982). A multiple criteria approach for evaluating information systems. *MIS Quarterly, 6*(1), March, 61-74.

Chervany, N.L., & Dickson, G.W. (1970). Economic evaluation of management information systems: An analytical framework. *Decision Sciences, 1*(3/4), 296-308.

Clemons, E.K., & Weber, B.W. (1990). Strategic information technology investments: Guidelines for decision making. *Journal of MIS, 7*(2), 9-28.

Davis, G.B., & Olson, M.H. (1985). Management information systems. New York, NY: McGraw-Hill.

Dickson, G.W., Senn, J.A., & Chervany, N.L. (1977). Research in management information systems: The Minnesota experiments. *Management Science, 23*(9), May, 913-923.

Dickson, G.W., & Wetherbe, J.C. (1985). *The management of information systems.* New York, NY: McGraw-Hill.

Dyer, J.S., & Sarin, R.K. (1979). Measurable multiattribute value functions. *Operations Research, 27*(4), July-August, 810-822.

Galletta, D.F., & Lederer, A.L. (1989). Some cautions on the measurement of user information satisfaction. *Decision Sciences, 20*(3), Summer, 419-438.

Goodhue, D. (1988). I/S attitudes: Toward theoretical and definitional clarity. Data Base, 19(3/4), Fall/Winter, 6-15.

Gremillion, L.L., & Pyburn, P.J. (1985). Justifying decision support and office automation systems. *Journal of Management Information Systems, 2*(1), Summer, 5-17.

Halbrecht, H.Z. (1977). Interview with R.E. McDonald. *MIS Quarterly, 1*(2), June, 7-11.

Hamilton, S., & Chervany, N.L. (1981a). Evaluating information system effectiveness — Part 1: Comparing evaluation approaches. *MIS Quarterly, 5*(3), September, 55-69.

Hamilton, S., & Chervany, N.L. (1981b). Evaluating information system effectiveness — Part II: Comparing evaluator viewpoints. *MIS Quarterly, 5*(4), December, 79-86.

Huff, S., & Munro, M. (1985). Information technology assessment and adoption:

A field study. *MIS Quarterly, 9*(4), 327-340.

Ives, B., & Olson, M.H. (1984). User involvement and MIS success: A review of research. *Management Science, 30*(5), May, 586-603.

Ives, B., Olson, M.H., & Baroudi, J.J. (1983). The measurement of user information satisfaction. *Communications of the ACM, 26*(10), October, 785-793.

Keen, P.G.W. (1981). Value analysis: Justifying decision support systems. MIS Quarterly, 5(1), March, 1-15.

King, J.L., & Schrems, E.L. (1978). Cost-benefit analysis in information systems development and operation. *ACM Computing Surveys, 10*(1), March, 19-34.

King, W.R. (1975). *Marketing management information systems.* New York, NY: Petrocelli/Charter.

King, W.R., & Epstein, B.J. (1983). Assessing information system value: An experimental study. *Decision Sciences, 14*(1), January, 34-45.

King, W.R., & Rodriguez, J.I. (1978). Evaluating management information systems. *MIS Quarterly, 2*(3), September, 43-51.

Kleijnen. J.P.C. (1980). *Computers and profits: Quantifying financial benefits of information.* Reading, MA: Addison-Wesley.

Kumar, K. (1990). Post implementation evaluation of computer-based information systems: Current practices. *Communications of the ACM, 33*(2), February, 203-212.

Martin, E.W. (1983). Information needs of top MIS managers. *MIS Quarterly, 7*(3), September, 1-11.

Money, A., Tromp, D., & Wegner, T. (1988). The quantification of decision support benefits within the context of value analysis. *MIS Quarterly, 12*(2), June, 223-236.

Montgomery, I., & Benbasat, I. (1983). Cost/benefit analysis of computer based message systems. *MIS Quarterly, 7*(1), March, 1-14.

Munro, M.C., & Wheeler, B.R. (1980). Planning, critical success factors, and management's information requirements. *MIS Quarterly, 4*(4), December, 27-38.

Pieptea, D.R., & Anderson, E. (1987). Price and value of decision support systems. *MIS Quarterly, 11*(4), December, 515-527.

Powers, M.J., Adams, D.R., & Mills, H.D. (1984). *Computer information systems development: Analysis and design.* Cincinnati, OH: South-Western.

Robertson, D.C. (1989). Social determinants of information system usage. *Journal of Management Information Systems, 5*(4), Spring, 55-71.

Rockart, J.F. (1979). Executives define their own data needs. *Harvard Business Review, 57*(2), March-April, 81-93.

Shank, M.E., Boynton, A.C., & Zmud, R.W. (1985). Critical success factor analysis as a methodology for MIS planning. *MIS Quarterly, 9*(2), June, 121-129.

Singleton, J.P., McLean, E.R., & Altman, E.N. (1988). Measuring information systems performance: Experience with the management by results system at Security Pacific Bank. *MIS Quarterly, 12*(2), June, 325-337.

Snitkin, S.R., & King, W.R. (1986). Determinants of the effectiveness of personal decision support systems. *Information & Management, 10*(2), February, 83-89.

Srinivasan, A. (1985). Alternative measures of system effectiveness: Associations and implications. *MIS Quarterly, 9*(3), September, 243-253.

Trice, A.W., & Treacy, M.E. (1988). Utilization as a dependent variable in MIS research. *Data Base, 19*(3/4), Fall/Winter, 33-41.

Weill, P., & Olson, M.H. (1989). Managing investment in information technology: Mini case examples and implications. *MIS Quarterly, 13*(1), 3-17.

Zmud, R. (1979). Individual differences and MIS success: A review of the empirical literature. *Management Science, 25*(10), October, 966-979.

CHAPTER 4

THE CHALLENGE OF IMPLEMENTING SIS ACROSS THE VALUE CHAIN: A CASE STUDY OF NEGATIVE IT CONSEQUENCES IN A SUPPLIER FIRM

C.R. Snodgrass, G. Rosenfelder and E.J. Szewczak
Canisius College

The challenges of implementing emerging information technologies into an integrated information system across a number of firms have been extensively analyzed by IS researchers and practitioners. The thrust of much of this work has been to describe the technical problems of implementation with some consideration to the political and behavioral barriers. However, little work has been done exploring the consequences of the implementation once it has been achieved. This is an oversight because these consequences can be quite powerful and, in some cases, quite negative for particular members of the information system.

This chapter is an initial step in remedying this oversight in the literature. The chapter explores the impact of the implementation of a strategic information system by a large supermarket chain. However, the chapter is not concerned directly with the consequences for the supermarket. Rather, the discussion is of the consequences for one of the small suppliers in the system, a small bakery. The consequences for the bakery were quite negative. In order to describe and explain these negative consequences, this chapter uses the concepts of the use of information technology to integrate activities of importance to the value chain of a firm (Porter & Millar, 1985). In this description of the strategic usefulness of information technology, the value chain activities are not confined to only those performed within the large firm. Rather, all parties to the information system become integrated links in the chain.

However, Porter & Millar assume economic maximization goals in order to achieve integration of the activities. In the case described in this chapter, the non-economic maximization goals of the bakery constitute a barrier to the smooth integration of the information system. The consequences of this goal conflict are quite negative for the bakery. The case study indicates the need to explore the critical factors in the implementation of an information system across a number of firms.

The competitive advantages of implementing emerging technologies such as strategic information systems (SIS) have been widely discussed in the IS literature. However the consequences of such implementation on non-competitors have not often been directly assessed by researchers, even though these consequences may be both significant and negative in individual cases.

This chapter presents a case study of a small, somewhat unique firm ("Young Workers Bakery") whose involvement in a SIS in a supplier capacity resulted in organizational changes in the firm that were far reaching and in some respects even threatened the survival of the firm itself. These negative information technology (IT) consequences have been identified as characteristic of one of the two "dark sides" of the development and implementation of IT. As Williams (1991, pp. 48-49) notes:

> First, there is the ever-present problem of performance failure. Performance failure occurs whenever the technology does not deliver substantially what was promised. These failures can take place in one or more of the development, implementation, or use phases of the technology. Generally speaking, this class of failures is referred to as systems failures. Second, however, is the problem of negative consequences which arise from the successful implementation of IT. In these cases, the technology may deliver what was promised, but the success of the technology causes problems for the firm or its industry.

This chapter proceeds by (1) describing the basic concepts underlying the SIS, (2) presenting summaries of representative cases of "successful" SIS development and use, (3) presenting a new case, Young Workers Bakery (YWB), which exemplifies how negative IT consequences can arise during SIS development even though the SIS performs adequately from a technical perspective, and (4) discusses the changes made at YWB in order to deal with these negative IT consequences.

BACKGROUND

In their discussion of information technology and competitive advantage, Porter and Millar (1985) develop a compelling model of the strategic value of IT. They show how IT can change the nature of competition and the ways in which value to the end user can be created. The nature of competition is changed by such upheavals as a change in industry structure itself. As an example, barriers to entry may change. On the one hand, barriers to entry may be heightened when the costs of investment in the necessary hardware and software to service a client are quite high, as in the case of the travel industry. On the other hand, barriers to entry may fall when the use of advanced software and hardware allows a small player to enter a big industry, as in the case of desktop publishing. As another example, the power of suppliers can increase as they take over more of the value added activities through CAD/CAM systems. The power of buyers may increase as on-line data bases allow them to comparison shop for supplies. Besides changing industry structure, IT can change the basis of competition itself. Thus rivalry may change from competition based on product quality to competition based on quality and speed of delivery. Porter and Millar (1985) also indicate how all the members of the value chain can improve their own competitive positions through the implementation of a SIS which links activities across the value chain.

Drawing on Porter (1980), Rackoff, Wiseman & Ullrich (1985, pp. 286-287) identified five basic strategic thrusts that represent major competitive moves that can be made by a firm:

1. Differentiation — Achieve advantage by distinguishing your company's products and services from competitors, or by reducing the differentiation advantage of rivals.
2. Cost—Achieve advantage by reducing your firm's costs, supplier's costs, or customer's costs, or by raising the costs of your competitors.
3. Innovation — Achieve advantage by introducing a product or process change that results in a fundamental transformation in

the way business is conducted in the industry.

4. Growth — Achieve advantage by volume or geographical expansion, backward or forward integration, product-line or entry diversification.
5. Alliance — Achieve advantage by forging marketing agreements, forming joint ventures, or making acquisitions related to the thrusts of differentiation, cost, innovation, or growth.

These basic strategic thrusts may be directed at three strategic targets: suppliers, customers, and competitors. As such, "[s]trategic thrusts represent the fundamental link between the firm's strategy and its use of information technology" (p. 285). SIS represent IT implemented to achieve competitive advantage.

Recent empirical results have been reported which support the attractiveness of the basic framework itself as a planning methodology (Bergeron, Buteau & Raymond, 1991), and representative case studies of SIS support this basic framework. The following case studies exemplify how various business advantages may accrue to a firm implementing SIS.

McKesson Drug Company (Clemons & Row, 1988). McKesson Drug Company is in the wholesale drug distribution industry. It implemented an electronic customer order entry system to which is attributed a sales increase of 424% while operating expenses have increased only 86%. Among the benefits from SIS implementation are the following:

- A reduction has been effected in the number of order entry clerks employed by McKesson from 700 to 15.
- Orders have increased sixfold while the number of sales personnel has been reduced by 50%.
- Various services are provided to the retail pharmacist, including management reports, based on electronic orders.
- The productivity of warehouse staff has increased fivefold, thanks to the optimization of daily warehouse operations based on electronic information collected.
- Fewer purchasing agents are required, with each able to place consolidated orders.
- Customers are tied electronically to McKesson, resulting in a larger share of the customers business.

The Health Care Industry (Kim & Michelman, 1990). Four minicases involving hospitals in the process of integrating SIS into their organization in order to achieve competitive advantages together reveal important factors in the use of SIS. These factors include:

- The integration of existing transactions processing systems (TPS) and information reporting systems (IRS).
- The overcoming of existing political barriers to SIS integration with the organization.
- The successful application of TPS/IRS to various areas strategic to the organization.

For the hospital which is successful in achieving SIS integration, the following strategic benefits may be expected (p. 211):

> (1) high switching costs incurred by community physicians when they refer their patients to other hospitals; (2) an effective barrier to entry because of capital requirements to invest in computer systems; (3) enhanced patient satisfaction because better services are provided in admission and clinical care; and (4) healthcare service differentiation as a defensive weapon against substitute services.

The Cotton Industry (Lindsey, Cheney, Kasper & Ives, 1990). The Plains Cotton Cooperative Association (PCCS) developed a computer-based system which originally acted as an electronic marketing system for PCCA's cotton. Today it has features resembling those of a major stock exchange. It provides a means of executing transactions between cotton buyers and sellers. Other commodity groups, such as cattle, grain and sugar, are considering adopting a similar approach to exchanging their goods. The system has helped PCCA grow dramatically over the past 15 years, from a relatively small low-tech company to an important example of a firm successfully implementing and using IT to achieve a competitive advantage.

Rosenbluth Travel (Clemons & Row, 1991). Following airline deregulation in 1978, Rosenbluth Travel continued its effort to invest in the building of an IT infrastructure to provide for continued innovation. This infrastructure contributed to lowering the cost and development time for new travel services. By continuing this investment effort over time, Rosenbluth Travel created an important resource barrier for its competition. Over the past 10 years, it has grown from a regional travel agency with $40 million in annual sales to one of the largest travel agencies in the United States, with sales of $1.3 billion. It is quickly becoming a global service company, in part through its linkage with the Apollo computer reservations system and its aggressive exploitation of the system's capabilities.

The discussion of the linkages in these cases assumes (implicitly or explicitly) that integration across the value chain will "naturally" occur. This would require that all links in the chain have congruent value systems and goal structures. However, this is not necessarily the case. As an example, the implementation of IT substitutes machines for human effort in the information processes (Porter & Millar, 1985). This can lead to cost savings and decreased errors. But it is not clear that all the organizations in the chain want to do this. For some, employment of as many humans as possible might be a goal either because the cost of labor versus the cost of capital might be low or they may be concerned with full employment in an economically depressed area. If a natural match of links in the chain does not occur, there are sure to be negative repercussions for the members of the chain.

As the above cases attest, much of the attention in the IS literature on SIS deals with the advantages that can (and often do) accrue to the developers of SIS, while neglecting the negative consequences of SIS implementation on "innocent" components of the SIS such as suppliers. This may be considered an unfortunate shortcoming of such IS research which tends to underestimate the "dark side" of IT (Williams, 1991). One of the main problems is that organizations in the value chain do not recognize that the implementation of a SIS entails an organizational change with all its attendant problems (Lederer & Nath, 1990). Thus in order to implement a SIS to the full advantage of all members of the value chain, issues of matching values and organizational change must be addressed. Without such a consideration, negative consequences are predicted.

The following presents the case of a somewhat unique firm whose company value system is threatened by its decision to join a SIS in the supermarket industry. In this case, membership in the value chain of a large, profit-maximizing firm (a supermarket chain) would be potentially beneficial to the supplier also seeking profit maximization. However, the strategic decision makers at one supplier firm (a small bakery) can be understood to be concerned with values other than profit maximization.

The consequences for the firm are both far reaching and in many respects negative, which points up the necessity of properly managing the implementation of new IT throughout the whole SIS. It should be noted that this case represents an interesting counterpoint to the previous cases. It does not refute the previous cases in any way, but rather it expands our understanding of the basic SIS framework in a positive fashion. One might even argue that the case contributes to theory formulation along the lines of scientific methodology as suggested by Lee (1989, p. 34):

> [A] scientific methodology, which applies the natural science model, actually complements and supports the methods traditionally associated with case studies. The natural science model is primarily a model for testing theories, not formulating theories in the first place. Methods traditionally used by case researchers to formulate theories ... may therefore still be applied in addition to the methods specified by the natural science model. Thus, ... the traditional function of case studies [is] in suggesting hunches and generating theories for later testing — a function recognized by scholars of all persuasions.

Young Workers Bakery [1]

Being a supplier in supermarket SIS is the last thing Jo Irving imagined would happen to the Young Workers Bakery (YWB). When asked her opinion of why her bakery was in business, she replied with simple sincerity, "To make a good loaf of bread." Jo is one of four collective owners ("the members") of YWB, a whole grain bakery located in a previously run-down and recently fashionable section of downtown Buffalo.

The YWB was started in 1976 to make both a political statement and a good loaf of bread while providing an environment in which people who were uncomfortable in a traditional corporate structure could earn a decent living. The structure of six people (three female and three male) working together informally and equally underwent some changes as members came and went. There have been 20 members over the bakery's history. All of the members are "full time". They work 8 hours per day, 4 days per week. In addition, they all attend a weekly meeting which deals with day to day operations of the bakery. These meetings discuss ways of improving the production process, efficiency, the quality of the supplies and any personal information. There are also monthly planning meetings at which long term goals are discussed.

As of 1985 the bakery has had "employees" who work at the bakery but do not have any ownership rights. The employees are all more or less part time. They do not attend the weekly and monthly meetings. The members are experimenting with ways to get the employees involved in meetings. The most appealing alternative is to have the employees meet with the members on paid time. Given the members' value system, it is important to them to have the employees and the members all participate in the decision making process. The decision to have employees was a difficult one for the members to make. They required a steady, reliable work force and they had a number of good people who were happy to work for them but who wanted none of the responsibilities of ownership. At present there are four members, six employees and a computer analyst. Of the four members, three have been there 5 years and one (Jo) has been there 11 years. The computer analyst was one of YWB's most recent hires.

The decision making at YWB is not cost driven. It is worker driven. One of the founding values of the bakery which has not changed is the goal of providing people with a decent living in an atmosphere of openness and mutual respect. Consequently job scheduling is done around individuals' needs, such as scheduling for day care. The jobs rotate from day to day. And even though some individuals have become specialized through skills and experience into certain tasks, people can still do whatever task they want, provided the bakery goods are produced. One developing exception to this has emerged in the area of sales where the computer analyst has become the predominant "sales person". This change has come about because of the nature of the market and the need to deal with that market in a uniform fashion. But it is still true that, with this one exception, titles are merely nominal and the structure is egalitarian. Power is shared along with responsibility. For the members of YWB, the value for the growth of the individuals is as important as the bread.

Because individual growth and support are so important, growth in sales has been used to support increased benefits for the members and the employees. As the needs of the people changed, so have the benefits. There is support for child care and for health insurance. There are paid vacations in addition to the unpaid ones they always had. In order to be sure that the bakery and the people are growing together, members have frequent meetings. There are weekly meetings to discuss general issues that people have put on the agenda. There are meetings away from the bakery where they discuss long term goals. They also have social get-togethers. Because this personal interaction is so important, screening new people is vital. Anyone who wants to be a member of the collective must first go through an apprenticeship. During this period, they attend all the meetings but they have no voting rights. After this probationary period, the members vote on admission into the collective. Employees only have to serve an apprenticeship if they desire to become members. Such care about the interactions of the members and employees has helped to sustain the bakery through all of its years of operation.

At present, the members of the bakery are at a cross roads. Growing awareness of the dangers of environmental pollution and a growing concern with health issues have made the pure products of

YWB very popular with a wide spectrum of consumers. There is the possibility of substantial growth. However, the very concept of such growth poses a challenge to the members' fundamental values for a cooperative, flexible, informal work place. In addition, the value system of the members is such that they have generally used excess profits to improve the benefits for their workers, not to support growth. Although the members do not believe a decision must be made immediately, there is a sense that the bakery is "riding the crest" of society's new concern for the environment and the members need to define for themselves how they want to be a part of this.

The Pre-Supermarket Era

When YWB opened, local coops were the main outlets, accounting for 98% of sales. The bakery also sold to a few health food stores. At that time YWB had a policy of not selling to supermarkets. To the members such markets were the embodiment of a corrupt food system, which exploited the relationships between the consumer, the employee and the environment. It was precisely from such a system that YWB wanted to break away. The members' values were for a cooperative, interactive relationship that integrated quality supplies, participative decision making, concern for the environment and the provision of pure foods at a reasonable price. The product line at that time was fairly simple. It consisted mainly of organic whole wheat bread with some cookies, muffins and specialty items.

From the beginning, everything at YWB was informal and everything was done as simply as possible. Its technology was "low tech". The dough was kneaded by hand. The food was packaged in simple wrappers and deliveries were made from the back of a station wagon. The members never budgeted for advertising. They relied on word-of-mouth advertising with the coops. Economics dictated that YWB not spend lavishly. However, the members' value systems would have called for such simplicity in any event. Their values for the bakery and its product line were part of the "politics of food". As a political statement, they wanted to make nutritional food with as few chemicals and pollutants as possible. Further, they would not engage in behaviors which they believed to be inappropriate -- behaviors such as advertising or merchandising. Kneading the dough by hand was done not just because a dough mixer was expensive. The members did it because kneading the dough by hand gave them a "spiritual" connection with their products.

However YWB's members have understood the need to be flexible in order to insure the survival of the bakery. As an example, although the members felt very strongly that they did not want to become alienated from their products, they recognized that some things had to become mechanized. Kneading the dough by hand is difficult and exhausting work. At first the members purchased a dough mixer for $300.00, but the mixer has proven inadequate given the level of demand for bakery products. However, adequate mixers cost between $5,000 and $10,000, and the members have not come to a consensus on the purchase of a new mixer. Some other steps in the production process are also tedious and unfulfilling. One such step is wrapping the products. Although this is now done by hand, the members believe that acquiring a packaging machine would be an appropriate use of resources. But they know intuitively that production volume is insufficient to make such a purchase cost effective. They do not know for certain what the break even point would be for such a purchase.

As another example, very early on YWB had problems with the consistency of both the quality and the quantity of the supply of organic flour. In addition to the problem of a consistent supply is the problem of costs. Organic flour is very expensive. The members have established a product line which is about half organic and half non-organic. However, they only use whole grain flour.

The product line has expanded to include approximately 47 different items. Eight products account for 74% of sales volume (Table 1). The staple of the product line is and always has been whole wheat bread which constitutes 20% of their sales volume. This is made with non-organic flour. Another 6% of sales comes from organic whole wheat bread.

Changes to the product line come from experimentation at the bakery, from recipes acquired through a nationwide cooperative network, and from customer suggestions. YWB produces a selection of products which are free of eggs, dairy products, salt, yeast and wheat. Any changes to the product line must fit into the members

PRODUCT NAME	PERCENTAGE OF SALES DOLLARS
Whole Wheat Bread	20%
Oatmeal Raisin Cookies	12
Three Seed Bread	11
Oat Bran Muffins	8
Granola	7
Organic Whole Wheat	6
Oat Sunflower Cookies	6
Bran Muffins	4

Table 1: Top Eight Products by Dollars of Sales Volume

value set and this is not always easy. As an example, in 1989 there was a great deal of national media attention given to oat bran because of studies showing the beneficial effects of oat bran on cholesterol. Consequently there was a great demand for oat bran in various forms. Because of the bakery's production flexibility and the fact they had already been doing some experimentation, YWB was in a position to begin production of oat bran muffins very quickly. It might seem that this is a marketer's dream — a product which has been shown to be healthful and for which there is now a tremendous demand and which could quickly be brought into production. YWB should simply launch into production and take advantage of the trend. But the members of YWB did not see it that way. They were concerned that introducing oat bran muffins might be a form of exploitation of a media event. They took the time to explore the ramifications of their decisions and to determine the appropriateness of what they were doing. YWB did decide to begin production of oat bran muffins, but only after the members were sure that the decision was in congruence with their value system. They produced oat bran muffins because one of their values is to be especially responsive to the dietary needs of their customers.

The customer base has grown over the years and covers a wide variety of people who are attracted to YWB for a number of reasons. Some customers have allergies or other health problems and they are seeking foods that will not harm them. Some are athletes who are seeking the high carbohydrate, sugar-free, no cholesterol foods. There are senior citizens who are concerned about their health. Many of the customers are students. There are still some customers who are "food political" such as some vegetarians. Some customers come for the fad. The members of the bakery themselves do not have a profile of their "typical customer" except to say that the typical customer is a health conscious, "main stream" person who wants a healthful product and is willing to pay for it.

YWB products typically cost 50% more than similar supermarket foods. As an example, four YWB oat bran muffins cost $1.89. A package of six store brand muffins (complete with chemicals and preservatives) costs $1.69. The two packages sit side by side on the shelf and customers buy out the YWB goods daily. In April, 1989 increased costs prompted YWB to raise prices as much as 50% on some products. There was no immediate decrease in demand. The demand and the customer base appear to be not only sustainable but capable of growth. Even though the products are considerably more expensive than the supermarket brands, they compare quite favorably with premium national brands, especially when the contents are considered. In addition, YWB compares favorably with other bakeries. As an example, YWB produces both a pecan and a pumpkin pie. Each pie sells for $8.30. Two other local bakeries also make pecan and pumpkin pies and they also claim to use pure ingredients. One bakery charges $9.50 for the pecan pie and $7.50 for the pumpkin pie. Another bakery charges $8.95 for a large pie and $6.95 for a small one.

There is no doubt that the YWB product line is quite popular. The bakery has seen constant increases in sales even though the members do not advertise and they do no marketing. One of the reasons that the bakery has seen no decline in demand is the fact that it has no direct competition. Few bakeries offer organic products. Non-organic bakeries which use processed sugar and flour are not perceived as direct competition. The customer who buys from YWB is not looking for just any loaf of bread.

The niche that YWB enjoys in the market is unique, but it is not a particularly profitable one. In addition, at the present scale of operations, the existing cost structure is not expected to change. Consequently, it is not expected that new competitors will emerge to take advantage of lower production costs.

The Supermarket Era

YWB's customer base has been growing steadily, and its distribution channels have been changing. There is very little retail done at the bakery itself. YWB has 43 outlets to supply with bakery goods. Whereas the coops used to be the main outlets, they now account for only 25% of sales. The other 75% comes from supermarkets and convenience stores.

Within the past two years, supermarkets have approached YWB for its products. This development prompted some changes at the bakery in terms of personnel, the development of new recipes, and technology. The changes came about because of the way large stores do business. Such stores pay by check and they pay on longer time schedules. Consequently the bakery had to have a way to keep good records, something it had never had to pay much attention to in the past. Secondly, the bakery needed to have some control over its finances. All of the financial decisions were made by the members together. But the increases in sales have made control of the relevant financial data more difficult. Consequently, the members hired a computer analyst to computerize their financial statements. The analyst (the husband of a member) recommended the purchase of a personal computer and the members approved his request.

The shift to the supermarkets also forced the bakery to formalize its product line. Because supermarkets have their own product lines and prices computerized, they require a stable supply of products. They also require at least three weeks to put a new product into their computer. Once it is in there, they do not want to have to change it. They also require UPC bar codes on all products which are scanned at checkout.

The stabilization of the product line has not been a welcomed change for the bakery because it has limited the amount of experimentation the members can do. Furthermore, the products they do develop must be more carefully chosen so as not to conflict with supermarket requirements. The members still do some experimentation and they use the coops as outlets for the new products. But in many ways the change to using the supermarkets has heavily constrained their freedom to experiment.

In the pre-supermarket era, members often produced new products and delivered them to coops in small batches to see how well they would be received by customers. If the product did not sell, then the members concluded that the experiment was a failure and the product was not produced again. The cost of such experiments was low and no consideration of lead times was necessary. If the product was successful, larger batches could be produced and distributed at will. No product coding was required. In the supermarket era, things have become more formalized both in terms of developing and distributing products and in the interactions with supermarket personnel. Products must be registered at least three weeks in advance and bar codes assigned. Also YWB's product lists are evaluated by supermarkets in terms of their own requirements, which are not always fully understood by YWB members. At one supermarket, the purchasing manager appeared to treat YWB's offering of products whimsically, picking and choosing items seemingly at random. In addition, YWB was unable to collect data on the types of people who were purchasing YWB products, though they believed that the supermarkets were able to collect this data as part of the checkout scanning process.

To deal with the more formalized way of doing business, the members agreed to allow the computer analyst to be the liaison between YWB and the supermarkets. After all, the personal computer he had recommended appeared to be fully satisfactory in meeting YWB's needs and even proved useful in developing programs for pricing YWB's products. And of all YWB people he was most familiar with information technology.

However, over a period of time, some of the members began to view the computer analyst's style to be brusque and somewhat intolerant. For example, when the idea was suggested that YWB find some way to develop customer profiles from the data collected routinely by the supermarkets, the computer analyst belittled the idea as not useful but did not fully explain why he felt this way.

The members generally have found that consensus is harder to achieve in the supermarket era. The computer analyst is perceived by some of the members as partly responsible for this. Some view him as "power hungry", autocratic, and wanting to "manage". Some members resent his "specialist" attitude and accuse him of not doing the hard work of baking expected of all members and employees. Even though the computer analyst is married to a member, he is not wanted as a member by the other members.

Growth for YWB has been slow and natural. As the bakery has grown, change has been absorbed gradually and without trauma. Until now, the informal, egalitarian structure of the business has not been threatened. Though the prospects for continued growth as a supplier to supermarkets look favorable, Jo Irving will not be participating in this anticipated growth. She left YWB at the beginning of 1991.

Discussion of the Problems

As can be seen from the discussion of the case thus far, the consequences to the bakery of implementing the SIS were devastating as valued members left and the cooperative atmosphere evaporated. The upheavals of the bakery also negatively impacted the supermarkets through the loss of a dependable supplier of wanted products. Because this is a lose/lose situation, it is important to understand what went wrong and how to prevent such a situation from happening in the future.

There are two points of analysis of the networking partners which can lead to useful information. First of all, the value structures of the members of the value chain must be discussed and matched. Secondly, the information needs of the members must also be examined. Both of these analyses can be used to develop the appropriate approach to organizational change for the successful implementation of the SIS across the value chain.

The first level of analysis is quite straight forward. This deals with a discussion of basic goals and values. The implementation of the SIS as discussed by Porter and Millar (1985) assumes that the basic goals of the partners are cost minimization and profit maximization. If all parties to the SIS are in agreement in terms of this, they can probably begin the implementation process. However, in the case of YWB, the owners did not have a profit goal. They wanted to be able to provide their pure products to a needy public while providing good jobs in a friendly atmosphere. Thus when the implementation of the SIS required that they make changes such as formalizing the internal structure (in order to maximize efficiency), these changes were not accepted. The required changes led to a disintegration of the internal environment and led to the loss of valued members and an increase in hostility. Such negative consequences may be anticipated if the basic goals of the members in the value chain are not congruent.

Another level of analysis is in terms of the information requirements of each firm which might enter into the SIS (Porter & Millar, 1985). In their analysis of the strategic value of IT, Porter & Millar examine two dimensions of information requirements of firms. The first is the information intensity of the value chain. This deals with the amount of information necessary to coordinate activities across the value chain. This might include the logistics of delivery schedules, the integration of CAD/CAM systems or even the timing of after sales service. The second dimension is the information content of the product or service. This includes everything the consumer needs to know in order to obtain and use the product or service. This might include contents, operation manuals, or assembly instructions. Firms vary from low to high on each dimension and thus vary in the degree to which IT may be viewed as a strategically important resource.

In the case of a large supermarket chain, supermarkets may be characterized as high on both dimensions. First of all, there is a great deal of use of IT across the value chain. Supermarkets lock themselves into their suppliers through computerized inventory control systems which automatically signal the need for deliveries. The logistics of the movement, warehousing and sale of perishable products are carefully controlled through computer systems. Point of sale scanners allow for automatic price changes without the need to reprice every unit on the shelves, and automatically perform inventory control without the need to close the store for two days in order to count everything manually. Point of purchase scanners also provide up to the minute information on consumers and do as much market research as most store managers can use. Secondly, there is a tremendous amount of information which is provided so that the consumer can make the correct purchase and use of the product. Supermarkets provide unit pricing for comparison shopping, nutritional information, suggested recipes and health warnings. Computerized displays allow shoppers to locate products anywhere in the store. Shopping cart TVs provide the shopper with both product information and light entertainment. Thus for the supermarket, IT is a strategic resource which allows the store to develop and maintain a strategic competitive advantage against all the other stores which are trying to sell exactly the same products to the same customer base. Because IT can provide such advantages as speed of delivery of perishable items, consumer profiles and instant price changes in an industry where 1/100 of a cent per unit can translate into $100,000 of profit, the strategic advantages of carefully managing IT are clear.

A bakery such as YWB is not in the same position. In fact, YWB is likely to be measured as low on both dimensions of information requirements. First, there is little use of IT across the value chain until it reaches the supermarkets. Up to that point the linkages of the value chain are informal and personal. Each day as the bakers use up supplies, they can make a note to order more. The arrival and warehousing of the supplies can also be characterized as *ad hoc* as the supplies arrive when the truck gets there and stored wherever there is room. Secondly, because YWB does no advertising and provides customers with only a list of ingredients, the information being processed by the customers is not intense. The bakery has done no market research so it is not even clear what information the consumers use when making the purchase decision. Thus IT would not be viewed by the bakery as a potentially strategic resource. IT has nothing in particular to offer to the bakery in terms of a strategic competitive advantage. Indeed, the bakery does not really perceive that they have much competition to have a strategic advantage over. Nor is it clear that a strategic competitive advantage would jibe with their egalitarian value system. Thus the bakery owners are not particularly driven to embrace IT.

This would seem to be a situation where there would be predictable problems. On the one hand, the supermarkets have a great incentive to manage IT as a strategic resource. For them, a well managed SIS can be the difference between survival and failure. They can be predicted to work hard on the SIS and to find ways of using it to advantage. The YWB, on the other hand, has no particular competitive incentives to become part of a supermarket's SIS. Indeed, it would seem they did not consider the full implications of what was required of them in becoming a supplier to a large supermarket. They did not seem to realize that becoming part of the supermarket's supplier network would require becoming part of their SIS as well. Entering the network provided them access to more customers — presumably a good outcome. However, it also required standardization, formalization and other changes which violated the owners' basic value system. Since the bakery is low on information requirements, the owners had no incentive to make the information system work to their benefit. In fact, any benefits of the SIS would be far outweighed by the damage to other aspects of the bakery.

Thus the information requirements of the links in the value chain should be analyzed before a SIS is implemented. If the levels of information requirements of the various firms in the chain are congruent, it may be assumed they will all view the use of the SIS as consistently valuable. However, if any links in the value chain are substantially different from the others in terms of information requirements, it may be anticipated that they will not all perceive the SIS as equally valuable. In this case, the underlying values and goals of the firms should be analyzed. If all the firms are profit maximizers, then the cost savings capabilities of the SIS may prompt them all to work on the efficient and effective use of the SIS anyway. This would be the case for a hypothetical other small bakery which also supplies a supermarket chain. Such a small bakery may also be low in information requirements and thus not be motivated by that to embrace the supermarket's SIS. But they might be motivated by profits to become part of the SIS anyway. In the case of YWB, they had neither the information needs nor the profit value to make the changes necessary to use the SIS to full advantage.

It must be stressed that becoming part of a SIS does require organizational change (Lederer & Nath, 1990). As each firm becomes part of the SIS, some things change for them organizationally. The power distribution changes as key personnel in the information system gain power. The authority structures change as the reporting channels and information processing requirements become formalized. Individual discretion diminishes as jobs, tasks and processes become more standardized. Such changes absolutely must be carefully managed. If they are not, the organization will change anyway — but rarely for the better. Instead, there will likely be demotivated workers, increased uncertainty and a decline in product and service quality. Obviously, such problems do not lead to any of the strategic competitive advantages attributable to the use of a SIS.

MANAGING THE ORGANIZATIONAL CHANGE

As the case stands, this is not a good situation. In order to save it, two changes would have to be undertaken by the bakery. The first is an internal change. If the bakery is to remain in the supermarket's value chain and thus in the SIS, the owners must find an internal configuration which can accommodate both their value system and the requirements of the SIS. The standardization and formalization required by the SIS are inherent in the system. They cannot be avoided. Thus the bakery owners must find a mechanism with which to buffer their core values from the required changes. Secondly, the bakery must change its external relationships. The owners must define what their relationship is going to be with their own suppliers and their other customers. In fact, they must also decide if they want to be a part of the supermarket's SIS.

The outcome for YWB emphasizes both these points. In fact, YWB did make both an internal and an external change in order to remain in the supermarket's SIS. Internally they retrenched along a number of dimensions. First of all, they eliminated the "employee" category. The owners decided that everyone needed to have the commitment to be an owner in order to work there. Thus they reduced to 8 the number of YWB owners/workers. They have also cut back on their product line. They now produce only their best selling items on a regular basis. In addition, they have cut back on the organizational commitment to the use of IT. They support only the simplest of inventory and financial software. All of the computer work is done in 4 hours/week as opposed to 40 hours/week previously. Besides divesting themselves of what they considered to be the unneeded software, the owners also "divested" themselves of the previous computer analyst. He has left the bakery. In order to accommodate the needs of being part of the SIS, the owners of the bakery have found an internal configuration which allows them to meet the needs of the supermarket without violating their values. They have done this by taking a minimalist approach to IT. The IT they have is utilized for a few basic activities. They have not sought to be anymore closely linked to the SIS through the use of IT.

Externally, the owners of YWB have also undertaken a retrenchment. They have cut back on the number of outlets they serve. Interestingly, the cutback has been in the number of health food stores and coops they serve. The bakery now sells a large percentage of its products through the supermarkets. In addition, the bakery has undertaken a limited geographic expansion. It now serves more stores of the supermarket chains with which it initially had agreements.

IMPLICATIONS

In the case of the YWB, becoming part of a SIS of a large supermarket resulted in some fairly significant changes at the bakery. Because the owners of YWB did not manage the implementation process, a number of unexpected negative consequences occurred. This constituted quite a threat to their value system. In order to maintain their internal environment of a cooperative workplace and remain part of the value chain, the owners of the bakery had to undertake some substantial restructuring. Had the owners been aware of the potential problems, they might not have chosen to link the bakery into the SIS. Or they might have undertaken a more controlled organizational change process which might have avoided the acrimony, disenfranchisement and conflict which characterized the months following the implementation of the SIS.

Entering into a SIS as a link in a large value chain is a process which requires careful management by all parties in the chain. This is true even if all the members in the value chain are in agreement on the cost minimization/profit maximization capabilities of the relationship. This is especially true if the members in the value chain are not in agreement on the use of the relationship. In this case, the supermarkets wanted a low cost, steady supply of a predictable product line. The owners of YWB wanted to provide their pure products to more people. These two goals can be congruent. But the match does not "naturally" lead to congruence. It can be achieved, as is seen in the outcome of the bakery's change process. But the costs of not addressing the matching process can be quite high, as is also seen in the upheavals at the bakery. Such problems can be lessened by careful management of the implementation process.

CONCLUSIONS

YWB had major problems to confront and to solve before its supplier role in the supermarket SIS could be considered a success. In particular, it had to adapt its value system to embrace the need for greater formalization dictated by the SIS. The supermarkets who value YWB as a supplier should also have become involved in managing this change. A steady supply of innovative products requires that YWB be allowed to maintain the creative atmosphere that has allowed it to grow and be successful. Otherwise one of the SIS opportunities available to the supermarkets ("Can we use information systems to improve the quality of products and services we receive from our suppliers?" — Rackoff, et al., 1985, p. 291) could in all likelihood have disappeared.

ENDNOTE

[1] This case is a reworking and expansion of a case entitled "Young Workers Bakery" by C.R. Snodgrass, G. Rosenfelder & E.J. Szewczak published in C.R. Ruthstrom & C.A. Dykman (Eds.), *Information Systems for Managers: Casebook*, West Publishing:St. Paul MN, 1992, 193-200.

REFERENCES

Bergeron, F., Buteau, C., & Raymond, L. (1991). Identification of strategic information systems opportunities: Applying and comparing two methodologies. *MIS Quarterly, 15*(1), 89-103.

Clemons, E.K., & Row, M. (1988). McKesson Drug Company: A case study of Economost — A strategic information system. *Journal of MIS, 5*(1), 36-50.

Clemons, E.K., & Row, M.C. (1991). Information technology at Rosenbluth Travel: Competitive advantage in a rapidly growing global service company. *Journal of MIS, 8*(2), 53-79.

Kim, K.K., & Michelman, J.E. (1990). An examination of factors for the strategic use of information systems in the healthcare industry. *MIS Quarterly, 14*(2), 201-215.

Lederer, A.L., & Nath, R. (1990). Making strategic information systems happen. *The Executive, IV*(3), 76-83.

Lee, A.S. (1989). A scientific methodology for MIS case studies. *MIS Quarterly, 13*(1), 33-50.

Lindsey, D., Cheney, P.H., Kasper, G.M., & Ives, B. (1990). TELCOT: An application of information technology for competitive advantage in the cotton industry. *MIS Quarterly, 14*(4), 347-357.

Porter, M.E. (1980). *Competitive strategy.* New York, NY: Free Press .

Porter, M.E., & Millar, V.E. (1985). How information gives you competitive advantage. *Harvard Business Review, 63*(4) , 149-1 60.

Rackoff, N., Wiseman, C., & Ullrich, W.A. (1985). Information systems for competitive advantage: Implementation of a planning process. *MIS Quarterly, 9*(4), 285-294.

Williams, J. (1991). Negative consequences of information technology. In Szewczak, E., Snodgrass, C., & Khosrowpour, M. (Eds.), *Management impacts of information technology.* Harrisburg, PA: Idea Group Publishing, 48-74.

Part II

Emerging Technologies in the 1990s

CHAPTER 5

EMERGING APPLICATIONS OF COMPUTER GRAPHICS IN SUPPORT OF MANAGERIAL DECISION MAKING

Jerry A. Van Os
Westminster College of Salt Lake City

Current management literature on computer graphics supports the utilization of graphics in decision-making environments. Many managers prefer the use of graphic presentations during the decision-making process and believe that overall decision quality and decision speed are enhanced. The use of graphics in information systems permit more rapid presentation and assimilation of data by managers and supports the knowledge worker with non-repetitive, ill-structured problems typical of decision-making and knowledge work.

While the literature can document the benefits of graphics usage, the need for standards of graphic excellence and application are essential if computer graphics are to have an important impact on the way managers and knowledge workers understand and interpret graphic data to support complex decision-making tasks.

Graphical presentation of computer output to support management decision making is most often associated with decision support systems (DSS). Future trends in computer graphic applications include executive information systems (EIS), hypertext and hypermedia, multimedia, graphic user interfaces (GUIs), and visual programming.

The traditional role of graphs are to answer questions about data. Most business and scientific graphs answer four basic types of data questions: comparing proportions and relative amounts, showing trends, highlighting what's typical or exceptional, presenting or predicting correlations.

Presentation graphics is an extension of traditional graphic analysis by formally communicating information that illustrates activities, accomplishments, or trends to groups of individuals in a meeting or report format. Current display technology and software application tools accommodate a manager's preferences for a graphical display of output in place of, or in addition to, traditional displays of information.

The availability of computer graphics has an important impact on the way managers think about information. Computer graphics is distinguished from traditional graph usage by the following: (1) utilizing graphic data presentations to actively support management decision-making and support, (2) providing a consistent and useful graphic metaphor in supporting knowledge workers in complex tasks, (3) supporting computer-based training and interactive presentations, (4) providing support to business applications that must have the ability to share and display images in addition to text, and (5) utilizing meaningful graphic representations to support programming applications.

The objectives of this chapter are threefold. First, we will review management literature on graphics as compared to traditional methods of data representation with regard to their effectiveness as decision aids. An understanding of prior research will serve as a starting point regarding the integration of graphics in management information systems to support executive decision making and support. Next, this chapter will focus on issues relative to graphic excellence in terms of graphic application, graphic construction, and graphic integrity. Graphic literature identifies specific contexts in which certain types of graphs are most useful to decision makers. A single graphic will not prove to be universally superior since each graphic format has its own domain of application. In addition, the development of useful computer graphic metaphors will be discussed to support knowledge workers in complex business processes. The relationship between the format of information presentation and its usefulness in decision making is vital to the design of management information systems. Finally, this chapter will look at future trends and applications of computer graphics.

BACKGROUND

The traditional method of data display in a business context has been tables, containing numbers listed in a column and row format. Tables have been the display method of choice for most data processing reporting and decision support applications. Consequently, the substitution of graphics for tables raises the question of the comparative effectiveness of the two methods.

The primary uses of graphs by mangers and decision makers are to determine trends and to make comparisons, either between actual and projected data or between different aspects of the activities of an organization. Graphics are used in an organization for a variety of purposes. Gafner (1981) cited six specific advantages for the use of computer graphics:

1. Making information more visible to managers who have limited time to review printouts of tabular data,
2. Developing graphs from data already in the computer database at a lower cost that can be produced manually,
3. Creating graphs from data not already in the computer when the cost of production is lower that the cost of manual production,
4. Improving the quality of presentations,
5. Increasing the rate at which data can be absorbed, so that more reliable, time-sensitive decisions can be made, and
6. Reducing errors in the comprehension and understanding of traditional data presentations.

A fundamental issue of graphic aids research concerns the ability of users to interpret accurately information presented graphically and to make effective decisions based on that information. Careful consideration of the use of graphics as a decision making aid is needed if systematic research on the managerial use of graphs is to emerge.

A goal of systems design is to develop information systems that are well suited to the tasks at hand. During the last decade, designers have developed many decision-enhancing systems categorized as decision support systems and, with the availability of inexpensive hardware, have begun to utilize graphics to improve performance.

DeSanctis (1984) stated:

> ...if graphs indeed have a summarizing effect and allow an additional perspective of a problem over what is available in a table or narrative, then comprehension of a problem and decision making speed should be enhanced by use of graphs during the decision process.

Mason and Mitroff (1973) stated that an information system consists of, at least, a person of a certain psychological type who faces a problem within some organizational context for which evidence is made available through some mode of presentation to arrive at a solution. This defines the key variables comprising a management information system (MIS). An argument made is that most research and development to date on MIS has assumed only one underlying psychological type, once class of problem type, one or two methods of generating evidence, and finally, one mode of presentation. With the development of computerized information systems, business graphics have become automated and their applications have been extended to include standard data reporting and decision support. Reasons for including graphics in a decision support system include: (1) to permit more rapid presentation and assimilation of data by managers, (2) to allow for the efficient management of large volumes of heterogeneous data, and (3) support the manager as he or she deals with non-repetitive, ill-structured problems typical of planning and decision making.

PREVIOUS RESEARCH COMPARING TABLES AND GRAPHS IN DATA PRESENTATION

The use of graphics as a format for information presentation instead of a tabular format has been a topic of study for many researchers. A number of research studies have focused on the comparison of tables versus graphics as independent variables.

For the most part, research comparing graphical formats with alphanumeric or tabular formats has been conducted by statisticians, educators, cartographers, psychologists, and human factors engineers. Each piece of research has taken a somewhat different perspective in considering how people use graphics.

Feliaciano (1963) and Moriarity (1979) found graphs to be superior to tables for interpretation accuracy and speed. Grace (1966) found tables to be better than graphs for both interpretation and user preference. Vicino and Ringel (1966), Zmud (1978), Ghani (1981), Tullis (1981), Lucas (1981), Zmud (1983), Stock and Watson (1984), Benbasat and Dexter (1985), Dickson (1986), Mckay and Villareal (1987), and Van Os (1992) found conflicting results or no differences when graphs and tables were compared for their effects on decision quality, decision speed, and user preference. Primary research results for major dependent variables are presented in Table 1.

The lack of consistency among research results for different outcome variables are not encouraging with regard to the potential of computer graphics as a decision aid. A goal of systems design is to develop information systems well suited to the decision task at hand. If a graphic presentation medium has a summarizing effect and allows an additional perspective of a problem over what is available in another format, them comprehension of a decision task and decision making speed may be enhanced by the use of graphs during the decision process. A summary of major dependent variables in research on graphs and tables, and the rationale for their use, is given in Table 2. Prior research indicates that interpretation accuracy, decision speed, and viewer preference have been studied most frequently by graphics researchers. Keen and Scott-Morton (1978) argued than an effective decision support tool is one that results in greater decision effectiveness or efficiency. If the success of a decision aid is measured in terms of its ability to improve decision quality or speed, then these are relevant dependent measures.

ISSUES OF COGNITIVE FIT IN GRAPHS VERSUS TABLE USAGE

A considerable amount of research has been conducted over the years into the effects of graphical and tabular representations on decision-making performance. As shown in Table 1, the literature is inconclusive with regard to the performance of graphics versus tables for particular decision variables. Vessey (1991) addressed some of these issues by presenting an information processing theory that complexity in a task environment will be effectively reduced when problem representation supports the strategies required to

Dependent Variable	Better With		No
	Graphs	Tables	Difference
Interpretation Accuracy	3	3	2
Problem Comprehension	4	2	0
Task Performance	0	3	1
Decision Quality	1	2	2
Decision Speed	5	1	1
Recognition and Recall	0	0	1
Viewer Preference	3	3	2
Total	**16**	**14**	**9**

Table 1: Summary of Research Results Comparing Graphs and Tables for Major Dependent Variables

Dependent Variable	Rationale
Interpretation Accuracy	Data displayed in a graph should be understood correctly by the reader.
Problem Comprehension	A graph has dimensionality. This provides the reader with a different perspective.
Decision Quality	Because comprehension of data is better, performance on a task involving the use of that data will tend to improve.
Speed of Comprehension	Graphs have a summarizing effect. They reduce information overload and can be processed faster by the brain.
Decision Speed	Because information can be com prehended faster with a graph, the time required to make a decision will be reduced.
Memory Recall	Graphs can be comprehended better because the spatial aspect of a graph provides additional information to a reader beyond the data itself.
Viewer Preference	Users prefer graphs over other forms of data presentation. The spatial aspect of a graph makes it visually appealing.

Source: DeSanctis (1984)

Table 2: Major Dependent Variables in Graphics Research

perform the task. This notion is termed cognitive fit.

While graphical and tabular representations may contain the same information, they present it in fundamentally different ways. Graphical representations emphasize spatial information, while tables emphasize symbolic representation. Spatial representations facilitate viewing information without addressing elements separately or analytically. Symbolic processes facilitate the extraction of specific data values. As a result, perceptual processes are facilitated by graphic representations whereas analytical processes are more appropriately addressed by tables. Clearly, graphs and tables are problem representations that emphasize different characteristics of a given data set.

Decision-making tasks need to be closely examined to determine that abstract characteristics facilitated by each problem representation. Subscribing to the paradigm of cognitive fit, graphical and tabular representations will each facilitate certain decision-making tasks, even though these representations support the solution of spatial tasks, and similarly, symbolic representations the solution of symbolic tasks. The concept of cognitive fit supports the theory that decision-making performance will be more effective and efficient if decision-making tasks are matched with the appropriate problem representation in a graph or table.

The ability of organizations to compete in an information economy is based on their ability to employ what is known as intellectual technologies. Such technologies are based on the handling of abstract information rather than materials. Work employing these type of information technologies is described as knowledge work. Employees who spend their work day creating, using, and distributing information are called knowledge workers.

As future applications serve knowledge workers more directly, they become more complex. The nature of knowledge work is complex, consisting of nonrepetitive tasks and decisions. As previously described, information must be represented in a format that supports the nature of the decision-making task. The underlying reason for this requirement is that knowledge workers often deal with complex objects that cannot be decomposed into simple parts, each of which can be processed independently. Rather, the knowledge worker needs to see relationships and patterns, which support spatial decision-making tasks. Two-dimensional graphic representations support this type of decision task more effectively and efficiently than one-dimensional strings of text.

THE USE OF GRAPHICS IN A DECISION SUPPORT SYSTEM

A decision support system (DSS) is described as a computerized aid designed to ease or enhance the decision making process. A DSS is geared toward facilitating unstructured or semistructured decisions and has the added benefit of making those decisions more structured. The literature frequently categorizes the structure of a DSS into three major components: (1) data, (2) models, and (3) dialogue (Stemp, 1985).

Data

Data are the heart of a DSS. Decisions are based on information about the operations of an organization and its environment. A successful DSS must allow for the efficient management of large volumes of heterogeneous data.

The database most useful for decision support may itself be a complex structure comprised of internal and external data. In an organization, the typical database of accounting and financial measures may need to be substantially supplemented with internal data about production, personnel, and marketing; and external data about competitors, customers, market conditions, suppliers, and economics. A DSS database needs to be flexible, easily accessible, and rich enough to satisfy the requirements of the system's models and users (Samson, 1988).

Models

Modeling is the attempt to represent and simulate segments of the decision making process. Models are representations of real world relationships which transform raw data into meaningful patterns, trends, ratios, or summary-level data.

Models assist decision makers dealing with ill-structured problems. Ill-structured decisions are defined by Stemp (1985) as decisions made when either the decision criteria or the decision variables are unknown, but not both are unknown.

Dialogue

Dialogue is the communication between the user and the system. This components distinguishes DSS from traditional transaction processing. Transaction processing is based upon the "input-process-output" paradigm. Because of the unstructured nature of the DSS process, the system needs guidance from the user. Interim decisions are made, and the results of particular transformations of data suggest other paths to follow. For this reason, information must be able to flow back and forth between the computer and user.

Dialogue can take many forms. Some of the more common are (Stemp, 1985):

Command Driven Systems: The user must learn a special vocabulary to run the DSS. Commands are issued and the DSS performs the requested course of action.

Menu-Driven Systems: The user is presented with a series of choices and must enter a desired course of action using an input device.

Question and Answer Systems: The system asks the user a predefined set of questions. The user directs the system through his or her responses.

Icon Representations: These are similar to menu systems, but instead of a verbal description of the options, the user is presented with pictorial representations of the actions performed.

Graphic Representations: Graphics may be used to represent many data relationships simultaneously.

GRAPHIC EXCELLENCE

The benefits of graphics and graphic usage is well documented, however, the literature does not support a universal definition for graphic excellence, which is a fundamental assumption for graphic usage and understanding. A study by Van Os (1990) showed that while a large majority of participants responded that they understood graphs very well or reasonably well, the vast majority of participants spend minimal or no time with graphs. The exposure of managers to graphic presentation formats, or lack thereof, can have an important impact on the way managers understand and interpret graphic data to support decision making.

Three aspects of graphic usage form a basis for determining graphic literacy and excellence: graphic application, graphic construction, and graphic integrity.

Graphic Application

The goal of a graph is transparency. Instead of calling attention to itself, it focuses the viewer's attention on the meaning of the data. Choosing the right graph type is dependent upon the type of questions to be answered. As a result, the first step in selecting a graph type is to phrase the data question precisely.

Most business applications answer four basic questions (Scoville, 1988): (1) comparing proportions and relative amounts, (2) comparing trends, (3) highlighting what is typical or exceptional, and (4) presenting or predicting correlations.

To compare proportions and relative amounts, acceptable graph types include a pie chart, a horizontal bar chart, or a data table. To show trends, a column (bar) or a line graph should be used. To show what is typical or exceptional calls for a histogram, a cumulative percent chart, or a box plot. Finally, to present correlations, a multiplot chart or a scatterplot should be used.

Graphic Construction

Graphic construction focuses on identifying basic standards for presenting statistical and quantitative data in graphic form. The objective is to identify basic standards of graphic construction that will enhance graphic usage and enhance speed and accuracy with which complex information may be imparted and interpreted.

The following general standards are commonly applied to computer graphics, and are consistent with the objectives of such organizations as the American National Standard Institute for enhancing graphic communications (ANSI Y15.2M, 1979):

Borders. Clearly defined borders should be used for each chart or graph. The borders or shape of the chart should not detract from the content.

Background. The background should be unobtrusive.

Color. If color is used, it should be used to identify or highlight.

Dimensions. In general, three-dimensional forms should not be used where the reader is asked to infer volume of the three-dimensional form.

Data. All data should be depicted as elements on the graphic statements and the numbers should be shown so that they can be footed to the absolute totals. The numbers should be located at the end of the horizontal bars and relatively small in size and separated from the bar.

Time-Series. A time series using bar charts should be shown with vertical rather than horizontal bars.

Width of bars and spacing. Bars should be of uniform width and evenly spaced. The bars should not be either disproportionately long and narrow or short and wide.

Legends and identification. The title, legend, and chart identification should always be in the same place.

Negative numbers. All chart formats should show negative numbers in the opposite direction of positive numbers.

Amount of data in a graph. No agreement exists within the literature regarding how much data can be input to the human brain using graphic presentations. A presumption exists, however, of an absolute limit to the amount of information that can be comprehended by the human brain at any given moment.

Mintzberg (1975) recognized that the manager suffers from cognitive limitations that restrict the amount of information that can be considered in complex decision processes. The evidence is that the brain is severely limited in its ability to handle complex decision making tasks. The brain simply cannot cope with the quantity of information relevant to such decisions.

In fact, evidence exists that information overload leads to many forms of dysfunctional behavior, of which, Miller (1956) cites seven:

> ...(1) omission, failing to process some of the information; (2) error, processing information incorrectly; (3) queuing, delaying during periods of peak loads in the hope of catching up during lulls; (4) filtering, neglecting to process certain types of information; (5) approximation, or cutting categories of discrimination; (6) employing multiple channels, using parallel channels, as in decentralization; and (7) escaping from the task.

Jarrett (1983) describes the following rules governing the amount of data that should be presented in a graph:

1. Show only one type of pattern per graph. Do not mix types of patterns or information.
2. Separate data with different scales. Use different graphs for different scales.
3. Compare items that have clear relationships, and the same basic data structure.
4. Use only the number of elements that fit gracefully with the standard presentation size and permit properly proportioned bars to be shown for the primary and comparative presentations.
5. Use two graphs if there is any doubt on the amount of data to be shown in a single graph.

Graphic Integrity

Graphic integrity addresses the issue of designing a graph that is an accurate representation of the underlying data. A graphics designer can either deliberately or inadvertently miscommunicate the meaning of data behind a graph by the way in which the graph is designed. The goal of a graph is transparency. Instead of calling attention to itself, it focuses the viewer's attention on the meaning and interpretation of data.

Tufte (1990) identified six principles of graphic design that ensure graphic integrity. This principles include:

1. The representation of numbers, as physically measured on the surface of the graphic itself, should be directly proportional to the numerical quantities represented.
2. Clear, detailed and thorough labeling should be used to defeat

graphical distortion and ambiguity. Write out explanations of the data on the graph itself. Label important events in the data.
3. Show data variation, not design variation.
4. In time-series displays of money, deflated and standardized units of monetary measurement are nearly always better than nominal units.
5. The number of information-carrying (variable) dimensions depicted should not exceed the number of dimensions in the data.
6. Graphs must not quote data out of context.

Developing a Common Standard for Graphic Metaphors

Pictures represent the oldest form of written expression. Hieroglyphics is a form of ancient writing practiced by such notable cultures as the Egyptians, Mayans, and Chinese. Chinese, the most ancient of living writing systems, has evolved from the pictographs that originated some four thousand years ago and have been used in their present form for more than two thousand years. Lessons learned from Chinese ideograms can be utilized in the use of computer icons and iconic systems of today.

As a literary writing system, the Chinese system is capable of expressing an infinite range of feelings, ideas, concepts, and thoughts. A vast number of words have been developed for that purpose. The icons necessary for computer programming and application purposes may never require the vast number of ideographic characters as the Chinese writing system does, nevertheless, both systems serve as a means of communication based on pictorial origins. Some lessons for emerging iconic systems are identified.

1. The clarity of meaning is not an automatic consequence of using pictorial expressions. Looking at the pattern in Figure 1 developed by the Danish psychologist Edgar Rubin, one person may see it as a picture of two men facing each other, while another may see it as a vase.
2. A common argument for employing graphics is that by doing so we can utilize the brain's powerful recognition

Figure 1

capabilities. As shown by Miller (1956), the brain is susceptible to information overload. It is important that graphics are not so overwhelming that they can no longer be efficiently processed.

3. Finally, it is very difficult to build an efficient dictionary for graphic metaphors. When the number of icons is small, it is possible to have them presented on a single screen so that the knowledge worker can point to the one he or she wants. This method will not work well when a large number of icons are used.

Although "a picture is worth a thousand words," there is no guarantee that people always interpret the meaning of a picture as intended by the designer. The increased usage of graphical representations in computer systems has generated a number of studies on the use of graphic metaphors. For example, Xerox Corporation expended enormous effort in the design of the icon-oriented interface of the 8010 'Star' Office Workstation (Bewley, 1983). Included in this work was a series of tests used in helping to decide what graphic icons should look like. The results of this pioneering effort had a significant influence on the development of the Apple, Lisa and Macintosh computers. Additional research by Maguire (1984), Marcus (1984), Carrol and Mazur (1984), Tanimoto and Glinert (1986) and Gittins (1986) represent some of the important work in this field.

The Graphic Manipulation Metaphor

A critical success factor for systems serving knowledge workers is that they most present a consistent and useful metaphor to users. Early business applications utilized form-filling as a metaphor. This initially, was extremely successful because it was familiar to users and easy to learn. Its primary drawback was that forms are limited in their applications. Any activity that did not specifically have a form associated with it was impossible to execute.

A more powerful metaphor was the spreadsheet created in the late 1970s. Users of spreadsheets have the impression of manipulating a two-dimensional document on the worksheet screen. A keyboard or pointing device, such as a mouse, enable the user to move around a spreadsheet larger than the 24 X 80 character screen so that different parts of the worksheet can be displayed. Each cell contains data, either explicit or virtual. Virtual data is presented in the form of formulas, allowing the cell to be calculated from other elements. The storing of formulas instead of actual data and the ability to present data in graphical form, made the electronic spreadsheet a more powerful metaphor than its manual counterpart.

The next step in successful metaphors was the desktop. The desktop is made up of folders that contain folders within folders or other types of objects such as programs and files. An object can be manipulated "directly" by selecting it and then specifying some action to be taken on the object. Selecting can be accommodated by moving a mouse, lightpen, joystick, or a tracking ball. Actions on objects can be selected from a menu, specified by a command, or executed directly with a mouse. To reinforce the illusion of direct manipulation, objects are represented not only by names, but also by icons.

An object-oriented interface has the following characteristics:

1. Files are true objects in the sense that they are packaged with the programs that created them and that can manipulate them. Opening an object also opens the application.

2. Objects are specified before actions. An object must be selected before the menu options become operative.

3. The graphical user interface is actually programmed in an object-oriented language, thereby, making it easier to implement with this type of technology. The utilization of graphical user interfaces is likely to be the primary area of object orientation in future applications.

STANDARDS FOR GRAPHICS SOFTWARE

Graphs produced on microcomputers can be divided into two categories: information graphics and presentation graphics. Information graphics are typically produced by people for their own use or for the use of their colleagues in solving a particular problem. The graphs are sometimes displayed only on the computer monitor or printed on a computer printer. The software most frequently used to produce these graphs are integrated software packages that contain graphics capability. These packages are used to analyze the data, and a graph is an extension of that analysis.

Presentation graphics are usually produced for formal presentations and often displayed on the screen or presented on color transparencies, color slides, or some other high-resolution medium. The following benefits are associated with graphics (Cushing and Romney, 1990):

1. Graphic presentations are more persuasive than verbal presentations.

2. Graphics shorten presentations. The same information can be presented in less time using graphics.
3. Graphics aid decision making and shorten the decision making process. They help managers spot trends, problems, and opportunities earlier, and they help in analyzing and interpreting data.
4. Graphics make a good impression. People using graphics are perceived as being better prepared, as being able to make clearer and more interesting presentations, and as being more effective, credible and professional.

Table 3 presents some of the more important features users should consider in selecting a graphics software package.

FUTURE GRAPHIC TRENDS AND APPLICATIONS

Ivan Sutherland, a well-known pioneer, whose "interest for some years has been the programming of computers to draw pictures on the face of a cathode ray tube, stated (Sutherland, 1970):

> ... I think of a computer display as a window on Alice's Wonderland in which a programmer can depict either objects that obey well-known natural laws or purely imaginary objects that follow laws he has written into his program. Through computer displays I have landed an airplane on the deck of a moving carrier, observed a nuclear particle hit a potential well, flown in a rocket at nearly the speed of light and watched a computer reveal its innermost workings.

Sutherland made this statement in 1970 during a time when the power of computer graphics was available to only a few members of an elite group of computer scientists and researchers. At the time, costs for computer graphics were prohibitive. The drastic decline in computing costs and the dramatic improvement in display technology has significantly changed this situation. The opportunity of exploring the "Wonderland" of computer graphics is becoming increasingly available to all kinds of users. The potential application areas of interactive computer graphics are now becoming bounded only by imagination.

Interactive computer graphics is well on its way to becoming a pervasive means of delivering information. Visualization of data and information about data is a manifestation of this recent trend. In the rest of this chapter, examples of future trends in computer graphics

User-oriented menus, prompts, and other ease-of-use features. Automatic sizing and scaling of all graphs, with the option of setting these scaling operations manually.

The variety of graph types (point, line, bar, stacked-bar, clustered bar, overlapping bar, pie, expanding pie, three-dimensional, organization charts, flow charts, Gantt charts, bubble charts, etc.).

The number of data ranges displayed simultaneously on the screen.

The ability to generate labels for titling the X and Y axes.

A variety of colors, font sizes, and styles.

The ability to draw lines of varying sizes.

The types of hardware and the amount of memory required to operate the software.

Statistical features such as regression analysis, etc.

Whether the package has free-hand drawing or animation capabilities.

The ability to generate multiple data sets (lines, bars) on one graph using different colors or shading.

The ability to accept data interactively from stored files, a separate application program, or an integrated application program.

A tutorial to familiarize the user with the software.

The ability to drive a large variety of printers, especially those the user is most likely to use.

Adequate program support (frequent updates, hot line, news-letter, etc.).

Well-written, comprehensive documentation to help users get started, learn the program's advanced features, and answer their questions.

The ability to enter data using light pens, digitizers, or a mouse.

Whether the package has a picture library that contains things like geometrical designs, maps, pictures, fancy designs, etc.

The ability to specify the length, width, and rotation of a graph to be transferred to an output device.

The ability to recall graphs and modify ranges, features and labeling without reconstructing the graph from scratch.

Source: Cushing and Romney, 1990.

Table 3: Graphical Software Considerations

are discussed to illustrate this point.

Executive Information Systems

Executive information systems (EIS) combine features of information reporting systems and decision support systems, but they are tailored to the strategic information needs of top management. The goal of executive information systems is to provide top management with immediate and easy access to information about a firm's critical success factors, that is, key factors, that are critical to accomplishing an organization's strategic objectives.

Management information systems (MIS) was the first attempt by information systems professionals to provide managers and other organizational personnel with the information needed to perform their jobs effectively and efficiently. While system originators of the MIS concept initially had high expectations for MIS, in practice MIS largely came to represent an expanded set of structured reports, and have had only a minimal impact on upper management levels (Sprague, 1980).

Decision support systems (DSS) were the next attempt to help management with its decision-making responsibilities. DSS have been successful within a limited extent, especially in regard to helping middle managers and functional area specialists. The primary reason for their limited use by top managers and decision-makers focuses on the trade-off between simplicity and flexibility of use. Simple systems tend to be less flexible, while more flexible systems are usually more complex. Because DSS's are typically used to support poorly structured decision-making tasks, the flexibility required to analyze these decisions comes at the cost of greater complexity. Consequently, hands-on use of DSS's are typically delegated to subordinates who perform desired analyses.

Executive information systems tend to have the following characteristics that differentiate them from management information systems and decision support systems (Houdeshel and Watson, 1987):

1. They are used directly by top managers without the assistance of intermediaries.
2. They provide easy online access to current information about the status of the organization.
3. They are designed with management's critical success factors (CSF) in mind.
4. The use state-of-the-art graphics, communications, and data storage and retrieval methods.

An executive typically has little interest in the hardware or software in a system. Rather, the dialogue between the executive and the system is what matters most. Information for a particular subject area is organized in a top-down fashion. A summary graph is presented at the top of a screen or first in a series of graphic displays, followed by supporting graphs, and then by tables and text. This approach allows executives to quickly gain an overall perspective while providing backup detail when needed. An interesting finding has been that executives prefer as much information as possible on a single display, even if it appears "busy," rather than having the same information spread over several graphic displays.

Executive usage of a Management and Information Decision Support System (MIDS) at Lockheed-Georgia illustrate how graphics usage can be incorporated in an executive information system. Standards exist for all graphic designs. Line charts are used for trends, bar charts for comparisons, and pie or stacked bar charts for parts of a whole. On all charts, vertical wording is avoided and abbreviations and acronyms are limited to those on an authorized list. All bar charts are zero at the origin to avoid distortions, scales are set in prescribed increments and are identical within a subject series, and bars that exceed the scale have numeric values shown. Comments are added to the displays to explain abnormal conditions, explain graphic depictions, reference related displays, and inform of pending changes (Houdeshel and Watson, 1987).

The gathering and sorting of critical information has become an strategic competitive weapon. An executive information system can furnish decision-makers with timely information so that significantly more time can be spent planning, solving problems, and making decisions. EIS designers focus primarily on so-called critical success factors—the few things that must go right if a business is to succeed.

Making all this timely, focused, critical information thoroughly useful to a busy senior executive requires graphic representations that make anomalies leap of the screen. Executives like to see trends highlighted and projected over long periods. Robert Wallace, recently retired president of Phillips 66, the refining and marketing arm of Phillips Petroleum, likens using an executive information system to his experience as a Navy anti-aircraft gunner during World War II. With practice he could scan enormous reaches of sky and quickly identify an enemy plane when it a was a speck on the horizon. Looking at his screen, he says, "I can see trends in seconds. I can't do that if I'm scanning a lot of tables on paper" (Main, 1989).

Hypertext

Hypertext has quickly become an established paradigm in the design of information systems. The success of products in the software market, benefits as reported by users, and the conclusions of related research activity attest to the power of hypertext-rich information systems (Bieber and Kimbrough, 1992).

The core idea of hypertext was described by Conklin (1987):

> The concept of hypertext is quite simple: windows on the screen are associated with objects in a database, and links are provided between these objects, both graphically (as labelled tokens) and in the database (as pointers).

Hyptertext pioneers Ted Nelson, Douglas Englebart, and Andries van Dam believe that current hypertext technology is embryonic, but that future developments will radically change the way people use information and computers. Hypertext's nonlinear interconnectivity more closely approximates human thinking than conventional computing. The technology facilitates access to desired information in large databases, improves the ability to share information, and redefines computers as gateways into an extended domain of shared resources (van Tyle, 1990).

Current understanding of the cognitive processes involved in handling tables and graphs is still somewhat limited. Johnson and Payne (1985) and Johnson, et al. (1988) concluded that if information is presented in a format difficult for the user to comprehend, the user may employ an easier but less effective decision strategy than one that requires more sophisticated reasoning but leads to a better result. An erroneous perception of hypertext technology is that it is strictly a tool to browse information. Hypertext is a generic term, referring to a method of accessing information via an organized collection of nodes and links. Hypertext systems differ from conventional knowledge in that they can include text, sound, graphics, and processes. Hypertext deals with knowledge that cannot easily be expressed as rules (Swift, 1991).

The central concept of hypertext is that of linked collections of information. A hypertext document may be seen as a graph, with *nodes* that are collections of information. *Links* specify relationships between nodes. They are maintained by the system, and are named or referred to by link icons (Conklin, 1987) which are found in the nodes.

Typically, a user sees a node displayed in a window, its link icons highlighted in some fashion. The user explores the hyperdocument by clicking on a particular icon thereby causing the system to find the internal representation of the link named by the icon.

Typical operations supported by hypertext systems include (Bieber and Kimbrough, 1992):

1. User-directed navigation of the hyperdocument.
2. Search and display.
3. Map-based navigation where the system displays a graph of the hyperdocument, and the user may direct navigation of the hyperdocument based on the map (graph), whose link icons, when selected, cause the corresponding node in the hyperdocument to be displayed.
4. Creation, modification and deletion of nodes, links and their attributes.
5. Display of link and node attribute information.

Because links and nodes may be created automatically based on a declaration from the application, it is possible to set up the declarations in a way that results in salient representation of the information. What determines a salient representation, of course, is difficult to determine and will likely be application and user dependent. However, by making application-specific declarations, including contextual information, in the right way, the hypertext system can be made to present information in cognitively useful representations in support of managerial decision-making (Bieber, 1991).

Multimedia

The future training needs of knowledge workers will be quite different from those of traditional system users. A single concentrated course just prior to system conversion is insufficient. Much more emphasis must be put on continuous training. Although no single approach applies to all circumstances, the extension of presentation software into the world of multimedia is becoming possible with multimedia authoring systems. Using an authoring system, a user can develop computer-based training courseware, customer presentations, and interactive business presentations (Raskin, 1990). This conglomerate of technologies, is intended to deliver what is often called infotainment: superior graphic imagery, computer animation, and motion video combined with high fidelity sound. Authoring software helps users to collect pieces for a training presentation from a variety of equipment (voice recorders, scanners, videotape, and videodisk players, and other sources) to produce a CD-ROM disk, which may serve as a master for duplication.

There are five main components of multimedia: sound, still images, live-action video, animation, and data. These five components can be combined to form a powerful information gathering and dissemination tool.

Sound can be created digitally on a computer or leaded from a keyboard with a Musical Instrument Device Interface (MIDI) or a compact disk (CD). The sound is manipulated with software to make new sounds, combine sounds, or playback the sound as various instruments.

Still Images are composed of graphs, slides or photographs, hand drawings, scanned images, video images, computer-generated images, or CAD drawings. Video boards are used to display the still images on the computer with up to several million colors and with resolution approaching photographic quality. The still images can also be manipulated, altered, enhanced, or combined.

Live-action video may be played back through the computer and its software can alter the images and play them back as believable computer-generated reality. Many television commercials and films use anthropomorphic metamorphosis to create fascinating special effects. For example, "morphing" of the liquid-metal cyborg of *Terminator 2* or the facial transmutations in Michael Jackson's *Black or White* video are examples of motion video.

Two approaches are used in computer *animation*. In the first approach, the computer plays back a series of two dimensional drawings. The second approach uses a three-dimensional model and the computer traces a predefined path around the model. The computer then animates the views of the model as it moves along the path. Computer animation is now easily generated by several software packages. The high-end packages can now match television-quality animation.

Finally, computers were designed to handle data. Handling data from files and databases and incorporated into multimedia presentations will continue to be the main thrust (Neeley, 1992).

Multimedia software supports the hypermedia method of information delivery, in which multiple linkages may be established among various entities in a large multimedia document. These linkages enable the user to move from one topic directly to a related one, instead of scanning information sequentially.

Graphic User Interfaces

Although menu, prompt, and screen template input are the most commonly used types of screen design, end users are increasingly working with graphical user interfaces (GUIs). In a GUI, verbal commands are replaced by the action of pointing an arrow (guided by a mouse, trackball, or a similar cursor-control device) at icons and menu selections. Users "point and shoot;" that is, they move the pointer to an icon and click a button on a mouse instead of using keyboard commands. Moving a pointer to an icon or a program to be run and clicking a mouse button is a lot simpler for the manager than learning and keyboarding a series of commands.

Users report qualitative rather than quantitative benefits to using GUIs. Information is presented in a way that is more intuitive to users; therefore, training time is substantially decreased.

A true GUI satisfies the following requirements (*PC Magazine*, 1989):

1. It exploits bitmapped displays, offering true what you see is what you get (WYSIWYG) screen representation of printed output.
2. It is a graphically oriented interface, making extensive use of icons.
3. It has good screen aesthetics; it looks good and is pleasant to work with.
4. It allows direct manipulation of on-screen elements.
5. It embraces the object-action paradigm, so that the user chooses an object first, then selects the action, freeing up the user from an action sequence that must be completed before moving onto the next task.
6. It offers standard expected elements—such as menus, standard window elements, and dialogue controls—to provide consistency across applications.

Additional elements GUIs should incorporate are:

1. A strong set of user-interface controls and tools to build applications.
2. Consistency across platforms as well as across applications.
3. Ease of use and visual appeal.
4. Information communicated through graphics.
5. Flexibility and support for a keyboard or mouse as well as for a range of devices and peripherals.
6. User customization and personalization.

Broad, convincing research that decisively demonstrates the superiority of GUIs is still lacking. One study found that experienced GUI users work 35 percent faster and make 17 percent fewer errors than experienced uses of character-based interfaces. Other studies have shown that GUIs are easier to learn, more enjoyable to use, and give users more confidence (Von Simson, 1990).

Many organizations are looking for an easy-to-use interface that minimizes training costs and increases manager productivity. Once an user has learned a GUI, all applications will look the same. There will no longer be a different way to do various features among different applications. As an example, two federal agencies, the Federal Aviation Administration (FAA) and Department of Defenses (DOD) recently purchased microcomputers equipped with GUI software to meet this objective (Marson, 1990).

Visual Programming

Visual programming is defined to mean the use of meaningful graphic representations in the process of programming. Programming can be defined as specifying a method for doing something that computer can do in terms the computer can interpret. Processable graphics refers to graphic representations whose components can be recognized and processed as such by a program.

The attempt to make programming an easier task in not a new concept. For years, people have been trying to design or improve application programs for ease of use. However, program language design has been evolutionary rather than revolutionary. Only in the last few years has it become apparent that a radical departure from traditional programming is necessary if programming is to be made more accessible to a larger user population.

A review of the last thirty years shows that programming languages have evolved form low level, to high-level, to very high level, to ultra high level. These four levels correspond roughly to the four "generations" of programming languages.

An examination of recent work reported in the literature shows that visual programming progressing in two major directions. In one direction, graphical techniques and pointing devices are used to provide visual environments for information retrieval and presentation. In another direction, to actually program with visual expression.

Visualization information and retrieval of data deals with information stored internally in traditional databases, but expressed in graphical form and presented to the user in a spatial framework. Users can traverse the graphical surface of a database or zoom into it to obtain greater detail with a pointing device (joystick or mouse). This approach permits many types of questions to be answered without the need for a keyboard. In essence, these systems are devoted primarily to using "direct manipulation" as a means of information retrieval, using a graphical view of a database for visualization of the information retrieved.

Visual programming describes an application where users can program with visual expressions such as icons or graphical symbols. Visual programming has gained momentum in recent years primarily because the falling cost of graphics-related hardware and software has made it feasible to use pictures as a means of communicating with the computer. Graphical representations and pictures have come into play in the programming process. This form of programming is stimulated by the following premises:

1. Graphics are more powerful than words as a means of communication. They can convey more meaning in a more concise unit of expression.
2. Graphics aid understanding and remembering.
3. Graphics may provide an incentive for learning to program.
4. Graphics do not have language barriers. When properly designed, they are understood by people regardless of what language they speak.

CONCLUSIONS

The objectives of this chapter were to identify current management literature on computer graphics with regards to their effectiveness as decision aids, describe characteristics consistent with graphic excellence, and look at future trends and applications of computer graphics in information systems.

Current management literature on computer graphics supports the utilization of graphics in decision-making environments. Many executives prefer the utilization of graphic presentations during the decision-making process and believe that overall decision quality and decision speed are enhanced. The use of graphics in information systems permit more rapid presentation and assimilation of data by managers and support the manager with non-repetitive, ill-structured problems typical of planning and decision making.

While the literature can document the benefits of graphics usage, the need for standards of graphic excellence and application are essential if computer graphics are to have an important impact on the way managers understand and interpret graphic data to support decision making. Managers must develop a basic understanding of graphics in order to be considered graphic literate. Three aspects of graphic usage form the basis for graphic literacy: (1) understanding the correct application given the type of data presentation to be addressed, (2) understanding minimal standards for presenting statistical and quantitative data in graphic form, and (3) designing graphs that accurately represent the underlying meaning and interpretation of data.

Graphical presentation of computer output to support management decision making is most often associated with decision support systems. Future trends in graphic applications that support managerial decision making will include executive information systems (EIS), hypertext, multimedia, graphic user interfaces (GUIs), and visual programming.

Executive information systems are now successfully providing computer support for senior executives in a growing number of organizations. EISs are tailored to individual executive users for the purpose of tracking critical data presented to users in graphical, tabular, and/or textual presentation formats. Computer graphics are an essential ingredient to an EIS due to its ability to display timely, critical information to senior executives.

Hypertext is a relatively low-cost microcomputer-based technology that allows users easy retrieval of random data by mimicking the human thought process. Hypertext's nonlinear interconnectivity more closely approximates human thinking than conventional computing. The technology utilizes graphics, in conjunction with text, animation and sound, to link relationships among collections of information.

Multimedia represents a conglomerate of graphic imagery, computer animation, motion video, and high fidelity sound to create sophisticated computer-based training software, customer presentations, and interactive business presentations. Multimedia programming tools, particularly those based on hypertext concepts will be vital to the development of applications that will drive the growth of multimedia microcomputing.

Graphic user interfaces represent a future application of graphics where "icons" will replace keyboard commands and provide a better interface for busy managers who are unable or unwilling to learn keyboard commands. By using a "point-and-shoot" methodology, managers will be able to directly access and manipulate data. Communication with the information system is communicated through graphics. It is anticipated that GUIs will minimize training costs for users and increase manager productivity. An objective of graphical user interfaces is that the use of standardized icons will result in no significant differences in accessing various features among different software applications. Managers will be able to access a variety of effective and efficient software tools to support decision making.

Finally, visual programming will provide managers a means to access data stored internally in traditional databases, but expressed in graphical from and presented to the user in a spatial framework. Managers will be able to address more types of ad hoc questions without the need for a keyboard and knowledge of database language commands. In addition, managers will be able to program computers with visual expressions represented as icons.

REFERENCES

American Society of Mechanical Engineers. Time-Series Charts. (ANSI Y15.2M - 1979) (ASA Y15.2 - 1960). *New York*, 1979, 1960.

Benbasat, I. and Dexter, A. S., "An Experimental Evaluation of Graphical and Color-Enhanced Information Presentation," *Management Science*, 1985, vol. 31(11), pp. 1348-1363.

Bewley, W. L., Roberts, T. L., Schroit, D., and Verplan, W. L., "Human Factors Testing in the Design of Xerox's 8010 'Star' Office Workstation," *Proceedings of CHI '83*, December, 1983, pp. 72-77.

Bieber, M. P. and Kimbrough, S. O., "Towards a Logic Model of Generalized Hypertext," *Proceedings of the Twenty-Third Hawaii International Conference on System Sciences*, 1990, pp. 506-515.

Bieber, M. P., "Issues in Modeling a 'Dynamic' Hypertext Interface," *Proceedings of Hypertext '91*, San Antonio, TX, December, 1991a, pp. 203-218.

Bieber, M. P., "Template-Drive Hypertext: A methodology for Integrating a Hypertext Interface into Information Systems," working paper, BCCS-91-4 Computer Science Department, Boston College, Boston, MA, 1991b.

Carrol, J. M., and Mazur, S. A., "Lisa Learning," *IEEE Computer*, November, 1986, Vol. 19, pp. 35-49.

Conklin, J. "Hypertext: An Introduction and Survey," *Computer*, *20*, 9, September 1987, pp. 17-41.

Cushing, B. E. and Romney, M. B., *Accounting Information Systems and Business Organizations*, 5th ed., Addison-Wesley Publishing Co., 1990.

DeSanctis, G., "Computer Graphics as Decision Aids: Directions for Research, " *Decision Sciences*, 1984, vol. 15, pp. 463-487.

Dickson, G., DeSanctis, G., and McBride, D. J. "Understanding the Effectiveness of Computer Graphics for Decision Support: A Cumulative Experimental Approach," *Communications of the ACM*, 1986, 29(1), pp. 40-47.

Feliciano, G. D., Powers, R. D., and Bryan, E. K., "The Presentation of Statistical Information," *Audio Visual Communication Review*, 1963, vol. 11(3), pp. 32-39.

Flaatten, P. O., McCubbrey, D. J., O'Riorden, P. D., Burgess, K., *Foundations of Business Systems*, 2nd ed., The Dryden Press, 1992.

Gafner, M. K., "Computer Graphics: Looking Sharp for the Eighties," *Administrative Management*, May 1981, pp. 29-31, 54-56.

Ghani, J. A., The Effects of Information Representation and Modification on Decision Performance, unpublished doctoral dissertation, University of Pennsylvania, 1981.

Gittins, D., "Icon-Based Human-Computer Interaction," *International Journal of Man-Machine Studies*, 1986, Vol. 24, pp. 519-543.

Grace, G. L., "Applications of Empirical Methods to Computer-Based System Design," *Journal of Applied Psychology*, 1966, vol. 50, pp. 442-450.

Houdeshel, G. and Watson, H. J., "The Management Information and Decision

Support (MIDS) System at Lockheed-Georgia." *MIS Quarterly, 11*, 2, March 1987, pp. 127-140.

Jarrett, I. M., *Computer Graphics and Reporting Financial Data*, New York: John Wiley & Sons, 1983.

Johnson, E. J. and Payne, J. W., "Effort and Accuracy in Choice," *Management Science, 31*(4), April, 1985, pp. 395-414.

Johnson, E. J., Payne, J. W., and Bettman, J. R., "Information Displays and Preference Reversals," *Organizational Behavior and Human Decision Processes, 42*, 1988, pp. 1-21.

Keen, P. G. and Scott-Morton, M., *Decision Support Systems: An Organizational Perspective*, Reading, MA: Addison-Wesley, 1978.

Lucas, H. C., "An Experimental Investigation of the Use of Computer-Based Graphics in Decision Making," *Management Science*, 1981, vol. 27, pp. 757-768.

Maguire, M. C., "A Review of Human Factors Guidelines and Techniques for the Design of Graphical Human-Computer Interfaces," *Computers and Graphics*, 1985, Vol. 9(3), pp. 221-235.

Main, J. "At Last, Software CEOs Can Use," *Fortune*, March 13, 1989, pp. 77-83.

Marcus, A., "Corporate Identity for Iconic Interface Design: The Graphical Design Perspective." *IEEE Computer Graphics and Applications*, April, 1984, Vol. 4, pp. 24-32.

Mason, R. O. and Mitroff, I. I., "A Program for Research on Management Information Systems," *Management Science*, 1973, vol. 19, pp. 475-487.

McKay, D. B., and Villarreal, A., "Performance Differences in the Use of Graphic and Tabular Displays of Multivariate Data," *Decision Sciences*, 1987, vol. 18, pp. 535-546.

Miller, G. A., "The Magic Number Seven, Plus or Minus Two: Some Limits on Our Capacity for Processing Information," *The Psychological Review*, March, 1956, pp. 81-97.

Mintzberg, H. M., *Impediments to the Use of Management Information*, National Association of Accountants, 1975.

Moriarity, S., "Communicating Financial Information Through Multidimensional Graphics,"*Journal of Accounting Research*, vol. 17(1), Spring 1979, pp. 205-224.

Neeley, D. "Multimedia," *Cadence*, March 1992, p. 36.

PC Magazine, "Graphical: The Better Interface," 1989, vol 8(15), pp. 97-157.

Raskin, R. "Multimedia: The New Frontier for Business." *PC Magazine*, July 1990, pp. 151-192.

Samson, D., *Managerial Decision Analysis*, Irwin Publishing, Chicago, Illinois, 1988.

Scoville, R., Ten Graphs (and How to Use Them), *PC World*, September, 1988, pp. 216-219.

Shu, Nan C., *Visual Programming*, Van Nostrand Reinhold Company, New York, 1988.

Sprague, R. H., "A Framework for the Development of Decision Support Systems, *MIS Quarterly*, June 1980, pp. 1-26.

Stemp, S. D., Minkin, J. E., Thomopoulos, J., Stemp, M. W., Howell, R., *Decision Support Systems*, National Association of Accountants, 1985.

Stock, D. and Watson, C. J., "Human Judgement Accuracy, Multidimensional Graphics, and Humans versus Models," *Journal of Accounting Research*, vol. 22, Spring 1984, pp. 192-206.

Sutherland, I. E.,, "Computer Displays," *Scientific-American*, June, 1970, pp. 57-81.

Swift, M. K., "Hypertext: A Tool for Knowledge Transfer," *Journal of Systems*

Management, June 1991, vol. 42(6), p. 35(3).

Tanimoto, S. L., and Glinert, E. P., "Designing Iconic Programming Systems: Representations and Learnability," *Proceedings of the IEEE Workshop on Visual Languages*, June 1986, pp. 54-60.

Tufte, E. R., *Envisioning Information*, Cheshire, Conn.: Graphics Press, 1990.

Tullis, T. S., "An Evaluation of Alphanumeric, Graphic, and Color Information Displays," *Human Factors*, 1981, vol. 23, 22-34.

Van Os, J. A., "The Effect of Information Format Within the Context of a Decision Support System, unpublished doctoral dissertation, Brigham Young University, 1990.

Van Os, J. A., "User Reactions to the Format of Information Presentation Within the Context of a Decision Support System," *Proceedings of the 1992 Information Resources Management Association International Conference*, Charleston, South Carolina, 1992.

Van Tyle, S., "A Whole New Way of Using Computers," *Electronics*, 1990, vol. 63(2), p. 70(2).

Vessey, I., "Cognitive Fit: A Theory-Based Analysis of the Graphs Versus Tables Literature," *Decision Sciences*, 1991, Vol. 22, pp. 219-240.

Vicino, F. L. and Ringel, S., *Decision-Making With Updated Graphic vs. Alpha-Numeric Information*, (NTIS, No. AD647623), Washington, D. C., Army Personnel Research Office, November, 1966.

Von Simson, C., "Graphical Upstart Quelled," *Computerworld*, June 25, 1990, pp. 39, 55.

Wang, W. S-Y., "The Chinese Language," *Scientific American*, 1973, Vol. 228(2), pp. 50-63.

Zmud, R. W., Blocher, E., and Moffie, R. P., "The Impact of Color Graphic Report Formats on Decision Performance and Learning," *Proceedings of the Fourth International Conference on Information Systems*, Chicago, Illinois, Society of Information Management, 1983.

CHAPTER 6

COMMUNICATION CHALLENGE IN DESIGNING, TEACHING AND USING EMERGING INFORMATION TECHNOLOGIES

Karen J. Pettingell
University of Texas at El Paso

The study of communication dates back to ancient times when scholars such as Aristotle studied rhetoric. In today's society with the proliferation of information technology (IT) communication is very crucial. One of the definitions of learning is when communication causes a change in behavior. This is important to managers because as plans and goals are communicated, management desires employees to learn new behaviors and technology to implement these plans.

To effectively teach and utilize IT, managers need to understand how these technologies can affect communication. Technology should be a tool to get information and to perform a task transparently. If there is ineffective communication or the user does not know how to use and communicate with the system then the technology is no longer a productive tool.

Throughout the ages man has been struggling with ways to effectively communicate with each other. Now this struggle is exacerbated by the introduction of information technology (IT) in the communication process. Very often as ITs emerge little is understood on how they influence communication between humans and also between groups in an organization.

Emerging ITs also present another communication problem—How do we communicate so that the users of these technologies learn to utilize these new tools? This chapter focuses on how communication and learning interact and affect the new computer software user. The goal in using new ITs is to produce quality results, not anomalies.

To better understand the very complex nature of communication when computer software or emerging information technology (IT) systems are involved, this chapter will first examine communication models, followed by IT in the communication model, then a background in learning and finally learning software systems and IT systems. The first section, communication background, covers various communication models.

COMMUNICATION BACKGROUND

This chapter first examines several communication models. One of the best known and most commonly used models employed is Shannon's Communication Model (Shannon and Weaver, 1949). Although Shannon's model was developed for the technical aspects of communication, it applies, as well, to other forms of technical and human communication interactions (see Figure 1).

An example of electronic mail demonstrates how Shannon's model works. First the desired message is selected, e.g. a memo to a colleague. The memo is then typed and converted to sound waves by a modem and the sound waves in the telephone lines become the signal. Static created by electronic disturbances in the lines is an example of potential noise. The modem at a colleague's computer is the receiver which decodes the memo (message) for the receiver (destination).

Schramm's Adaptation of the Shannon Model

Schramm (1954) modified Shannon's model to emphasize the sender's and receiver's fields of experience in communication. It would be erroneous to assume that effective communication has occurred because a message was sent and received. Holt (1987) has stated: "Effective communication strengthens relationships, reinforces goal-directed behavior, and helps create a bond of confidence among individuals working in organized groups" (p. 464). To expand upon this, parts of Figure 2 will be briefly examined.

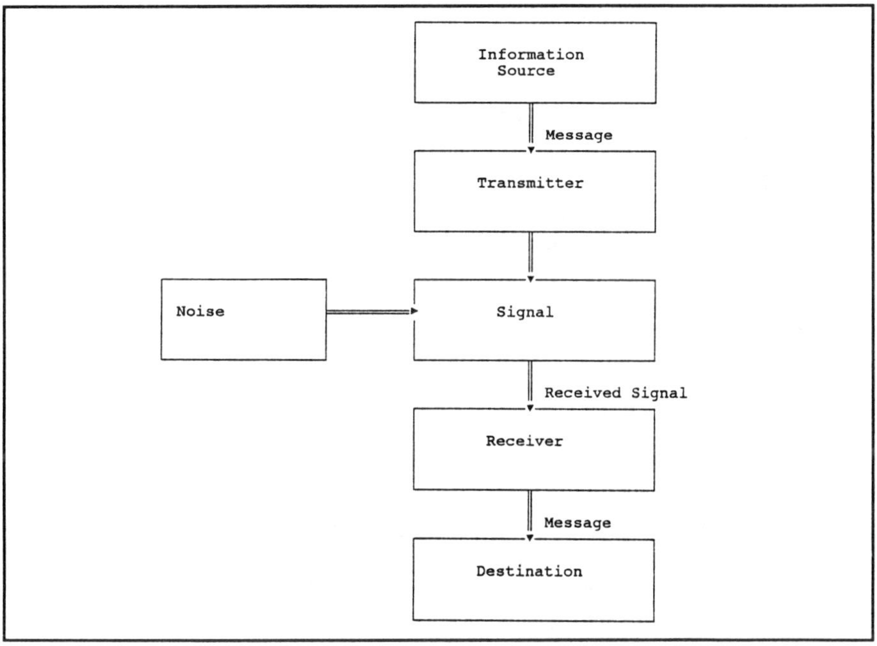

Figure 1: Shannon's Model

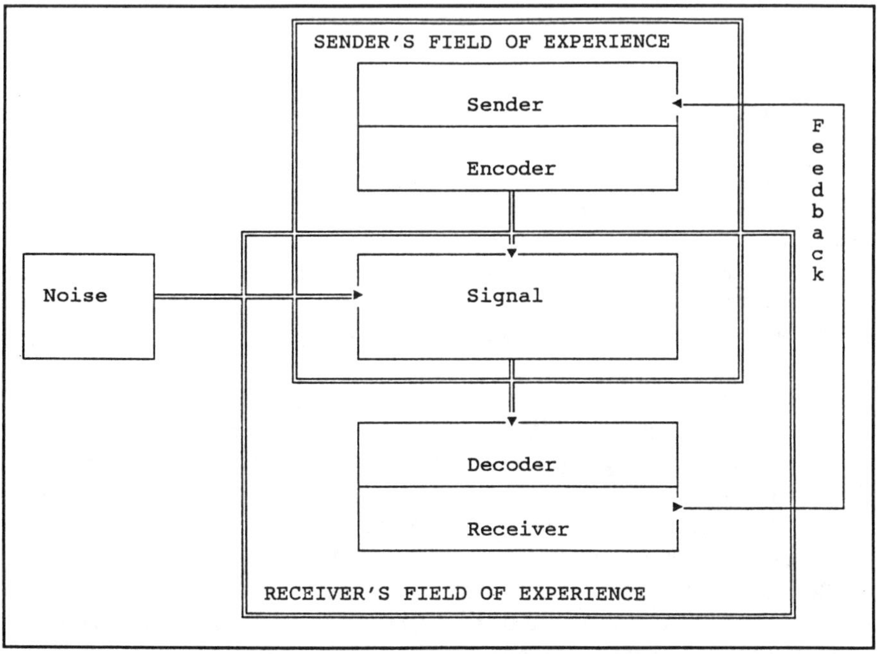

Figure 2: Schramm's Adaptation of the Shannon Model

Encoding and Signal

Encoding is the process whereby the sender encapsulizes the message to be sent in symbols such as words, pictures, and nonverbal communication. Holt (1987) has this to say about the encoding process: "The encoding process is crucial to ensure that our intended receiver has every opportunity of understanding what we are transmitting. Improper encoding can distort a message and confuse the other person" (p. 466). The signal, channel, or medium of transmission influences how communication is transmitted as well as how it is encoded. It may be words, graphs, TV, or gestures. Because the signal greatly influences the design and transmission of the message, it is vital to select the correct channel for the signal.

Decoding and Feedback

Once the message has been transmitted over the channel, the receiver decodes, or translates, the signal as an input message. The decoding process is greatly influenced by the receiver's interpretation of the signal; therefore, to ensure that the message received was the one sent, a feedback loop is necessary. This loop is crucial if there is to be a mutual understanding between the sender and the receiver. Ideally the sender can use the feedback loop data to fine tune the message and then resend the corrected message.

Fields of Experience and Noise

This fine tuning to the communication model is necessary because the fields of experience of both the sender and the receiver are influences that can distort or enhance the encoding/decoding process. Fields of experience include knowledge, skill, age, and the sender's/receiver's personal environment. New ITs must consider these factors in the designing process. These will be discussed more in the learning section.

Along with the fields of experience, noise can distort the signal. Noise factors can include the technical quality of the encoding device, channel integrity, decoder reception and the decoder itself. Environmental factors such as noise adjacent to the receiver can detract from the decoding process. Another example of environmental noise factor is the receiver not listening or paying attention to the incoming signal. These noise factors change the message by adding input from the distractions to the message and obliterating parts of the message. Noise in emerging technologies can be poorly designed devices that cause the user to focus on them rather than on the task or information. With this distraction, train of thought is disturbed and there is a chance of lost data, information, and continuity. Designers of new IT need to focus on communication so that the technology is transparent rather than cluttered with noise.

Other Communication Models

This section expands the previous two communication models by discussing some other models in the context of the key parts of Figure 2. The first part of Figure 2 examined is the sender. The sender of a message is also called the source and is the originator of the message. In some cases the sender also encodes the message which is transmitted by the communication system (Infante, Rancer and Womack, 1990; Berlo, 1960). Berlo (1960) includes communication skills, attitudes, knowledge, social system and culture in the source/sender. These are part of the field of experience of Figure 2. Hanneman (1990) goes further and says; "The concept that meanings are in people, however, implies that unless someone was raised in an environment similar to yours, the probability of perfect communication can never be high. Two people must share at least some of the same experiences for any type of meaningful communication to occur" (p. 29). In IT a third field of experience—the field of experience of the system designer/developer—complicates the communication model further. If the fields of experience of the sender, receiver and developers do not mesh closely, noise can enter the system. This is discussed in more detail later in this chapter.

In Figure 2 there is no direct mention of the message but the message is a very important part of the communication model. The message may be verbal, nonverbal or a combination of these. Humans tend to use both verbal and nonverbal messages in communication. When the channel cannot carry this full combination of verbal and nonverbal components the full message is not transmitted. In most uses of IT this is the case. Because the message is only partially transmitted, IT developers and users need to be aware of this limitation.

The next component of the models to be considered is the channel. The channel includes the lines carrying the message signal between the encoder and decoder. In Berlo's model (Berlo, 1960) the five senses are considered to be the channels. Berlo had this to say, "It is correct to say that messages can exist only in *some* channel; however, the *choice* of channels often is an important factor in the effectiveness of communication" (p. 31). Again, IT choice in communication is limited by the channel used in the technology.

The effectiveness of communication is often limited by noise.

Noise inhibits the accurate transmission of the signal. Noise can enter the encoding and decoding process. This is especially important when IT is part of the communication process since limitations are place on the coding and decoding process. This is discussed more later.

The receiver is the target of the channel/decoding processor. In some cases the receiver decodes the message. The same traits Berlo considers in the source/sender are included in the receiver and need to also be considered in the receiver's field of experience of Figure 2. The receiver often transmits feedback to the sender as a form of reinforcement. This feedback in psychology and communication fields can be either negative or positive feedback. Learning models consider the feedback loop of communication to be the changed behavior that has been learned. Berlo (1960) observed that sender and receiver may be the same person as in the case when a person talks to himself. Often in IT the user is both the sender and final receiver, as in cases where the user is using IT as shown in Figure 5 later in this chapter.

The Westley-MacLean model (Infante, Rancer and Womack, 1990) has an interesting addition to the communication model—the gatekeeper. Gatekeepers are especially important in mass communication, for example a newspaper editor. In IT the software and hardware often become gatekeepers. We especially see this in Executive Support Systems and Group Decision Support Systems.

These additions to the communication model enhance our understanding of the communication process and give a better understanding to communication. The next section expands these models further to examine a model where the sender and receiver are the same, and also discuss IT's role in the communication model.

IT IN THE COMMUNICATION MODEL

Information Technology (IT) can be viewed as the channel or signal in the communication model. IT can take the form of group decision support systems (GDSS), executive information systems (EIS), software packages, and multimedia packages. Each of these has special capabilities and can place limitations on the communication process. For example, suppose a multimedia sales presentation is to be made using a combination of CD, video tapes and computer graphics. The message is the desirability of the product (its features and benefits) to the audience. The goal of the message is to make a sale. Limitations of the presentation include the cost and time needed to make (encode) the presentation and the field of experience of the designer (sender) and the audience (receiver). If the sender does not know good design techniques for the IT being used, then noise (technical distractions) may enter the encoding process and limit the effectiveness of the communication.

Likewise, if the receiver does not understand IT in the same framework, the message could be short circuited and not received. This may occur if the receiver is missing one of the IT components (such as the CD player, VCR, or compatible computer in the multimedia sales example above). In these cases, the feedback loop could be used to notify the sender of the problems to help him circumvent the decoding limitations.

A more serious short circuit could be a breakage in the link between the signal and the decoder. An example of this would be the limitation of incoming messages in an executive information system (EIS). A manager may limit the groups of people from whom he will receive messages. A vital message from such a blocked person not only would not be received but, more importantly, no feedback would be sent notifying the sender of the blockage, thus allowing the sender to select another channel.

Another example of a communication/IT illustration is where the sender and the receiver are the same person. Figure 3 shows how the communication model is influenced in these cases. The second field of experience now becomes the IT system. Before the user can encode his message to the IT system he must be aware of the encoding and use of his input by the IT system. The encoding process is greatly influenced by two factors: 1) the technology's inherent assumptions and definitions and 2) IT's limitations and enhancements.

IT Assumptions and Definitions

In the design of the IT system, certain assumptions are made. An example of this is in simulation when the user is deciding which simulation variables are to be controlled and which variables are to be included in the random variables. These assumptions are made to make the IT systems a manageable size, but they in turn can be limitations. Probably the most important IT system factors are the system assumptions and definitions such as variable definitions in simulation. Definitions include the system variables and how they are used in calculations. A user may not use the same definition of a variable when he encodes his system request, and thus the communication of the system output to the user may not be valid. For example, a user defines sales as both sales and returns, yet the system defines sales as items sold with a ten percent return rate for the final sales figure. The user may rely on the sales figures from the system and not make as good a decision as he would if both his and the system's definitions were the same. A very serious problem with emerging technologies is that they often fail to state and teach these assumptions and definitions.

IT Limitations and Enhancements

Hardware and software may provide limitations to the system. A hardware restriction could be the use of a two dimensional CRT when the system is simulating a three dimensional system. A software limitation would be only allowing the entering of discrete numbers for a continuous variable.

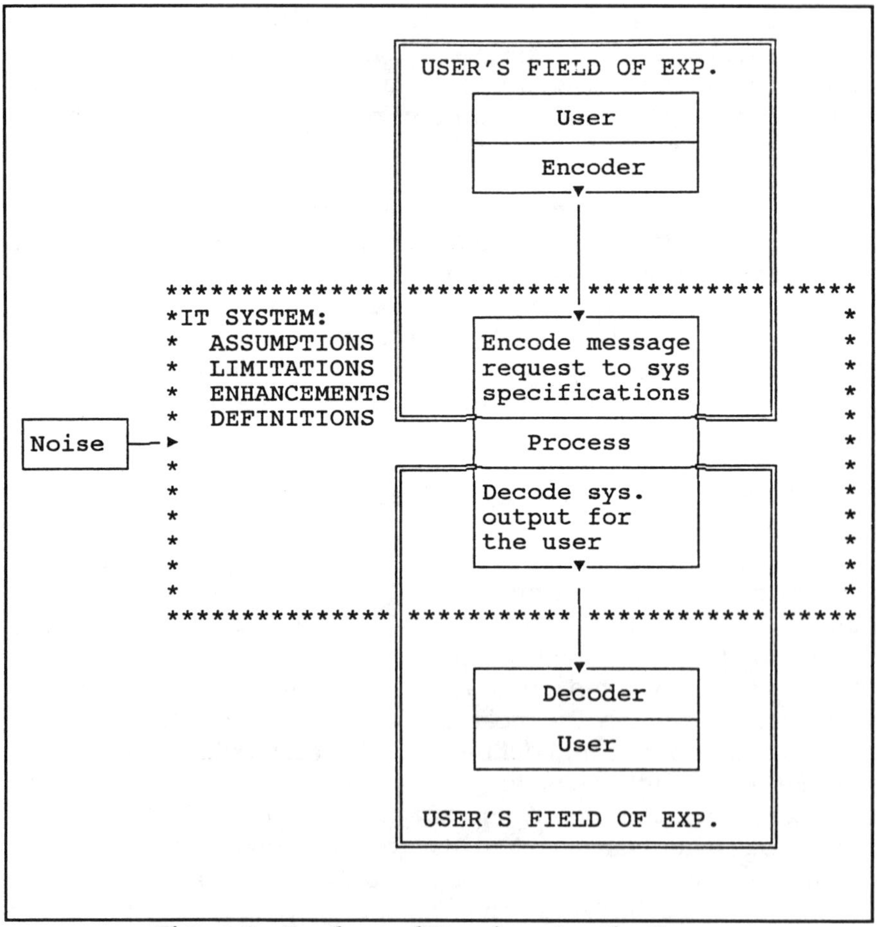

Figure 3: Sender and Receiver Are the Same

A potentially serious drawback or limitation is the experience of the IT system development team. The developers' fields of experience influence the communication between them and the system owners. These extraneous fields of experience are an insidious noise factor to the system since they often get embedded into the system and can cause an unexplainable breakdown in the communication process.

Just as there are limitations there are also IT enhancements that increase the system's value. Enhancements to the IT communication model include features such as presentation media. Such features could include using color graphs to present salient ideas, or allowing the user to zero in on crucial details and focus on their influence on a decision.

Users of new technologies need to analyze the output of the system and learn the consequences of their input parameters. One way the user can become aware of the need to alter input parameters is through the feedback loop. The feedback loop occurs when the user decodes the system output and realizes that fine tuning or re-entry of system messages is required. These changes may be necessary because the user has become aware of some of the system's design assumptions and limitations. Additionally, the user may realize that an error was made in encoding parameters. Users then are given the option to recode their message in another attempt at generating effective communication throughout the system. As the user becomes more aware of how to encode/decode and communicate with the system, he/she is learning to use the system more effectively.

LEARNING

The focus of this chapter is on communication and IT. The previous two sections focused on communication and IT in the communication model. The following sections will emphasize learning IT and computer software "systems" rather than using IT and computers in the learning process (such as computer aided instruction [CAI]). Learning to use an IT system is vital if the system is to be used successfully. Nelson (1991, p. 514) made this observation: "In essence, training end users to handle data, applications, and communication may be considered a form of *preventive maintenance*."

Not all researchers agree that training end-users is necessary (e.g. George and Theis, 1991). The IT system, especially transaction processing, is often designed for uniform data input and handling. In these systems users have to be trained how to use the system. Furthermore, users often desire and respond to training. For these cases, training the user to utilize the system is discussed here. First there is a discussion on learning and those characteristics that influence the learning process.

Learning Background

Learning has been defined as a relatively permanent process that is inferred from performance changes due to practice (Ellis, 1974; Heinich, Molenda and Russell, 1985). Four features of this definition are important. The first feature is that learning is inferred rather than directly observed. The second is that learning is tied to performance but is not the same as performance. Thirdly, learning is tied to practice in contrast to changes due to such factors as fatigue or maturing. The fourth feature is that learning is a permanent process rather than temporary processes which might involve just sensory or short-term memory.

Mathers defined learning in theoretical terms as "...frequently in theoretical definitions of learning one treats the phenomenon as one closely related to perception and defines it in terms of a reorganization of the perceptual, psychological, or behavioral world of the learner..." (as quoted in Mock, Estrin and Vasarhelyi, 1972 p. 133). Training documents and systems focus on this definition by trying to teach users to define their tasks in the same terms used by the (software) system.

Learner's/User's Field of Experience

The learner's field of experience very directly affects communication. With this in mind, a study was conducted on the learning of a time management software package using a procedural manual. Forty-five subjects participated in the training sessions. The results of the study are given in the following sections. For more details on the study see Pettingell (1991). The following section covers cognitive style, knowledge, and specific experience aspects of the learner's field of experience.

Cognitive Style

Research shows that the brain's hemispheres have different functions (e.g. Robey and Taggart 1982). The left brain is usually described as the language hemisphere and is alleged to specialize in serial or analytical processing. The right hemisphere operates intuitively and is described "as essentially mute and specialized for processing nonverbal information holistically" (Friedman and Polson,

1981, p. 1031; see also Robey and Taggart, 1982).

The software documentation must complement the user's cognitive system if the software is to be used successfully. Dillon (1983) had this to say:

> System designs often erroneously assume that it is easy for users to learn a new system using reference manuals written for other purposes or tutorials written without an understanding of either the learning process or the user. Human-factors specialists recognize the need for training and the need for understanding the cognitive process involved in the transition of users from novice to experts (p. 197).

In a study of U. S. Navy yeomen (Enochs, Handley and Wollenberg, 1986), CAI programs were preferred by those with an arithmetic reasoning, a desire for qualitative learning, a preference to work with inanimate objects, and a higher achievement in reading comprehension. The traditional self-paced training method was preferred by those yeomen with reading as a learning style, with a desire to work with people and learn from people, with more of an aptitude for general science, and with less interest in organization of preferences. Trainers of new technologies need to be aware of individual mental processing to benefit from the strengths of these differences. Also, these differences influence how to communicate in the training process since cognitive style influences the encoding/decoding process.

Knowledge

Knowledge in the learning process is discussed in the following sections from two points of view—system/user interfaces and a focus on the learner/user. The system/user interface has two layers, the know-what and know-how (Bullinger and Faehnrich, 1984; see also Chi, 1981).

The know-what layer includes pragmatic and semantic knowledge while the know-how layer includes syntactical and interaction knowledge. The second focus on the learner/user is explained by Gott, Bennett and Gillet (1986) to include three dimensions—procedural knowledge, conceptual knowledge and critical mental models. Procedural knowledge is used to act on the environment. Procedures are followed in performing a task (Umanath and Scamell, 1988). In learning to use a computer software system or learning to use some form of IT, the user needs to not only learn to use procedures but needs to know how to use the system to accomplish some specific goal (Von Papstein and Frese, 1988). This is another way of saying that the user has to communicate with the system.

The second dimension, conceptual knowledge, is the knowledge base that supports the technical skill (Gott, Bennett, and Gillet, 1986; Umanath and Scamell, 1988). Included are background knowledge, specific knowledge, and scientific laws. Dillon (1986) calls conceptual knowledge "declarative knowledge" and defines it as the content and fact of a discipline.

Concept learning is an activity where the learner must classify two or more different events of objects into a single category (Ellis, 1974). Conceptual learning as a topic in the psychology of learning is more complex than procedural learning. The focus is on developing more general many-to-one associations (Ellis, 1974). Furthermore, conceptual knowledge also includes contextual information which embraces the shaping and selecting of an environment with respect to one's life.

Finally, mental models are in effect road maps for problem solving and interpretation. Mental models reflect the understanding and mental formation of the information the software user desires to glean from using the computer (Murray, 1988; Turner and Karasek, 1984). Whitefield (1987) describes the user's model of the system in terms of predicting the user's behavior or how the user characterizes the system. Other researchers label the model as a conceptual model (Sein, 1988; Bayman and Mayer, 1984) and visualize one of the functions of the model as a help to the novice in becoming more expert in the usage of the system (Kieras and Bovair, 1984). Users of a computer system form mental models of the system they are using. These models provide a predictive and explanatory basis to help guide the user in learning and using software (Sein, 1988).

Emerging ITs can use the different types of knowledge to enhance communication. Designers of the technology and manuals need to know their users so that they can design the system to build on the users' existing knowledge. Good communication between the system and user/learner can form accurate mental models.

Specific Experience

The final variable in the learner's field of experience is specific experience (e.g. computer experience). The learner/user brings his experience:

- in the field he is learning,
- in the use of the technology used in the learning process, and
- in the learning process.

The learner's experiences can both expedite the learning process as well as hinder it. If previous experiences, knowledge and mental models complement the current learning goals, they will enhance learning. On the other hand, previous learning that is contradictory or uses very different procedures can cause a blockage in the learning process.

These differences are demonstrated by research in human computer interaction (HCI), especially in the use of menus and commands by software. Novice users have trouble learning a command system more so than do experienced users. Several researchers (Norman, 1984; Pettingell, 1991; Potosnak, 1985) observed that commands were harder to use than menus because specific syntax has to be learned. In addition, exploring a system is more difficult using commands than menus.

Designers of IT, documentation and training tools as well as teachers need to be aware of the learner's cognitive style, knowledge and field of experience if they are to develop effective training. Teachers and users must be aware of the level of expertise needed for the system they need to teach and use. If there is not a match on users' expertise and system requirements, learning is complicated and communication between the user and IT system is blocked.

Once the system and the learner/user are defined, the software and IT system as well as the teaching system can be designed. The next sections will focus on learning a computer software or IT system in the context of the communication model.

LEARNING SOFTWARE AND IT SYSTEMS

Figure 4 shows the relationship between the learner/user and the computer software or IT system. Notice the feedback in the learner/user box. Heinich, Molenda and Russell (1985) have stated "the basic principle of instruction: learning means appropriate change in response, or performance" (p. 10). Learning takes place when the learner/user mentally processes a stimulus and then responds to it. The feedback fine tunes and corrects previous messages to both enhance the learning process and to reflect previous learning.

Another addition to this model is the documentation/help/training box. If these tools are well done they can greatly aid learning and the formulation of the learner's mental model of the system. A further benefit of these aids is that they are used in the encoding and decoding of messages to and from the system. Unfortunately, if these

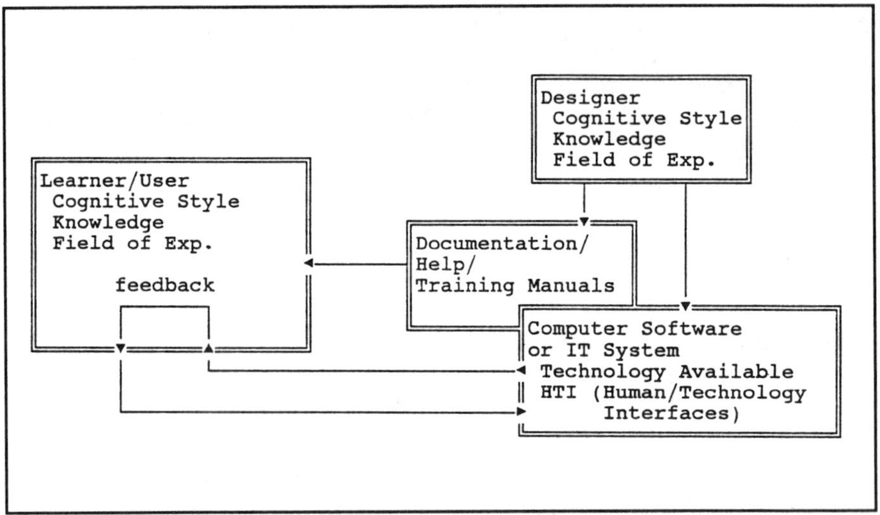

Figure 4: Learner and Teaching System

tools are not well constructed or have weaknesses they cause noise to enter the system.

In a survey of end-user and information system personnel regarding knowledge and skill needs, Nelson (1991) found conflicting documentation needs. End-users rated use and understanding of documentation in the middle of their current deficiency list, while IS personnel rated documentation as their lowest. This conflict on documentation needs illustrates a conflict in perceptions. Documentation is not only written texts but also is a subsystem in IT. An illustration of this is the system message that appears on the screen or the choice of words used in the menu system. Documentation is a form of communication and Nelson's survey reflects noise in the system. This conflict is potentially a serious point of failure in the use of an IT system.

Noise can also enter the system if the IT system designer's traits cause encoding errors. This occurs when the designer does not hear system requirements correctly and introduces errors into the system. Another problem can happen when the designer flawlessly follows the system specification but the learner/user has different variable and process perceptions. Training and documentation can alleviate this latter difficulty. Unfortunately, the first problem of system errors is not always easily detected or corrected.

Nelson (1991) observed that the level of knowledge of the IS professional of the organization and its environment was lacking. End-users, on the other hand, expressed a deficiency in their IS/IT knowledge. These two different deficiencies influence the knowledge components of the Learner/User and Designer boxes in Figure 4. Top managers and Chief Information Officers (CIOs) must be aware of differences between the user/learner and designer if communication is to flow through the system. Another point to consider is the fact that these two knowledge deficiencies can cause a failure of a new IT in an organization.

The last area of interest in Figure 4 is the computer software or IT system. Two factors are considered here: the technology available and the human/technology interfaces (HTI). The first factor— technology available—is a factor first when the system is being designed and equipment and software are being purchased, then once the technology is in place it influences methods of decoding incoming messages and encoding outgoing messages. An example of the influence of decoding on an incoming message is the use of a scanner to input a picture. The digitized picture would then be modified using specialized software to improve scanning shortcomings. An example of the limitation of the encoding of an outgoing message could be demonstrated by only allowing the user to see summarized information when he might want more detailed information.

The second factor —HTI —has been studied much in emerging technologies. Aykin and Aykin (1991) reviewed studies involving individual differences in human-computer interaction. They list four characteristics that affect user performance: 1) level of experience, 2) personality traits, 3) demographic characteristics and 4) others. Other parts of this chapter have focused on the user's cognitive style, knowledge and field of experience. Whichever list is preferred, the users of technology need to remember that these factors influence communication and learning.

Communications Influences on Learning when the Sender and Receiver Are the Same

Figure 5 shows what the communication loop would look like if the sender and the receiver were the same person. Notice the decoding and processing of the incoming message by the IT system. When this has been done the output of the processing is then encoded and transmitted back to the user (receiver).

Communication is much more complicated in IT systems than in Schramm's model (see Figure 2). In the model shown in Figure 5, there are two communication loops. The first is when the user enters (encodes) and transmits a message into the system. The software or IT system then decodes the message and processes it. In the process cycle a message may have to be encoded and transmitted back to the

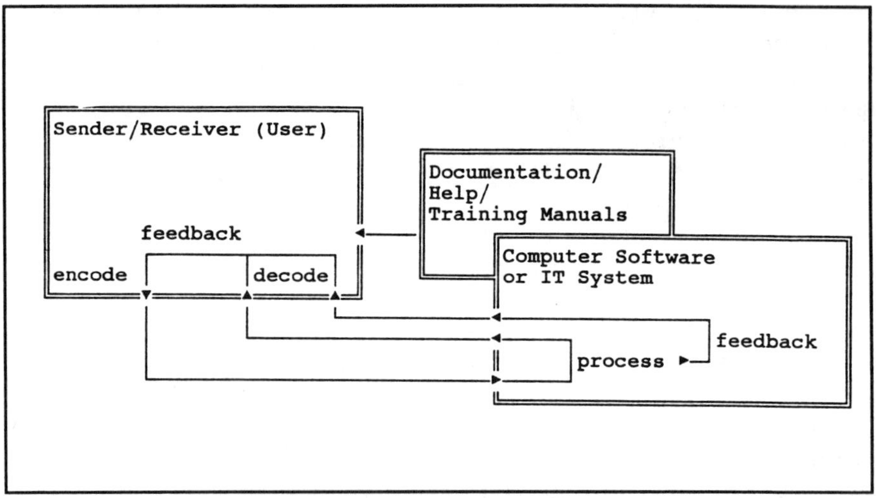

Figure 5: IT System Communication
Sender/Receiver Are the Same

user notifying him of an error. This is shown in the feedback loop from the process in the Computer Software box. When this occurs, the user has to decode the error or warning message and recode his message to the system for further processing. When processing is complete the software encodes the output and transmits it to the user who then decodes the system message. If the incoming information (message) is judged to be incorrect, the user then recodes his message to the IT system and repeats the process until either correct information is received or the user gives up.

Documentation and Noise

The documentation in Figure 5 is a source for the user for both encoding and decoding. Documentation can be used to help the user learn to use the system in both of these coding procedures. Learning occurs when the user discovers that he has encoded a message to the system and received the expected information (message) back from the system. Furthermore, learning can occur when the user has to analyze why the message he encoded did not produce the expected results and he has to respond and reformulate a message to the system.

Complicating the learning process is noise in the system. Noise can enter the system through:

- the documentation,
- the limitations on how messages can be encoded for the system and by the system,
- the limitations on how the messages are transmitted to and from the system, and
- the field of experience of the software design team.

Furthermore, the field of experience of the user is now a triple threat. His experience affects encoding and decoding of the messages plus the learning process. Just as communication systems between two humans are complicated, communication involving IT is complex also.

Nelson (1991, p. 513) observed: "... it appears that organizations need to pay more attention to the IS-related education of all employees regardless of functional area. It is apparent that both IS and end-user personnel need to know more about such issues as the use of IS/IT for competitive advantage, the fit between systems and technology within the organization." This fit of IT in the organization and its influence on communication is discussed in the next section.

IT SYSTEM INFLUENCE ON GROUP COMMUNICATION

Organizations that use ITs within subdivisions and between subdivisions complicate the communication between IT users even more. Figure 6 illustrates a possible scenario of IT communication in this environment in the relationships between the Subdivision/ Group and IT Systems boxes. These will be discussed more in the following sections.

Subdivision/Group and the Individual

Group dynamics not only influence but are influenced by the individuals in the group as well as how individuals interact and react. Figure 6 shows three areas of concern in examining communication in the IT environment. Group Policies/Procedures influence how individuals are to formulate (encode) messages and parameters to the IT system. An example of this is the policy to select a lead on a bid for a construction company. Once it is decided that the lead fits the organization's policy, the procedures to make the bid are followed. A team is formed to complete the bid. The fields of experience of the team members are combined to form the team's field of experience. Each member enters the IT system parameters he is responsible for in order for them to be processed. The output of the processing is then encoded as a message and sent to the team. The team then decodes the output from the IT system to make sure valid communication has taken place. If not, then the team has to recode some of its parameters and run the system again.

A third group factor mentioned in Figure 6 is group demographics. These factors have a definite influence on the group's communication within itself and the organization. If the group has little power or is low in the organization, it may not be heard. For example, in the bid process above if the group submitting the bid had little power, its bid would receive lower priority. The IT system would list bids from departments with more power before those with less power.

Another demographic variable is the group's leader. A sophisticated system and users would have less value if the leader of the

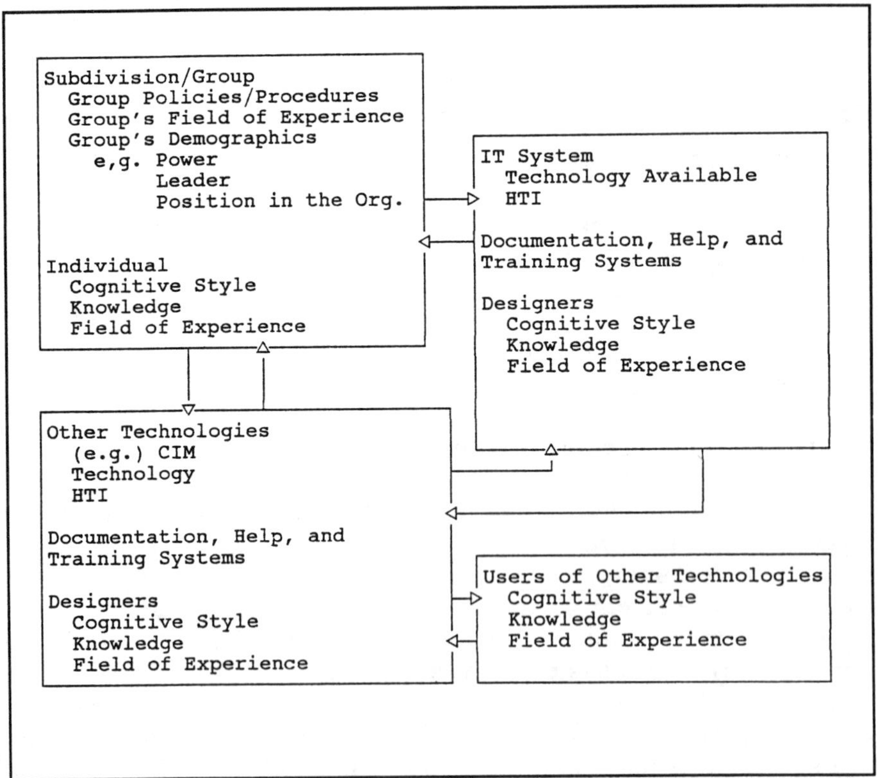

Figure 6: IT Systems in Group Environments

team were an ineffective champion. Another demographic might be the energy of the team. If the group is perceived as energetic go-getters, then the project might carry more weight and gloss over weaknesses in the IT system. In these cases the group communicates success that may not really exist in the system.

Individual

Along with the group's traits, individuals in the group have their own traits. As mentioned in the Learning section of this chapter, individuals bring their own characteristics to the communication process. The biases the individuals bring to the process greatly influence the use of the IT system and the communication process. Individuals have the responsibility to encode their part of the IT system parameters and then decode part of the system output. The IT system combines input from group members so that each member has to communicate with each other. In the bid example, one team member may be responsible for the electric specifications and another the plumbing. Members have to communicate with each other to be sure they do not conflict. The IT system would then test for programmed errors. Not all possible checks can be built into a system; humans are needed to do the non-routine checking. Communication between individuals and the system is necessary to compile a valid bid.

Another individual trait that affects communication in the group environment is the knowledge of the individual. As individuals work together they may have different mental models of the IT system. As a result, conflicting parameters may be fed into the system. As the team tries to decode and analyze the system's output, they may not realize they are not communicating with each other. In cases such as these the IT system appears to have failed but in reality communication outside the system is the problem. User training can help correct these types of problems.

FUTURE TRENDS

The future of IT will include the integration of other technologies and IT systems. The following sections cover the two remaining parts of Figure 6 —Other Technologies and Users of Other Technologies.

Other Technologies

Other technologies such as CIM have to consider the human and technology interface (HTI). Some systems provide reports on the status of the system on such topics as downtime and defects. These are fed into other IT systems to generate management reports. If there is a breakdown in communication, poor decisions may be made by managers. Future designers of systems will need to have to communicate with the designers of systems they feed. This is illustrated by the IT team talking to the CIM team to see how they define downtime and collect the raw data. If the CIM definition does not match managements' definition, then the IT team will have to write a conversion algorithm before the CIM data is used. This type of conversion and integration has been going on for many years in IS. The problem here is that IT and CIM teams are often in very different divisions of a company and so communication is not easy.

This problem of communication between divisions points out another problem. IS and developers of other technologies often do not read each other's research and findings. Often each discipline has to reinvent the wheel. Future IT developers can progress much faster if they read what is going on in a field they have to design a system for. An example of this is to study findings in management on group dynamics and power when IS is designing and implementing a GDSS.

Users of Other Technologies

These other technologies also present a communication problem for emerging IT. These other technologies have users who are removed from the IT system. Their traits influence a system which in turn influences IT. Communication problems in this case are outside the IT system and usually not detectable by the system. An example may be an employee on the shop floor working a lot of widgets and then scanning each widget to save time and steps. The IT system looks at the scan time stamp and calculates the time to produce the widget. The first widget of the lot would have a long production time while the rest in the lot would have very short times. Designers of the CIM technology and IT system either did not train the floor employee or failed to observe his work patterns. In any case, there has been a breakdown in the communication process.

FUTURE RESEARCH IN IT/COMMUNICATION RELATIONSHIPS

As in the CIM production and bid examples above, there are

many points where communication failures can cause IT systems to falter. Future researchers may want to compare and contrast cases where there has been successful and unsuccessful communication. Much research has already been done on the HTI communication links but most of these focus on correct use of the system features. Research should be done on the encoding and decoding done by users and IT systems to examine the influence of the fields of experience on these processes with regard to the communication model. Some of the current IT research done to date may have been found to have insignificant results because communication links confounded the results. Individual communication variables such as field of experience may need to be factored into research design. In fact, more work may have to be done on how fields of experience influence the use and interactions of IT, communication and learning.

Conclusion

Basic communication models such as Shannon's and Schramm's provide a foundation to analyze communication with and within an IT system. Some areas to consider when examining communication and the IT relationship involve the user, group of users, IT itself and the designers of the system. Each user brings his cognitive style, knowledge and field of experience to the process. These variables apply to the group of users as a whole along with the group's policy/ procedures and demographics. One of the group's demographic variables that has a strong influence on successful use and communication is its power. If the IT does not carry the identity of the group with its message then the technology may not be used in the communication process.

Variables to study in the IT system include the technology being used, HCI, documentation, and help and training subsystems. The final set of variables to examine are those of the designers of the IT system. These variables are like the user's variables but are troublesome since they are not as obvious as the user's since they get coded into the system.

Along with these variables, relationships have to be considered. In some IT systems the user is the sender and receiver in the communication model. In the middle is the IT system which receives a message from the user, decodes it, processes it, and then encodes the results and sends them back to the user.

Another relationship that is examined is the integration between IT and other technologies such as CIM. These other technologies have their own set of variables plus their own users. These are external to the IT system but greatly influence communications from IT to its users. All these factors demonstrate the complexity of communication when an IT system is involved. Designers of emerging ITs can not ignore the influence communication has on how successful their system will be. More important, users of IT need to understand communication so that any technology they use will enhance and facilitate getting tasks completed.

REFERENCES

Aykin, Nuray M. and Aykin, Turgut. (1991). Individual differences in human-computer interaction. *Computers and Industrial Engineering, 20*(3), 373-379.

Bayman, Piraye, & Mayer, Richard E. (1984). Instructional manipulation of users' mental models for electronic calculators. *International Journal of Man-Machine Studies, 20*(2) 189-199.

Berlo, David K. (1960). *The Process of Communication: An Introduction to Theory and Practice.* New York, New York: Holt, Rinehart and Winston.

Berlo, David K. (1990). The context for communication. In *Communication and Behavior,* ed. Gerhard J. Hanneman and William J. McEwen, 3-20. Reading, MA.: Addison-Wesley Publishing Company.

Bullinger, H. J., & Faehnrich, K. P. (1984). Symbiotic man-computer interfaces and the user assistant concept. In *Human-Computer Interaction: Proceedings of the First U.S.A.-Japan Conference on Human-Computer Interaction* held in Honolulu, Hawaii, August 18-20, 1984, ed. Gavriel Salvendy, 17-26. Amsterdam: Elsevier.

Chi, Michelene T. H. (1981). Knowledge development and memory performance. In *Intelligence and Learning, Proceedings of a NATO Conference on Intelligence and Learning,* held July 16-20, 1979, in York, England, ed. Morton P. Friedman, J. P. Das, and Neil O'Conner. 221-229. New York, N.Y.: Plenum Press.

Dillon, Richard F. (1983). Human factors in user-computer interaction: an introduction. *Behavior Research Methods & Instrumentation, 15*(2), 195-199.

Dillon, Ronna F. (1986). Issues in cognitive psychology and instruction. In *Cognition and Instruction,* ed. Ronna F. Dillon and Robert J. Sternberg. 1-12. Orlando, FL: Academic Press.

Ellis, Henry C. (1974). *Fundamentals of Human Learning and Cognition.* Dubuque, Iowa: Wm. C. Brown Company.

Enochs, J. R., Handley, H. M., & Wollenberg, J. P. (1986). Relating learning style, reading vocabulary, reading comprehension, and aptitude for learning to achievement in the self-paced and computer-assisted instructional modes. *The Journal of Experimental Education, 54*(3), 135-139.

Friedman, Alinda, & Polson, Martha Campbell (1981). Hemispheres as independent resource systems: limited-capacity processing and cerebral specialization. *Journal of Experimental Psychology: Human Perception and Performance, 7*(5), 1031-1058.

George, Joey F. and Theis, James W. (1991). Microcomputer training: do trained users differ from non-trained users? *Data Base.* Winter/Spring, 1-10.

Gott, Sherrie P., Bennett, Winston, & Gillet, Alex (1986). Models of technical competence for intelligent tutoring systems. *Journal of Computer-Based Instruction, 13*(2), 43-46.

Hanneman, Gerhard J. (1990). The study of human communication. In *Communication and Behavior,* ed. Gerhard J. Hanneman and William J. McEwen, 21-46.

Reading, MA.: Addison-Wesley Publishing Company.

Heinich, Robert, Molenda, Michael, & Russell, James D. (1985). *Instructional Media and the New Technologies of Instruction.* New York: John Wiley & Sons.

Holt, David H. (1987). *Management Principles and Practices.* Englewood Cliffs: Prentice-Hall, Inc.

Infante, Dominic A., Rancer, Andrew S., & Womack, Deanna F. (1990). *Building Communication Theory.* Prospect Heights, IL: Waveland Press, Inc.

Kieras, David E., & Bovair, Susan (1984). The role of a mental model in learning to operate a device. *Cognitive Science, 8*(3), 255-278.

Mock, Theodore J., Estrin, Teviah L., & Vasarhelyi, Miklos A. (1972). Learning patterns, decision approach, and value of information. *Journal of Accounting Research,* Spring, 129-153.

Murray, Dianne M. (1988). *A survey of user cognitive modelling.* NPL Report DITC 92/87. Teddington, Middlesex, UK: National Physical Laboratory.

Nelson, R. Ryan. (1991). Educational needs as perceived by IS and end-user personnel: a survey of knowledge and skill requirements. *MIS Quarterly,* December, 503-525.

Norman, Donald A. (1984). Design principles for human-computer interfaces. In *Human Factors in Computing Systems: Proceedings of the CHI '83 Conference Sponsored by the ACM Special Interest Group on Computer & Human Interaction* (SIGCHI) and the Human Factors Society held in Boston, Massachusetts, December 12-15, 1983, ed. Ann Janda, 1-10. New York: North-Holland.

Pettingell, Karen (1991). *An experiment on the interactions of the learner, HCI, and training manual in learning a computer software package,* Ph.D. diss., University of North Texas.

Potosnak, K. M. (1985). Choice of interface modes by empirical groupings of computer users. In *Human-Computer Interaction*—Interact '84: Human-Computer Interaction held in London, UK, September 4-7, 1984, ed. B. Shackel, 27-32. Amsterdam: Elsevier.

Robey, Daniel, & Taggart, William (1982). Human information processing in information and decision support systems. *MIS Quarterly,* June, 61-73.

Schramm, Wilbur (1954). Procedures and effects of mass communication. In *Mass Media and Education Fifty-Third Yearbook of the National Society for the Study of Education,* Part II. ed Nelson B. Henry, Chicago: University of Chicago Press.

Sein, Maung Kyaw (1988). *Conceptual models in training novice users of computer systems: effectiveness of abstract vs. analogical models and influence of individual differences.* Ph.D. diss., Indiana University.

Shannon, Claude E. & Weaver, Warren (1949). *The Mathematical Theory of Communication.* Champaign, ILL: University of Illinois Press

Turner, Jon A., & Karasek, Robert A. (1984). Software ergonomics: effects of computer application design parameters on operator task performance and health. *Ergonomics. 27*(6), 663-690.

Umanath, Narayan S., & Scamell, Richard W. (1988). An experimental evaluation of the impact of data display format on recall performance. *Communications of the ACM, 31*(5), 562-570.

von Papstein, Patricia, & Frese, Michael (1988). Transferring skills from training to the actual work situation: the role of task application knowledge, action styles, and job decision latitude. In *Human Factors in Computing Systems: Proceedings of the CHI '88 Conference* held in Washington, D.C., May 15-19, 1988, ed. Elliot Soloway, Douglas Frye, and Sylvia B. Sheppard, 55-60

Whitefield, Andy (1987). Models in human computer interaction: a classification with special reference to their uses in design. In *Human-Computer Interaction-Interact '87: Proceedings of the Second IFIP Conference on Human-Computer Interaction* held at the University of Stuttgart, Federal Republic of Germany, September 1-4, 1987, ed. H. J. Bullinger and B. Shackel, 57-63. Amsterdam: Elsevier.

CHAPTER 7

EXPERT SYSTEMS TO SUPPORT MANAGERIAL DIAGNOSIS AND EVALUATION

Nancy Green Hall
Kennesaw State College

P. Mohan Rao
Salisbury State University

Expert systems' potential to support higher level business decision making remains unfulfilled. Two systems demonstrate impediments to progress. PET (Productivity Evaluation Technology) interprets precise productivity measurements to extract their meaning for the firm. STRATASSIST (The Strategist's Assistant) assembles natural language descriptions of the firm, its product, and its industry, and processes these values to rate various strategy alternatives available to the firm. Each system presents technical challenges for implementation. With PET, productivity results must be interpreted and evaluated by production rules providing necessary contextual nuances. The more complete the descriptive framework, the more programming lines multiply. STRATASSIST sidesteps the foregoing problem by obtaining the manager's assessment of strategic variables in natural language forms which subsume the shadings of context in the expression itself. Savings on programming lines are offset by the processing problems non-numeric values present. Expert systems which seek to emulate human evaluative and judgmental thought processes encounter difficulties in digital computer environments. Developments in hardware and software may yet allow expert systems to effectively support managers with higher level business decisions.

Expert systems technology has been applied in many areas of human endeavor from industrial controllers to medical diagnosis. This technology moved computer processing closer to human thought and created a great deal of interest in areas of decision making where expertise and judgment are important. Unfortunately, the potential for expert systems to support higher level business decision making has not been realized.

Since the success or failure of a firm depends on the overall quality of managerial decisions, many analytical models, problem solving techniques and other decision aids have been developed for business managers over the past several decades. A veritable arsenal of tools exists to assist managers with routine (well-structured) decisions to be made in the work place. Because such tools lend themselves to computer implementation, managers enjoy the added benefits of the computer's speed, tirelessness and accuracy when they use these models.

Researchers have pushed the envelope of analysis to create expert systems and other knowledge-based technologies which go beyond identifying and measuring what is quantifiable, seeking ways to evaluate observed conditions and emulate human thought processes which result in judgments and choices. In a parallel shift, rigorous algorithms are now augmented by heuristics based on human experience. These knowledge-based techniques can assist managers with the information processing necessary for interpretation and evaluation of the work place and the broader competitive environment. Unfortunately, current computer technology does not adapt so comfortably nor so easily to situations in which important variables may be difficult to quantify and relationships may be very complex or poorly understood.

This chapter will examine some aspects of the challenge presented by efforts to create expert systems to help managers with higher level business decision making. Specific points will be illustrated by two existing systems: PET (Productivity Evaluation Technology) and STRATASSIST (The Strategist's Assistant).

BACKGROUND

Managers in organizations at all levels must plan how to accomplish their objectives and carefully control activities to ensure successful attainment of these goals. Computerized software exists to assist the quantifiable aspects of these two managerial functions: e.g. IFPS is a popular strategic level planning decision support system available from Execucom, and productivity measurement packages such as SCOREBORD by Virginia Production Center are marketed to support control of the production process. These packages focus on numerical processing within a fairly well-structured decision environment.

The situation managers face in planning and controlling a firm contains elements that are well known, partially known, and unknown. This constitutes what Leigh and Doherty (1986) call a semi-structured problem. There are no firm rules to determine whether conditions warrant an affirmative or a negative decision. A manager must reach a subjective decision in his own mind, but an expert system can help by providing an expert's knowledge and judgement for the manager to consider (Tom 1991, p.77).

Advantages of Expert Systems for Managers

Currently expert systems are growing in popularity. Many businesses are attempting to invest at least small sums of money in various applications transferring expertise from man to machine. This knowledge can include what to look for, where to find supporting data, how to interpret values observed, how to put together an accurate portrayal of performance, how to diagnose problem areas, and how to choose an appropriate set of solutions. Expert systems offer distinct advantages to managers who must diagnose problems and evaluate possible solutions.

Expert Systems and Incomplete Information. One of the strengths of expert systems in semi-structured decision situations is that they can function despite missing or incomplete information. An ordinary mathematical model must have values for all of its variables in order to produce any output. An expert system will use whatever information is available in the database or from the user. It can process any production rules for which cues are provided and return those results to the user. There is no necessity for every rule to fire. One can argue that some answers are better than no answers at all.

Expert Systems and Uncertain Information. The information available for a particular managerial decision is not only incomplete at times, but it may also contain an element of uncertainty. A firm may expect that sales revenue will be higher next year than this year, but there may be some question as to how much higher they will be, and there may even be a chance that results will be the same or lower. This type of uncertainty is handled in expert systems by use of a certainty factor entered as a separate value with the sales revenue estimate. When inputs are uncertain, expert systems can still produce output for the user. The certainty factor associated with the result will simply reflect a degree of uncertainty as determined by the individual system.

Symbolic Processing in Expert Systems. The interpretation and evaluation which connects output from computerized measurement systems with management decisions and action implementation require a different kind of processing which Liebowitz calls symbolic processing (1988). This involves manipulating strings of characters rather than crunching numbers. For example, one can combine the information that a firm's revenues are up and costs are down to arrive at the conclusion that the firm's profit potential is improved. Alternatively, viewing a time series of declining labor productivity numbers and concluding that this is a serious problem also can be considered symbolic processing.

An expert system can be of great value to derive benefits from computerized measurement systems. This currently requires manual intervention to perform the necessary symbolic processing which analyzes and diagnoses the real problems and recommends appropriate solutions. The focus on symbolic processing, which is a strength of expert systems, is one reason that many researchers recommend them for managers who need help with poorly structured problems (Goul, 1985) (Green-Hall, 1985) (Oral, 1987) (Sviokla, 1986).

Less Structured Processing in Expert Systems. Expert systems technology is a major departure from mathematical algorithms whose output is strictly determined for given inputs. This new technology allows the discovery of potentially significant relationships in the knowledge base without human assistance (Silverman, 1987). It is quite possible that some of these relationships might have eluded the less systematic human mental processing and thus have been missed entirely. As Negoita observes, "Propositions, production rules, and frames allow unplanned interactions with facts." (1985, p.69)

Expert Systems and Limitations on Human Thought. A human decision maker can handle only so much information at one time, so he unconsciously or consciously limits what he works with to just a few major chunks. A computer can search a huge database for items which match a given pattern in a short time and with little programming effort. Thus the amount of information which can contribute to the decision process is limited only by the system designer's listing of propositions, production rules, and frames based on expert opinion and the volume of information supplied to the database (Tom, 1991) (Green 1984). An expert system can rapidly examine many aspects of a decision and reduce the number of cues a manager must consider (Duhaime and Schwenk, 1985).

Another potential problem introduced by human processing of information is bias or narrowness of focus. Grant and King (1979) recommend a systematic data collection and structuring procedure in order to protect the organization from arbitrary and unwarranted constraints which might be imposed unconsciously by the analyst. Tom (1991) points out that expert systems pay attention to all details available to them and do not overlook any relevant information or potential solutions. Both Utterback (1979) and Klein (1979) favor a prescriptive method for directing attention to a broad range of interactions and relating them to the particularities of a firm's products, resources, and competitive environment. As Whalen and Schott (1983) observe, a computerized system can elicit from the planner, store, and process more chunks of information than is possible for human memory, while imposing minimal restrictions and distortions on the way the knowledge is represented.

Although the foregoing advantages are not an exhaustive listing of the reasons why expert systems have excited so much interest among information systems researchers and practitioners, they serve to illustrate expert systems' potential as an aid to higher level business decision making. PET and STRATASSIST have been developed to bring these benefits to managers.

Description of PET

PET is the acronym for Productivity Evaluation Technology. This expert system prototype was developed using GoldWorks. PET is designed for use at the operations control level of a production organization. Its purpose is to accept crisp measurements of many aspects of a firm's production processes over time and then to identify profit centers where a productivity problem may exist. It then proceeds to a category level assessment to identify problem areas. At the element level it finds the factors creating the problem and identifies causes for these factors which the manager can then match with possible corrective actions. PET runs on a 286 or 386 PC. GoldWorks requires a minimum of 5-MB memory.

PET is an interactive, user-friendly system which is menu based and uses windowing and graphics capabilities associated with an electronic spreadsheet. The expert system component includes an inference engine, a knowledge base, a working memory, a user interface, and data interfaces. The ability to access and use data from various sources can facilitate a more precise identification of problems.

PET begins with input from a multi-period productivity measurement system based on the PPP model "Profitability = Productivity + Price Recovery" (Miller, 1984). This measurement model is implemented on a Lotus 1-2-3 spreadsheet. As PET scans the file imported from the spreadsheet and proceeds through the various levels of its analysis, additional information is elicited from the user and the user has the opportunity to choose among options available. When the analysis is finished, PET has identified any productivity problems and their possible causes.

Description of STRATASSIST

STRATASSIST is a prototype fuzzy decision support system designed for use by small- to medium-sized firms with predominantly a single product/market. It is designed to support the manager charged with formulating a strategy for the firm to pursue. STRATASSIST acquires information on strategic variables from the user and judges how likely it is that the firm would have success with certain generic strategies. It is currently based in Lotus 1-2-3 and can be run on a 286 or 386 PC.

STRATASSIST assembles a data base containing the user's knowledge and opinions about his firm and its competitive environment via an interactive menu-driven questionnaire based on Porter's (1980) structural theory of competition in an industry. The decision maker answers the questions in English rather than in precise numbers or ratios. A fuzzy expert system processes the information provided by the user and reasons approximately to evaluate the likelihood of success of specific strategic alternatives. A visual representation of the user's values on a related set of strategic variables compared to the expert specified values for this set enables the user to make his own assessment of the degree to which his firm's situation predisposes to success with a particular strategy.

Both PET and STRATASSIST have demonstrated potential as decision supports for higher level business decision making. Nevertheless, implementation questions remain which impede progress.

FAILURE OF EXPERT SYSTEMS SUPPORT FOR HIGHER LEVEL DECISION PROCESSES

When so many capabilities of expert systems match the requirements of managerial decision making, why have expert systems failed to achieve their potential as aids to middle and upper level managers? This section will examine some of the problems which continue to plague developers of expert systems to assist managerial diagnosis and evaluation, and will propose some recommendations and solutions.

Obstacles to Successful Expert System Support of Higher Level Managerial Decisions

Developers of expert systems for middle and upper level managers encounter problems of various sorts when attempting to automate the interpretation, evaluation, and diagnosis that managers must do in order to judge which actions should be undertaken in the best interests of the firm. The two systems discussed below illustrate some aspects of these problems.

Challenges for PET as Expert System. PET provides a good illustration of difficulties for expert system development posed by the productivity control decision process. Inputs to the control process are generally crisp numbers derived from the productivity measurement system. Because of the precise nature of these data, one might assume that the control decision could be characterized as well-structured and therefore easily modeled and encoded for computer processing. Unfortunately, interpreting and evaluating performance measurement results over time cannot be done so easily as one might think.

Productivity Evaluation Decision Process With PET. The first task PET performs is to identify changes in performance results. It interprets time series data from a minimum of 5 periods using standard statistical control techniques with control limits to identify trends, runs, and outliers. This identification is not limited to one level, but takes place at the macro-level, the category-level, and the element-level of performance.

Once the performance results are identified, PET assesses the significance of the performance changes. Information about problem significance allows problems to be ranked according to their severity. Without such information a minor problem and a serious problem would receive the same attention. Moreover, some variations in performance may be purely random variations without any assignable causes. PET applies process control techniques to identify non-random variations such as a multi-period trend and converts numerical values into a descriptive term such as "4-period downward trend." PET must next evaluate this interpretation and make a value judgement about the significance of the problem, *e.g.*, very serious, serious, significant, moderate, minor, insignificant or no problem. Expert opinion prioritizing performance variations and evaluating implications of trends can be extremely useful from a management standpoint and adapts easily in principle to expert system technology.

PET uses the information developed so far to present a complete performance "story" rather than just a number or a single word, such as SERIOUS. The system displays at least a one-sentence statement such as "There is a SERIOUS PROFITABILITY-PROBLEM with [situation-specific descriptor] with a 0.7 certainty." It also tells the cause(s) of performance change. With causes identified, it is just a step in the mind for the manager to find possible corrective actions.

PET and Automation of Symbolic Processing

In the case of PET, problems for implementation begin to emerge when the crisp data from the productivity measurement system must be interpreted to extract their meaning in the productivity context. This must be done before further evaluation is possible. For instance, a production rule to interpret sales figures might read as follows in English: "If the reported sales is up and deflated sales is down, then there is a volume decline with 0.85 certainty." Unfortunately, to get from actual numbers in a time series of sales results to the conclusion that on a deflated basis, volume is actually down, requires a sequence of 28 programming lines in GoldWorks code.

Expert systems for value judgments require additional efforts on implementation because of questions such as what constitutes a SERIOUS problem and what constitutes a MINOR problem. Multi-period data and process-control techniques are invaluable in making such value judgments. For example, if there is a DOWNWARD-TREND since the base period, then the problem is SERIOUS. There will be no debate whether or not the problem is SERIOUS if the downward trend is sharp. But what if the downward trend is slight? Should it be considered a SIGNIFICANT problem rather then a SERIOUS problem? If so, what about a trend that is in between? How far should one go with such classifications? Should not a downward trend in a key factor indicator for a critical success factor be interpreted as more serious than a downward trend in another performance area? Clearly, developing logic rules to execute such value judgments is a very complex task, and as illustrated above, results in reams of programming when implemented on a computer.

Consider further the fact that numbers themselves, whether represented in percent or in the underlying metric of dollars, hours, units, and so forth, should really be placed in a context of threshold amounts (or acceptable levels) on a case by case basis as an aid to interpretability. One must never forget the context when interpreting and evaluating data about a firm, yet the number of production rules and other code which are required to capture all the salient details of an individual situation is daunting.

This serves to illustrate how very cumbersome is the process required to automate what an experienced, trained analyst can do at a glance. Evaluating the broader implications to the firm of a decline in sales is no less important nor less cumbersome to automate. The more ambitious a system such as PET becomes, the more programming lines expand with all the accompanying headaches.

Strategy Formulation With STRATASSIST. At the other end of the organizational spectrum is the strategic planning problem faced by the senior managers of an organization who must design and implement a grand strategy for a firm. As Porter describes the process, "...the broadest guidance for the formulation of strategy is stated in terms of matching a firm's strengths and weaknesses, particularly its distinctive competence, to the opportunities and risk in its environment." (1980, p.149)

The strategy formulation decision process begins with a survey of the firm, its product, and its competitive environment, to identify and evaluate strengths and weaknesses on the one hand, and opportunities and risk on the other. The matching process is where managers most need the benefits of experience and the judgment of experts. Porter points out that competitive strategy depends "...critically on a subtle understanding of industries and competitors." (1980, p. ix)

STRATASSIST supports this top management decision in the following way. First it assembles a data base containing the user's knowledge and opinions about his firm and its competitive environment via an interactive menu-driven questionnaire based on Porter's (1980) structural theory of competition in an industry. This procedure directs the user's attention in an organized and comprehensive fashion to those strategic variables which should be considered in formulating a strategy for the firm. The decision maker answers the questions in English rather than in precise numbers or ratios. This provides a benefit in both time and ease of use since most senior managers of a small or medium sized firm can respond quickly and confidently in qualitative terms to questions about the performance of the firm and its rivals.

Values accepted by the system are as follows: Very high, High, Medium high, Medium, Medium low, Low, and Very low. In answer to a question such as "What is your firm's market share?", a manager might respond, High. Since a manager may not always be one hundred percent certain of a value provided, the system also allows two modifiers: *More-or-less*, to indicate uncertainty as to the precise location of the value itself; and *Possibly*, to express a user's perception that the quality of the information provided may be open to question.

Two types of processing are provided to help the manager match his firm's strategic position with one of Porter's generic strategies. An expert system processes the input values and produces ratings of the success potential for a specific strategy. A visual representation of the firm's profile of values plotted against the expert's set of required values gives a snapshot for the manager to interpret. The manager uses either the ratings or the graphs, or both, to determine what broad strategy has the most potential for his firm.

Challenges for Strategic Expert Systems. Although STRATASSIST evades the questions raised above with PET regarding interpretation and evaluation of crisp input values, the nature of the strategic decision environment introduces a panoply of new problems and challenges for implementation in an expert system to support the strategic decision process.

Quality of Information. The future orientation of strategic planning leads to quantification problems even in areas, such as financial performance, in which a firm historically has precise measurements available. Forecasting can provide estimates of future values in these instances, however, the greater the precision of the estimate, the greater the chance of error in the value predicted (Hall, 1988).

Strategic planning is complicated by the fact that some decision variables, though very important to the strategic decision, have no automatic domain on the number line. For example, managers can express market share as a percent of total market. Competitive position, which includes market share, also includes intangible aspects of a firm such as market reputation and the nature of its distribution channels. One can qualify competitive position as either strong or weak but to assign a numerical value to it would be both arbitrary and artificial. Nevertheless, competitive position is an extremely important strategic variable which should be included in any comprehensive strategic planning effort (Hall, 1988).

Modeling Vagueness and Complexity. Managers who are formulating a strategy for their firm have to deal with many aspects of the competitive environment which, like competitive position, are complex ideas made up of many subcomponents whose relationships are not well defined. What is meant by a concept such as reputation is even more difficult to specify, yet managers understand what it is and can immediately characterize it for their firm and its rivals. Such vagueness and complexity make it very hard to model the strategy formulation decision process. Researchers struggle constantly with specification and measurement, frequently discarding elements which are intractable to traditional approaches.

Negoita calls it a misunderstanding that a model cannot be built unless every parameter is known to high accuracy. He points out that this often causes the omission of very significant subjective evaluations. "Vagueness need not be eliminated in models if we can use a mechanism to model vagueness" (Negoita, 1985, p.120). As early as 1965, Lotfi Zadeh published the first paper in what has since become known as fuzzy sets theory. Zadeh (1972, p.131) remarked that "In general, complexity and precision bear an inverse relation to one another in the sense that, as the complexity of a problem increases, the possibility of analyzing it in precise terms diminishes." In an effort to cope with this situation, Zadeh developed a theory of fuzzy sets in which an element could have partial membership in a set. He suggested using values in the range between 0 and 1 to represent this degree of membership in the set for any single element.

Linguistic Variables. The idea of using linguistic values such as high or low to characterize a degree of membership in a fuzzy set emerged as a natural progression from Zadeh's approach. Goguen characterized what he called L-fuzzy sets in a paper by that name in 1967. Gaines pointed out that the use of modifiers such as very, somewhat or moreorless in combination with natural language values for linguistic variables allows expressions which connote both degree of precision and expected value. Words are less precise than numbers, but they do "exactly express our thoughts." (1976, p. 662) Zadeh concurs, "Since words...are less precise than numbers, the concept of a linguistic variable serves the purpose of providing a means of approximate characterization of phenomena which are too complex or too ill-defined to be amenable to description in conventional quantitative terms (1975, p. 313). A computerized system "able to work with fuzzy parameters, offers users a superb gain in human effectiveness" (Negoita, 1985, p. 120). For this reason the planning aid, STRATASSIST, accepts and processes natural language values of linguistic variables in its expert system.

Approximate Reasoning. Processing the strategic information provided by the user, the fuzzy expert system reasons approximately to evaluate the likelihood of success of strategies and strategic actions for consideration. The prototype contains production rules based on opinions expressed by Porter in his book, *Competitive Strategy* (1980). The majority of these rules relate certain firm or environment characteristics to one or another of Porter's three generic strategies: Cost leadership, Differentiation, and Focus. A typical production rule has the form, "If *Market share* is *High* then *Cost leadership* strategy is possible." From the user's point of view, the more production rules relating to any one strategy, the better, so that "...multiple weak and individually fallible chains of reasoning...converge into an accurate solution" (Whalen and Schott, 1983, p. 128). In the prototype described below, each of 14 rules relating to Porter's cost leadership strategy produces a number between 0 and 1 reflecting the degree of match between the user's descriptions of specific firm and environment characteristics and the expert's opinion about desirable levels on the same variables if a firm is to experience success as a low cost leader. The list of 14 variables can be viewed as necessary ingredients for success. A good match on most of these would suggest to a user that the firm is in a good position to pursue a Cost leadership strategy. A mediocre match on most, even with one or two "hits," would be unlikely to induce pursuit of the strategy.

As with PET, the production rules for expert system processing of the strategic cues and strategy alternative matches can be stated succinctly in English language expressions. Problems emerge when implementing the inference engine appropriate for approximate reasoning on natural language values with existing computer software.

Problems With Initial Implementation of STRATASSIST. STRATASSIST does not have the benefit of crisp inputs, for reasons explained above. Instead, the system relies on the user for interpretation of observed strategic variables. Benefits achieved in reduced programming lines at this point are off-set by the difficulty encountered while attempting to adapt existing expert system software to non-crisp value inputs.

STRATASSIST in an Expert System Shell. Since the major processing module within STRATASSIST is an expert system, an obvious approach to implementing it on the computer would be to use one of the many expert system shells now on the market. Currently, many expert system shells are available, such as VP-Expert and ExSys. The writers chose to explore possibilities for implementing STRATASSIST in one of these software environments to see whether a satisfactory fuzzy expert system could be developed without programming from scratch.

VP-Expert provided several challenges relative to implementing STRATASSIST. Although the system lends itself to the sort of question and answer between user and software which assembles the information to be processed, VP-Expert does not lend itself to examining many rules related to one objective and then aggregating the results. Instead, VP-Expert will cycle through a set of rules until it finds one satisfactory response and it then moves on to another objective entirely. This proved to be a very vexing problem. To solve this problem the writers defined a goal variable which could only be found by examining the entire set of related production rules.

A second problem involved the use of linguistic variables. The expert system shell processes categorical designations on a match / no match basis. This method defeats the purpose of these values in STRATASSIST. Since the system has no means of reasoning approximately, it was necessary to translate an English language value offered by the user into a number of some sort. Zadeh (1975) first suggested using a number between 0 (no resemblance) and 1 (identity) to describe the degree of resemblance between a user-observed phenomenon and a defined set characteristic for the phenomenon. This allowed a sort of quantification for variables which are not easily measured. Wenstop (1980) carried the quantification of linguistic variables a step further by using a profile approach which represented a resemblance measure such as "high" by a ten cell vector of numbers between 0 and 1 to indicate the general area of resemblance (*i.e.*, higher values clustered at the right hand or "high" end of the vector and zeros in the low range). Wenstop's profile represented uncertainty about the actual location (precision) of the value on the low to high continuum by spreading non-zero entries to either side of the best estimate and tapering off more gradually to zero entries. The user's uncertainty that the description is true, as distinguished from precise, is shown by the same profile but with lower values in each cell (*i.e.*, .5 in place of 1 for the best estimate location). The Zadeh approach produces a "pseudo-number" which must be approached with caution regarding mathematical operations. Many theorists will not accept operations upon these numbers except by very conservative, non-parametric algorithms. The Wenstop elaboration further complicates the situation by providing a "pseudo-vector". The VP-Expert inference engine was not well suited for the types of calculations preferred for a pseudo-number and had no mechanism whatever to manipulate a pseudo-vector of numbers.

Although this implementation of STRATASSIST in VP Expert collected the desired strategic information from the manager and processed it to produce some assessment of strategy alternatives, it was not satisfactory because of the compromises made. A standard off-the-shelf expert system shell cannot model appropriately the decision variables and judgment process required for STRATASSIST.

Solutions for Better Expert System Support

The complexities of higher level management decision processes represent obstacles which expert systems must overcome before they can achieve their potential as decision aids to managerial planning and control. As shown above, both PET and STRATASSIST are designed to assist managers with the interpretation and evaluation required for productivity control and strategy formulation. Problems discussed regarding implementation of the systems can be addressed as follows.

Revising PET for Better Productivity Evaluation. Interpreting productivity numbers and evaluating their implications for the firm create two types of problems when programming the system. The large numbers of programming lines required to assess what certain combinations of numbers actually mean to a particular firm will become less problematical as greater speed and memory capacity become available at lower prices. Therefore, this is not really a constraint to expert system assistance for managerial control.

Capturing and storing all the specifics of a particular firm so that correct and complete interpretation and evaluation of productivity measurement data becomes possible represents a much greater obstacle for expert systems. Knowledge engineering is a very important area within the field of knowledge-based systems. According to Silverman (1987, p.9) it is "...a potentially powerful approach to the identification of productivity problems and corrective opportunities..." The problem for PET becomes one of incorporating the results into the expert system for maximum portability from firm to firm.

Ideally, there should be a maintenance module in the expert system to store and update context parameters so that they are neither hard-coded nor supplied by the user for each session. Hard-coded parameters do not allow portability. On the other hand, supplying these values for each session is tedious for the user and can allow "game playing" with the numbers themselves. Acquiring necessary context data from the user could be part of the installation procedure for PET when a manager commits to using the system as an aid to productivity evaluation. The manager would subsequently update the module only as needed.

Additional knowledge engineering and price/performance improvements in PC hardware should allow PET to achieve its full potential to help managers with the productivity control decision process.

A New Software for STRATASSIST. Because the goal for STRATASSIST is to be able to reason approximately to assess the degree of match between a user-supplied value for a strategic variable and the desirable expert-specified value, the writers chose to explore other software which might be more adaptable to the mathematical manipulations suitable to non-crisp data.

A Spreadsheet-based STRATASSIST

The search for a readily available software home for a fuzzy expert system has led to an electronic spreadsheet environment such as Lotus 1-2-3, in which logical and mathematical operations may be specified by the user at will. Using macros and writing appropriate formulas in cells, it is possible to perform the operations necessary for a fuzzy expert system while presenting a user-friendly interactive interface to the user.

An interactive macro can acquire the user's qualitative assessment on the variables of interest for a Cost leadership strategy. The spreadsheet system can then display all fourteen of the firm / environment cues Porter relates to a Cost leadership strategy as the identifying labels on the horizontal axis for a Cost leadership profile. The height of the vertical axis would be the maximum linguistic value, Very High; the low point would be Very Low. Using one color or symbol, Porter's required levels could be indicated. Another color or symbol could be used to display the user-supplied value. The user can assess for himself the degree to which his firm's values match the Porter values and thus, the possibility that a Cost leadership strategy might be appropriate for his firm to pursue.

This profile assessment relies on the user's interpretation of spatial relationships rather than semantics or mathematics to assist strategic planners in selecting a strategy for their firm (Sage, 1981). Experienced managers are accustomed to being in control. They may be unwilling to accept direction from another source, such as a computer (Hall, 1988).

For the sake of those users willing to consider expert opinion, it is possible in the spreadsheet environment to actually process user-supplied qualitative values against the expert production rules using max-min composition of relations. A real strength of the electronic spreadsheet in this application is that the user can write any desired formulas as cell entries. The linguistic values provided by the user and the expert-specified values from the production rules can be translated using the Wenstop methodology described above. A simple approximate reasoning inference engine can be modeled in the spreadsheet environment using logical @ functions to process the translated natural language values as follows.

The Wenstop vectors representing user and expert measures can be composed using the @MAX and @MIN functions provided by the spreadsheet. For each rule, a value between 0 and 1 would be returned representing the degree to which the user-supplied value and the expert-specified value resemble each other. By implication, the value would suggest how well the firm satisfies this necessary ingredient for the strategy's success. Numbers approaching 1 on a majority of the 14 rules supporting Cost-Leadership strategy would encourage a user to seriously consider this strategy for his firm, while numbers approaching 0 would surely lead the user to search for more promising strategic alternatives. Tabular presentation of fuzzy expert system processing results might be more satisfying than the graphical representation described above, for managers who like to see tables with numbers.

Given an appropriate software host, STRATASSIST can effectively support top managers as they formulate a strategy for their firm. Expert systems' failure to achieve their full potential as aids to higher-level business decisions can be overcome with new modeling approaches such as linguistic variables and approximate reasoning, but the solutions create new problems until expert systems and/or spreadsheet software is developed for such technology.

FUTURE DEVELOPMENTS

A large body of researchers continue to expand the scope of expert systems applications to assist managers with higher level decisions involving interpretation and evaluation. For the two systems discussed in this chapter, certain developments follow naturally from current research.

Proposed Directions for PET and STRATASSIST

Enhancements for PET. PET can be improved by facilitating through the data interface the capability to access other sources of data within the organization. A system for productivity analysis should be able to determine the causes of identified problems. For example, if labor productivity has been identified as a problem, then the system should be able to determine if the problem is related to motivation or training or other causes. An expert system can determine such causes by gathering information from company data bases or from the user. To discover whether absenteeism and tardiness point to motivation as the cause of reduced productivity in the labor force, actual absenteeism and tardiness data for recent periods should be obtained from company data bases and examined for tell-tale patterns.

A great deal of work remains in order for PET to be able to recommend corrective actions based on the causes identified above. A simple cause and treatment might be, for example, that if lack of training is lowering labor productivity, then training is the appropriate corrective action. A comprehensive treatment may not be that simple. In the first place, there may not be a single cause. When several factors contribute to a problem each may have to be addressed separately. Sometimes, when several causes are put together, there may be a single appropriate treatment. On the other hand, one cause may require several types of treatments. A systems approach must be flexible, capable of recognizing inter-relationships and synergies, and, if at all possible, capable of anticipating longer-term consequences of solutions suggested. All of this will require much effort to build the knowledge base from experienced analysts and to program production rules, frames and instances in order to automate this type of management thought.

Expansion of STRATASSIST. STRATASSIST must be expanded to include as broad a base as possible of expert opinion about appropriate strategy-firm matches. This will involve some increase in the size of the questionnaire that the user completes to build the database. It will require many more production rules to use in processing the user-supplied information. Graphs may be more difficult to devise because of the larger volume of information which may have to be represented. Time to load the spreadsheet and perform required tasks may expand to the point that the user must wait an unreasonable amount, as is now the case with PET.

The search for a better software home for STRATASSIST will continue. Some promising software is coming to market which incorporates fuzzy logic: TILShell from Togai InfraLogic, Inc.; NET-Link+ from NORRAD; NEXPERT OBJECT from Neuron Data Inc.; CubiCalc from HyperLogic; and FuziCalc from FuziWare. Concerns and frustration expressed above may find solutions in one of these packages.

Updating the rule bases. One of the important advantages of expert systems over conventional systems is that expert systems allow easy modification or upgrading of the knowledge base. For example, new techniques for productivity improvement are discovered over time; these techniques can be readily added to the system's knowledge base. As strategic theory advances, new insights can be incorporated in the system. Managers can even distill their own experience into heuristics to add to the knowledge base. The expert system that recommends solutions for a given set of problems can have up-to-date knowledge of new improvement techniques. The decisions of managers can therefore become even more effective. More importantly for the long term survival of the firm, senior managers using STRATASSIST can benefit from the best and most recent expert knowledge about appropriate strategies.

Areas For Further Research

For PET and STRATASSIST, ongoing research will focus on

further refinements, enhancements, and validation of both systems as aids to managerial diagnosis and evaluation. Each system will have to demonstrate its usefulness and acceptability to line managers of business organizations.

A research area which seems most pressing in light of the foregoing discussion, is a validation of the claim made by Lotfi Zadeh, "Humans have a remarkable ability to assign a grade of membership to a given object without a conscious understanding of how the grade is arrived at." (1984, p. 26) Whenever a user supplies a value for a variable, this "remarkable ability" comes into play. For those areas in which user judgement must be employed, there is a critical need to establish that users can correctly and consistently evaluate observed phenomena. In the near term, a group approach which solicits several opinions and aggregates them may enhance the credibility of linguistic variables with natural language values. Nevertheless, this approach to non-quantifiable variables will never achieve true scientific respectability unless a great deal of research demonstrates the validity and reliability of human judgement for natural language measurement.

CONCLUSION

Expert systems such as PET and STRATASSIST have much to offer business managers as they interpret and evaluate conditions in and around their firms to judge which actions should be taken to ensure organization success. PET automates much of the interpretation and evaluation which managers would ordinarily have to do themselves before they could judge which actions are necessary to maintain desired productivity levels in the firm. STRATASSIST provides comprehensive strategic scanning for the firm and matches firm-specific values on important variables with expert suggested levels on strategy alternatives. Both help managers make important decisions.

Other advantages of an expert system approach to productivity analysis with PET include cost reductions due to the reduced need for staff manpower, faster analysis of pressing productivity problems, and more consistent appraisals and interpretations of productivity performance. Perhaps the most significant benefit is the likely increase in management inquiry into productivity performance and the resulting impact on the firm's competitiveness. The challenges detailed above for developing PET from a research prototype to a full scale software aid for managerial control can be met and should provide benefits well worth the cost in time and effort.

Strategic managers will benefit from letting STRATASSIST help them formulate an appropriate strategy for their firm. As Moser and Christoph observe, "The complexity of business problems and the critical nature of the decisions to be made make management one of the most important application fields for expert systems." (1987, p. 19) This applies even more to the area of strategic planning, which touches the very survival of the firm. Unfortunately, the nature of much important strategic planning information makes the use of fuzzy expert systems desirable, but the state of the art in terms of expert system software shells presents some serious problems for the use of non-crisp data. A more appropriate choice at the present time is a software such as Lotus 1-2-3. The graphical capability to visually represent relationships combined with the ability to freely define mathematical and logical operations make this software a reasonable off-the-shelf home for STRATASSIST.

Emerging technologies such as expert systems offer great promise for creation of computer aids to managerial diagnosis and evaluation. Creating software for this purpose presents distinct challenges as illustrated in this chapter with two existing systems: Pet and STRATASSIST. These two systems illustrate reasons why expert systems have failed to reach their potential as supports for higher level managerial decision making.

REFERENCES

Duhaime, I. and Schwenk, C. (1985). Conjectures on cognitive simplification in acquisition and divestment decision-making. *Academy of Management Review, 10*(4), 287-295.

Gaines, B. (1976). Foundations of fuzzy reasoning. *International Journal of Man-Machine Studies, 8*, 623-668.

Goguen, J. A. (1967). L-fuzzy sets. *Journal of Math Analysis and Applications, 18*, 145-174.

Grant, J. H., & King, W. R. (1979). Strategy formulation: Analytical and normative models. In D. E. Schendel & C. W.Hofer (Eds.), *Strategic management* (pp. 104-122).

Green, N. L. (1984). Interfacing interactive graphics with fuzzy production rules in a DSS. *Proceedings of the 1984 IEEE International Conference on Systems, Man, and Cybernetics*, 226-228. IEEE Catalog No.: 84CH2063-6.

Green-Hall, N. (1985). Using a fuzzy expert system for decision support of the strategic planning process. Ph.D dissertation, Georgia State University, Atlanta.

Green Hall, N. L. (1986) A fuzzy decision support system for strategic planning. In E. Sanchez & L. A. Zadeh (Eds.), *Approximate reasoning in intelligent systems, decision and control* (pp. 77-90). Oxford: Pergamon Press.

Goul, M. (1985). The inclusion of expertise in a decision support system for strategic planning: An empirical study. Doctoral dissertation, Oregon State University, Corvallis.

Hall, N. G. (1988). Diagnosing problems with the user interface for a strategic planning fuzzy DSS. *IEEE Transactions on Systems, Man, and Cybernetics, 18*(4), 638-

646.

Hall, N. G., & Rao, P. M. (1992). STRATASSIST - A Strategic Planner's Fuzzy Expert Consultant. *Proceedings of the 1992 Information Resources Management Association International Conference*, (pp. 181-184).

Klein, H.E. (1979). Commentary. In D.E. Schendel & C.W. Hofer (Eds.), *Strategic Management* (pp. 144-151). Boston: Little, Brown & Co.

Leigh, W. E., & Doherty, M. E. (1986) *Decision Support and Expert Systems.* Ohio: South-Western Publishing Co.

Liebowitz, Jay. (1988). *Introduction to Expert Systems.* California: Mitchell.

Miller, David M. (1984). Profitability = Productivity + Price Recovery. *Harvard Business Review, 62*(3), 145-153.

Moser, J. and Christoph, R. (1987). Management expert systems (M.E.S.): A framework for development and implementation. *Information Processing Management, 23*(1), 17-23.

Negoita, C. V. (1985). *Expert Systems and Fuzzy Systems.* Menlo Park, CA: Benjamin/Cummings.

Oral, M. (1987). A DSS design framework for competitive strategy formulation. *European Journal of Operations Research, 28*(2),

Porter, M. E. (1980). *Competitive Strategy.* Boston: Little, Brown & Co.

Rao, P. M. & Miller, D. M. (1992). Expert systems approach for productivity analysis. Manuscript submitted for publication.

Sage, A. P. (1981). Behavioral and organizational considerations in the design of information systems and processes for planning and decision support. *IEEE Transactions on Systems, Man, and Cybernetics, SMC-11*(9), 640-673.

Silverman, B. G. (1987) Should a manager "hire" an expert system? In B. G. Silverman (Ed.), *Expert systems for business.* Massachusetts: Addison-Wesley Publishing Company.

Sviokla, J. (1986). Business implications of knowledge based systems. *Data Base, 18*, 5-19.

Tom, P. (1991). *Managing information as a corporate resource.* New York: Harper Collins Publishers.

Utterback, J. M. (1979). Environmental analysis and forecasting. In D. E. Schendel & C. W. Hofer (Eds.). *Strategic management* (pp. 134-144). Boston: Little, Brown & Company.

Wenstop, F. (1980). Quantitative analysis with linguistic values. *Fuzzy Sets and Systems, 4*, 99-115.

Whalen, T. and Schott, B. (1983). Representing and manipulating fuzzy knowledge about forecasting problems and techniques. In *Proceedings of the International Conference on Systems, Man, and Cybernetics*, (pp. 127-131), Bombay.

Zadeh, L. A. (1965). Fuzzy sets. *Information and Control, 8*, 338-353.

Zadeh, L. A. (1972). Fuzzy languages and their relation to human intelligence. *Proceedings of the International Conference on Man and Computer*, 130-165, Bordeaux, France. Basel: S. Karger.

Zadeh, L. A. (1975). The concept of a linguistic variable and its application to approximate reasoning, Part II. *Information Science, 8*, 301-57.

Zadeh, L. A. (1984, August). Making computers think like people. *IEEE SPECTRUM*, 26-32.

CHAPTER 8

EXAMPLE-BASED INFORMATION SYSTEMS FOR EXPERT, MANAGERIAL DECISION SUPPORT

Aaron Patula
Memphis State University

High level, managerial decision making requires a great deal of rich and varied experience in the decision domain as well as access to a wide range of data about the present problem. Research into the process of advanced decision making has discovered that these experts utilize example-based thinking to solve such complex problems. This suggests that the computer based decision support of example-based thinking could improve the decision outcomes for managers. But before this question can be examined directly, one must know what an example-based information system might be like. The following research reviews the relevant literature, describes the components and functions of an example-based information system, proposes a model for future research and provides an example of how such a system can be used in business decision making. Example-based decision support may be a path by which managerial expertise is amplified and improved, resulting in greater business success.

The increase in global competition is a great challenge for U. S. business. The world-wide availability of advanced technology and efficient transportation as well as low labor costs abroad has the effect of forcing U.S. companies to lower wages. A strategy for U. S. companies which do not want to lower their employees' standard of living is to increase labor productivity (Madnick, 1991). One way of accomplishing this is to increase the level of individual employee expertise and effectiveness. Having mastered the knowledge and skills associated with their jobs, experts are extremely effective producers and are responsible for a disproportionately large part of an organization's success. Augustine's (1979) study of expertise and decision correctness (cited in Turban, 1990) concluded that the top 10% in terms of expertise made correct decisions three times more frequently than individuals of average expertise. The implication is that increases in the level of expertise will yield huge gains in individual and organizational effectiveness.

The literature shows that expertise is created by exposure to numerous examples or cases. Experts solve problems by reasoning in terms of examples. The kind of expertise created by example-based[1] thinking allows the decision maker to progress beyond mere rule following to a highly effective, context sensitive decision making method which may, more appropriately, be called judgment or wisdom.

Experts reason from examples when solving a problem: they apply past cases and examples to the present problem through analogical reasoning (Chi et al., 1989). The advantage of reasoning by example is that the decision maker can use a parallel, pattern matching thinking process which facilitates rapid solutions. An example is a device by which a large amount complex, interrelated knowledge can be gathered into a single, unified chunk, allowing the decision maker to simplify problem solving (see Chase and Simon (1973) on knowledge 'chunking').

The expert normally encounters the examples which create expertise by real world experience. However, expertise gained by raw experience may be inefficient and incomplete. Decision makers learn by solving difficult or unusual problems. The decision maker, relying upon raw experience, may have to wait a long time before coming across such problems. It could happen that real world experience may never provide a good range of problems which are necessary to develop true expertise. For example, an expert stock trader who learned trading during the bull market of the 1980's may suddenly find that expertise to be irrelevant in the sideways market environment of the 1990's. Therefore, the use of an example base having a wide range of problems could result in an increase of expertise within a firm.

Furthermore, experts solve problems by comparing the present problem to a bank of past examples stored in memory. This ability to effectively use past examples to solve problems even though those examples often do not exactly fit the present situation is called analogical reasoning (Keane, 1988; Novik, 1988). The past examples sketch the characteristics of a problem domain. The significant elements of the present problem are compared with the significant elements of past examples. The past examples with the closest match to the present problem are used as a guide for solving the problem. However, experts know that the past does not always repeat itself. So, they are alert to problems in which one must break with what past experience suggests and try something new.

Example-based information systems (E-bIS) might be used to support expert, managerial decision making. An E-bIS can store, organize and retrieve a collection of examples. It can also function as a blackboard style, process independent decision support system which aids decision makers by using stored examples to solve problems. Example-based reasoning has been called a cutting edge technology (Turban, 1991), but it has also been noted there is a dearth of research on the topic (Turban, 1990).

Example-based information systems (E-bIS) could teach expertise to non-expert decision makers (Cook, 1989). An E-bIS can expose experts-to-be to a variety of examples, thus simulating a broad range of experience which ordinarily might require a number of years to acquire otherwise. E-bIS can automatically and repeatedly expose novices to examples in order transfer expertise to them, raising the overall expertise level within an organization.

The central task of this chapter is to systematically relate example-based information systems to the creation of expertise and the support of decision makers in an organization. "The Skill-Knowledge Distinction" points out a distinction important to the remaining discussion and corrects a common misconception about expertise. "Literature Review" examines the association between expertise and example-based thinking as well as a brief review of example-based systems. "The Example-based Information System: An Emerging Technology" is the central topic of the chapter and describes the components and functions of a generic example-based system. "A Model of Operational Factors in an E-bIS" describes the factors relating to E-bIS outcomes. "How Would E-bis be Used by a Managers" describes a fictional session with an E-bIS. The chapter concludes with an outline of future E-bIS trends.

A DISCUSSION OF GENERAL BACKGROUND ISSUES

The following discussion is about concepts important in example-based systems such as expert decision making processes, philosophical background issues and examples of actual example-based systems.

The Skill-Knowledge Distinction

It is often thought that expertise is the accumulation or memorization of facts and knowledge. However, that is a misconception. In fact, expertise has two components: skill and knowledge (Cook, 1989). The knowledge component is made of explicit facts, procedures, inferences, rules, objects and attributes. Knowledge is most often communicated in the form of propositions. Today, knowledge can be stored and communicated via computer based systems in the form of inference bases in an expert system, conceptual networks or Object-Attribute-Value triplets. Skill is the implicit ability to apply the appropriate knowledge in an intelligent, flexible and effective manner to solve problems. Skills are not communicated explicitly (in propositional form) but are taught implicitly, by example.

For instance, much knowledge is required in order to appraise art. An art appraiser cannot define exactly how to select good art. But an art appraiser can give some general principles which guide appraisals. Also, examples of art which have been properly appraised can be cited. The example base of art works previously appraised defines the functioning of expertise within that problem domain. Skill in appraising art is not acquired through the memorization of facts and procedures but through practice and experience in applying that knowledge.

The following model summarizes the previous section and describes the two components of expertise and the manner in which these components are related. Both skill and knowledge are important to expertise but very often present day information systems only treat knowledge and ignore the skill component. It is hypothesized that an E-bIS can address both aspects of expertise and support decision making more effectively.

Knowledge is created by learning explicit facts, concepts and relationships in a problem domain. Knowledge becomes active and usable by being exercised through the faculty of deductive reasoning. Skill is created by experience with many examples. The problem solver learns to reliably apply past examples to present problems through the faculty of analogical reasoning.

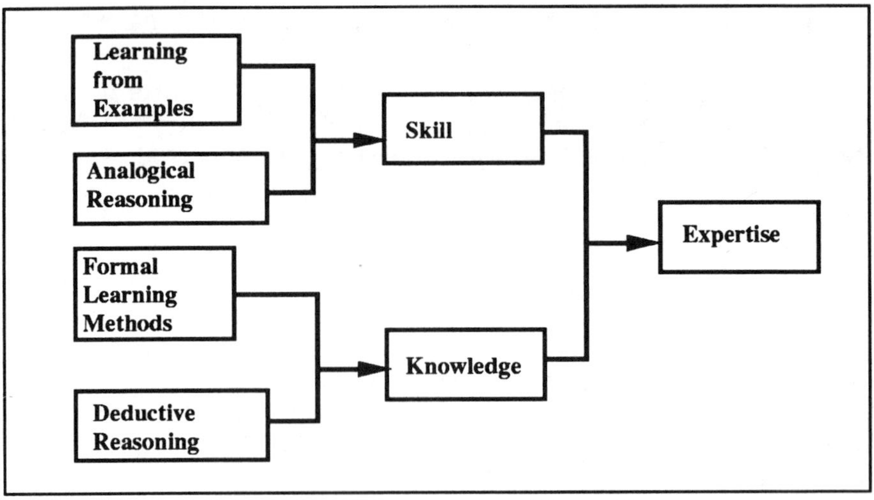

Figure 1: Components of Expertise

Many decision support systems and expert systems focus upon the explicit, formal knowledge component alone. This may account for the limited success that traditional ES and DSS have enjoyed. Example-based information systems can focus upon the skill component as well as the knowledge component; therefore such systems, theoretically, may be able to truly support decision making at the expert level. E-bIS are uniquely able to fulfill this role because they alone handle information at the level of the example.

Literature Review

Having explored the skill-knowledge distinction, the literature which relates example-based thinking to expertise and the literature on actual systems with example-based features will be discussed.

Exposure to numerous cases is necessary for the creation of expertise. Chess experts see about 50,000 different chess positions over a period of ten years before they attain expertise (Chase & Simon, 1973). Radiologists have studied about 200,000 X-ray pictures also over a ten year period before attaining expertise (Lesgold et al., 1988). Studies examining the nature of expertise have related superior problem solving abilities to the practice of thinking from cases or examples (Chi et al., 1989; Chi, Glaser & Farr, 1988). These experiments show that expert problem solvers were able to learn from example problems better than novices. Experts are better able to understand the deep structure of example problems. This implies that expert problem solvers got to be experts after much experience with example-based thinking. An analysis of the verbal protocols of managers showed that expert managers reasoned from examples more than non-experts (Isenberg, 1986). The link between expertise and example-based thinking is empirically established.

There is also a link between learning and examples. Dreyfus and Dreyfus (1986) believe that the learning of managerial decision making skills can be facilitated by training which uses information in the example format. In the exploratory phase of decision making, learning the problem domain can be improved when the relevant features of past examples are marked and indexed as an aid to explanation building (Redmond, 1991). Schank uses example-based reasoning to improve the learning of strategic planning skills (Emrich, 1990).

Five Stages to Expertise

The creation of judgment making ability at the expert level is marked by the decision maker's advance through five stages: novice, advanced novice, competent, proficient and expert (Dreyfus & Dreyfus, 1986). A description of these stages will help to explain the nature of expertise and expert managerial decision making.

The novice is familiar with the basic entities in a problem domain and is able to apply formal, literal, context free rules to make decisions. A novice chess player knows the basic elements of the game and conducts play by rote. The advanced novice has learned many more rules than the novice and also knows in which contexts these rules are applied and knows some exceptions to the rules. However, the advanced novice tends to be bogged down by the large number of rules and facts which must be mastered. The competent decision maker is able to reduce the number of items which are consciously considered because the competent decision maker understands which subset of rules and facts are relevant to solving a problem given a certain context. The proficient decision maker is able to automatize the earlier stages of problem solving but still uses rule-based thinking at the choice and implementation stages of the decision. The expert decision maker no longer reasons with explicit rules at any stage of the decision. Instead, all the entities and their interrelationships in a problem are viewed as a single pattern and decisions are made under a holistic, visual, pattern matching paradigm.

Now consider the five stages with respect to the two components of expertise: skill and knowledge. The novice and advanced novice learn the basic entities and relationships in a problem domain. This we recognize as the knowledge component which is taught using explicit instruction paradigms such as textbooks or lectures. Next, the novice must learn the contexts in which the explicit knowledge is used. The novice must learn when there may be exceptions to the rules. This is done by learning to identify the context in which a problem occurs. This is accomplished when one learns how to make complex, subtle, categorical judgments which is the skill component. Horgan et al. (1989) identifies this as the predecision process. Before chess masters make a move, they quickly evaluate board positions in terms of powerful, abstract categories. The experts do this by inspection, by considering the entire board position as a single pattern. Experts have learned how to efficiently apply their knowledge.

Information Systems With Example-based Features

Although fully functional example-based information systems are rare, there are systems which have some example-based features. Such features are the use of meaning sensitive rather than formal indexing, the storage of information in complete, knowledge level chunks and the use higher order features to classify information.

Example-based reasoning in the legal field has been long recognized due to the obvious feature that the trials are recorded in the form of a series of cases or examples. Hence the use of example-based methods is natural. An example-based database for legal information has been created by Kevin Ashley (1990). The primary functions of this database involve matching the present legal problem to the most relevant stored cases and indexing cases according to a set of legally significant features.

In business, instances of example-based technology can be found but in a more indirect form. One may consider any neural network system to be example-based because a neural network learns from a series of examples. New example-based expert system products using neural networks are beginning to be introduced ('Pair of expert systems tools debut,' 1991). A new database for storing mechanical drawings has been proposed. The key to this system is a meaning sensitive index which groups the drawings according to the engineering problem solved and the technique used to achieve the solution (Jea & Lee, 1990). Several systems were suggested which use higher order, meaning sensitive indexing to order a textual database (Schwarz, 1990; Trawinski, 1989). Example-based methods of planning are of note because they promise to reduce the computational demands placed upon planning systems (Sycara,1990; Hammond, 1990). A review of computational models of example-based reasoning can be found in Reisbeck and Schank (1989). The point to recognize is that computer models of analogical or example-based reasoning have difficulty doing what humans do easily: People can take past examples and use them to solve problem even though the past examples do not precisely fit the present problem. The lesson is that E-bIS should be constructed to support human decision making rather than make decisions for people.

A Complete Example-based Information System

Example-based systems have been studied by cognitive psychologists for some time. But one of the first, complete example-based systems to be studied in business appears in Mukhopadhyay, Vicinanza and Prietula (1992). This seems to be the initial stage of a new trend in business research.

This example-based system, ESTOR, estimates the cost of software development projects based upon the stored examples of successful cost estimates. From the verbal protocols of experts, a representation scheme for the examples was developed. Then examples of successful solutions were entered into the system's example base. Also, the knowledge of how to match the present problem to past examples was stored in an analog retrieval base and a rule base was used so that the system could make adjustments when the present problem did not exactly match the stored example.

This system solved cost estimation problems in five stages:

1. A representation of the target problem is generated.
2. A stored example is matched with the target problem and retrieved.
3. The solution in the retrieved example is used as an initial solution of the target problem.
4. The differences between the retrieved example and the target problem are identified.
5. A final solution is found after adjustments are made based upon the differences identified in stage 4.

The experimental findings were that ESTOR made better cost estimates than those of the standard alternatives but not as good as those of a human expert.

Although this system's performance is impressive, one must note that the emphasis of this author's research is the support of human decision making rather than the development of automated, expert systems. Keeping the human decision maker in the loop is important because automated systems tend to be bound by past examples and cannot use world knowledge to know when to ignore experience as a human expert might (Senge, 1990; Dreyfus & Dreyfus, 1986).

Related Literature from Philosophy

There is much literature addressing the philosophical issues related to decision making. The philosophical assumptions associated with example-based thinking will be contrasted with those of rule-based thinking. It is important to address philosophical issues because the philosophical assumptions of the decision maker affect the kinds of solutions sought and perhaps decision quality. The key point in the following discussion is the issue of interpretation. Example-based thinking is more involved with the interpretation of a problem domain. Once a problem domain becomes well understood, rule-based thinking is employed and the issue of interpretation is forgotten. However, some decision makers are so accustomed to rule-based thinking that the possibility of re-interpreting a domain is overlooked. This section serves as a reminder.

Philosophical Assumptions of Rule-Based Decision Making

Expert systems, decision payoff matrices and management science models are considered rule-based because some formal process is triggered upon the input of hard data having certain values. The philosophical basis of rule-based problem solving is called the Cartesian view under which thinking is understood as objective observation (Descartes, 1978; Dreyfus & Dreyfus 1986; Dreyfus, 1982; Flores & Winograd, 1989). The decision maker is thought of as in a subject-object relationship to the world. Decision making is viewed as the detection or observation of objects, qualities and relationships in the world. Since the world stands to the decision maker as an object, the various entities and relationships which register upon the senses are often regarded as a fixed, canonical, correct and unassailable understanding of the world.

This philosophical view effects managerial decision making in the following manner. Since problem solving is seen as observation, decision makers will tend to interpret the problem domain using the concepts which are already in common use without investigating the possibility that new concepts may exist. Managers having such a philosophical view tend less to review the terms by which the world is interpreted. In the case of a paradigm shift, the Cartesian manager may resist the new paradigm because the variables by which world has been understood are considered objectively determined and not subject to change.

Consider a stock investment problem. A Cartesian style manager might take the commonly used information from stock tables and financial reports as the sole, canonical, atomic terms upon which to base a decision. Then, this manager would relate these variables to each other by some model or set of rules which is used to solve the problem. The result is that the decision maker becomes fixated in the way the problem is construed. So, there is less chance of advancing the paradigm by which stock investment problems are solved.

Philosophical Assumptions of Example-Based Reasoning

The assumptions of example-based reasoning are that the problem solver is not a detached observer of the world but is tightly coupled to it (Flores and Winograd, 1989; Heidegger, 1968). Under this view, the world exists as an undifferentiated background of possibilities. Entities, variables and relationships of a problem domain are not considered to be inherent in the world, discoverable purely by observation, but are partly the result of some interpretation by the decision maker. Under the Heideggerian concept, thinking is not passive perception, but active judgment making. The entities and relationships which one discovers in the background are not solely a matter of observation, but also of interpretation. However, this is not relativism or subjectivism. One cannot create a reality merely by wishing it. Nevertheless, the Heideggerian view understands that reality is, in part, the result of the kinds of questions one asks about the world together with the way the world responds to one's inquiries and efforts.

According to this view, problem solving begins in an exploratory phase in which the decision maker discovers some aspect of the background upon which it is useful to focus. This discovery is called a 'breaking down' and is a process through which separable objects and qualities are identified out of the undifferentiated background and become 'present-at-hand' or usable to a decision maker. Once an interpretation of the world has been made, the present-at-hand entities are used to solve a problem. At this point, one could return to rule-based methods. But by thinking in terms of interpretations rather than in terms of fixed variables, the possibility of discovery is more present in the mind of the example-based thinker than the rule-based thinker. New discoveries and new interpretations can be made at any time which would result in new entities 'breaking down' and becoming 'present-at-hand.' The Heideggerian manager is searching for solutions never considered which are hiding in the background. This manager knows that the potential for a radical revision in the interpretation of a problem domain always exists.

Consider the stock investment example. An example-based manager using Heideggerian assumptions would be looking for new and better ways to understand the problem of stock selection. For example, rather than just examining the standard financial ratios and plugging them into formal math models, the manager may seek to reconstrue the problem in psychological terms.

The Heideggerian basis of decision making is consonant with present day business themes such as the search for constant improvement, strategic advantage or Kuhnian paradigm shifts. All these themes indicate that a seeking after innovation is valued and this value is supported more by the Heideggerian outlook.

THE EXAMPLE-BASED INFORMATION SYSTEM: AN EMERGING TECHNOLOGY

The term 'example' has been used until now without being defined. This section will define the example which is the fundamental unit of information under E-bIS. It will also describe how examples can be formed into an information system which can aid managerial decision making. The components and functions of an E-bIS will be described. There has been much discussion and research about E-bis from a theoretical approach. However, this section will show how actual example-based systems for decision support may be constructed.

What Is an Example?

An example is the basic until of information in an E-bIS. An example is made of a series of components called snapshots. Consider the following figure which is a diagram of the snapshot. The snapshot is a data structure made of a set of variables and the relationships among those variables. They describe the problem domain at a specific time. The snapshot has a boundary which means that some variables are considered relevant to the problem domain and are included in the snapshot while other variables are excluded.

The small rectangular symbols represent a set of domain variables. These variables are free format variables and may include

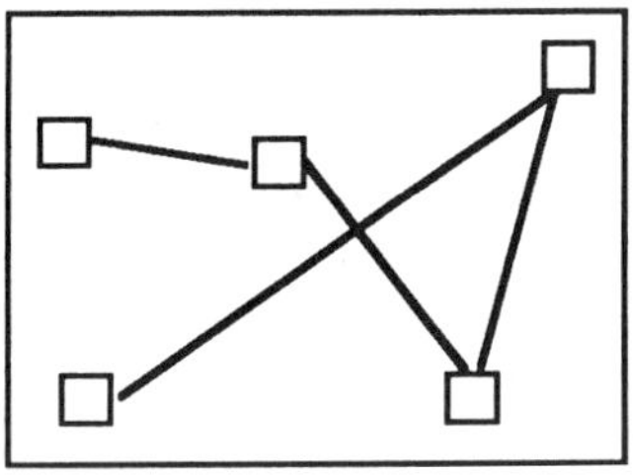

Figure 2: Snapshot

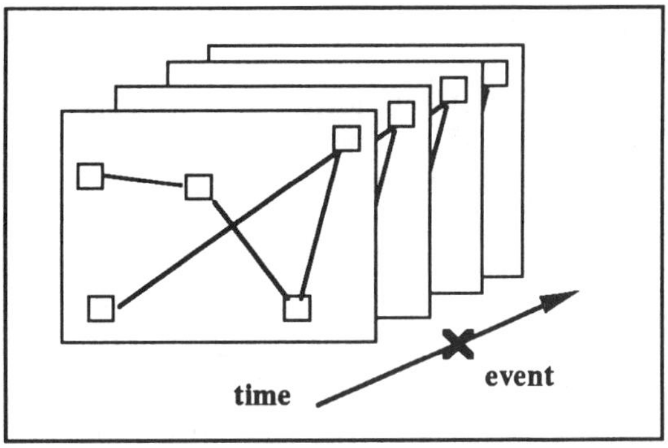

Figure 3: Example

graphics, text and numbers. The lines in the diagram represent relationships among the variables. These relationships can be statistical or math models or expert systems as well as expert opinion expressed in text format. However, it is not as likely that formal models will be used in semi-structured and unstructured domains. In that case, the relationships between variables can be expressed by qualitative mental models or narratives.

The variables which are selected to make up the snapshot are not fixed according to a formal template but may have a flexible structure. Variables may drop out or be added to the snapshot as understanding of the problem domain improves (Koton & Chase, 1989). However, all snapshots within an example are structurally identical. Therefore, the set of snapshot variables may vary only from example to example.

The above figure portrays an example which is constructed from a series of snapshots across a period of time. A series of snapshots is used to capture an event or experience by recording the same variables before, during and after the event or experience of interest. The example is a single, integrated unit of information and is the level at which the E-bIS is organized. For instance, if the decision maker is interested in learning about stocks which rise steeply, a collection of examples of rising stocks would be made. Each example would consist in a series of snapshots which describe the stock and its market environment before the price rise, during the price rise and after the price rise. The example can bracket the phenomenon of rising stocks and capture it, making this knowledge available to the decision maker for problem solving.

Components and Functions of an Example-based IS

This section details the functions and components of an example-based IS. The E-bIS has a graphical interface which allows the decision maker to compare the present problem with past examples to aid decision making. The graphical interface depicts examples as an integrated presentation of patterns, graphs and text. The decision maker uses a visual, pattern matching method of problem solving. The benefit of the graphical interface is that large amounts of information can be scanned and processed quickly. An E-bIS has two modes: the first provides computerized support for decision makers and the second provides tutoring for novice decision makers by using the expertise stored in the examples to simulate decision making situations. The system has checklist and blackboard functions as well. The checklist function reminds the decision maker of certain issues which should be considered in the decision. The blackboard function records the comments and actions of the decision maker so that others can know the reasons for decisions which have been made. The figure below represents such a system, and a more detailed discussion follows.

Example Base

An example base is a set of stored examples which are organized in a manner so that the decision maker can retrieve them in order to facilitate problem solving. A good set of examples is like markers in the sand of decision space. They outline key features of the problem domain. They describe important categories of the domain and clarify ambiguous cases (Hunter, 1989; Redmond, 1989; Weber, 1991). The example base is a map of the problem domain which can be used as a guide in decision making. The decision maker looks at the present problem as matches it with the 'map' which is the example base. The 'map' tells the decision maker how to solve the present problem.

Each example base has an organization or structure. The organization of the example base helps the decision maker retrieve the relevant cases. There are a number of methods of organization which will be discussed later. However, the basic point of example base organization is that it should aid the decision maker in retrieving a set of examples solving the problem at hand.

For example, a stock investor may organize the example base by gathering examples into groups of rising stocks, falling stocks and neutral stocks. The investor may want to evaluate a stock. This is

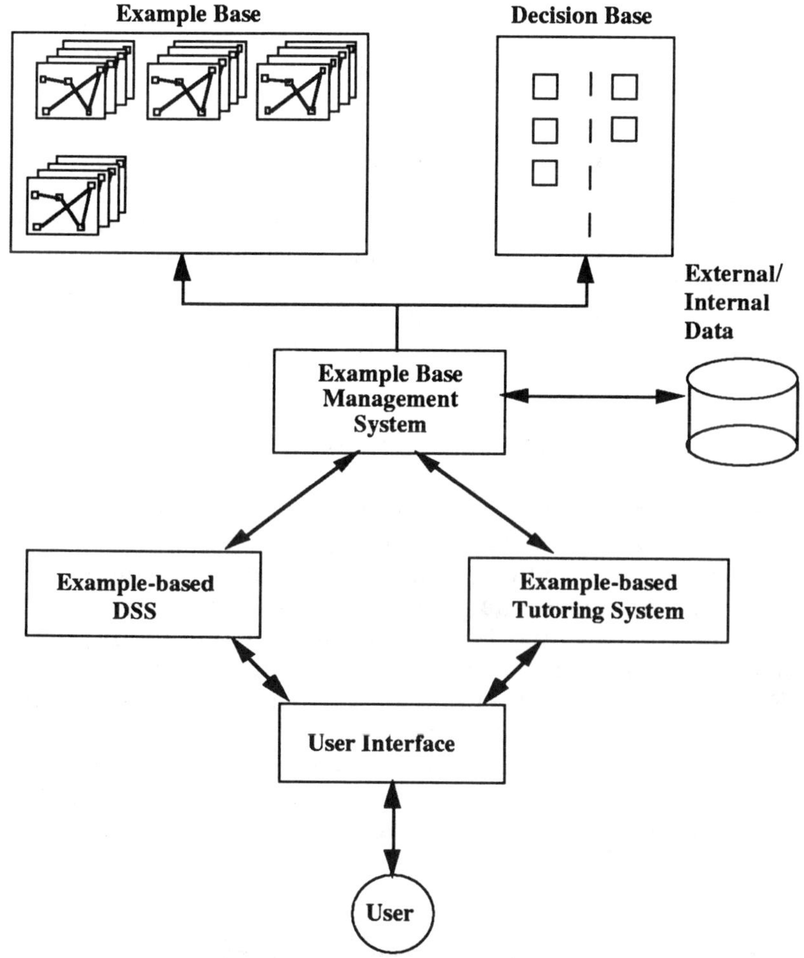

Figure 4: Model of Example-based Decision Support System

accomplished by comparing that stock to examples from the three groups. The evaluation of the stock is made by deciding which group is closest to the stock under consideration. If that stock looks more like the examples from the 'rising' group, then the decision maker would conclude that the stock will go up. Here the organization of the example base is designed to help the decision maker to preselect plausibly relevant examples.

Decision Base

The decision base preserves the expertise of decision makers and makes that expertise available for other decision makers (Cook, 1989). The system records the decisions made. The problem to be solved, the examples cited and the reasons for making the decision are combined into a stored decision. The decision is rated for accuracy and usefulness and placed into the decision base. Recalled decisions could be used for training. Ongoing decisions can be retrieved in order to revise them or to perform quality assessment upon them.

The Management of the Example-base

The example-base management system (E-bMS) creates, stores and retrieves examples. The E-bMS can extract and tie together information of varied data types from a number of data sources into a snapshot. It organizes snapshots into an example and sends that example to the example base. This system maintains example consistency , example indexing and the example retrieval scheme. The E-bMS should have access to external data sources so that the creation of examples can be partially automated. Data can also be entered manually by the decision maker or some other support personnel. The E-bMS also manages the decision base. The E-bMS may include a journaling function so that changes made in the example base or decision base could be rolled back if they prove to be in error.

Example-based Decision Support System

The example-based decision support system (E-bDSS) coordinates and operates the example base in a manner to support managerial decision making. The E-bDSS includes checklist and blackboard functions. The blackboard is an idea generator, a space in which to do brainstorming. The blackboard also records the decision maker's reasons why certain stored examples were chosen and why certain decisions were made. The checklist function identifies specific questions or issues that the decision maker should consider in the decision. It is a means for providing some level of structure to the decision making process. The checklist function can be used to remind the decision maker of errors that were made in the past and how to avoid them. The also DSS controls the presentation of stored examples so that the user can solve the problem-at-hand by having the stored examples easily available for comparison.

Example-based Training Support System

The Example-based Training Support System (E-bTSS) controls the presentation of stored examples and decisions to facilitate the transfer of expertise to novice decision makers. A set of stored decisions can record the expertise of proficient decision makers. By presenting past decisions and stored examples, expertise might be taught to others in an organization. The E-bTSS could support a simulation function by which the novice is given a realistic problem solving situation. The novice can use the stored examples and decisions to practice problem solving. The novice's decision can be recorded and then evaluated. A stored list of decisions can chart the novice's progress to expertise. Of course, these benefits are hypothetical at this time. The effectiveness of such a system should be determined with empirical research.

User Interface

The user interface is an icon and menu based system with graphical support. The icon and menu interface will allow the decision maker to use an intuitive point and click method of controlling the system. The interface should allow decision makers to use different methods of problem solving. That is, it should be a process independent interface.

Personnel

The personnel one might use to support an example-based system are similar to those in any DSS except in two positions: the system designer and a new position called the advocate. The designer has special responsibility for the success of the system more so than in traditional DSS or expert systems. The organization scheme of the example base and the core variables chosen for the snapshots relate to the success of the system. The example base organization and the snapshot variables selected are the result of the designer's interpretation of the problem domain. A designer who does not have a good interpretation of the problem domain or who does not understand the issue of domain interpretation will irrevocably build flaws into key elements of the system.

The proper use of an example-based system has certain prerequisites. The users must know about analogical reasoning and the stages of expertise. The use of stored examples and analogical reasoning to solve problems may encounter resistance, especially among people fixated on rule-based reasoning methods. The advocate does not merely generate acceptance for the system, but must guide the users in learning analogical reasoning and example-based thinking. These additional duties make the responsibilities of the advocate much greater. The advocate's job is more critical because maximum system success is predicted only when analogical reasoning is used. Therefore, the advocate must get users to adopt this new kind of thinking which is very difficult to accomplish.

A MODEL OF OPERATIONAL FACTORS IN AN E-BIS

The following model, based upon previous research and logical analysis, describes the factors relating to E-bIS. The factors are listed and described and relationships among these factors are then hypothesized. The main relationship proposed can be summarized as a trade-off between flexibility and efficiency. Flexible systems are highly customized for the individual user but have example bases that are difficult to search and, therefore, are less efficient. Example bases which are designed for efficient searches are more structured and less flexible. Smaller systems, built for an individual in an unstructured problem domain, can be highly customized, designed to meet the user's needs. Public systems, designed to function in the more structured domains, will be larger and more efficient but less flexible. This trade-off must be considered when designing the system. The following model should help in resolving this trade-off and can serve as a guide for future research.

System Client

Who or what is the example-based system client? The E-bIS can have a human or a computer client. The E-bIS can support human decision making or it can be an input for another computer based system.

Support for Human Controlled Decision Making

An E-bIS supports the presentation of examples to a human decision maker to aid problem solving. The following user arrangements are anticipated to be the most common.

1. Single user- Small, highly flexible, *ad hoc* systems may be developed for a single user. Such systems are suitable for exploring unstructured problem domains.
2. Many users- A public, multi-user system such as a database of legal cases is less flexible but more efficient. Example data structures are well defined and the problem domain is more structured. The size of the example base is hypothesized to be negatively related to search efficiency and flexibility.

Support for Computer Controlled Decision Making

An E-bIS may supply an input for another computer based expert system which uses analogical or example-based reasoning to solve problems. This E-bIS is expected to be the least flexible, the most structured, having the fewest options for user initiated innovation, but with the greatest example base search efficiency.

Software Implementation

The E-bIS can be created with a variety of software applications beginning with relatively simple word processors and draw programs and ending with highly sophisticated systems which were developed with object-oriented programming languages.

1. Object Oriented Language- A number of features in object oriented languages make it a good candidate for implementing large, multiple user, public E-bIS. The examples and snapshots can be defined as objects in the programming language and inheritance allows for the easy creation of new examples while automatically maintaining data integrity. E-bIS which support another computer based system should be created with an object oriented language.
2. HyperCard- The HyperCard application by Apple Computer is a hypertext program that includes graphics, sound and programming capabilities. This software is good for implementing single user, small, ad hoc systems because the software is flexible and the hypertext features can be used to support the creation and

maintenance of examples and example bases.

3. Relational DB, Text Processors, Paint/draw applications- It is possible to implement E-bIS with more commonly available software such as word processors and relational database programs. In that case, the example base is maintained as a computer version of the paper file folder and is categorized, indexed, and searched manually.

Integrity of Example Base

Although flexibility is an advantage to the E-bIS, a certain level of integrity must be maintained across examples and across decisions in the decision base.

1. Maintained by People- Small, *ad hoc*, flexible systems which are designed for single users have data integrity maintained by users. Small gaps in data integrity can be spotted and corrected by the users themselves.
2. Maintained by System- In large, multi-user systems or in systems which support another computer-based system, data integrity should be maintained by the E-bIS. The disadvantage is that the computational overhead and system complexity is considerably greater.

Organization of the Example Base

The organization of the example base aids in the retrieval of examples. There is much discussion concerning the role of indexing. While the view of Thagard and Holyoak (1989, 1990) that indexing is not needed for retrieval has merit, from a practical point of view indexing is helpful at times. The following section is a synthesis of Ashley (1989), Kolodner (1989), Parsaye (1989), Sycara and Navinchandra (1989) and Waltz (1989).

1. Manual Indexing- A human operator examines and categorizes a new example according to a pre-established indexing scheme. Textual databases such as bibliographic databases are the most common type of system which use this method. Variability across and within human operators is a cause of misclassification and the inconsistent use of index terms. This is a problem for large example bases; however, manual indexing seems to be well suited for small, single user E-bIS since the user would be familiar with the content of the example base and the use of indexing terms.
2. Automatic Indexing- Artificial intelligence can analyze cases and

classify them according to an indexing scheme (Trawinski, 1989). Variability is reduced and classifications are more consistent which is important for large example bases. However, computer based intelligence cannot classify and interpret cases in a very sophisticated manner because such programs lack extensive world knowledge. This may cause unexpected or improper classifications. The automatic indexer takes a very literal approach and is not able to make classifications which depend on a deep understanding of the domain.

3. No Index- In this organization scheme, the examples are not classified by some pre-defined index (Thagard & Holyoak, 1990). The problem-at-hand is compared with examples in the example base using some automated metric. The examples which are closest to the problem-at-hand are retrieved for study by the problem solver. Neural networks are often used for this purpose; the patterns of variables in the problem-at-hand are compared with the patterns of stored examples by an auto-associative network. The neural network retrieves the closest matches which will be used for problem solving by the user.

The no index organization method is useful for large example bases in unexplored problem domains. Recall from the section on philosophical assumptions that a problem domain must be interpreted before problem solving can take place. Whenever an index for an example base is established, a definite, implicit interpretation of the problem domain is utilized in forming that index. When the problem domain is being explored, many interpretations of the problem domain may be tried. Hence, it is counterproductive to arbitrarily establish some index scheme in the exploratory situation because it enforces a single interpretation when many interpretations should be tried. Therefore, the no index method is best in the exploratory situation.

The drawbacks with the no index method are that the metric which retrieves stored cases may not be very sophisticated and will not perform the retrieval task as well as a knowledgeable human decision maker. A strategy to counter this problem is to use a simplified retrieval metric which has very loose criteria. The result will be an expanded subset of possible matches which then can be searched manually by the human decision maker.

There is no ideal indexing or retrieval system for example-based systems. The retrieval and storage of complex knowledge structures is much more difficult than the retrieval of information or data. However, this should not result in the abandoning of example-based systems. There are trade-offs between flexibility and efficiency. The designer must create a system which balances the various system characteristics in order to effectively support managerial decision making.

Structuredness of Decision Support System Interface

Example-based systems may provide structure to the decision making process or they may simply provide access to the example base without guiding the decision maker in the problem solving process.

1. Process Independent- This system does not structure the decision process but simply provides the storage and retrieval of examples in order to support decision making. Such as system would be created if its users were domain experts and already knew how to make good decisions. Also, if the system is used for exploring a problem domain, then a process independent system should be installed because the decision making interpretation is still in flux.
2. Process Dependent- This type of system leads the decision maker through the problem solving methods which have been shown to be most effective. Process dependent E-bIS should be used with problem domains which are understood. The users of such systems would most likely be novice or competent decision makers who may be learning the domain while making decisions at the same time.

Problem Domain Structuredness

Various problem domains have varying degrees of structuredness. Problems in highly structured domains are solved by relating specific variables to well defined rules and procedures. Unstructured or semi-structured domains are solved by informed human intuition or judgment making based upon experience which cannot be devolved into explicit rules and procedures.

1. Unstructured- Problem domains that are unstructured are pre-eminently the ideal situation for decision support using E-bIS. E-bIS are the means by which computer support can immediately be supplied to human decision makers working in unstructured domains.
2. Semi-structured- E-bIS can be used here, but they must be integrated with statistical models, management science tools and rule-based expert systems.

3. Structured- E-bIS are not the most efficient method of problem solving in domains which are well understood and have well defined and explicit problem solution methods.

Flexibility of the Example Template

Recall that an example base is a collection of examples which are made from a set of snapshots which are in turn made up of a set of variables and interrelationships. As the understanding of a problem domain improves, the set of variables which comprises a snapshot may change. E-bIS whose examples have different snapshot variables are said to have example templates with high flexibility. Examples whose snapshots have the same sets of variables, have example templates with low flexibility.

1. High- Highly flexibility example templates should be used with systems that have few users or a single user; flexibility implies that the system is highly personalized which limits the number of effective users. Systems which are used by humans and not used as inputs for other computer based systems can have a high template flexibility. Systems which support problem solving in domains that are unstructured or semi-structured or which support exploratory thinking should have high flexibility. Highly flexible example templates can best be used in systems which have a small number of stored examples. Flexible templates increase the system complexity and makes search and retrieval less efficient.
2. Low- E-bIS whose outputs are used by another computer-based system should have example templates with a low flexibility because computer based systems require inputs which are well defined. E-bIS that have large example bases should have templates with a low flexibility in order to make example retrieval more efficient. Systems which support a large number of users or are used publicly would tend to have lower template flexibility because such a system is easier for casual users to master and will cause fewer errors due to user confusion.

SYSTEM CONSTRUCTION

E-bIS can be built either by an E-bIS designer or by the system user. In the latter case, a shell system would be provided which would be filled with examples by the user. The former may typically involve a larger, multi-user system implemented by an object oriented language.

1. Built by User- Small, highly flexible, private E-bIS maintained on applications such as Apple's HyperCard or on applications such as relational databases, word processors and draw programs can be built by the system user. The ease of system generator use and lack of system size are the criteria which permit user built systems.
2. Built by E-bIS Designer- Designer built systems are larger systems having many users and are more likely to be implemented with an object oriented programming language. Such a system will depend much more upon the computer to maintain example integrity, retrieve relevant examples and display information in graphical, user friendly ways. An E-bIS designer should build systems where a large amount of programming skill and development time is required.

LIMITATIONS OF EXAMPLE-BASED TECHNOLOGY

There are reasons why example-based technologies may be undesirable. Example-based databases are difficult to search. Example-based applications are often ad hoc developments and lack standardized, common functions. Example-based databases are difficult to maintain and example-based decision making may be difficult to integrate into rule-based systems.

Should example-based systems be used in every problem domain? Should we abandon management science models and rule-based expert systems? In short, no! There are many instances in which rule-driven decision making and formal models can obtain all the benefits that are possible. Example-based systems are useful only where the problem domain is complex, dynamic and semi-structured or unstructured; where it has both quantitative and qualitative dimensions; where the problem domain has not been exhaustively defined and the potential for discovery is real. Example-based technologies should be used in the exploratory phases of problem solving or when decisions must be made while the problem domain is still being investigated.

HOW WOULD AN E-BIS BE USED BY A MANAGER?

A manager or researcher may be interested in experimenting with a small example-based system without making a large investment in programming a new system. This section outlines a possible fast track for the construction of a small E-bIS suitable for research or use as a prototype business system. First, the platform best suited to implement a small E-bIS will be described. Second, the basic functions which must be supported will be detailed. Lastly, the manner in which this system can be used to support decision making will be described.

The best platform with which to implement a small E-bIS is something like Apple's HyperCard for the Macintosh computer which is a hypertext application having graphics, sound and basic programming features. This application is easily programmed; many users learn to program it as the natural outcome of repeated usage. Note that if HyperCard or some equivalent is not available a small system can be created with word processors or draw programs. In that case, the system would be basically a manual system which uses a computer for document creation and storage. However, the remaining discussion will assume the E-bIS designer is using HyperCard.

Note that HyperCard uses the index card paradigm. HyperCard also has stacks which are a series of cards. The cards contain buttons, windows and messages which allow the user to initiate programs, to input and display information. The HyperCard features which will be utilized in E-bIS construction are the ability for a series of cards in a stack to inherit similar features, the ability for a card in a stack to bring up other stacks and the ability to integrate text, graphics and data. However, the programming abilities of HyperCard are not utilized to automate retrieval. In this E-bIS, the user manually retrieves stored examples aided by a simple index scheme.

The system characteristics are the following: The E-bIS has a small example base and decision base. It is built for one or a few users. The examples and decisions are searched with the manual index method. Data integrity is enforced by the user. This small system will most probably be built by the user. It provides process independent decision support. The client of this system is a human user and not another computer-based system. All of these characteristics allow the system to be quickly constructed with HyperCard.

The feature allowing the user to retrieve other stacks permits a super stack to form an example base and a decision base. This super stack can be used to recall stored examples and decisions (which are themselves subordinate stacks), implement a simple index and add new examples and decisions.

The checklist and blackboard functions are stacks which are called up from the main stack. The checklist and blackboard are essential decision support functions. The checklist and blackboard are the medium through which the problem is investigated and solved. The checklist is a stack of cards which lists the issues or questions the user should consider in problem solving. Each issue or question is linked to a blank card on which the user's responses are recorded. The blackboard is a stack which records the decision maker's brainstorming efforts and preserves decision progress over time. The retrieved examples and the checklist and brainstorming stacks make up the decision which then can be entered into the decision base.

How would this system be used to solve a problem? The following is a fictional session with the E-bIS. Suppose a stock investor found a company in a turnaround situation. The problem with turnarounds is that their stock can go up like a rocket or down like a rock. The investment decision is an attempt to predict in which direction the turnaround will be resolved. The following assumes that the decision maker already has developed an example base which describes a variety of past turnaround situations, both successful and failed. Also, assume there exists for consultation a decision base which describes past investment decisions relating to turnarounds. Hence, in the this discussion, the basic parameters of the E-bIS have already been established. It is assumed that the design and construction of the E-bIS has already taken place.

First the decision maker would copy an empty set of example cards onto the working memory. Then, the decision maker would consider the problem-at-hand which is the decision to invest or not invest in a certain company involved in a possible turnaround situation. Naturally that investment decision rests upon a prediction of the company's future; will it thrive or fail? The decision maker would now enter the present problem into the E-bIS by filling out the appropriate snapshot slots in the empty example cards. Examples from the example base which are similar to the problem-at-hand are marked by the user. The user retrieves the marked examples and compares them with the problem-at-hand. The various issues raised by the checklist are dealt with and the deliberations involved in comparing the present problem with past examples are written down in the blackboard. The examples which are most like the present problem serve as guidance for the decision maker, but one should be wary of merely repeating past decisions. The present situation is no doubt unlike any situation encountered before, so it is the mark of a decision maker skilled in analogical reasoning to profitably use examples which are close to the present problem but do not fit it exactly.

After making the decision, the user may wish to review past decisions in the decision base to make sure that old mistakes are not being revisited and that useful insights have not been overlooked. When this oversight function has been performed, the user may wish to copy the problem which was just solved into the decision base for future reference and evaluation.

FUTURE TRENDS

The above model of E-bIS serves as a guide for future empirical research. The initial research phase should concentrate on the general question of E-bIS effectiveness. The basic claim is that example-based systems will support expert decision making better than present systems which use more formal data models. Experiments should establish the relative performance of E-bIS and the general parameters under which they can be profitably used. The second phase should study the links among the specific factors listed in the above model. This would entail more detailed experimental work in which the relationships between example base size, retrieval efficiency, flexibility and decision outcomes would be precisely measured and determined. The third phase, for which a number of extant E-bIS is necessary, would be a study of the E-bIS design methodology and life cycle. This phase should result in a validated methodology that shows in which circumstances one should use an E-bIS and with what results. Also this methodology should recommend how best to design and implement an E-bIS.

The trend for the increasing use of example-based systems is foreseen because of the fact that example-based systems are a way of storing, communicating and using the collected wisdom of domain experts and that users are demanding systems with more 'intelligence.' This trend will proceed along three streams. First, research will continue into the process of human, example-based thinking. In particular, the unique ability of human experts to use past examples as an aid in solving a new problem with features not exactly found in stored examples begs for closer study. Second, fully automated expert systems which use stored examples to solve problems will be developed, studied and used more. Example-based expert systems should make knowledge acquisition much easier since examples of solved problems are more quickly generated than the rules used by experts to solve those same problems. However, automated systems presently do not have enough world knowledge to make adjustments in the case that the target problem is novel. That is, these systems are bound by past experience, unlike human experts. Third, example-based systems which are designed to support human judgement making should be developed. Such systems have the potential for increasing the effectiveness of highly productive, expert managers. They also may be used to store and communicate expertise and to engender expertise in others resulting in the betterment of the entire organization.

Example-based systems are a way in which the demand for information systems can be increased. As information systems become more 'intelligent,' there will be more uses for them and a greater demand for the services of information systems developers.

CONCLUSION

Example-based decision support, theoretically, has the potential for being a means of improving expert, managerial problem solving. However, one is immediately made aware that little research has been done on example-based systems for business. To that end, this paper concretized the concept of example-based systems by creating a specific model of example-based support for human decision making. Furthermore, a model which related various E-bIS factors was created as a guide for future research. Then, a fictional session for investment decision making on a small E-bIS was written to give the reader a better feel for example-based technologies in action. The challenge for the future is to verify the hypotheses presented here by building and testing actual E-bIS for business problem solving.

ENDNOTE

[1] The term example-based is more commonly known outside of business as case-based. However, due to confusion with the business term computer aided software engineering (CASE), the phrases example-based reasoning and example-based information systems will be used instead of case-based reasoning and case-based information systems.

REFERENCES

Ashley, K. D. (1989). Indexing and analytic models. *Proceedings of the Second Case-based Reasoning Workshop*, 197-202.

Ashley, K. D. (1990). *Modeling legal argument: Reasoning with cases and hypotheticals*. Cambridge, MA: MIT.

Augustine, N. R. (1979, Spring). Distribution of Expertise. *Defense System Management.*

Chase, W.G., & Simon, H.A. (1973). Perception in chess. *Cognitive Psychology, 4*, 55-81.

Chi, M. T. H., Glaser R., & Farr, M. J. (Eds.). (1988). *The nature of expertise.* Hillsdale, NJ: Lawrence Erlbaum.

Chi, M. T. H., Bassok, M., Lewis, M. W., Reimann, P., & Glaser, R. (1989). Self-explanations: How students study and use examples in learning to solve problems. *Cognitive Science, 13*(2), 145-182.

Cook, L. K. (1989). Teaching expertise: using case-based systems to transfer real world experience. *Proceedings of the Second Case-based Reasoning Workshop*, 235.

Descartes, R. (1978). Principles of philosophy. In *The Philosophical Works of Descartes* (E. S. Haldane and G. R. T. Ross, Trans.). Cambridge: Cambridge Univ. (Original work published 1644)

Dreyfus, H. L., & Dreyfus, S. E. (1986). *Mind over machine: The power of human intuition and expertise in the era of the computer.* New York: Free Press.

Dreyfus, H. (Ed.). (1982). *Husserl, intentionality, and cognitive science.* Cambridge, MA: MIT.

Emrich, M. (1990). Future training with a pair of practical visionaries. *Manufacturing Systems, 8*(1), 30-35.

Flores, F., & Winograd, T. (1989). *Understanding computers and cognition: A new foundation for design.* Norwood, NJ: Ablex.

Hammond, K. S. (1990). Case based planning: a framework for planning from experience. *Cognitive Science, 14*(3), 385-445.

Heidegger, M. (1968). *What is called thinking?* (J. G. Gray, Trans.). New York: Harper & Row. (Original work published in 1954)

Horgan D. D., Millis K., & Neimeyer, R. A. (1989). Cognitive reorganization and the development of chess expertise. *International Journal of Personal Construct Psychology, 2*, 15-36.

Hunter, L. (1989). Finding paradigm cases or when is a case worth remembering? *Proceedings of the Second Case-based Reasoning Workshop*, 57-61.

Isenberg, D. J. (1986). Thinking and managing: A verbal protocol analysis of managerial problem solving. *Academy of Management Journal, 29*(4), 775- 788.

Jea, K. J., & Lee, Y. (1990). Building efficient and flexible feature based indices. *Information Systems, 15*(6), 653-662.

Keane, M. T. (1988). *Analogical problem solving.* Chichester, UK: Ellis Horwood.

Kolodner, J. (1989). Selecting the best case for a case based reasoner. *Proceedings of the 11th Annual Conference of the Cognitive Science Society*, 155-162.

Koton, P., & Chase, M. P. (1989). Knowledge representation in a case-based reasoning system: Defaults and exceptions. In R. J. Brachman and H. J. Levesque (Ed.), *First International Conference on Principles of Knowledge Representation and Reasoning* (pp. 203-211). Ontario, Canada: Morgan Kaufman.

Lesgold, A., Rubinson, H., Feltovich, P., Glaser, R., Klopfer D., & Wang, Y. (1988). Expertise in a complex skill: Diagnosing X-ray pictures. In M. T. H. Chi, R. Glaser and M. J. Farr (Eds.), *The Nature of Expertise* (pp. 311-342). Hillsdale, NJ: Erlbaum.

Madnick, S. E. (1991). The information technology platform. In M. S. Scott-Morton (Ed.), *The Corporation of the 1990's: Information Technology and Organizational Transformation* (pp. 27-60). New York: Oxford Univ.

Mukhopadhyay, T., Vicinanza, S. S., & Prietula, M. J. (1992). Examining the feasibility of a case-based reasoning model for software effort estimation. *MIS Quarterly*, (2), 155-170.

Novik, L. R. (1988). Analogical transfer: Processes and individual differences. In D. H. Helman (Ed.), *Analogical Reasoning: Perspectives of Artificial Intelligence, Cognitive Science, and Philosophy* (pp. 125-145). Boston: Kluwer.

Pair of expert systems tools debut. (1991, March 18). *PC Week*, p. 55.

Parsaye, K. (1989). *Intelligent databases.* New York: Wiley.

Redmond, M. (1989). Learning from others' experience: Creating cases from experience. *Proceedings of the Second Case-based Reasoning Workshop.*

Redmond, M. (1991). Improving case retrieval through observing expert problem solving. *Proceedings of the 13th Annual Conference of the Cognitive Science Society*, 516-521.

Riesbeck, C. K., & Schank, R. C. (1989). *Inside case-based reasoning.* New York: Lawrence Erlbaum.

Schwarz, C. (1990). Content based text handling. *Information Processing and*

Management, 26(2), 219-226.

Senge, P. M. (1990). *The fifth discipline: The art and practice of the learning organization.* New York: Doubleday.

Sycara, K. P., & Navinchandra, D. (1989). Index transformation and generation for case retrieval. *Proceedings of the Second Case-based Reasoning Workshop,* 324-328.

Sycara, K. P. (1990). Negotiation planning: An AI approach. *European Journal of Operational Research, 46*(2), 216-234.

Thagard, P., & Holyoak, Keith J. (1989). Why indexing is the wrong way to think about analog retrieval. *Proceedings of the Second Case-based Reasoning Workshop,* 36-40.

Thagard, P., & Holyoak, K. J. (1990). Analog retrieval by constraint satisfaction. *Artificial Intelligence, 46,* 259-310.

Trawinski, B. (1989). A methodology for writing problem structure abstracts. *Information Processing and Management, 25*(6), 693-702.

Turban, E. (1991). Top MIS issues. Presentation at Memphis State University, Dept. of MIS, Memphis, TN.

Turban, E. (1990). *Decision support and expert systems: Management support systems* (2nd ed.). New York: Macmillan.

Waltz, D. L. (1989). Is indexing used for retrieval? *Proceedings of the Second Case-based Reasoning Workshop,* 41-44.

Weber, G. (1991). Explanation-based retrieval in a case-based learning model. *Proceedings of the 13th Annual Conference of the Cognitive Science Society,* 522-533.

CHAPTER 9

EXPERT SYSTEMS DEVELOPMENT ISSUES CONFRONTING ORGANIZATIONS IN THE EVOLVING GLOBAL MARKETPLACE

Brenda L. Killingsworth and Michael E. McLeod
East Carolina University

The literature regarding expert systems research in business and industry is examined to generate propositions for future research which address development issues confronting organizations in the evolving global marketplace. A brief review of the expert system domain environment is presented followed by a discussion of performance suppositions suggested in the literature from results on individual case studies or by conceptualizations about expert systems based on practical experience. To gain a better understanding of how environmental and organizational factors impact on the success of expert systems, more extensive empirical research is needed. Specific areas explored include four factors which the literature suggests influence the success of expert systems in business: the decision setting, management, the users, and the experts modeled. Further, conjectured interactions among these factors (as well as two others - expert systems and information systems) are explored including: MIS integration capability, user interface, expert system networking capability, expert system development strategies, and interrater reliability between the experts modeled and the users. Propositions for further research are offered for each of the areas addressed along with

An earlier version of this paper was published in the Proceedings of the 1992 Information Resources Management Association International Conference.

recommended research methods.

Over the past several years there has been a noticeable increase of interest in business applications of expert systems. Research has indicated that there is considerable investment in expert system technology (New Science, 1987; Nisse, 1987; Rauch-Hindin, 1984). However, few studies have appeared in the literature which examine the issues involved in the development and implementation of expert systems in organizations (Sviokla, 1990).

These expert systems are a subset of artificial intelligence (AI), which is concerned with the employment of human thought processes to computer technology (Barr & Feineguam, 1981). An expert system (ES) is defined as an AI program whose performance is meant to emulate that of human experts and "depends more on the explicit presence of a large body of knowledge than on the possession of ingenious computational procedures" (Duda & Shortliffe, 1983, p. 267). It is designed to store and apply the knowledge of experts to aid a non-expert or provide second opinions to other experts.

While few empirical studies have been published, there has been a growing number of suppositions appearing in the expert system literature which need to be addressed if organizations are to rely on them. For the most part, these suppositions have been suggested in the literature by the results of individual case studies or by conceptualizations about expert systems based on practical experience. Very few suppositions are supported by empirical studies. The results of this literature investigation are presented as: a classification of these suppositions in an effort to provide a beginning reference point for assessment and expansion of expert system research in a dynamic global environment; and, a series of propositions representing the central positions on the suppositions explored.

The propositions are meant to be general research questions requiring a more comprehensive empirical examination and are not offered as formal hypotheses. Many of the measures recommended to test these propositions were derived from frequently cited information system's articles but should be tested for validity prior to a full-scale study. The literature references supporting the propositions were obtained from a survey of academic and trade literature identified in the *Social Sciences Citation Index*, the Calgary Surveys Query System (Newsted, Munro, & Huff, 1992) as well as other sources available to the authors.

This chapter begins with a brief review of the expert system domain environment and a review of related literature providing general support for the entities and interactions addressed. Next, research suppositions derived from results on individual case studies or by conceptualizations about expert systems based on practical experience are identified and developed into research propositions along with recommended research methods. By addressing these research propositions, a greater understanding should be gained with respect to how environmental and organizational factors affect success of expert systems development and implementation. It is hoped that this increased understanding will assist in promoting a more rapid development and acceptance of expert systems in business.

BACKGROUND

Waterman (1986, p. 33) identifies the nature of problem domains that can be supported by expert system technology as those that require "interpretation, prediction, diagnosis, design, planning, monitoring, debugging, repair, instruction or control." These decision activities can be supported to varying degrees with the current state-of-the-art technology. While there are many business domains that require the above listed activities, relatively few actually incorporate expert systems in their decision making processes.[1]

Little research has been conducted in expert systems which identifies factors impacting on success of expert systems. Thus, to develop a foundation for initially identifying this set of factors, this chapter relies not only upon expert system literature, but also upon previous empirical and theoretical support from traditional information systems literature, decision support system literature, and cognitive literature.

A major area of traditional information systems research which has been shown to impact on success of technology is concerned with issues on the management of information within an organization. Issues which have special relevance to expert system management include: the awareness and acceptance of information technology by top management (Coats, 1988), the policies established to manage information (Markus & Robey, 1988), the level of involvement of end users in the development of information systems as well as the level of training provided (e.g., Grindley, 1988; Robey, 1979), and the use of cost-benefit analysis in the planning of information systems (Barua, Kriebel, & Mukhopadhyay, 1991; Bauer & Griffiths, 1988). Further, information systems literature has addressed the impact of information characteristics, or the decision setting, on decision making tasks (Ettenson, Shanteau, & Krogstad, 1987) as well as the level of integration within the corporate information system.

The decision support system literature can offer guidance in understanding how the user interface design impacts on the acceptance of expert systems. A number of researchers have investigated the impact of user interfaces (Lehner & Zirk, 1987, Thensen & Beringer, 1986). While the impact of cognitive styles on acceptance of a decision support system interface has stimulated controversy (e.g., Huber, 1983), the methods used to test different interfaces may still provide guidance to evaluating the impact of different explanation facilities. In addition, office information systems literature has investigated the impact of tailoring an interface (tutorials and help features) to domain skill levels. Their findings suggest that the tailoring of expert systems explanation facilities may also improve acceptance of expert systems.

One difference between expert systems and traditional information systems is that the latter models relatively structured and well-understood procedures while the former models problems in which there may be disagreement among experts regarding exactly what knowledge is needed to solve a problem and how a problem should be approached. For decades, the cognitive research literature has tackled the problems of measuring interrater reliability (the level of agreement (or disagreement) among experts) and of promoting convergence of opinions between different experts (e.g., Cohen & Cohen, 1983). Thus, one possible factor impacting on success of expert systems is the level of agreement between experts for the domain that is modeled within an expert system.

With the preceding background, this chapter concentrates on four environmental and organizational factors or entities which could influence success of expert systems in business: decision setting, management, users and experts modeled. In addition, conjectured interactions among these entities (as well as two others - expert systems and information systems) are explored including: MIS integration capability, user interface, expert system networking capability, expert system development strategies, and interrater reliability between the experts modeled and the users. The latter two entities, expert systems and information systems, are principally technology concerns and are beyond the scope of this chapter. Figure 1 diagrams these entities and interactions. This figure will serve as the basis for discussion of the propositions within the body of this chapter.

The propositions incorporate five surrogate measures for expert system success which have been suggested or implied in the expert system literature and which are founded in information systems theory: (a) acceptance of expert system technology by top management; (b) acceptance rate of the expert system's recommendations by

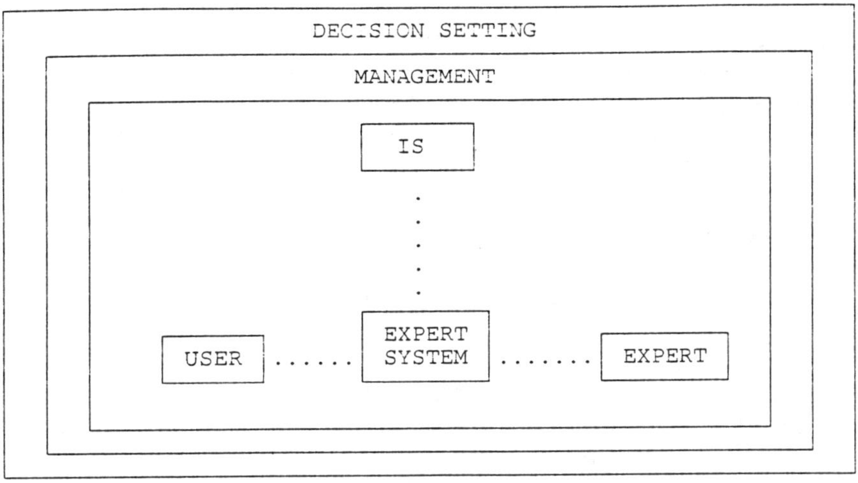

Figure 1: Factors Affecting Expert System Success

the user; (c) utilization level of expert systems by decision makers; (d) the change in the number of expert systems developed; and, (e) the change in the number of domains for which expert systems have been developed (Benbasat & Schroeder, 1977; Grindley, 1988; Harmon, Maus & Morrissey, 1988; Leonard-Barton & Sviokla, 1988; O'Keefe, Belton & Ball, 1986; O'Leary, 1987; Waterman, 1986; Zahedi, 1987).

Based on information systems success literature, research has indicated that the utilization measure is frequently employed as a measure of success (Cheney, Mann, & Amoroso, 1986; Ives & Olson, 1984; Maish, 1979; Robey, 1979; Swanson, 1976). In addition, because the field of expert systems is in its early stages, acceptance of technology as well as expansion of expert system applications into new domains are important to the success of expert systems in a broader sense. Unlike traditional information system research on success, the user's acceptance of an expert system's recommendation is important as a separate measure of success (Killingsworth, 1987), in addition to utilization, because of the current techniques used in expert system validation.

PROPOSITIONS FOR EXPERT SYSTEM RESEARCH

The following propositions represent suggestions for future research in the area of expert systems. The entities and their interactions are discussed in the context of previous research in the area of expert systems as well as related information systems literature. Table 1 summarizes the citations and their related propositions. The research methods used in the previous research cited (Table 1) as well as the recommended research methods are categorized as either a case study (C), an experimental/empirical study (E), a descriptive survey study (S), or a theoretical conjecture or argument (T).

Entities

Decision Setting. The first proposition is derived from the work done by McKee (1988) on the environmental setting conducive for expert system development and from the information resource management and strategic planning literatures. McKee (1988) identifies candidates for expert system development through the description of the decision making environmental setting in which expert systems would be most effective. This setting must have one or more of the following conditions:

1. The decision must be made quickly.
2. The decision is recurring in nature.
3. The expert is not available at all times.
4. The expert knowledge can be lost.
5. The decision must be made consistently.
6. The expert knowledge must be shared.
7. The expert knowledge must be pooled with other expert knowledge.

As worldwide competition ensues, more domains will be confronted with the above conditions and fall into the realm of domains which are feasible for expert system development. This expansion in domains will partly result from the recent orientation towards using information for productivity improvement in an effort to be competitive in worldwide markets (Marchand & Horton, 1986). The characteristics of many business decision making environments are changing to parallel those of currently viable expert system domains.

Increasingly more decisions are required to be made in *shorter decision times* (Rockart & Treacy, 1982). Strategic decisions are becoming *more frequent in occurrence;* for instance, product life cycles are becoming shorter in many manufacturing concerns, thus requiring more product introduction decisions. Information, and as such, expert knowledge is being recognized as a *valuable* resource that should be managed. Organizations are realizing the value associated with expertise (or the cost associated with the *loss* or *lack*

Author(s)	Area	Research Method	Decision Setting 1	Corporate Management 2	3	4	Users 5	Experts 6	MIS Integration 7	User Interface 8	9	ES Dev. Strategies 10	User-Expert Agreement 11
Adeli & AL-Rijleh (1988)	ES	C											
Bailey, et. al. (1981)	IS	C											
Barr & Feineguam (1981)	ES	E											
Barua, Kriebel & Mukhopadhyay (1991)	IS	T											
Bauer & Griffiths (1988)	ES	T											
Benbasat & Schroeder (1977)	IS	E											
Benjamin (1982)	IS	T			T								
Cheney, Mann & Amoroso (1986)	IS	E			T					T			
Coats (1988)	ES	T											
Cohen & Cohen (1983)	COG	T											T
Davis & Olson (1985)	IS	T			T								
DeSanctis & Gallupe (1985)	DSS	T	T										
Dickson, et. al. (1984)	IS	S					S						
Dologite (1987)	ES	C											
Duchessi, Shawky & Seagle (1987)	ES	C											
Duchessi, Shawky & Seagle (1988)	ES	C											
Duda & Shortliffe (1983)	ES	T											
Dungan (1983)	ES	C											
Ellis & Brown (1987)	ES	C											
Entemann & Cannon (1987)	ES	C											
Ettenson, Shanteau & Krogstad (1987)	COG	E											
Fried (1987)	ES	T				T							
Gannon (1979)	COG	T	T										
Grindley (1988)	IS	S	S	S									
Guterl (1986)	ES	S/C											
Hansen & Messier (1986a)	ES	C											
Hansen & Messier (1986b)	ES	C											
Harmon, Maus & Morrissey (1988)	ES	T								T			
Harrington (1988)	ES	T						T					
Heinrich & Chrysler (1988)	ES	C						C					
Herbert & Hartog (1986)	IS	S	T										
Hoffman (1987)	COG/ES	T						T					
Holsapple, Tam & Whinston (1988)	ES	T							T				
Huber (1983)	IS/DSS	T											

Legend
Research Method: C - Case Study; E - Experimental/Empirical; S - Survey, Descriptive; T - Theoretical Conjecture/Practical

Area: COG - Cognitive; DSS - Decision Support Systems; ES - Expert Systems; IS - Information Systems

(table continues)

Table 1: Literature Citations and Related Propositions

Author(s)	Area	Research Method	Decision Setting 1	Corporate Management 2	3	4	Users 5	Experts 6	MIS Integration 7	User Interface 8	9	ES Dev. Strategies 10	User-Expert Agreement 11
Ives & Olson (1984)	IS	T											
Keim & Jacobs (1986)	ES/DSS	S/T									T		
Killingsworth (1987)	ES/DSS	C/E											E
Killingsworth & Kletke (1991)	ES/DSS	C/E											E/T
Lamberti & Wallace (1990)	ES	E									E		
Lehner & Zirk (1987)	ES	E									T		
Leonard-Barton (1987)	ES	T							T			T	
Leonard-Barton & Sviokla (1988)	ES	T										T	
Lieberman (1980)	IS	C											
Lucas (1973)	IS	T								T			
Maish (1979)	IS	E											
Marchand & Horton (1986)	IS	T	T										
Markus & Robey (1988)	IS	T											
McDermott (1980)	ES	C											
McDermott (1982)	ES	C											
McKee (1988)	ES	T	T			T							
Michaelsen (1982)	ES	C											
Michaelsen (1984)	ES	C											
Moad (1987)	ES	T							T				
Nelson & Balachandra (1991)	ES	T										T	
Nelson & Cheney (1987)	IS	E											
New Science (1987)	ES	T											
Newsted, Munro & Huff (1992)	IS	S											
Nisse (1987)	IS	T											
Nolan & Wetherbe (1980)	IS	T											
O'Keefe, Belton & Ball (1986)	ES	T								T			
O'Leary (1987)	ES	T											
Parker, Benson & Trainor (1988)	IS	T	T										
Rauch-Hindin (1984)	ES	T											
Robey (1979)	IS	E						E					
Rockart & Treacy (1982)	IS	T	T										
Shaw & Gentry (1988)	ES	C											
Simon (1987)	ES	C				C							
Sprague (1980)	DSS	T									T		
Steinbart (1987)	ES	C											
Sviokla (1990)	ES	C											
Swanson (1976)	IS	T											
Thesen & Beringer (1986)	IS	T									T		
Turban & Watkins (1986)	ES	T							T		T		
Waterman (1986)	ES	T											
Wiseman & MacMillan (1984)	IS	T	T										
Zahedi (1987)	ES	T											

Legend
Research Method: C - Case Study; E - Experimental/Empirical; S - Survey, Descriptive; T - Theoretical Conjecture/Practical
Area: COG - Cognitive; DSS - Decision Support Systems; ES - Expert Systems; IS - Information Systems

Table 1: Literature Citations and Related Propositions Contd.

of available expertise) (Parker, Benson & Trainor, 1988). Further, the organization's constituents (stockholders, owners, customers, government, and suppliers) are requiring more *consistent* and accurate decision making (i.e., an expert's decision would be identical to another expert's decision) (Wiseman & MacMillan, 1984).

There is a growing interest in group decision making in an effort to pool and to share knowledge among experts for a number of business domains (DeSanctis & Gallupe, 1985). Fewer decisions are being made by individuals as organizations become increasingly complex. Instead, more and more decisions are requiring the input from two or more individuals (Gannon, 1979). This pooling of knowledge will permit refinement of expert knowledge to further the state of a given domain (and its degree of *accuracy*). As a result of these environmental changes, organizations are placing more emphasis on strategic planning and policy making (Herbert & Hartog, 1986; Wiseman & MacMillan, 1984), and as such, domains previously less affected by these policies are becoming likely candidates for expert system development.

In addition to domain characteristics identified by McKee, expert system literature suggest two other characteristics: the amount of knowledge to be stored (knowledge intensiveness) and the frequency with which knowledge must be updated (knowledge dynamics). Knowledge intensiveness involves the amount of knowledge needed to produce an expert opinion on a specific decision task. While there are a number of well-known expert systems reported to contain several thousand rules (i.e., MYCIN, XCON), most reported expert systems have been much smaller in size. Another area gaining an increasing amount of attention is the issue of knowledge maintenance. The term used here to describe the volatility of knowledge within a knowledge base is knowledge dynamics. Expert systems whose knowledge base requires frequent maintenance to protect against entropy in their rule base specification or fact base definition require a large amount of resources to maintain.

The field of expert systems is not a static one. Neither is the environment of corporate decision making. One major complaint of executives is their inability to find applications suitable for expert system development (Grindley, 1988). To assist corporate leaders in identifying potential applications, an index of domain potential for expert system development, or domain viability index, could be developed along with weights for each factor which affects the feasibility, or viability, of a domain to be supported by an expert system.

Proposition 1

The decision setting characteristics of a domain (timeliness, frequency in occurrence, availability, consistency, knowledge interconnectivity, knowledge intensiveness, and knowledge dynamics) significantly influence the perception of whether the development of an expert system is feasible for a given domain.

One method for determining domain viability for potential expert system development would be to:

(1) develop measures corresponding to McKee's (1988) domain characteristics;
(2) identify a representative list of domains, or decision tasks, within a business setting;
(3) using a questionnaire, have a group of experts
  (a) specify their weights associated with the measures,
  (b) classify each domain on a scale of 1 to 20 in terms of its feasibility for expert system development (with endpoints of "very feasible" and "very unfeasible"),
  (c) specify values for each of the measures characterizing the domain, and,
  (d) at the end of the questionnaire, specify the degree of viability which must be met prior to developing an expert system for any given domain task; and
(4) conduct a regression analysis to determine the weight of each factor on expert system viability and its statistical significance.

Several possible avenues for developing specific measures to test this proposition are offered below. Timeliness could be assessed by determining the length of time between the point a decision task is identified and the point in which the decision is required. Frequency could be assessed by determining the number of times a decision must be made for a specified period - possibly on a yearly basis. Availability could be addressed in two ways: (a) the percentage of time the expert is available during the period in which that decision task must be made; and, (b) the probability that knowledge could be lost (i.e., factors affecting turnover in field, such as age, job stress, and job dissatisfaction). Consistency could be assessed by examining the level of interrater reliability of methods or decision outcomes for a given task. The degree of knowledge interconnectivity could be determined by examining factors such as (a) the number of different types of information shared for a given decision task, (b) the number of different individuals involved in a given task, (c) the amount of information that must be shared, and (d) the manner in which the decision is made —group decision making or organizational decision making (in which a decision is made up of a sequence of decisions made by different individuals). The degree of knowledge intensiveness could be measured by the number of anticipated rules and required to produce an expert system. Knowledge dynamics could be measured by computing the ratio of the number of rules and fact definitions updated over a given period of time to the number of rules and fact definitions at the beginning of said period.

Management. Many management decisions are made which impact on the development, acceptance, and usage of expert systems. The literature suggests three prominent areas of concern regarding management's involvement or direction in the expansion of expert systems within an organization: the lack of management awareness on expert system potential, the lack of expert system policies, and inadequate or nonexistent cost-benefit analysis.

Proposition 2

As awareness of expert system potential increases, management's acceptance of expert system technology will increase.

In a recent *Datamation*/Price Waterhouse Survey on expert systems, 64% of the information systems executives surveyed in the U.S. indicated that the lack of awareness of expert system potential limited the acceptance of that technology (Grindley, 1988). Management's acceptance of expert system technology could be measured by determining the percentage of expert system projects accepted relative to the number of expert system projects proposed which met an organization's required rate of return on investments or cost savings. Management's awareness could be measured by surveying top executives on their knowledge and the uses of expert system technology within their own industry or related industry.

Proposition 3

The establishment of corporate policies and goals covering the creation and operation of expert systems will increase the likelihood of acceptance and utilization.

Just as with other forms of end-user computing, policies and guidelines need to be established to direct the development, maintenance, and utilization of expert systems (Benjamin, 1982; Cheney, Mann & Amoroso, 1986; Davis & Olson, 1985). In fact, expert systems are especially vulnerable in that users expect the system's recommendations to be accurate. If there are no controls to ensure a high degree of accuracy then users could lose confidence in expert system technology. The decentralized approach to expert system development creates a special control problem; ensuring that adequate validation tests are conducted. The controls used in traditional development of information systems should also be incorporated on expert systems. The corporation should establish controls to ensure that validation of the knowledge, problem processing strategies, and recommendations offered by the expert system is performed on all expert systems. A survey of corporations to determine the type of corporate expert system policies established and their relationship to user acceptance and utilization would be appropriate to explore this proposition.

Proposition 4

The percentage of expert systems utilized relative to expert system projects initiated will increase if the development phase is based on a cost/benefit analysis.

In prioritizing expert system development projects, each of the decision setting conditions (McKee, 1988) that are met should be quantified to determine the benefits that are expected from the proposed expert systems. Many expert system development projects are started without a full assessment as to the cost and benefits expected from the proposed product.

The average cost for developing a system is approximately $700 per rule (Fried, 1987). This cost excludes any hardware and software tool costs as well as the costs associated with the time an expert contributes in the development of the knowledge base and the testing of the system. Expert systems can contain 50 to 10,000 rules. In total, a moderate size ES with about 300 rules will typically cost $250,000 to $500,000 just to develop; and, manual update expenses can be huge as indicated by DEC's $2 million expenses per year to maintain its XCON system (Simon, 1987). Without a realistic estimation of both initial and recurring expenses, many economically infeasible expert system development projects may be undertaken, causing a drain on technical and economic expertise resources. Some organizations indicate that there is little need for a cost/benefit analysis when utilizing a rapid prototyping approach.

One possible research design might involve a survey of organizations to determine the number of expert system projects initiated, scrapped, completed, and in progress and whether these projects included an adequate cost benefit analysis.

Users. A recent study of key information system issues identified user education as the sixth most important issue (Dickson, Leitheiser, Wetherbe & Nechis, 1984). Other researchers also include user education as an important component of information systems research (Cheney, Mann & Amoroso, 1985; Ives & Olson, 1984; Lucas, 1973; Nolan & Wetherbe, 1980).

Proposition 5

The availability of expert system training for users will result in a greater number of domains identified for expert system development.

Techniques for training users to develop expert systems would be similar to those used in training other end-user computing activities: tutorials, seminars, computer-aided instruction, interactive training manual, resident experts, help component, and external classes from universities or vendor sponsored seminars (Nelson & Cheney, 1987). A survey of different methods used to train decision makers about expert system development and its impact on the number of expert system applications proposed would be relevant to the testing of this proposition. Also, a more in-depth field study of different training methods within a given company would permit additional factors, such as cognitive style, to be considered.

Experts. The success of an expert system lies not only with the abilities of a knowledge engineer to extract knowledge from an expert but also with the capability of the expert(s) being modeled (Harrington, 1988; Hoffman, 1987). Involving multiple experts (even with varying levels of capabilities) from within an organization in the knowledge acquisition or identification stage should produce synergistic effects. As with information system development (e.g., Robey, 1979), encouraging participation by a pool of experts who will later be expected to use the expert system should improve the acceptance rate.

Proposition 6

There will be a higher acceptance level for expert systems developed or selected using a pool of experts from within an organization than for those expert systems developed or selected without the involvement of an organization's own experts.

To test this proposition, a survey of expert system users regarding their level of participation during the development or selection of a given expert system, whether they are required to use the expert system, as well as the frequency with which they accept or reject the expert system's recommendation would be appropriate.

Interactions

Degree of Integration with MIS. The Price Waterhouse/ *Datamation* survey further indicated that most companies believe the integration of expert systems with existing information systems will provide sufficient payoff to justify developing them (Grindley, 1988). Lack of expert system integration is cited as one of their major problems. Most existing expert systems in business have been developed as stand-alone systems and are not designed for integration (Holsapple, Tam & Whinston, 1988; Leonard-Barton, 1987; Turban & Watkins, 1986). However, software houses are beginning to concentrate on the issue of integration and have made it a primary focus for expert system tool development (Harrington, 1988; Moad, 1987). With the ability to integrate expert systems with existing databases, more opportunities will be available for expert system development. Further, the integration will increase convenience for the end user and thus increase the likelihood of expert system usage.

Proposition 7

The utilization and feasibility of expert system applications will vary directly with an expert system's ability to interface with the existing corporate database(s).

To test this proposition, a survey of organizations regarding the economic value, utilization, and number of expert systems developed with respect to the degree of integration with existing information systems would be germane.

User Interface. The number of questions posed to the user is an area of concern as well as an expert system's inability to represent natural language in a more realistic manner are growing areas of concern for expert system users. One reason is the current consultation procedure followed within most expert systems. The logical technique known as backward chaining is frequently used to direct the consultation session. With this technique, the inference engine works from the goal backward using the stored rules to determine the questions it must ask the operator to obtain all of the information needed to recommend a decision (Harmon, Maus & Morrissey, 1988). This consultation method of decision support has limited the use of expert systems to problem areas which require relatively few questions to produce a solution. O'Keefe, Belton and Ball (1986, p.

664) suggest that any expert system which "asks about 15 questions before responding with some advice is unlikely to be acceptable as a frequently used tool, although this number is obviously dependent upon the perceived benefit of the information".

Proposition 8

Minimizing the number of questions posed to the user will increase the utilization of expert systems by the user.

Proposition 8 could be researched by developing several expert system interfaces for a given domain task which have a different number of questions posed to the user and conducting an experiment to determine the impact of the number of questions on the utilization of the expert system. Determining the "minimal" number of questions is currently specific to a given application and may more accurately be referred to as satisficing, or finding an acceptable number of questions, rather than minimizing, or finding the least amount of questions. Further research needs to be conducted on developing a minimizing algorithm for the number of questions posed by an expert system. In developing this algorithm, one must consider the risk associated with not asking certain questions or not repeating questions that are used to ensure accurate information is being provided by the user (as in many medical expert systems). Removing redundant questions or questions whose information have only a small amount of influence on the recommendation should be weighed against the risk associated with a less reliable recommendation.

Another potential method for reducing the questions posed to the user is the interfacing of functionally adjacent expert systems, or those expert systems which could share knowledge. Questions could be minimized across expert systems and not just within a stand-alone expert system by sharing common knowledge. The idea of sharing information between information systems is not new. However, little effort has been directed at linking expert systems so that knowledge or rules could be shared. Developing a method to link this knowledge would reduce the amount of information needed. Also, the development of common sense heuristics and automated knowledge acquisition techniques would help to reduce the number of questions posed to a user.

Proposition 9

User satisfaction and the utilization of expert system applications will increase as the user interface more adequately matches the user domain skill level.

In addition to the large number of questions posed to the user, many expert systems utilize a user interface which could only be considered "friendly" to computer scientists (Keim & Jacobs, 1986). Much work needs to be done to match the user interface to the skill level of the expected user. Just as an expert would tailor a problem solution's presentation to the level of expertise of the listener, an expert system's interface should be developed with consideration given to the extent that the user can interpret its recommendation and reasoning pattern.

Considerable research has been conducted on decision support systems interfaces which could be used as a guide in initially attempting to evaluate the relationship between an expert system's interface and a user's skill level (e.g., Sprague, 1980; Thesen & Beringer, 1986; Turban & Watkins, 1986). In addition, several studies have been conducted on knowledge presentation in expert systems (Lamberti & Wallace, 1990, Lehner & Zirk, 1987). Proposition 9 could be tested by developing an explanation facility with different degrees of complexity and conducting an experiment with different levels of user skill.

Expert System Development Strategies. Choosing the right expert system development strategy is an important issue facing developers because of the need to maintain control of knowledge while encouraging the proliferation of the technology throughout an organization (Nelson & Balachandra, 1991). Two strategies to expert system development are emerging in business: decentralization and centralization. Firms taking a decentralized approach are encouraging their users to develop their own expert systems by training them to use expert system shells. For other firms, the expert system development has been found primarily in the information services division.

Proposition 10

There is an interaction between expert system scope (knowledge intensiveness and knowledge interconnectivity) and expert system development strategies on expert system acceptance and utilization.

Specifically, for large scale expert system projects spanning multiple decision tasks, a centralized approach to expert system development will result in a higher level of acceptance and utilization than a decentralized approach. For small scale expert system projects, a decentralized approach to expert system development will result in a higher level of acceptance and utilization than a centralized approach.

Some firms advocating a decentralized approach have developed extensive, refined training sessions in an effort to streamline the development of expert systems. One such organization is E.I. Dupont de Nemours and Company which is reported to have had 150 expert systems being utilized in 1986. DuPont introduced a training program which produced twenty knowledge engineers a week, each capable of constructing a fully tested expert system in a period of just one month. Ed Mahler of DuPont states "[T]he last ten systems we started have given us 800% return on investment" (Guterl, 1986, p. 36). Companies which report the most success in expert systems have delegated the task of finding applications to the users (Grindley, 1988).

For other firms, expert systems have originated from the information systems division or from an outside consulting service. Usually, these expert systems are much larger in scale than the ones developed by users with shells. The firms that develop these larger expert systems in-house tend to have established a pattern of successfully supporting and implementing user-initiated systems and have the necessary talent and skill to develop expert systems (Leonard-Barton & Sviokla, 1988). Firms without the appropriate expert system development knowledge have commissioned outside consulting services.

Regardless of the expert system strategy followed, expert systems are characteristically developed by rapid prototyping using trial and error techniques, unlike conventional information system development (Leonard-Barton, 1987). This technique permits the development of small, workable systems in a relatively short period of time.

These observations suggest there is an interaction between expert system scope (i.e., knowledge intensiveness and/or knowledge interconnectivity) and expert system development strategies. To research this interaction, a survey of organizations to determine the strategies followed, the level of knowledge intensiveness and interconnectivity of expert systems developed, and the number, acceptance, and utilization of these expert systems would be appropriate. A more in-depth case study also would be desirable to determine additional factors associated with expert system scope, expert system development strategies and success.

User-Expert Agreement. The degree of interrater reliability, or agreement among experts, recently has been proposed as an additional validation measure of an expert system (Killingsworth & Kletke, 1991). Research dealing with audit program planning, which has a low interrater reliability relative to other audit related tasks, suggests that experienced decision makers in an auditing situation are less likely to change their decisions after reviewing a knowledge-based decision support systems recommendations than are inexperienced auditors (Killingsworth, 1987). These initial findings suggest additional research needs to be conducted to determine the impact of interrater reliability on expert system utilization.

Proposition 11

Interactions will occur between the level of interrater reliability of an expert system's domain and the task experience level of a user on acceptance of an expert system's recommendations.

It is expected that there will be a significant difference on acceptance of an expert system's recommendations between levels of task experience for decision makers that are provided with an expert system whose domain has a low degree of interrater reliability. Specifically, users with a high level of domain experience will be less likely to accept the expert system's recommendations than users with a low level of domain experience. Further, there will not be a significant difference on utilization between levels of task experience for decision makers that are provided with an expert system whose domain has a high degree of interrater reliability.

This proposition could be tested through a laboratory experiment on other domains with varying levels of interrater reliability using experts with varying levels of experience.

CONCLUSIONS

A set of environmental and organizational factors which could potentially affect the success or failure of expert system development, acceptance, and usage within an organization have been identified. These factors should be analyzed by management and information systems executives in strategically planning, implementing, and managing expert system technology within an organization. By analyzing these factors, organizations will be better equipped to develop an environment within which expert system development may thrive. Further, a set of propositions for research has been advanced. The expert system research that has been conducted represents only a modest amount of the research necessary to develop the full potential of expert systems in business. In the past several years, interest in expert systems research has increased significant use, as evidenced by the growing number of trade and academic articles published. The set of factors and the set of propositions are not offered as exhaustive, but are provided as a mechanism for facilitating development of expert systems aimed at satisfying the needs of business. Additional research needs to be conducted to address the research questions raised by this chapter and to expand this set of variables and propositions.

ENDNOTE

[1] Representative examples include: Accounting and finance (Bailey, Duke, Ko, Meservy, & Whinston, 1981; Duchessi, Shawky & Seagle, 1987, 1988; Dungan, 1983; Ellis & Brown, 1987; Hansen & Messier, 1986a, 1986b; Lieberman, 1980; Killingsworth, 1987; Killingsworth & Kletke, 1991; Michaelsen, 1982, 1984; Shaw & Gentry, 1988; Steinbart, 1987); Marketing (Entemann & Cannon, 1987; McDermott, 1980, 1982; Production (Adeli & AL-Rijleh, 1988); Information Systems Development (Heinrich & Chrylser, 1988) and Strategic Planning (Dologite, 1987).

REFERENCES

Adeli, H., & AL-Rijleh, M. N. (1988). An expert system for design and manufacturing of roof structures. In M. D. Oliff (Ed.), *Expert Systems and Intelligent Manufacturing*, (pp. 385-400).

Bailey, A. D., Duke, G. L., Ko, C., Meservy, R. D., & Whinston, A. B. (1981). TICOM and the analysis of internal control systems. *Auditing: A Journal of Practice and Theory* (Summer), 38-52.

Barr, A., & Feineguam, E. A. (Eds). (1981). *The handbook of artificial intelligence*, (Vol. 1). Reading, MA, Addison-Wesley.

Barua, A., Kriebel, C. H., & Mukhopadhyay, T. (1991). An economic analysis of strategic information technology investments. *MIS Quarterly*. *15*(3), (September), 313-332.

Bauer, R. J., & Griffiths, M. D. (1988). Evaluating expert system investment: An introduction to the economics of knowledge. *Journal of Business Research*. *17*, 223-233.

Benbasat, I., & Schroeder, R. G. (1977). An experimental investigation of some MIS design variables. *MIS Quarterly*. *1*(1), 37-50.

Benjamin, R. I. (1982). Information technology in the 1990s: A long range planning scenario. *MIS Quarterly*, *6*(2), 11-31.

Cheney, P. H., Mann, R. I, & Amoroso, D. L. (1986). Organizational factors affecting the success of end user computing. *Journal of Management Information Systems*, *3*(1), 65-80.

Coats, P.K. (1988). Why expert systems fail. *Financial Management*. *17*(3), 77-86.

Cohen, J., & Cohen, P. (1983). *Applied multiple regression/correlation analysis for the behavioral sciences*. Hillsdale, NJ: Lawrence Erlbaum Associates.

Davis, G. B., & Olson, M. H. (1985). *Management information systems: Conceptual foundations, Structure, and Development*, (2nd Ed.) New York: McGraw Hill.

DeSanctis, G., & Gallupe, B. (1985). Group decision support systems: A new frontier. In J. C. Wetherbe, V. T. Dock, S. L. Mandell (Eds.) *Readings in Information Systems: A Managerial Perspective,* (pp. 346-357). West Publishing Company, (1988). [appeared in Data Base (Winter 1985)].

Dickson, G. W., Leitheiser, R. L., Wetherbe, J. C., & Nechis, M. (1984). Key information systems issues for the 1980's. *MIS Quarterly. 8*(3), 135-162.

Dologite, D. G. (1987). Developing a knowledge-based system on a personal computer using an expert system shell. *Journal of Systems Management, 38,* 30-37.

Duchessi, P., Shawky, H. A., & Seagle, J. P. (1987). Commercial loan analysis: An application of knowledge-based systems. In J. Feinstein, J. Liebowitz, H. Look, & B.S. Luerman (Eds.) *Proceedings of the First Annual Conference on Expert Systems in Business,* (pp. 55-62). Nedford, NJ: Learned Information.

Duchessi, P., Shawky, H. A., & Seagle, J. P. (1988). A knowledge-engineered system for commercial loan decisions. *Financial Management, 17*(3), 57-65.

Duda, R.O., & Shortliffe, E.H. (1983, April 15). Expert systems research, *Science,* pp. 261-268.

Dungan, C. (1983). *A model of an audit judgement in the form of an expert system.* Unpublished doctoral dissertation, University of Illinois, Urbana-Champaign.

Ellis, Q., & Brown, D. E. (1987). Values: A venture analysis expert system for small telecommunications companies. In F. Feinstein, J. Liebowitz, H. Look, & B.S. Luerman (Eds.) *Proceedings of the First Annual Conference on Expert Systems in Business,* (pp. 63-70). Nedford, NJ: Learned Information.

Entemann, C. W., & Cannon, H. (1987). A rule-based expert system for sales promotion management. In *Proceedings of the 1987 Conference of the American Academy of Advertising.* Las Vegas, NV: American Academy of Advertising.

Ettenson, R., Shanteau, J., & Krogstad, J. (1987). Expert judgement: Is more information better? *Psychological Reports. 60,* 227-238.

Fried, L. (1987, June 29). The dangers of dabbling in expert systems. *Computerworld,* pp. 65-72.

Gannon, M. J. (1979). *Organizational Behavior: A Managerial and Organizational Perspective.* Boston: Little, Brown, and Co.

Grindley, K. (1988, April). End users are key to success. *Datamation, 34*(7), pp. 100-101.

Guterl, F. V. (1986, October). Computers think for business. *Dun's Business Month, 128,* pp. 30-37.

Hansen, J. V., & Messier, W. F., Jr. (1986a). A knowledge-based expert system for auditing advanced computer systems. *European Journal of Operations Research,* (September), 371-379.

Hansen, J. V., & Messier, W. F., Jr. (1986b). A preliminary investigation of EDP-XPERT, *Auditing: Journal of Practice and Theory,* (Fall), 109-123.

Harmon, P., Maus, R., & Morrissey, W. (1988). *Expert Systems Tools and Applications.* New York: Wiley.

Harrington, S. J. (1988). Implementing expert systems: Approaches and caveats. *Journal of Systems Management.* (November). 26-29.

Heinrich, S., & Chrylser, E. (1988). An expert system for system design. *Journal of Systems Management.* (November), 17-25.

Herbert, M., & Hartog, C. (1986, November 15). MIS rates the issues. *Datamation,* pp. 79-86.

Hoffman, R. R. (1987, September). The problem of extracting the knowledge of experts from the perspective of experimental psychology. *AI Magazine. 8,* pp. 53-67.

Holsapple, C.W., Tam, K.Y., & Whinston, A.B. (1988). Adapting expert system technology to financial management. *Financial Management.* 7(3), 12-22.

Huber, G.P. (1983). Cognitive style as a basis for MIS and DSS designs: Much ado about nothing? *Management Science. 29*(5), 567-579.

Ives, B., & Olson, M. (1984). User involvement and MIS success: A review of research. *Management Science, 30*(5), 586-603.

Keim, R.T., & Jacobs, S. (1986). Expert systems: The DSS of the future? *Journal of Systems Management. 37*(12), 6-14.

Killingsworth, B. L. (1987). *The design of a knowledge-based decision support systems enhancing audit program planning.* Doctoral Dissertation (The University of South Carolina).

Killingsworth, B. L., & Kletke, M. G. (1991). The design and implementation of intuitive support for knowledge-based decision support systems: A theoretical and empirical investigation through audit program planning. In J. Carey (Ed.) *Human Factors in Information Systems: An Organizational Perspective* (pp. 135-150). Norwood, New Jersey: ABLEX Publishers.

Lamberti, D. M., & Wallace, W. A. (1990). Intelligent interface design: An empirical assessment of knowledge presentation in expert systems. *MIS Quarterly. 14*(3), 279-312.

Lehner, P. E., & Zirk, D. (1987). Cognitive factors in user/expert systems interaction. *Human Factors. 29* (February), 97-109.

Leonard-Barton, D. (1987). The case for integrative innovation: An expert system at Digital. *Sloan Management Review, 29*, 7-19.

Leonard-Barton, D., & Sviokla, J. J. (1988, March-April). Putting expert systems to work. *Harvard Business Review. 66*(2), 91-98.

Lieberman, A. Z. (1980). Mechanized analysis of entity-relationship design databases. In P. P. Chen (Ed.) *Entity-Relationship Approach to Systems Analysis and Design*, North-Holand, International Conference on ERA.

Lucas, H. C., Jr. (1973). A descriptive model of information systems in the context of the organization. Proceedings of the Wharton Conference on Research on Computers in Organizations. In *Data Base, 5*(2), 27-36.

Maish, A. M. (1979). A user's behavior toward his MIS. *MIS Quarterly. 3*(1), 39-52.

Marchand, D. A., & Horton, F. W., Jr. (1986). *Infotrends: Profiting from Your Information Resources.* New York: John Wiley & Sons, Inc.

Markus, L. M., & Robey, D. (1988). Information and technology and organizational change: Causal structure in theory and research. *Management Science. 34*(5), 583-598.

McDermott, J. R. (1980). R1: A rule-based configurer of computer systems. Computer Science Department, Carnegie-Mellon University. Rept. CMU-CS-80-119 (April).

McDermott, J. R. (1982). R1: A rule-based configurer of computer systems, *Artificial Intelligence 19*(1), 39-88.

McKee, T. E. (1988). Does your practice have a place for an expert system? *The CPA Journal. 58*(1), 114-118.

Michaelsen, R. H. (1982). *A knowledge-based system for individual income and transfer tax planning.* Doctoral Dissertation (University of Illinois at Urbana-Champaign).

Michaelsen, R. H. (1984). An expert system for federal tax planning. Expert Systems: *The International Journal of Knowledge Engineering. 1*(2), 149-167.

Moad, J. (1987, January 1). Building a bridge to expert systems. *Datamation, 33*(1), pp. 17-19.

Nelson, C. W., & Balachandra, R. (1991). Choosing the right expert system building approach. *Decision Sciences. 22*(2), 354-368.

Nelson, R. R., & Cheney, P. H. (1987). Training end users: An exploratory study. *MIS Quarterly. 11*(4).

New Science (1987). Expert system: New opportunities for financial services. Conference Report, Stanford, CT: New Science Associates (March).

Newsted, P. R., Munro, M. C., & Huff, S. L. (1992). Data acquisition instruments in management information systems. In K. L. Kraemer (Ed.) *The Information Systems Research Challenge: Survey Research Methods,* (Vol. 3). (pp. 187-209). Boston, Massachusetts: The Harvard Business School.

Nisse, J. (1987, July). Banking tomorrow big spenders. The Banker, pp. 64-67.

Nolan, R. L., & Wetherbe, J. C. (1980). Toward a comprehensive framework for MIS research. *MIS Quarterly. 4*(2), 1-9.

O'Keefe, R. M., Belton, V., & Ball, T. (1986). Experiences using expert systems in O.R. *Journal of the Operational Research Society,* 37(7), 657-668.

O'Leary, D. E. (1987). Validation of expert systems -With applications to auditing and accounting expert systems. *Decision Sciences, 18*(3), 468-486.

Parker, M. M., Benson, R. J., & Trainor, H. E. (1988). *Information Economics: Linking Business Performance to Information Technology.* Englewood Cliffs, N.J.: Prentice Hall.

Rauch-Hindin, W. (1984, October). Bankers and AI experts team up for greater resources. *Systems and Software.*

Robey, D. (1979). User attitudes and management information system use. *Academy of Management Journal, 22*(3), 527-538.

Rockart, J.F., & Treacy, M.E. (1982). The CEO goes on-line. *Harvard Business Review.* (January-February). 82-88.

Shaw, M.J., & Gentry, J.A. (1988). Using an expert system with inductive learning to evaluate business loans. *Financial Management. 17*(3), 45-56.

Simon, R. (1987, October 19). The morning after, *Forbes*, pp. 164-168.

Sprague, R. H., Jr. (1980). A framework for the development of decision support systems. *MIS Quarterly. 4*(4), 1-26.

Steinbart, P. (1987). The construction of a rule-based expert system as a method for studying materiality judgments, *Accounting Review,* (January), 97-116.

Sviokla, J. J. (1990). An examination of the impact of expert systems on the firm: The case of XCON. *MIS Quarterly, 14*(2). 127-142.

Swanson, E.B. (1976). Measuring user attitudes in MIS research: A review. *Omega, 10*(2). 157-165.

Thesen, A., & Beringer, D. (1986). Goodness of fit in the user-computer interface: A hierarchical control framework related to friendliness. *IEEE Transactions on Systems, Man, and Cybernetics. 16*(1), 158-164.

Turban, E., & Watkins, P.R. (1986). Integrating expert systems and decision support systems. *MIS Quarterly. 10*(2), 121-136.

Waterman, D.A. (1986). *A Guide to Expert Systems.* Reading, MA: Addison-Wesley.

Wiseman, C., & MacMillan, I.C. (1984). Creating competitive weapons from information systems. *Journal of Business Strategy,* 5(2).

Zahedi, F. (1987). Artificial intelligence and the management science practitioner: The economics of expert systems and the contribution of MS/OR. *Interfaces. 17*(September-October), 72-91.

Part III

Strategies for Emerging Technologies

CHAPTER 10

STRATEGIES FOR INFORMATION RESOURCE MANAGEMENT: DEVELOPING CORPORATE-WIDE INFORMATION SYSTEMS

Richard M. Kesner
Babson College

This chapter briefly considers three of the key computer mediated tools in effective organizational communications: (1) electronic mail [one-to-one communication], (2) electronic conferencing [many-to-many communication], and (3) corporate-wide information systems or CWIS [one-to-many communication]. It then proceeds to explore in greater detail the practical issues associated with the design and implementation of a CWIS. In so doing, the author considers the operational, organizational, and technological dynamics of the modern organization, the implications of these factors on the delivery of information services, and some promising strategies that one might employ in response to these emerging requirements. The author will illustrate his points through the use of three case studies. The first and primary example will be that of CWIS development at Babson College, supplemented by short references to the use of CWIS within a global consulting firm and within a large insurance organization.

Opening Scenario: Paul Smith is your typical busy executive. While simultaneously managing a number of complex assignments, he must also keep abreast of all the comings and goings of the larger organization. Mr. Smith does not have the luxury of a research staff to assist him in this regard. Fortunately, he does not require such services. Instead, he merely flicks on his desktop work station. Within seconds the corporation's electronic information library menu pops onto his screen. This library, generically referred to as the "corporate-wide information system (CWIS)," provides menu-driven access to the latest corporate news, personnel and policy changes, sales data, scheduled events and activities, and many other files of valuable information. He may pick and choose with ease, addressing his immediate "need to know." As a result, Mr. Smith stays well informed in an efficient and cost effective manner and in so doing enhances his personal contribution to the corporate team effort.

Information is the life blood of the modern organization. Yet it is increasingly difficult to devise effective and efficient data delivery systems that reach the appropriate end users in a timely manner. As part of his/her responsibilities, today's information resources manager must find ways to address this challenge. Increasingly, three of the key computer-mediated tools in this effort are: (1) electronic mail, (2) electronic conferencing, and (3) corporate-wide information systems or CWIS. The implications and potential benefits of these services for corporate IRM are significant. The purpose of this chapter is to consider the operational, organizational, and technological dynamics of the modern organization; to discuss the implications of these factors on the delivery of information services; and to develop strategies in response to these emerging requirements. The author will then examine corporate-wide information systems (CWIS) in more detail, identifying the practical steps in its implementation on a college campus. To supplement this illustration, the author will provide two other examples: one, a global engineering consulting firm, and the other, a large insurance company. While the reader's own work environment and organizational context may differ widely from the case studies presented by the author, he/she will find that the operational concerns and IRM opportunities address in this chapter are common to most business settings. Furthermore, the chapter's basic premises apply universally. In the first place, successful organizations increasingly achieve this distinction through individual employee and work group empowerment. Worker empowerment is achieved—at least in part—through easy and timely access to appropriate information. More of this information comes from global sources in a myriad of formats. These resources in turn are costly to obtain and use, and are difficult to manage.

For the information resources management professional,these circumstances pose an interesting set of challenges:

- What resources are required by the organization?
- How do we obtain them in an affordable and timely manner?
- How do we provide easy and economical access to these information resources?
- How do we encourage our customers (i.e. information resource end users) to take full advantage of these capabilities.

Within the confines of this chapter, the author cannot hope to deal with each of these subjects in great detail. Instead, he provides a context for the establishment, design, and implementation of a CWIS, including critical success factors leading to a successful deployment. In so doing, he has developed a foundation upon which the reader may build a CWIS strategy in keeping with the needs of his/her organization.

BACKGROUND

During the winter of 1990, the author was invited to join Babson College as its first chief information officer (CIO). Concurrently, the entire College community was in the throws of a detailed self-evaluation culminating in a new strategic plan. This process helped to restate and clarify Babson's mission as a educational institution dedicated to the development of innovative leaders capable of initiating, managing, and implementing change.[1] Furthermore, the College committed itself to teaching with a global perspective and to integrating information technology (I/T) throughout all aspects of the Babson learning experience(Babson, 1991).

To achieve the latter objective, the chief information officer was charged with creating and maintaining a "realworld" information resource environment for the use of students, faculty, and administrators. In establishing this new office, the College brought together all of the campus's existing information service departments, included: Academic Computing, Administrative Computing, Media Services, the Babson College Telephone Company (BABTELCO), and the Library. These functional areas had not operated in concert before. Each reported to a different senior administrator; possessed its own personnel structure, policies, and procedures; and provided services according to its own sense of customer requirements. To fashion a new environment within which to realize the College's strategic objectives,the CIO was obliged to reshape the operating units that now reported to him, provide his staff with a common sense of mission, and to instill in them a sense of customer service that transcended their specific job assignments. The organization that emerged from this effort was named the Information Technology and Services Division (ITSD). Its newly defined mission and strategic plan began as follows:

> Consistent with the overall strategic plans of the College, it is the mission of Babson's Information Technology and Services Division (ITSD) to provide in partnership with the Babson Community information and services to proactively support the educational programs, operational requirements, and business plans of the College. To achieve these ends through innovation and excellence, ITSD will deploy the best in proven information technologies (ITSD 1990; ITSD 1991).

In brief, the ITSD intended to deliver on this challenging assignment through the innovative exploitation of an integrated information services organization. The model for such a structure, the so-called "Information Utility," was already present in private industry and was in fact emerging in leading U.S. colleges and universities.

Within any organization, the information utility includes all of those resources, services, and facilities that comprise, process, and deliver information to the enduser. More than computer hardware and software, *an information utility is an approach to customer service that emphasizes availability, ease of access, economy, efficiency, and accountability to the community* (Woodsworth, 1991; Szewezak, 1991; Khosrowpour, 1990; Hawkins, 1989B; Arms, 1988). Babson's IRM team adapted this approach to their own institutional setting and in so doing provided their colleagues with a practical illustration of how to effectively restructure information services to enhance performance and competitive advantage.

These accomplishments were not achieved without some pain. To create the information utility, Babson was obliged to restructure the various organizational units servicing its information resource management requirements, redefine individual employee responsibilities, invest greater financial resources in I/T management, and break with past institutional practices. For a more detailed consideration of the human resource implications of the information utility strategy, see Kanter, 1991 and Kesner, 1993. As the Division explored innovative ways to deliver information resources and services, the ITSD team inventoried the College's communications infrastructure. The campus already employed highly successful voice- and electronic-mail systems. To supplement face-to-face meetings, ITSD also installed an electronic conferencing product (VAXNotes). However, most mass communications still went out in paper formats. Periodically, the institution employed voice-and electronic-mail to reach the community, but these applications proved inefficient. In the first place, "broadcast" messages of even the shortest length annoyed end users. They clutter mail boxes with unwanted information, consumed computer disk space needed to store more important data, and at times never reached those for whom the broadcast was intended because the recipients were not regular users of electronic mail.

After some consideration of the information technology options, ITSD identified an opportunity to automate much of this information exchange through a CWIS, thus reducing operating costs while delivering up-to-date information to end users in a more timely fashion. This approach entailed the establishment of a corporate-wide information system for the use of the entire Babson community. Though the specific features of any given CWIS may vary from one organization to another, they all provide ready electronic access to a broad range of shared information resources, including for example: parent organization calendars and schedules of events, corporate policies and procedures, widely used manuals and handbooks, internal telephone directories, and in many instances stock quotes, news and weather services, train schedules and the like.

Due to its newness, published information about corporate-wide (also know as "campus-wide") information systems is somewhat limited. Perhaps the most valuable source of data on CWIS applications, and one that this author relies upon throughout this chapter, is the CWIS List Server that may be accessed via BITNET or INTERNET. Though the List Server's contributors are largely university IRM personnel, their insights will prove useful to anyone venturing into CWIS development and implementation regardless of their particular institutional settings. In brief , CWIS is analogous to an "electronic library" that provides online access to a wide range of data and documents.

Perhaps the most useful concept behind a CWIS design is that it attempts to address a broad range of information resource end-user requirements. However, it leaves the final decision of what information to access when to the customer, thus eliminating both paper and electronic "waste" while improving the flexible servicing of end-user needs. This chapter examines the rationale behind

Babson College's CWIS efforts in some detail, supplemented by briefer case studies of an engineering consultancy firm and a major insurance carrier. This study identifies the process employed to involve the community in CWIS design, the project's implementation schedule, and a summary of critical success factors for CWIS deployment.

To achieve this end, the author begins with a brief consideration of the forces at work within the modern organization that drive information resource managers toward solutions like CWIS. Global information needs, the increasing diversity and complexity of available information resources and systems, the emergence of the "knowledge worker" as the IRM professional's primary customer, and the escalating "utility" costs of service maintenance are all factors influencing these developments. From this more general discussion, the author will focus upon the use of CWIS for information distribution and intra/interorganization communication.

THE MODERN ORGANIZATION, IRM, AND THE KNOWLEDGE WORKER

The modern organization is less bureaucratic, more complex, and global in its orientation. Increasingly, its management structure is flatter, with senior executives playing a larger role in the direct management of people, processes, and resources (including information resources). Typically, these players map out the strategic programs for their organization, often employing external alliances, resource sharing, outsourcing, and new information technologies to enhancing overall corporate performance. Correspondingly, middle management is growing thinner. Many now serve primarily as technical specialists, developing policies, procedures, and applications for "hands-on" workers. The vast majority of those remaining directly contribute to value creation for the organization's ultimate customers. In this more-fluid, less-hierarchical environment, most if not all employees will have both information resource management and production responsibilities (Davis, 1991; Morris, 1990; Naisbitt, 1990;Peters, 1987).

Information technologies have and will continue to play a central role in this restructuring of the enterprise. They facilitate streamlining and encourage a more entrepreneurial operating mode among managers now freed from dependence onothers for vital information. They also tend to foster linkages with external global partners. Operationally, I/T's allow senior management involvement in day-to-day business processes and communication with players throughout the organization. These developments in turn will transform the way assignments are accomplished and will place a demand for new skills and greater flexibility on the part of both managers and workers. Furthermore, the ubiquitous and increasingly user-friendly nature of emerging information technologies has meant that line managers rather than technologists can now take charge of these resources, refocusing IRM requirements on core services and strategic business objectives on a "real-time" basis (Tom 1991,Targowski, 1990; Emery, 1987). The proliferation of I/T and information resources throughout the organization is illustrated in Exhibit I. No functional area in this representation of an organization is without its IRM capabilities and responsibilities.

As represented in Exhibit I, each operating unit of the XYZ Organization has control of its own information systems.This structure is indicative of the worker empowerment andmanagerial flattening of the corporation alluded to above. Similarly, each unit has its own information processing capabilities, ranging from individual personal computer workstations to large corporate databases run on typically shared mainframe computers. They also have access to if not complete control over the I/T tools, hardcopy and online information resources, and associated support services deemed necessary to satisfy the requirements of their customers.

The organization's administrative units are similarly endowed as the "owners" of human resource, financial, real estate, purchasing, insurance, and other corporate data. In this context, the information services arm of the organization acts as the I/T standards watch dog, the keeper of networks and operating environments (i.e. the I/T infrastructure), access to external information utilities(e.g. bibliographic utilities and extra-corporate electronic mail networks), and the developer and supporter of new I/T capabilities.

From this author's perspective, information resource management encompasses the economical and efficient management, servicing, and support of all information (in whatever format) that is of value to the organization. The value-added component of IRM is the information utility's ability to deliver accurate, specific, information to the end user in a timely manner. Similarly, we must redefine what we mean when we refer to an information services professional. While the terms librarian, archivist, records manager, and systems analyst have relevance in today's information technology (I/T) environment, the Twenty-First Century information utility requires the services of cross-trained, highly-integrated staffs of I/T professionals to act as facilitators, catalysts for change, standards monitors,

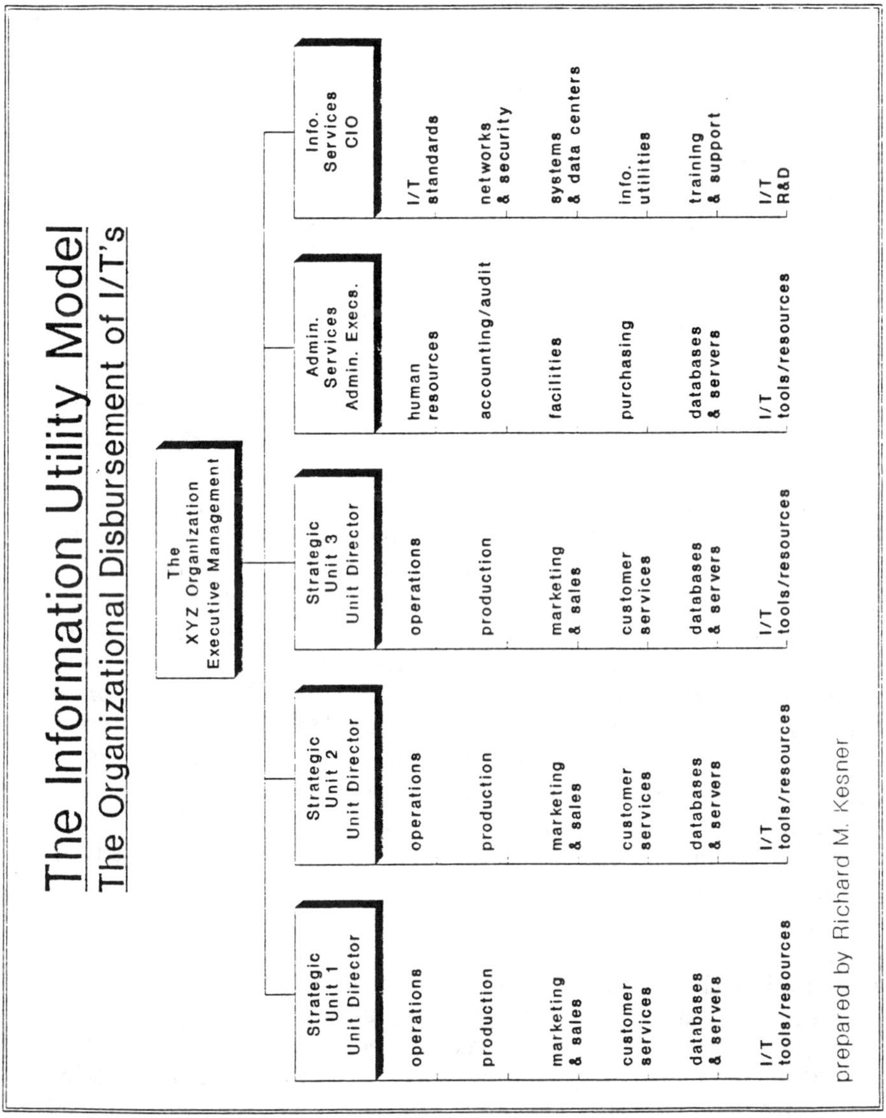
The Information Utility Model
The Organizational Disbursement of I/T's
The XYZ Organization Executive Management
Strategic Unit 1 Unit Director
operations
production
marketing & sales
customer services
databases & servers
I/T tools/resources
Strategic Unit 2 Unit Director
operations
production
marketing & sales
customer services
databases & servers
I/T tools/resources
Strategic Unit 3 Unit Director
operations
production
marketing & sales
customer services
databases & servers
I/T tools/resources
Admin. Services Admin. Execs.
human resources
accounting/audit
facilities
purchasing
databases & servers
I/T tools/resources
Info. Services CIO
I/T standards
networks & security
systems & data centers
info. utilities
training & support
I/T R&D
prepared by Richard M. Kesner

Exhibit I

and resource managers for complex, user-driven and controlled, information delivery systems.

As a result of these envisioned reallocations of I/T responsibilities, the organization's information service providers are concerned less with such secondary issues as the efficient and economical storage of data, and spend more of their productive time proactively delivering knowledge. Thus, the IRM shopping list includes such products as: intelligent, personal computer-based tools for end users; future-focused decision support systems; business simulation software; and expert systems (Index Group, 1991, 1988).Throughout, the objective of these I/T scenarios is to empower the end user and to put this person in touch with the appropriate data to address immediate customer needs today and plan for tomorrow. These same operational requirements necessitate the development of such mechanisms as electronic mail networks, electronic and video conferencing, and electronic information libraries for information sharing and the communication of decisions.

We often think of "information" in terms of documents, records, files, etc., but these are merely formalized vehicles for the delivery of data to an end user. Historically, these information products were/are self supporting and generally sufficient in terms of satisfy theneeds of the end user. With recent developments in I/T, "information" alone is not satisfactory—primarily because there is too much of it and the "products" in question are insufficiently focused and unadaptable. Instead, users seek knowledge, that is: a higher level of information, at times in multi-media formats, that are tailored and processed to address a specific requirement. Correspondingly, knowledge tools, such as artificial intelligence systems, and hyper-text databases, facilitate the manipulation of information to meet end user needs. The *knowledge worker* is an end user who employs a wide range of information technologies to draw upon diverse information resources in a variety of formats to address his/her immediate needs through the sophisticated sifting, search,and reassembly of data into highly usable formats.

Given this view of the modern organization and IRM operations, it is clear that the information services professional must come to know and understand the needs of the "knowledge worker" whose information resource and service requirements are the driving force behind the design and functionality of the information utility model. Here again, it is helpful to begin from the perspective of IRM dynamics in the work place. These processes may be summarized as follows:

(1) raw data is created/collected - "input,"

(2) the data is enhanced through value-added services "data processing applications;" data is replaced when more current information is available or purged when it is no longer of use to the organization.
(3) the enhanced data "information" is distributed via electronic networks to the desk top,
(4) the information is then received and manipulated by a worker or a work process, and
(5) the resulting creation is a "knowledge product orprocess that exists for a specific purpose in time (Tom, 1991; Targowski, 1990; Emery, 1987).

To actually operationalize this flow of information resources, the knowledge worker needs access to a complex array of information resources, including: printed publications of all kinds, information systems documentation, bibliographic and other information utilities, proprietary and public databases, and the thoughts and voices of colleagues. But access alone is not enough. To be "empowered" and indeed to add value to the information at hand, the knowledge worker requires independent data processing capabilities, including: a personal computer workstation with local and wide-area network connectivity, relational database tools, a multi-media receipt and transmission capacity, and even artificial-intelligence-based IRM applications. With this functionality at hand, the worker can more readily address his/her self-managed assignments, adding value to the greater organization's products and services, and further enhancing the "knowledge base" of the organization through data sharing and group work. The knowledge-worker scenario described here reflects agrowing desire within the modern organization to enhance the productivity and corporate contribution of each individual employee. To achieve this end, information services must betailored to the specific needs of the worker and readily accessible, preferably at the desk top. The implications of this design for CWIS are immense. The IRM staff must look for innovative ways of promoting and providing value-added access to corporate-wide information resources. It must tailor its activities in concert with the strategic and tactical direction of its parent institution to deliver these resources efficiently and economically. In so doing, it must involve data and system "owners" in the establishment and maintenance of CWIS services. These types of activities challenge establish paradigms of information utility operations and funding. Indeed, they call for a different approach to overall IRM administration, dissolving many of the artificial distinctions that separate I/T professionals from end users and hence affording easy and economical access a vast array of information through electronic libraries and CWIS delivery mechanisms. By way of orientation, examine Exhibit II.[2] This exhibit graphically represents the follow of raw data in various media and formats to intermediate data collection and distribution platforms (e.g. databases) (United Nations, 1990; Kesner, 1984A; Martin, 1982). From there, it is manipulated by higher-level information processing ("knowledge") tools (i.e.computer applications) and then transmitted through various networks to the desk top of the end user, who in this illustration is either a living person or an automated process further along the value chain. The ultimate delivery of "knowledge" as defined above may then lead to specific, informed actions. This entire set of transactions (Exhibit II) constitutes the range of information resource management and use within the modern organization. The unique character of these processes defines the institutional context and corporate culture within which people work. Like the role of IRM itself, the modern organization is also transforming in light of this technological innovation and adaptation. For example, the personal computer has dramatically altered the way individuals work, communicate, and manage (Kanter, 1991; Kesner, 1988; Kesner, 1984B). Similarly, the more recent emergence of sophisticated electronic networks have revolutionized corporate and even interpersonal communications (Woodsworth, 1991; Hawkins, 1989B; Arms, 1988; Wiseman, 1988). Perhaps no where is the impact of these developments more obvious than in the use of electronic mail where traditional pecking orders are ignored and creative alliances are established through the informal electronic exchange of news, gossip, hard data, and documents (Sproull, 1991; Whitaker, 1989; ACRL, 1988). If the benefits of electronic mail (e-mail) are generally recognized, the same may not be said for corporate wide information systems. Though as easy to use as e-mail, a CWIS requires a more determined, resource-intensive approach to implementation. Its initial maintenance costs are higheras well. On the other hand, the potential benefits of CWIS to the user community are considerable. In the first place, a successful installation will reduce the corporate-wide use of paper documentation and the associated costs of printing and distribution. Secondly, the information sources themselves are communicated through a common computer-based "library" delivery system. Thus, all authorized personnel would have ready access to the most current version of a given document. The updating of files is easily and efficiently accomplished. Delivery is always timely. Most importantly, if the CWIS affords easy user access and if it carries information that is vitally important to the organization, it will encourage even the most non-technical members of the community

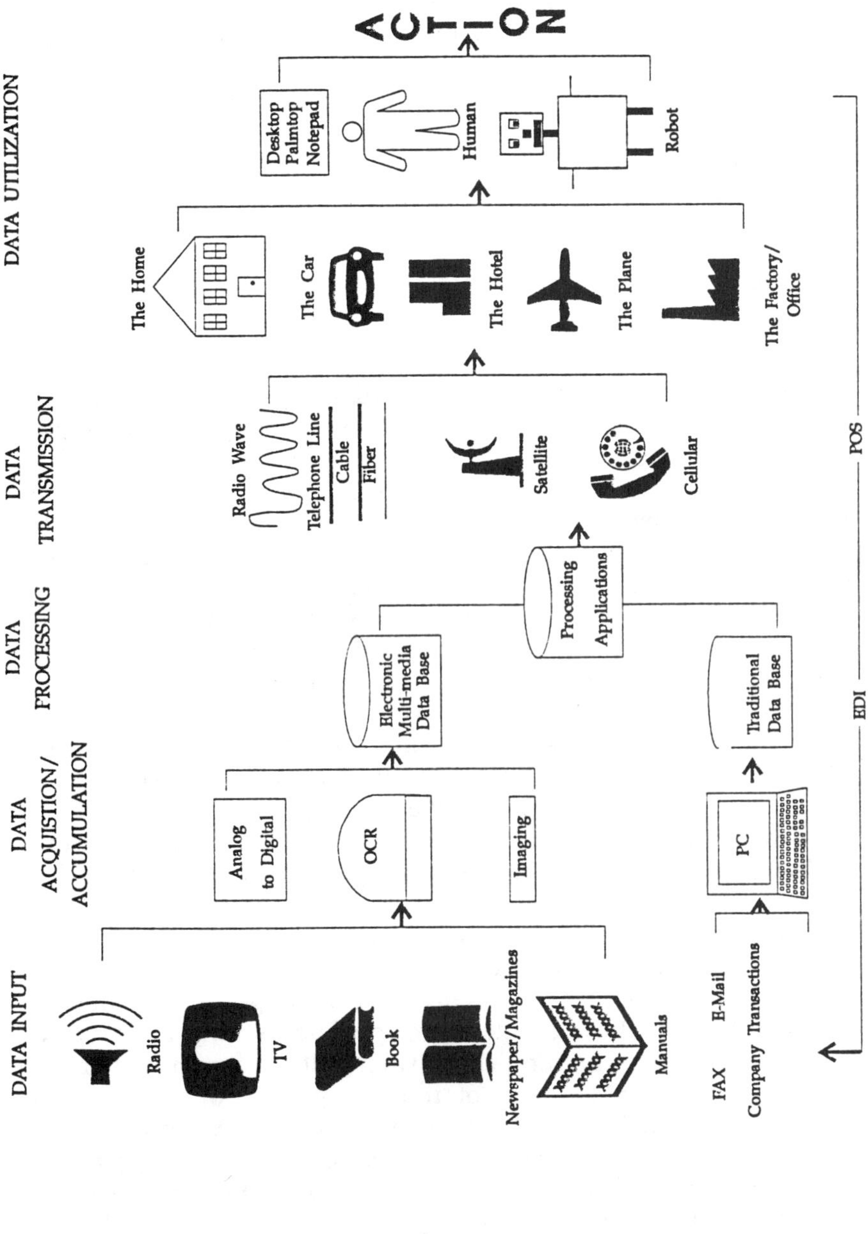
DATA INPUT
Radio
TV
Book
Newspaper/Magazines
Manuals
FAX
E-Mail
Company Transactions
DATA ACQUISTION/ ACCUMULATION
Analog to Digital
OCR
Imaging
PC
DATA PROCESSING
Electronic Multi-media Data Base
Traditional Data Base
Processing Applications
DATA TRANSMISSION
Radio Wave
Telephone Line
Cable
Fiber
Satellite
Cellular
DATA UTILIZATION
The Home
The Car
The Hotel
The Plane
The Factory/ Office
Desktop Palmtop Notepad
Human
Robot
ACTION
EDI
POS

Exhibit 2

to get on the network. Indeed, in the long run, the CWIS is perhaps the most effective vehicle for bringing the total organization into the I/T loop by making information access through the network a necessary condition of corporate survival. Unfortunately, the CWIS implementation process is not an intuitive one (Laderman, 1990; Finnegan, 1990; Hawkins,1989A; Emmett, 1989). The remainder of this chapter will explore the CWIS development process in more detail. In this regard, Babson College's experience, as well as those of a global consulting firm and a major insurance company, will serve as illustrations as to how one might go about CWIS deployment.

THE CORPORATE-WIDE INFORMATION SYSTEM (CWIS): THE STRATEGY

Most organizations are buried in information. Much of this information is communicated via paper even though it may exist simultaneously in an electronic format. Document distribution tends to be costly and dysfunctional. Thus, knowledge workers do not get what they need when they need it. Furthermore, data tends to come to the end user in a static form that may be altered only after a process of wasteful rekeying. To avoid these pitfalls, many information resource managers, especially those in geographically disbursed organizations, have turned to electronic delivery systems (Palvia, 1991). The most familiar of these approaches is electronic mail. E-mail has repeatedly demonstrated its worth as a means of shipping messages and documents throughout an organization in an efficient and economical manner. It is expressly designed to afford electronic communication between a given individual "sender" and one or more recipients.While e-mail systems are often used to share "broadcast"messages within a large group, they are not always suited for the transmission of large, complex documents on an "as needed" basis. Nor do most e-mail systems lend themselves to interactive exchanges. To address this type of information sharing requirement, many organizations are now turning to electronic- or video conferencing where a select group of users may review and comment on data and the remarks of their fellow team members in an interactive manner. This type of "many-to-many"communication works well within well-defined groups of knowledge workers. However, like electronic mail, video-and electronic-conferencing systems are not designed for corporate-wide information sharing. Furthermore, these conferencing products place time and financial constraints on their users and do not typically deliver information "on demand." To this end, organizations are investing in electronic libraries and bulletin boards for information dissemination.These vehicles store both time-sensitive data, such as events and schedules, as well as voluminous documents, such as software and hardware specifications, in machine-readable formats. Employing a limited number of keystrokes or a mouse, the end user accesses these files through a simple, menu or icon-driven interface. In busy public-access areas,a touch-tone screen might replace more conventional mechanisms to encourage wide-spread use of the service. To ensure success, the system must provide information that is in demand. If the data in question also changes regularly, is time-sensitive, and needs to reach a broad cross section of the organization, it belongs in the CWIS. On the customer side of the equation, ready access to online, timely, and accurate information will prove irresistible even among hitherto non-users of the network. Indeed, a CWIS is a sure way to bring over those resistant to I/T within the organization to a more sympathetic view of electronic-data exchange. In terms of cost, a CWIS is highly affordable, assuming of course that the organization already has a network in place. Like e-mail, a CWIS system is merely a delivery shell with various rules for the storage and retrieval of electronic files. Most, like Digital Equipment Corporation's"VideoTex," have a relatively "friendly," menu-driven interface for user access. But unlike e-mail, a CWIS system stores all of its information centrally. The user calls in to the system, selects items of interest, views them, and then signs off (with the option of printing portions of or whole CWIS files off line). Under e-mail, the system would need to ship individual copies of each file to all end users to have something approximating the same result. Data delivery would not be driven by customer requirements and would clutter the "mail boxes" of all network users regardless of their interests/needs. Clearly, CWIS is less consumptive of data processing resources while being more responsive to user requirements.Post-implementation system maintenance by I/T personnel is minimal because, as the author will detail below, this responsibility is largely distributed among the organization's information providers ("owners"). Finally, the associated reduction in a reliance on paper-based documents leads the author to conclude that a successful CWIS will lead to lower operating costs, better use of information resources, and an overall improvement in corporate performance. However, to realize these benefits, the IRM team must work in concert with their customers to design and implement a CWIS.

THE CORPORATE-WIDE INFORMATION SYSTEM (CWIS): IMPLEMENTATION

As a starting point, the organization must already have in place an operating electronic network, one that provides access to e-mail and various other computer-based resources. End user knowledge and heavy use of this network are not prerequisites. The CWIS itself must be extremely simple to access and will over time encourage wide-spread exploitation of the organization's information utility as the richness of its CWIS offerings increase. The next two steps in the process may occur concurrently, namely: the development of aCWIS implementation strategy and the selection of CWIS software.

The initial plan will in all likelihood take shape under IRM team leadership. However, I/T personnel should involve their customers in the process as soon as they can. The basic elements of such a CWIS strategy may be summarized as follows:

1. establish the IRM CWIS team.
2. develop specifications for selection of a CWIS shell.
3. identify key information providers throughout the organization.
4. educate information providers as to the benefits and responsibilities of CWIS participation.
5. win information provider support for CWIS; that is: *their commitment to provide information products for delivery through CWIS.*
6. obtain and install a CWIS-shell product.
7. test the CWIS shell and insure that the IRM team assigned to CWIS are familiar with its functionality.
8. prototype and test a limited number of high-priority (i.e. high-interest), real-life applications on the CWIS.
9. establish format and content standards for CWIS information files; establish a CWIS User Group.
10. obtain information provider approval of standards.
11. develop information provider and user-community documentation and training for CWIS as needed. Note: Training is critical to the overall success of a CWIS application. Through comprehensive, customer sensitive training programs, one will develop both a critical mass of receptive users and information "owners." Their joint participation is essential for long-term CWIS viability.
12. along with information providers, tie informationresources into CWIS interface on a prioritized basis; work with information providers to convert their data to more user-friendly CWIS formats.

13. locate public-access CWIS terminals (also known as "information kiosks") in strategic locations around the organization.
14. publicize the availability and benefits of CWIS to the community at large; and provide training as needed to encourage use of CWIS. Note: To succeed, CWIS must be provide a very simple—indeed effortless—interface, such as an icon or menu driven access system.
15. ensure information provider compliance with CWIS standards.
16. search for additional information resources to be delivered through CWIS.
17. monitor CWIS use (most CWIS systems will provide product-specific usage statistics); expand outreach and educational efforts of IRM-CWIS team.
18. add more information resources to the CWIS menu and enhance CWIS features based upon customer feedback.

The CWIS team should be lead by an I/T professional with extensive project management and "customer-relations" experience. Strong people and salesmanship skills are essential. While he/she needs to understand the organization's I/T capabilities, it is even more important that this individual work effectively with those who will provide information for the CWIS. The chief I/T executive of the organization need only be involved directly at the outset to win senior management support for the CWIS effort. The remaining I/T personnel commitment to the CWIS project will be that of the programmer(s) involved in tying each information resource into the CWIS and in working with information providers to ensure the compatibility of their data files with the CWIS format.

The CWIS shell itself might be home grown, run off the organization's e-mail system, or operate as a stand-alone, off-the-shelf product. For example, on many college and university campuses where Digital Equipment Corporation (DEC) computers may be found, the product of choice is often DEC's "VideoTex." Alternatively, Microsoft, Lotus, Apple and others have issued or are about to release a new generation of desk-top-based IRM products that will readily facilitate end user access into both internal and external multi-media information resources. The final selection should make the best use of the organization's network and must be as user friendly as possible. If the network supports color and graphics, find a CWIS shell that does likewise. Similarly, products with a graphical user interface and touch-screen capabilities are highly desirable as long as they can be supported by the corporate information utility.

However, the key to a successful CWIS implementation has less to do with technology than it has to do with people. The team must involve the organization's information providers from the outset. These players might include: the library (owners of holdings information and other bibliographic data), human resources (owners of employee handbooks, benefits information, and holiday schedules), public relations (owners of special events calendars), and so forth. Each of these groups must be educated as to how CWIS will provide wider and better access to their information and services. Since in most cases they are already generating documents, schedules, and lists via word processing or some other computer-mediated system, the point should be made that all they need do is electronically transfer their existing files to CWIS for subsequent "on-demand" distribution to the community. (Note: In some instances, the CWIS team may need to coax users to adopt a standard format so as to afford the merging of data, such as event schedules. If the team meets with initial resistance, they should point out that compliance with a standard will lead to wider dissemination and hence better communication of the "owner's" information. This ought to "make the sale.")

Typically, a hard-sell by the I/T team is not required. A general overview of the CWIS product followed by a group brainstorming session on potential CWIS applications will generate plenty of interest. Once these information providers realize that CWIS does not add much, if any, additional work to their other responsibilities, the team will face a fairly receptive audience. To ensure ongoing support, establish a CWIS User Group comprised of all of theorganization's participating information providers. Get them to spread the word and assist in the team's end-user marketing efforts. For pilot CWIS applications, choose among the most enthusiastic of the information providers. Be sure to consider which applications will win broad end-user support. Events calendars, phone directors, operating hours, and cafeteria menus are examples of popular and easily implemented CWIS applications.

Begin with these and other heavily-used information resources. To make the best use of the system, the team should require information providers to conform to a standard data entry format. In most instances, the offsetting advantages of wide-spread information dissemination will more than compensate these providers for any perceived inconveniences associated with conformity. As part of the CWIS role out, the implementation team must pay special attention to the marketing of the service. The key to success is an easy-to-use shell that incorporates a critical mass of the information viewed by the customer as essential for corporate existence. Even if some of these highly desirable CWIS applications are not initially available, the team should list them in the CWIS menus as"upcoming attractions." Furthermore, the team should not neglect the provision of training for end users. These sessions may be exploited to promote CWIS and to get nonparticipating information providers involved in the process. With the application interfaces in place, I/T personnel need only police CWIS standards, maintain the shell software,and look for additional information sources. Those creating the data and therefore those best informed of its currency, accuracy, and relevance to the user community will be vested with the responsibility to update their respective CWIS files. In this way, the burden of maintenance is well distributed and the ongoing resource drain on I/T is limited. To add further value to CWIS services, I/T personnel might develop mechanisms to consolidate information from various files. For example, if each operating unit publishes its own monthly calendar of events over CWIS, I/T might establish a daily calendar of corporate-wide events that merely draws its data from these other, more specialized listings. In so doing, the team will realize the CWIS's full potential as an internal IRM tool.

THE CORPORATE-WIDE INFORMATION SYSTEM (CWIS): EXAMPLES

Babson College is implementing its first CWIS in a manner similar to that outlined above. After an initial presentation to executive management, the I/T team, led by the Director of Libraries and the Manager of Systems Development, met with the College's Senior Management Committee. This group comprises all of Babson's primary information providers (also known as "owners"). Together with I/T personnel, this assemblage settled upon the following mastermenu of CWIS applications:

1. Academic Programs
2. Campus Electronic Conferences
3. Campus Events
4. Career Information
5. Employee Policies and Procedures
6. Library/Media/Computer Services
7. News (UPI)
8. Stock Quotes
9. Student Services
10. Telephone Directories
11. INTERNET (global information network)

By selecting one of these menu items, the user moves to a more specific menu of information offerings. For example,under the "Academic Programs" sub-menu, a CWIS user can access the College's academic calendar, class schedules, course descriptions, exam schedules, and a listing of open classes. The "Campus Events" sub-menu provides today's, this week's and this month's events as automatically culled from the more specialized calendars that appear in this directory (e.g. Academic Events, Athletic Events, Cultural Events, and so forth). The "Career Information" offerings include job postings on and off campus as well as schedules of visiting corporate recruiters. The "Library" menu provides access to Babson's automated library system and a directory of services and hours for the entire Information Technology and Services Division (ITSD). It will eventually link the end user directly into our CD-ROM resource library holdings as well as off-campus bibliographic utilities. The "Student" menu offers information about housing, student evaluations of college courses, and even cafeteria menus and operating hours. One could go on. In summary, the Babson CWIS affords immediate access to the most current information pertaining to all on-campus activities and services.

The College currently employs DEC's VideoTex running on a VAX cluster as its CWIS shell. Students may access CWIS from their dormitory rooms or from computer labs and study rooms in the Horn Library/Computer Center complex. Faculty and staff may access CWIS from their office machines or may dial into a modem pool from any off-campus location. Since CWIS access is controlled by user identification numbers, Babson can tailor its CWIS offerings to the needs and security clearances of its end users. For example, students on the one hand, and faculty and staff on the other view different menu offerings when they sign on to CWIS. The College is also considering the implications of providing individual alumni and possibly corporate sponsors with access to CWIS on a limited basis. Finally, ITSD and the CWIS User Group are contemplating the locating of CWIS terminals in such public places as the Library, the Special Events and Recreation Center, and the student dining facility. It is too early in its development cycle for Babson to evaluate the benefits of CWIS but the community is certainly excited about the prospects and quite willing to join with the I/T team in CWIS's further elaboration. As Babson College completes the installation of a new campus wide voice/data network, we will undoubtedly move to a client server-based CWIS solution, employing a graphical user interface and standard icons for our various CWIS offerings.

To conclude this section, the author would like to briefly mention two further illustrations of how CWIS might benefit an organization.[3] In the first instance, a global engineering consulting firm established a number of research and development functions in support of its core businesses. Each of these units prepares detailed specifications, architectural and engineering drawings, and project management data, employing CAD/CAM and word processing technologies, for the use of field personnel. The information in question is voluminous and highly specialized. It would be impractical, and indeed wasteful, for each outlying office to store this entire body of data on site. Since all of the field personnel are linked through an electronic network, the firm has decided to establish an electronic library for the transmission of the aforementioned information to the field on an as-needed basis.

Their CWIS interface will provide ready access to appropriate technical data. All the end user needs to do is specify the nature of his/her particular engineering assignment. Once delivered, these CWIS files may be drawn down from the network and integrated with the documentation for the current project, saving the corporation time and money, and insuring a uniform product based upon the input ofthe firm's specialists. In this example, CWIS brings the unique expertise of the firm to bear on specific problems without concern for the geographical location of the information provider or the end user. The arrangement results in a distinct competitive advantage for the firm, both in terms of the quality and timeliness of the work as delivered and in terms of lower overhead costs for the firm.

A large commercial insurance company faces a similar IRM challenge to that of the engineering firm mentioned above. In this case, the organization maintains a wide-range of market data, rate tables, technical information, and policies and procedures. All of these resources are currently paper based, even though they are created through the mediation of automated tools. To access this data, each district office must keep its own information resource library. Ensuring that the files are current and complete is a costly and not always successful task. For that matter, the timely retrieval of information is problematic, especially in those offices without a proper records management system. CWIS is the obvious solution to this situation. By transferring all of this documentation to CWIS subdirectories and by providing user-friendly interfaces, the company has streamlined information retrieval and eliminated its single largest source of errors while significantly reducing regional and district office operating costs. The productivity of field personnel has also improved as has customer satisfaction. No doubt, the company's CWIS strategy will win additional adherents as time goes on.

In each of the three examples cited above, CWIS effectively

addressed major IRM issues for the organization. This accomplishment did not come without some effort and investment, but clearly, the benefits far outweighed the costs. The author therefore encourages his colleagues to consider a CWIS as they fashion their own IRM strategies for the future. With that in mind, he would like to conclude by considering future I/T developments that will impact the viability of CWIS as well as offer a list of critical success factors for any CWIS implementation.

FUTURE TRENDS AND CONCLUSIONS

Many organizations are now in the process of shifting their IRM paradigms. Previously, they created and established information systems along functional lines. As end-user and work group empowerment has become more of an issue, this "stove-pipe" approach to IRM has proven inadequate. In response, these organizations are investing in information architecture redesigns, relational databases that tie disparate older information systems together, and a tool-rich desk top for end user manipulation of information resources.

Many of these developments will have a dramatic impact on the evolution of "corporate-wide information systems." In the first place, all corporate information resources of any consequence will reside in an electronic format, rendering the concept of a CWIS all the more viable. Secondly, corporate information architectures will overtly connect or build linkages between these resources, making them more accessible. Thirdly, to abet these developments, organizations will invest in such information utilities as client-server-based networks, powerful relational-database tools, and versatile desk-top platforms. Fourthly, the costs associated with PC-based videoconferencing and multi-media information transmissions are plummeting. Multi-media CWIS capabilities will surely follow.

Indeed, the clear worth of CWIS as a facilitator of worker empowerment and corporate communications suggest that it will rapidly become a strategic feature of corporate I/T planning. Thus, the model offered by Babson College as a first step in CWIS evolution will in all likelihood evolve further, grow, and prosper as the corporation invests in its development. For our part, we at Babson look forward to the expansion of our initial foray into CWIS. At present, our Network Development Team is prototyping a graphical useri nterface that provides "point-and-click" access to standard office productivity tools, customer-specific IRM applications (e.g.

"Admissions," "Registration," "Alumni Management"), and a wide range of CWIS utilities. For those who would follow, the author offers these concluding recommendations:

Critical Steps in The Development of a CWIS

1. Build with what you have; exploit existing corporate data network and electronic mail capabilities.
2. Keep the I/T team small: one project manager/analyst and a programmer as need be.
3. Keep user involvement broad; involve as many information providers ("owners") as possible.
4. Get the public support and commitment of executive management.
5. Involve both information providers and end users throughout the process; brainstorm with them.
6. Select a CWIS shell that exploits the best of existing network capabilities and is extremely easy to use; supplement with an aggressive training program.
7. Select CWIS applications for implementation in order of their importance to the community. Choose first those that will give the project the biggest "return on the investment" in terms of community interest and use. You may need to work with the files to get them into a CWIS-compatible format. Make sure that the file is useful to the community before investing the effort.
8. Prototype the initial applications; release nothing to the end user until it works perfectly and only then after you have installed a "critical mass" of information resources.
9. Make certain that your information providers understand that they "own" their CWIS files and are therefore responsible for their ongoing maintenance. At the same time, remind them that they are already creating the data for hard copy distribution and that little if any additional work is required to ship it to CWIS.
10. Establish a CWIS User Group of information providers to provide a vehicle for their input and ongoing participation in the CWIS enterprise.
11. Market like crazy!! Enjoy!!
12. Maintain the CWIS environment and the information resources that feed it. This assignment encompasses such activities as data backup and disaster recovery. In general, as CWIS evolves into your organization's repository of information assets, due diligence must be exercised to ensure data integrity and long-term viability.

Like the preceding narrative, the aforementioned "critical success factors" are based upon the practical,hands-on experience of the author. There is nothing magical in these recommendations. Rather, their intent is to serve as a checklist for those information service professionals who are about to embark on the establishment of a CWIS within their own organizations. In each instance, the reader will find that his or her own institutional culture and context will necessitate the tailoring of this methodology. However, the key to success remains *listening to the customer* and building one's corporate-wide information systems on a foundation of those information services in greatest demand.Good luck!

ENDNOTES

[1] This process involved some fourteen, so-called "Excel" groups comprised of a cross-section of students, faculty, administrative staff, and members of College governance. Each group examined an aspect of College operations, such as the graduate program, the executive education, or the management of fiscal resources; benchmarked what other schools were doing; and offered suggestions as to how Babson should proceed. The research associated with the "Excel" process was developed into a strategic plan that enjoyed broad community support. It also served as a useful starting point in Babson's accreditation self-evaluation.

[2] Exhibit II was prepared by Richard Wilson, the late and deeply missed Manager of Multi-Media Production,Information Technology and Services Division, Babson College at the request of Jerome Kanter, Director of the Center for Information Management Studies, Babson College.

[3] My distinguished colleague, Jerome Kanter, Director of the Center for Information Management Studies at Babson College has reminded me that the CWIS model may take on many different forms. For example, the State of Michigan has implemented a CWIS-like system for the status of legal legislation, court decisions, amendments to state law, and so forth. The New England, one of New England's venerable insurance companies, has what they refer to as "JIT" or "Just in Time Education," where agents can access new corporate policies and procedures from their desk-top work stations. Fidelity and other fast-paced investment firms keep their financial advisors abreast of changes through a CWIS system. In each of these examples, individual and corporate performance are enhanced thanks to easy and timely access to constantly changing information via CWIS.

REFERENCES

ACRL, "The Use of Electronic Mail in Research Libraries,"*ACRL Spec Kit #149* (November/December, 1988).

Arms, Caroline, ed., *Campus Networking Strategies* (Maynard, MA: Digital Press, 1988).

Babson College, Strategic Plan, 1990-1995 (Babson Park, MA: Babson College, 1991).

Davis, Stan and Davidson,Bill, *2020 Vision* (New York: Simon & Schuster, 1991).

Emery, James C., *The Strategic Imperative* (Oxford: Oxford University Press, 1987).

Emmett, Arielle, "Carnegie-Mellon Forges Standard Look for Multivendor Network," *Computerworld 23*,4 (January, 1989): S8.

Finnegan, Gregory A., "Wiring Information to a CollegeCampus: A Port for Every Pillow," *Online 14*,2 (March, 1990):37-40.

Hawkins, Brian L., "Campus-Wide Networking at BrownUniversity," *Academic Computing 3*,5 (January, 1989A): 32-3, 36-9, 44, 46-9.

Hawkins, Brian L., (ed.), Organizing and Managing Information Resources on Campus(McKinney, TX: Academic Computing Publications, 1989B).

The Index Group, *Critical Issues of Information Systems Management for 1991* (Boston: The Index Group, 1991).

The Index Group, "Europe in 1992, Winning Through Technology, Indications (Fall 1988).

TSD, *Babson College Information Utility* Working Paper (Babson Park, MA: Babson College, 1990).

ITSD, *Strategic Plan 1991/6 & Action Plan 1991/2* (Babson Park, MA: Babson College, 1991).

Kanter, Jerry and Kesner, Richard M., "The CIO/GIO as Catalyst and Facilitator: Building the Information Utility toMeet Global Challenges," Shailendra Palvia, et al., eds., *The Global Issues of Information Technology Management* (Harrisburg, PA: Idea Group, 1991): 465-83.

Kesner, Richard M. Automation for Archivists and Records Managers (Chicago: American Library Association, 1984A), pp. 12-31,

Kesner, Richard M. Microcomputer Applications in Libraries (Westport, CT: Greenwood Press, 1984B), pp: 49-80.

Kesner, Richard M. "Integrating the Library into the Information Utility," *Library Trends* (1993, forthcoming).

Khosrowpour, Mehdi and Yaverbaum, Gayle, (eds.), *Information Technology Resources Utilization and Management: Issues and Trends* (Harrisburg, PA: Idea Group, 1990).

Laderman, Diane Aiken and Parker, Anne, "Student-Friendly Networking," *TH E Journal 17*,8 (April, 1990): 53.

Martin, James, *View data and the Information Society* (Englewood Cliffs, NJ: Prentice-Hall, 1982).

Morris,Charles R., *The Coming Global Boom* (New York: Bantam Books, 1990).

Naisbitt, John and Aburdene, Patricia, *Megatrends 2000* (New York: William Morrow, 1990).

Palvia, Shailendra, et al., eds., *The Global Issues of Information Technology Management* (Harrisburg, PA: Idea Group, 1991).

Peters,Tom, Thriving on Chaos (New York: Knopf, 1987).

Sproull, Lee and Kiesler, Sara, *Connections: New Ways of Working in the Networked World* (Cambridge, MA: The MIT Press, 1991).

Szewczak, Edward, et al., (eds.), *Management Impacts of Information Technology: Perspectives on Organizational Change and Growth* (Harrisburg, PA: Idea Group, 1991).

Targowski, Andrew, The Architecture and Planning of Enterprise-Wide Information Management Systems(Harrisburg, PA: Idea Group, 1990).

Tom, Paul L., *Managing Information as a Corporate Resource*, 2nd ed., (New York: Harper Collins, 1991).

United Nations, Advisory Committee for Coordination of Information Systems, *Management of Electronic Records: Issues and Guidelines*, (New York: United Nations, 1990).

Whitaker, Becki, "Electronic Mail in the Library: Perspective," *Library Trends 37*,3 (Winter, 1989): 357-65.

Wiseman, Charles, *Strategic Information Systems* (Homewood,IL: Irwin, 1988).

Woodsworth, Anne, *Managing Information Technology on Campus* (Chicago, American Library Association, 1991).

CHAPTER 11

SYMBIOSIS: A THEORETICAL FOUNDATION FOR THE DEVELOPMENT OF STRATEGIC INFORMATION SYSTEMS ALLIANCES

Gregory B. Turner, Mark A. Mitchell, and Ronald L. Berry
Mississippi State University

The increased utilization and recent popularity of information systems partnerships dictates the necessity of a robust and soundly constructed theoretical foundation for examining these alliances. Towards achieving this goal, this chapter proposes and develops the concept of the symbiotic information systems (SIS). Symbiotic information systems occur when two or more organizations develop a synergistic relationship(s) within their information systems function(s) in order to enhance each firm's ability to serve the demands of their ultimate consumer. Provided the needs of the ultimate consumers are fulfilled, a symbiotic information systems relationship remains a win-win proposition for the participants. The underlying factors behind the development of these relationships are explored. The potential impediments to the successful implementation of symbiotic information systems are examined as well as recommendations for resolving these difficulties.

Increased levels of environmental uncertainty, competition, and governmental regulation, coupled with shorter product life-cycles and increased consumer demand for quality and service, has prompted many organizations to form strategic business alliances or partnerships in order remain competitive in a changing marketplace. Such alliances may be defined as a mutual recognition by two or more separate business entities that the potential success of each firm depends, in large part, on the actions of other firms. As such, the actions of each firm are aimed at a coordinated effort focused on jointly satisfying the requirements of the customer to the mutual benefit of all parties involved (Anderson & Narus, 1990).

The logistics function serves as a prime candidate for the possible formation of these strategic partnerships. In fact, in an attempt to develop a distinct competitive advantage, many organizations are awakening to the benefits of a well-designed, integrated system of logistics management (Shapiro, 1984). While the effects of changes in other components of the marketing mix (i.e., product, price, promotion) may be easily duplicated by competitors, the competitive advantages available to the possessor of a well-designed, integrated logistics system are not (Heskett, 1977).

The logistics function exists to create time and place utility for a product. This utility-generation is commonly referred to as the level of customer service provided. Thus, customer service serves as a measure of the effectiveness of the logistics system (Stock & Lambert, 1987). Customers are growing increasingly demanding and unwilling to accept less than adequate levels of service. As such, the logistics function, whose main "output" is customer service, is enjoying a new prominence within the business community (Sharman, 1984).

As in the case of logistics management, many firms are awakening to the benefits resulting from a well-designed, integrated system of information management (Porter & Millar, 1985). Indeed, successful firms have begun to effectively utilize information as a weapon in their "battles" to gain a distinct competitive advantage (Hussain & Hussain, 1988). This increased focus on the strategic use of information has prompted great change in the typical firm's internal operations, as well as reshaping the relationship between the firm and its suppliers and customers (Porter & Millar, 1985).

In fact, the argument may easily be made that increases in information technology are indeed THE driving force behind the formation of a successful strategic partnership. Timely communication is the glue that holds these alliances together while serving as the basis for increased mutual inter-dependance.

An excellent example of information technology's impact upon strategic alliances is the concept of Just-In-Time (JIT) exchange relationships. JIT fosters a sense of co-destiny between the firm and its suppliers by focusing on building long-term relationships. Within a JIT framework, the firm minimizes its inventories by relying on the supplier to deliver the needed materials just-in-time for production.

Due to the potential disastrous effects of a bad JIT relationship (e.g., idle assembly lines), accurate and timely communication of production plans and schedules is imperative. Such a communication process is made possible through the utilization of well-designed and integrated information systems.

Given the increasing importance attached to effective logistics and information systems management, this chapter will synthesize the concepts of symbiotic marketing and symbiotic logistics to propose the development of symbiotic information systems. Specifically, the purpose of this chapter is to examine the development of symbiotic relationships between the information management systems of two or more organizations in an effort to realize competitive advantages not individually attainable to the participants.

First, the rationale for the development of the symbiotic information systems concept is discussed. Second, the conceptual foundations of both symbiotic marketing and symbiotic logistics are presented. Next, the symbiotic information systems concept will be proposed as a logical extension of these two evolving research streams. The nature of symbiotic information systems relationships are explored as well as the impetus for their development. Next, potential impediments to symbiotic information systems relationships, and recommendations for their resolution, are presented. Finally, the future trends of these relationships are explored.

Background And Justification For The Symbiotic Information Systems Concept

The concept of forming strategic information systems partnerships is by no means a revolutionary idea. Various debates on this topic have occurred in the past, usually in the form of discussions concerning the benefits of interorganizational information systems (IOS). Cash and Konsynski (1985) define an IOS as "automated information systems shared by two or more companies" (p. 134). An IOS allows information to cross organizational boundaries which facilitates the sharing of stored data and application programs by the participants (Johnston & Vitale, 1988).

The common thread within most discussions of IOS is a micro view of the strategic alliance relationship. In other words, discussions tend to highlight the competitive benefits of IS cost, scale, and risk sharing while merely alluding to the potential organization-wide benefits. By viewing information systems as only one part of the logistics mix, the symbiotic information systems (SIS) concept offers a macro framework in which to examine these IS partnerships. Within this framework, success is measured not only in terms of cost savings and scale benefits, but also by the ability to satisfy the ultimate consumer.

THEORETICAL FOUNDATIONS OF THE SYMBIOTIC INFORMATION SYSTEMS CONCEPT

Importance of Building Relationships

Historically, relationships between buyers and sellers have been viewed as "transaction marketing," whereby each transaction among the participants is considered to be an isolated event. However, transaction marketing is part of a larger idea, namely relationship marketing. Relationship marketers attempt to establish "win-win" relationships with customers, distributors, dealers, and suppliers.

By strengthening the economic, technical, and social ties between two or more organizations, the parties involved become more trusting, knowledgeable, and interested in assisting one another (Kotler, 1991). Given the complexity of the current business environment, the need to cultivate relationships with trading partners is of utmost importance. Symbiotic marketing provides the foundation from which the concepts of symbiotic logistics and, ultimately, symbiotic information systems evolve.

Symbiotic Marketing

The term symbiosis, when applied to contemporary business, refers to a working relationship between two seemingly dissimilar organizations such that the parties benefit equally from their interaction. It has been nearly twenty-five years since the original discussion of symbiotic marketing appeared in the marketing literature (Adler, 1966). As defined by Adler (1966), symbiotic marketing is "the alliance of resources or programs between two independent organizations, designed to improve the marketing potential of each" (p. 60). In essence, the whole becomes greater than the sum of the parts.

At the time of Adler's writing, areas cited for possible symbiotic relationships included (a) sales organizations, (b) physical distribution facilities, (c) entry into a market, (d) technical know-how and research and development staffs, (e) marketing expertise and knowledge of complex markets, (f) finances, (g) equipment, (h) purchasing power, and (i) marketing research programs. Adler (1966) accurately predicted that symbiotic marketing would assume an important position as a means of developing a distinct competitive advantage in the marketplace.

Varadarajan and Rajaratnam (1986) provide an update on symbiotic marketing's diffusion as a viable competitive strategy. In addition to presenting recent examples of this phenomenon, the researchers provide an outline of the nature and scope of symbiotic marketing, as well as an overview of the environmental and organizational factors which have contributed to its wide-spread acceptance. Indeed, Adler's prediction of an increasing presence of symbiotic marketing relationships is confirmed.

An example is in order here. Pinnacle Publishing has succeeded in the publishing industry by building symbiotic relationships with software firms. The company publishes independent publications featuring the computer software of its strategic partners. The win-win relationship provides the software firm with the market acceptance that flows from an independent publication while Pinnacle obtains potential new customers from the software registration lists ("Symbiotic Software," 1990).

Symbiotic Logistics

The logistics system can be viewed as the customer service component of the firm's marketing mix. The firm desires to provide (a) the maximum level of customer service for a given cost or (b) the desired level of customer service for the lowest possible cost. Components of the logistics system include (a) procurement, (b) transportation, (c) warehousing, (d) inventory, (e) order processing and information systems, (f) salvage and scrap disposal, (g) return goods handling, and (h) parts and service support.

The cornerstone of a system of integrated logistics management is total cost analysis, whereby the firm seeks to minimize the total cost of the logistics mix while providing the desired level of customer service (Stock & Lambert, 1987). Management must make cost trade-off decisions within the components of its logistics mix in order to provide the desired level of customer service within the prescribed cost/price range.

Toward achieving greater efficiency within the logistics function, many organizations are forging strategic alliances with other firms in an attempt to realize benefits not available to the parties individually (Bowersox, 1989). Symbiotic logistics systems, then, can be defined as "an alliance of two or more independent marketing entities designed to provide the desired level of customer service in accordance with the total cost concept of integrated logistics management" (Mitchell, LeMay, & Arnold, 1991, p. 1). In this context, logistics is viewed as a means of developing a competitive advantage rather than merely a cost center to be controlled.

Symbiotic Information Systems

Driven by the desire to better manage and utilize information for strategic business purposes, many organizations are attempting to integrate their IS with those of other organizations to realize competitive advantages not individually attainable. It is suggested here that these symbiotic relationships are merely an example of the integration of the order processing and information systems component of the logistics mix.

Symbiotic information systems are defined here as the relationship formed through the strategic alliance of two or more independent business entities designed to gain competitive advantages through some level of combined information systems management. A quick example should clarify the concept.

Suppose a large manufacturer elects to expand its information systems capabilities. The firm purposely selects a system with a larger-than-needed capacity which will accommodate its expected growth. However, the increased capacity will yield short-term operating inefficiencies. In an effort to increase its operating efficiency, the firm solicits processing arrangements with smaller local manufacturers. Such relationships provide a win-win situation for the participants. The larger manufacturer better utilizes the capacity of its system while the smaller manufacturer(s) lessen their dependence upon their own primary processing capacity.

Nature Of The SIS Relationship

In the purest sense, SIS relationships are market-driven. That is, one product or service provider (primary party) has formulated a competitive strategy designed to best fulfill the demands of its target market. As such, the satisfaction of the ultimate consumer provides for the continuation of the symbiotic relationship. Provided the parties continue to satisfy the needs of their ultimate consumer(s), it is desirable to maintain the symbiotic relationship.

As mentioned earlier, the increased interdependence between firms involved in business transactions has focused more attention on the establishment and maintenance of long-term relationships. This is clearly evidenced in the formation of SIS relationships. For example, the firm that elects to have portions of its IS needs met by outside sources must be confident of that source's capabilities. The firm is in essence depending on the source's ability to control quality and its ability to maintain reliability ("Symbiotic Software", 1990).

Antecedent Conditions For The Development Of SIS

Implicit in our definition of SIS is the development of synergistic relationships between two or more dissimilar organizations with compatible strategic objectives. In this context, we view the exchange between the parties as a process rather than a discrete event. This perspective permits the examination of those antecedent events which motivated the parties to transact (Dwyer et al., 1987). Accordingly, some of the environmental forces which have contributed to the diffusion of SIS relationships are discussed below.

Competitive. As noted earlier, SIS relationships are market-driven. Today's manager faces a myriad of competitive pressures, such as contracting product life cycles, expanding product lines, changing patterns of distribution, emerging technologies, and the globalization of markets (Sharman, 1984). The competitive demands of the marketplace are forcing many managers to review their existing information systems in an attempt to gain operating leverage.

Consider the case of United Services Automobile Association (USAA), a financial services firm. The company operates the largest mail order business in the United States as well as the largest automatic call distribution telephone system in the world. Each day the company receives over 100,000 letters and mails over 250,000 items. In order to stay abreast of the massive amounts of paper and to gain an edge on the competition, USAA initiated an alliance with IBM for the joint development of an imaging system. Before the system was developed, 39,000 square feet of office space was required to store active files while 80,000 boxes held inactive files. After introduction of the system, the same information requires only 100 square feet of office space (Lasher et al., 1991). The system has increased USAA's ability to respond to customers in a timely manner.

Technological. The pace of technological change, along with the resultant changes in the costs of computing, has been rapid over the past thirty years. This increased pace of change provides incentive for those firms considering a symbiotic relationship. For example, the interest in developing uniform guidelines and standards for data storage has made it easier for firms to exchange information, and, consequently, to participate in strategic partnerships (Cash & Konsynski, 1985).

Consider the case of General Motors. The company requires all of its primary suppliers to adhere to the standards and protocols recommended by the Automotive Industry Action Group (Cash & Konsynski, 1985). By conforming to the standards, the suppliers solidify their position and GM receives quick, accurate information concerning supplies.

Economic. The concepts of risk and return are central to most business decisions. The economic uncertainty of the past decade has motivated many firms to seek synergistic relationships with both suppliers and competitors in an attempt to pool their risk. By combining activities with other organizations, the individual firm lowers the level of risk to which it is exposed. Additionally, the return realized by the firm from in-house operations may be insufficient to warrant their continuance. The scale economies may prompt the organization to redeploy assets to more profitable ventures (Varadarajan & Rajaratnam 1986).

Potential Impediments and Suggested Solutions

It would indeed be naive to assume that strategic alliances occur effortlessly without causing friction within and between participating organizations. Since people are naturally resistant to change, conflicts in culture and style are to be expected when groups from different organizations attempt to achieve a common goal (Bowersox, 1990). Some of the impediments to the successful development of a SIS include issues of (a) trust, (b) control, and (c) culture. Each of these issues are more fully explored in the following section along with suggestions for resolving the conflicts.

Issues of Trust. Ironically, the highly competitive mind-set of American business is one potential SIS stumbling block. The irony lies in the fact that a key impetus for SIS relationships is to gain competitive advantages. However, a certain level of trust must be present before these long-term relationships can succeed. The trust issue is a stumbling block for most managers who have been "schooled in an adversarial tradition" (Bowersox, 1990, p. 44). For these managers the idea of sharing ideas and information with those outside the boundaries of the organization is instinctively wrong.

Trust may also constitute a stumbling block when a disproportionate share of the risk or commitment is carried by one of the participants. Within this context, it is only natural for the firm with higher levels of exposure to be concerned with the level of commitment by the other participants given their relatively lower level of risk.

Solving the Trust Issue. In order to foster a trustful mind-set among adversarially-schooled managers, training is needed which stresses the benefits of forming long-term alliances. If this is not sufficient, then a mediator or facilitator may be utilized during the developmental stages of the alliance. The facilitator should be acceptable to all parties involved and connected to none of them

(Bowersox, 1990).

Trust may be a by-product of the relationship. That is, as the length of the association grows, the level of trust between the participants will naturally increase (Lasher, Ives, & Jarvenpaa, 1991). However, the key is to develop the needed levels of trust in the formation stage of the relationship. The easiest way to achieve this goal is to seek potential partners based upon compatibility (Henderson, 1990). That is, each participant must possess some unique attribute which allows for synergistic benefits. This will ensure that each partner is equally committed to the success of the relationship.

Issues of Control. Another potential stumbling block is the degree of control each participant has in key management decisions (Cash & Konsynski, 1985). The very nature of an alliance is the shared decision making process. By definition, shared decision making necessitates the loss of some degree of control over the decision making process for all participants. This may be a hard pill to swallow for those used to the lone decision maker role. The sense of co-destiny fostered by these relationships contradicts with the "natural law" of having complete control over the destiny of the firm.

Additionally, conflicts over accountability and responsibility may arise from the control issue. Persons previously responsible for overseeing the completion of a particular task may be reluctant to see that responsibility shifted to others. Also, friction may develop over procedures and methods of operation (Konsynski & McFarlan, 1990). For example, the attitude of 'that's not how we do it around here' may arise.

Solving the Control Issue. Clear, precise, and comprehensive operating procedures are imperative to alleviate any ambiguities. These guidelines should explicitly outline what tasks are expected of each partner and how to accomplish them. The necessary actions to take when things go wrong should also be included in these procedures (Bowersox, 1990).

Additionally, the key roles within the partnership should be identified early in the process. The persons appointed to these roles should also be given the appropriate decision making authority. To avoid potential conflicts within the partnership, this authority should be legitimized by all of the firms in the alliance (Henderson, 1990).

Issues of Culture. Each firm possesses a unique set of values and beliefs referred to as its organizational culture. According to Daft (1989), an organization's culture helps provide organizational participants with a clear understanding of how to act and think. It also gives direction to participants and helps build commitment to something larger than the individual.

Given that each firm has its own individual culture, clashes between the guiding principles and norms of the participant firms is a potential impediment to the successful SIS implementation. A distinct culture, composed of parts of the character of the firms involved, will have to evolve. During this culture formation stage, the potential for conflict will be high.

Solving the Culture Issue. It should not be assumed that organizational culture is just another organizational subsystem or variable that can be molded easily or changed quickly. Cultural beliefs, values and norms of behavior are enacted by individuals throughout the organization, not simply by managers. These outlooks may be widely shared, or may vary across groups or subcultures within the organization. Although managers can tap into shared symbols and daily rituals to increase their understanding and promote commitment to the organizational mission and strategy, they cannot impose their preferred interpretations on all organization members.

Given the difficulty involved in managing cultural change, the easiest resolution to potential cultural impediments is to seek out partners with similar cultural norms. One key to the success of the USAA and IBM imaging project partnership was their similar cultures. "Both were strongly committed to customer service, respect for individual employees, and continued pursuit of excellence" (Lasher et al., 1991, p. 556). However, if differences do exist, then operating procedures must incorporate the values of all participants.

FUTURE TRENDS

Given the impetus for the development of SIS discussed earlier, we anticipate the use of SIS to increase in the future. As the globalization of markets increase and the boundaries between organizations continue to blur, the "one corporation" concept comes closer to being reality. The following quote from Digital Equipment Corporation's Metaframe Group policy statement aptly describes this phenomenon.

> We look forward to the evolution of the business world to the "one corporation" concept, in which the information flow between departments of two different companies is as easy as that between equivalent departments in the same company. This interaction would make clear that the primary long-term added value of a company is the processes which it has; if those processes are not clearly superior to those available externally, then the company should seriously consider using the external

processes instead of its internal ones (Jenster, Bidault, & Cummings, 1992, p. 144).

Symbiotic information systems truly reflect the emergence to the "one corporation" concept. As companies continue to share information concerning products, markets and customers, productivity will increase as tasks are solely performed by the most efficient source. As global partnerships emerge and national as well as organizational boundaries blur, we may one day approach the "one world corporation".

SUMMARY AND CONCLUSIONS

The driving force behind the symbiotic information systems relationship is the ultimate consumer. A product or service provider (primary party) develops a synergistic relationship with other organization(s) to enhance its ability to service the demands of the consumer. Similarly, those outside organizations are motivated to participate in the SIS relationship to improve the performance of their own information systems. Provided the needs of ultimate consumers are fulfilled, the SIS relationship remains a dual-win proposition for the participants.

Roadblocks to the successful implementation of these relationships do exist. However, the potential rewards may well be worth the time and effort required to solve these impediments. The proverb "the early bird gets the worm" could not be more appropriate. The early entrants into these alliances may find themselves as the new leaders in a world economy. Conversely, those obstinate firms that wait too long to explore the benefits of SIS relationships may find themselves locked out of potentially profitable markets as the alliance of other firms create unsurmountable entry barriers.

Approximately twenty-five years have passed since Lee Adler correctly predicted that symbiotic marketing would increase in prominence within the coming years. Consistent with this statement, we expect symbiotic information systems to play an increasing role in the activities of today's operators as they seek to develop a distinct advantage within an increasingly competitive marketplace.

REFERENCES

Adler, L. (1966). Symbiotic marketing. *Harvard Business Review, 44*(6), 59-71.

Anderson, J. C., & Narus, J. A. (1990). A model of distributor firm and manufacturer firm working partnerships. *Journal of Marketing, 54*, 42-58.

Bowersox, D. J. (1989, February). Strategic alliances: a new opportunity. *Distribution Center, Inc.*, pp. 1-4.

Bowersox, D. J. (1990). The strategic benefits of logistics alliances. *Harvard Business Review, 68*(4), 36-45.

Cash, J. I., Jr., & Konsynski, B. R. (1985). IS redraws competitive boundaries. *Harvard Business Review, 63*(2), 134-142.

Daft, R. L. (1989). *Organization theory and design.* St. Paul, MN: West Publishing.

Dwyer, F. R., Schurr, P. H., & Oh, O. (1987). Developing buyer-seller relationships. *Journal of Marketing, 51*, 11-27.

Henderson, J. C. (1990). Plugging into strategic partnerships: The critical IS connection. *Sloan Management Review, 31*(3), 7-18.

Heskett, J. L. (1977). Logistics - essential to strategy. *Harvard Business Review, 55*(6), 85-96.

Hussain, D., & Hussain K. M. (1988). *Managing computer resources.* Homewood, IL: Irwin.

Jenster, P., Bidault, F., & Cummings, T. (1992). Digital equipment corporation international: Competing through cooperation. In R. D. Buzzell, J. A. Quelch, & C. Bartlett (Eds.), *Global Marketing Management* (pp. 132-157). Reading, MA: Addison-Wesley.

Johnston, H. R., & Vitale, M. R. (1988). Creating competitive advantage with interorganizational information systems. *MIS Quarterly, 12*(2), 153-165.

Konsynski, B. R., & McFarlan, F. W. (1990). Information Partnerships - shared data, shared scale. *Harvard Business Review, 68*(5), 114-120.

Kotler, P. (1991). *Marketing management: Analysis, planning, implementation, and control* (7th ed.). Englewood Cliffs, NJ: Prentice-Hall.

Lasher, D. R., Ives, B., & Jarvenpaa, S. L. (1991). USAA-IBM partnerships in information technology: Managing the image project. *MIS Quarterly, 15*(4), 551-565.

Mitchell, M. A., LeMay, S., & Arnold D. (1991). Logistics, symbiosis, and Europe 1992. *Proceedings of Academy of International Business* - Northeast, Bermuda.

Outsourcing: who pulls the strings. (1990, September 15). *Datamation*, pp. 103-106.

Porter, M. E., & Millar V. E. (1985). How information gives you competitive advantage. *Harvard Business Review, 63*(4), 149-160.

Shapiro, R. D. (1984). Get leverage from logistics. *Harvard Business Review, 62*(3), 119-126.

Sharman, G. (1984). The rediscovery of logistics. *Harvard Business Review, 62*(5), 71-79.

Stock, J. R., & Lambert D. M. (1987). *Strategic logistics management* (2nd ed.). Homewood, IL: Richard D. Irwin.

Symbiotic Software. (1990, October 29). Forbes, p. 136. Varadarajan, P., & Rajaratnam D. (1986). Symbiotic marketing revisited. *Journal of Marketing, 50* , 7-17.

CHAPTER 12

MANAGING INFORMATION TECHNOLOGY: AN INTEGRATIVE INFORMATION TECHNOLOGY ACQUISITION/DIFFUSION CONTINGENCY MODEL

Mathew J. Klempa
California State University, Dominguez Hills

This chapter presents a contingency model which causally relates information technology acquisition and diffusion (IT/AD) to the interaction of three primary driving forces: organization culture, organization learning, and knowledge sharing. These three literatures of the model are well-grounded in prior streams of research encompassing the disciplines of communication, sociology, diffusion of innovation theory, causal agency theory, organization development and organization intervention theories, control theory, systems theory, and strategic planning and information resource management theories.

The contingency model is further delineated by an eight sector taxonomy. The taxonomy utilizes ten specific measurement categories, well grounded in prior research. These measurement categories are of interest to both practitioner and academic. For the practitioner they enable application of the model as a managerial tool, both for normative planning purposes, as well as diagnostic assessments, both external and internal to the firm. As such, the taxonomy can be used for IT/AD planning and control, as well as suggesting organizational intervention strategies. For the academic, they serve as a guideline for future research endeavors.

The model is additionally explicated by consideration of moderating variables, impacting the three heuristically interactive IT/AD driving forces. Consideration of moderating variables suggests IT/AD patterns. Future venues of research utilizing cross-sectional and longitudinal research modalities, as well as simulation, is proposed.

> There is nothing more difficult to plan, more doubtful of success, nor more dangerous to manage than the creation of a new order of things....
> **Niccolo Machiavelli**
> ***The Prince* (1513)**

Since Leavitt and Whisler's (1958) "Management in the 1980s", much conceptualization has dealt with management of information technology (IT) and its impacts on organizations, e.g., Drucker's (1988) synchrony, Applegate, Cash and Mills'(1988) cluster organization, Huber's (1984) post-industrial organization, Huber's (1991) semi-permanent symbiosis, Peters and Waterman's (1982)[1] permeable membrane, Toffler's (1980) adhocracy, and Naisbitt's (1982) collapsed pyramid. IT, as used by Leavitt and Whisler, included abilities to process large amounts of information rapidly (high speed computer), application of statistical and mathematical methods, and simulation. Today, management of a much expanded family of information technologies is an infinitely more complex task, as evidenced by:

- the increasing panoply of information technologies (IT), e.g., office automation (E-mail, voice mail, FAX, word processing), image processing, teleconferencing, telecommunications, CAD/CAM, fourth generation languages, artificial intelligence technologies, and multimedia technology (text, numbers, voice, image, and full motion video).
- substantive improvements in IT price/performance (Raho, Belohlav, and Fiedler, 1987). Examples include IT industry cost performance improvements of 30-40% compounded annually (Benjamin and Morton, 1988), as well as improvement in the power/cost ratio of technology by up to as much as a factor of 10 (Emery, 1991).
- an increasing rate of adoption of new technologies. Research from Frand and Britt (1991), Boynton and Zmud (1987), Dixon and John (1989), and Raho, Belohlav, and Fiedler (1987) indicates increasingly rapid rates of adoption for new information technologies, as evidenced by compressed S-curves.
- levels of investment in IT. Appendix A summarizes prior research findings concerning levels of investment[2,3] in IT. Surveys underes-

timate firm-wide investment in IT, since decentralization of IT often embeds IT expenditures within functional departments' operating budgets (Weill and Olson, 1989).

- the focus on management of creativity, synergy, and leverage. Porter's (1985) value chain analysis, Wiseman's strategic thrust (1985), and the research of Dixon and John (1989), Raho, Belohlav, and Fiedler (1987), Johnston and Vitale (1988), Bergeron, Buteau, and Raymond (1991) focus on the importance of managing investment in IT so as to create comparative efficiency, effectiveness, and bargaining power for the firm. High conversion effectiveness is associated with creativity, synergy, and leveraging in the management of IT.

Prior theorists provide two divergent causal linkages between technology and the organization, which explain information technology acquisition/diffusion[4] (IT/AD). In the first perspective, technology pushes the organization, e.g., the price of technology pushes investment in IT/AD. By contrast, in the second perspective, organization drives technology, i.e., the demand for technology from organization forces pulls IT/AD.

Prior research findings based on these divergent perspectives is both inconclusive, as well as generally unable to resolve inconsistent findings. Both practitioners such as Dixon and John (1989), as well as the academicians included in Table 1, call for proposed research which examines IT/AD as both an antecedent and consequence of organizational action.

This chapter unfolds a conceptual IT/AD contingency model and its particulars which employs such a research perspective. The objectives of this chapter are to:

- provide a critical appraisal of the role of organization culture, organization learning, and knowledge sharing as primary causal mechanisms driving IT/AD
- synthesize two primary previous research streams, the rational and the political, so as to establish these as research foundations for the integrative IT/AD contingency model
- explicate and ground in prior research five categories of rational measures and five categories of political measures which serve as a basis for operationalizing the contingency model

These three objectives are of interest to both the academician as well as the practitioner. Other objectives, of particular interest to the academician, include to:

Author(s)	Quotation
Dixon & John, 1989	"There is a need to integrate ... existing and evolving technologies into a... vision of their combined macrofinancial, competitive, organizational structure, and power impacts" (p. 250).
	"The partnership ... will require ... that both sides ... carefully plan - the political and organizational consequences ... of technology ... to understand and communicate the gestalt impact of many interacting technologies and their synergisms ..." (p. 253).
Boynton & Zmud, 1987	Robust views of organizational IT contexts and management planning approaches, based upon a variety of theoretical perspectives ... are required. Thus, research that examines the planning agenda and behaviors from strong theoretical perspectives is advocated." (p. 69).
	"Organizational Learning Analysis ... the capabilities of subunits to accept, use and institutionalize the technology must be assessed" (p. 63).
	"Planning must consider the organization's current culture and anticipate how this culture may impact or be used the affect information technology efforts" (p. 63)
Mohrman & Lawler, 1984	"... we need more theoretical underpinnings to help us generalize beyond our atomistic knowledge of IT impacts in unrelated situations ... these models need to address the themes running through most past research studies ..." (p.139).
Mason, 1984	"Social implications ... of IT ... require interdisciplinary research ... and a holistic perspective" (p. 186 - 187).
Orlikowsky & Robey, 1991	"Information technology ... is the social product of human action... and ...simultaneously ... rules and resources ... in mediating human action" (p.151).
Orlikowsky & Baroudi, 1991	"We examine two other research philosophies, the interpretive and the critical... the interpretive emphasizes the importance of subjective meanings and social-political as well as symbolic action ... the critical [philosophy] is concerned with critiquing existing social systems and revealing any contradictions and conflicts that may inhere within their structures. (p. 13,19).

Table 1: Proposed Research Characteristics

- focus research attention on these five rational and five political measurement categories, so as to encourage development of robust taxonomies for these ten measurement categories
- identify operational measures/measurement issues utilized in previous research
- identify future primary research foci, including
    - types of proposed research
    - levels of proposed research analysis
    - specification of moderating variables to be included in future research
    - suggestions for application of models from other research disciplines

BACKGROUND

Initial Explication of the Model's Research Foundations

The research of Gresov (1984), DeLisi (1990), Dixon and John (1989), Rogers (1983), Fiol and Lyles (1985), Weick (1984), Argyris and Schoen (1978, 1982), Galbraith (1973, 1974, 1977), Huber (1984, 1990, 1991), Saffold (1988), and Walsh and Ungson (1991) suggests three primary driving forces of IT/AD, interacting dynamically across time. Through such interaction creativity, synergy, and leveraging effects of IT will either be intensified or diminished. Each of the three is summarized below.

Organization Culture[5]

Organization Culture Construct. Development of the epistemology of organization culture is an on-going process, as reflected in the following research examples: culture is the pattern of basic assumptions, values, beliefs, and symbols invented, discovered, or developed (DeLisi, 1990), (Barney, 1986); culture simultaneously determines and reflects values, beliefs, and attitudes, i.e., the shaper of human interaction and the outcome of it (Kerr and Slocum, 1987), (Jelinek, Smircich, & Hirsch, 1983); culture is learned, shared, and transmitted (Duncan, 1989); culture is holistic, socially constructed, soft, and changeable[6,7] (Hofstede, Neuijen, Ohayv, and Sanders, 1990).

Primacy of Organization Culture. Several theorists' research attests to the primacy of organization culture, i.e., cultures are real and should be dealt with in a serious manner (Appendix B). Prior research also identifies risk seeking versus risk averse organization cultures[8], e.g., Ein-dor and Segev (1982), Gresov (1984), DeLisi

(1990), Dixon and John (1989), Damanpour (1991), Leifer (1988), Gordon (1991), Kerr and Slocum (1987), Shaw, Fisher, and Randolph (1991), Levsen and Fry (1987), Child (1987), Douglas and Wildavsky (1982), Cox and Blake (1991), and Sitkin and Pablo (1992). Organization cultures that foster a risk seeking propensity are seen as maximizing creativity, synergy, and leverage. Sitkin and Pablo (1992) cite 3M's (Minnesota Mining and Manufacturing) emphasis on continually trying out innovative and risky ideas as a core tenet of the firm's culture values. In contrast, risk averse organization cultures are associated with minimal creativity, synergy, and leverage. Both Sitkin and Pablo (1992) and Dean and Snell (1991) identify organization inertia as a major force in determining the degree to which an organization is risk seeking or risk averse.

For purposes of conceptual simplification, the contingency model presented in this chapter treats organization culture at the level of the firm. The contingency model classifies organizations on a mutually exclusive dichotomy, heterogeneous versus homogeneous[9]. Heterogenous organizations are risk seeking; homogeneous organizations are risk averse. Table 2 summarizes organization culture characteristics associated with the heterogenous versus homogeneous organization culture dichotomy.

Organization Learning

Weick (1984), Daft and Weick (1984), Schein (1984), Fiol and Lyles (1985), Argyris (1976), Argyris and Schoen (1978), and Walsh and Ungson (1991) have researched organization learning. Fiol and Lyles[10] (1985) identify four contextual factors that affect organization learning: organization culture, the organization's strategic posture, organization structure, and the organization's internal as well as external environments[11]. Thus, organization learning results from a creative and recursive dynamic, arising from new insights, new knowledge, and new structures. Who learns what and in what order is important. For example, Gurbaxani and Mendelson (1990) researched IT/AD, examining both price and learning effects. They found learning effects to dominate IT/AD processes in the earlier stages of IT/AD. Organization characteristics and processes, such as mentoring, gatekeepers, control processes, feedback characteristics, and dyadic linkages impact organization learning.

Argyris (1976) and Argyris and Schoen (1978, 1982) provide the concept of single loop versus double loop learning, i.e., organization learning with respect to the detection and correction of error. Specifically, the detection of error produces learning. A double loop organization learning modality consciously seeks out inner contra-

Researcher(s)	Heterogeneous	Homogeneous
Main & Short, 1989; Dixon and John, 1989; Boynton & Zmud, 1987	Risk seeking	Risk averse
Huber, 1990	Holistic view: internal and external	Segmented view
	Cognitive characteristic:	*Cognitive characteristic:*
Neumann & Neumann, 1992	Innovative (Kirton A/I)	Adaptive (Kirton A/I)
Klempa, 1983	Intuition Feeling (Myers-Briggs)	Sensing Thinking (Myers Briggs)
Rowe & Mason, 1987	Intuition Feeling (Myers-Briggs)	Sensing Thinking (Myers-Briggs)
Huber, 1990	Multidirectional information flows	Vertical information flows
Ives & Mason, 1990; Boynton & Zmud, 1987	Assumptions surfacing and testing	No assumptions surfacing and testing
Dixon & John, 1989	Synergy: internal and external	Synergy: internal
Dixon & John, 1989	Effectiveness	Efficiency
Bergeron, Buteau, & Raymond, 1991; Johnston & Vitale,1988	Leveraging ideas/products/processes	Minimal leveraging
Rogers, 1983	Heterophilious (dissimilar units)	Homophilious (similar units)
Dixon & John, 1989	Gestalt impact of technology	Economic impact of technology
Damanpour, 1991	Product (new) flows	Process focus
Dixon & John, 1989	High tolerance for ambiguity	Low tolerance for ambiguity
Johnston & Carrico, 1988 Damanpour, 1 991;Huber, 1990; Dean & Snell, 1991; Stevenson & Gilly, 1991	Shared data/information	Parochial husbanding of data/information

Table 2: Organization Culture Dichotomy: Previous Research - Organization Characteristics Associated With Creativity, Synergy, and Leverage

Researcher(s)	Heterogeneous	Homogeneous
Hannan & Freeman,1977; Kelly & Amburgey, 1991; Dean & Snell, 1991	Low organization inertia	High organization inertia
Child, 1987	High information codification	Low information codification
Dean & Snell, 1991	Cross functional problem solving	Localized problem solving
Dixon & John, 1989	Reward mechanism: accomplishment	Rewards mechanism: authority
Dixon & John, 1989	Coordination: mutual adjustment	Coordination mechanism: standardization
Dixon & John, 1989; Raho, Belohlav, & Fiedler, 1987	Control system: behavior based, flexible partnerships	Control system: outcome based, formal rules
DeLisi, 1990	Flexible mentoring/gatekeeper team-oriented	Rigid mentoring/gatekeeper linkages, individual-oriented
Dean & Snell, 1991	Interrelated goals (compatible)	Disparate goals (opposing)
Dixon & John, 1989	Manage through knowledge and influence	Manage through formal power
Dixon & John, 1989	Utilize "soft" skills, e.g.,listening	Utilize "hard" skills
Damanpour, 1991	Decentralization: authority, responsibility, locus of decision making	Centralization: authority, responsibility, locus of decision making
Weill & Olson, 1989	Conversion Effectiveness: High	Conversion Effectiveness: Low

Table 2: Organization Culture Dichotomy: Previous Research - Organization Characteristics Associated With Creativity, Synergy, and Leverage (Contd.)

dictions, i.e., presence of error, in order to resolve them. Contradictory assumptions are purposefully formulated in order to frame a challenge (dialectic). Double loop learning results in changing the underlying governing variables, policies, and assumptions of either the individual or the organization. Double loop learning is linked to organization characteristics such as flexibility, insightfulness, heuristic control mechanisms, dynamic agenda setting, and proactive organization actions. The contingency model presented in this chapter classifies organizations employing double loop learning as innovative.

In contrast, single loop learning ignores such inner contradictions. Thus, organizations exhibiting single loop learning exhibit minimal change, if any, in their underlying governing values, variables, policies, or assumptions. Single loop organization learning is associated with characteristics such as rules, routine, repetition, and reactive organization actions. The contingency model classifies organizations whose organization learning is single loop as adaptive. Table 3 summarizes the organization learning innovative/adaptive dichotomy.

Knowledge Sharing. This dimension of the model considers information processing, i.e., knowledge sharing [12] within the organization (Daft and Weick , 1984; Daft and Lengel, 1986; Huber, 1982, 1984, 1990, 1991; Yates, 1990; and Walsh and Ungson, 1991). Organizations both process information from the environment, in addition to serving as interpretive mechanisms (Walsh and Ungson, 1991). As delineated by Drucker (1988) and Huber (1982, 1984, 1990, 1991), knowledge sharing is achieved via a diverse set of knowledge specialists. Knowledge sharing can be both internal as well as external to the organization, i.e., tacit knowledge (Huber, 1991). Such knowledge specialization leads to increased interdependencies, e.g., knowledge inflows and knowledge outflows among subsidiaries in a multinational corporation (Gupta and Govindarajan, 1991).

Knowledge sharing includes, but is not limited to Huber's (1984) C^2, computing and communication technologies. At a threshold level, organization knowledge sharing will be impacted by choices pertaining to C^2, i.e., the technologies involved. However, knowledge sharing[13] is a gestalt concept, i.e., knowledge sharing is viewed as flows through a social network, the strength and characteristics of individuals' ties affecting the transmission (Stevenson and Gilly, 1991), Rockart and Short (1989). Thus, knowledge sharing is also impacted by modalities and characteristics of mentors, gatekeepers, control processes, feedback characteristics and dyadic linkages.

Further, knowledge sharing can focus on the organization's

Innovative	Adaptive
Double loop	Single loop
New products, structure, processes	Modified products, structure, processes
Effectiveness	Efficiency
Gatekeepers influence incentives, adoption	Gatekeepers monitor incentives, adoption
Strategic assumptions surfacing and testing	Does not use strategic assumptions surfacing and testing
Dynamic/creative interpersonal, group, intergroup dynamics	Defensive interpersonal, group, intergroup dynamics
Use of empowerment	No use of empowerment
Early adoptors of IT	Late adoptors of IT
Rewards: longer term based, creativity	Rewards: shorter term based, incrementalism
Recursive adaptations of IT	Non-recursive adaptations of IT
Mentors: proactive	Mentors: maintenance
Control: Behavior, dynamic	Control: Outcome, rigid
Feedback: Second order, third order	Feedback: First order
Dyadic linkages: Short, few non-cadre	Dyadic linkages: Long, many non-cadre

Table 3: Organization Learning Dichotomy

processes or the organization's form. Toffler's (1980) adhocracy illustrates the former; Huber's networked form of organization illustrates the latter. In this chapter, the contingency model networked classification includes both process knowledge sharing, as well as organization knowledge sharing. The contingency model utilizes a networked/hierarchical knowledge sharing dichotomy, with characteristics as shown in Table 4.

Hierarchical knowledge sharing is typified by the vertical, pyramid organization[14]. Networked knowledge sharing is typified by Drucker's (1988) synchrony, Applegate, Cash and Mills'(1988) cluster organization, Huber's (1984) post-industrial organization, Huber's (1991) semi-permanent symbiosis, Peters and Waterman's (1982) permeable membrane, Toffler's (1980) adhocracy, and Naisbitt's (1982) collapsed pyramid.

Further Explication of the Contingency Model's Research Foundations

This chapter dichotomizes prior IT/AD research into two perspectives, a rational and a political. From the rational perspective,

Networked	Hierarchical
Multidirectional information flows	Vertical information flows
Many communication technologies	Few communication technologies
Behaviorally-based decision-aiding technologies	Rationally-based decision-aiding technologies
Dynamic locus of decision making	Well defined locus of decision making
Specialization coupled with increased interorganizational dependencies	Minimal interorganizational dependencies
Multiple co-ordination mechanisms	Singular co-ordination mechanisms
High media richness	Low media richness
Message equivocality	Message unequivocality
Strategic-oriented technologies	Transaction-oriented technologies
Decreasing knowledge costs	Non-decreasing knowledge costs
Gamma change	Alpha change
Extensive and mediating technologies	Long-linked technologies
Synergy: internal and external	Synergy: internal

Table 4: Knowledge Sharing Dichotomy

technology serves as an exogenous force which drives the organization. In contrast, from the political perspective, organization drives technology. Each of these research perspectives is discussed below.

The Rational Perspective. Markus and Robey (1988) identify a technological imperative, with technology seen as an exogenous force, determining the behavior of individuals and organizations. Since action is viewed as the result of external demands, rational and analytical techniques are applied in order to better understand such externalities, e.g., BSP, Zachman (1982); SAST, Mason and Mitroff (1981); strategic thrust, Wiseman (1985); CSFs, Bullen and Rockart (1981), and value chain Porter and Millar (1985). Research associated with these techniques includes: BSP - Whetherbe (1991), Lederer and Sethi (1988); SAST -Henderson and Sifonis (1988), Ives and Mason (1990); strategic thrust - Davamanirajan, Kriebel, and Mukhopadhyay (1991), Dos Santos and Pfeffers (1991), and Bergeron, Buteau, and Raymond (1991); CSFs -Whetherbe (1991); and value chain - Bergeron, Buteau, and Raymond (1991), Ives and Mason (1990), Johnston and Carrico (1988), Johnston and Vitale (1988), and Wightman (1990).

The organization's effort is directed toward identification and recognition of opportunities for using IT, specification of resource requirements necessary to exploit these opportunities, and development strategies and actions to accomplish the targeted objectives. The application of such rational models attempts to systematically assess creativity, synergy, and leveraging effects of IT both internal and external to the organization.

Prior research from Porter (1985), Porter and Millar (1985), Mohrman and Lawler (1984), Macy and Petersen (1983), Gersick (1991), Rogers (1983), Makridakis and Wheelwright (1983), Gurbaxani and Mendelson (1990), Jarvenpaa and Ives (1990), Weill and Olson (1989), McKeen and Smith (1991), and Mason (1984) suggests five categories for the rational forces identified as drivers of IT/AD. The five, value chain, extent of change, patterns of IT investment, IT performance measures, and technology type, are summarized separately below.

Value chain. As noted in the introduction to this chapter, management of IT demands creativity, synergy, and leveraging in both its strategic and operational implementations, both internal and external to the firm. Cash and Konsynski's (1985) competitive advantage research, Porter's (1985) and Porter and Millar's (1985) value chain, and Wiseman's (1985) strategic thrust research are illustrative of the search for creativity, synergy, and leveraging of IT to gain competitive advantage. Johnston and Carrico (1988), Johnston and Vitale (1988), Bergeron, Buteau, and Raymond (1991), and Ives and Mason (1990) have researched creativity, synergy, and leveraging in IT.

Johnston and Carrico's (1988) research examined performance improvements in the value chain by relating importance of IT, as measured by external competitive pressures, and the integration of IT with strategy. Their results suggest that both organization learning which is translated into action, as well as organization culture characteristics, establish an innovation process that continues to generate performance improvements in the value chain. Johnston and Vitale (1988) employ a comparative efficiency (both internal and intraorganizational) and bargaining power framework in analyzing competitive advantage. Bergeron, Buteau, and Raymond (1991) compared the value chain methodology and the strategic thrust methodology in terms of their abilities to generate ideas worthy of implementation. Although limited in nature, their research suggested companies in more stable environments might prefer the value chain approach; those in more dynamic environments the strategic thrust approach.

Figure 1 is a decision tree representation of the value chain

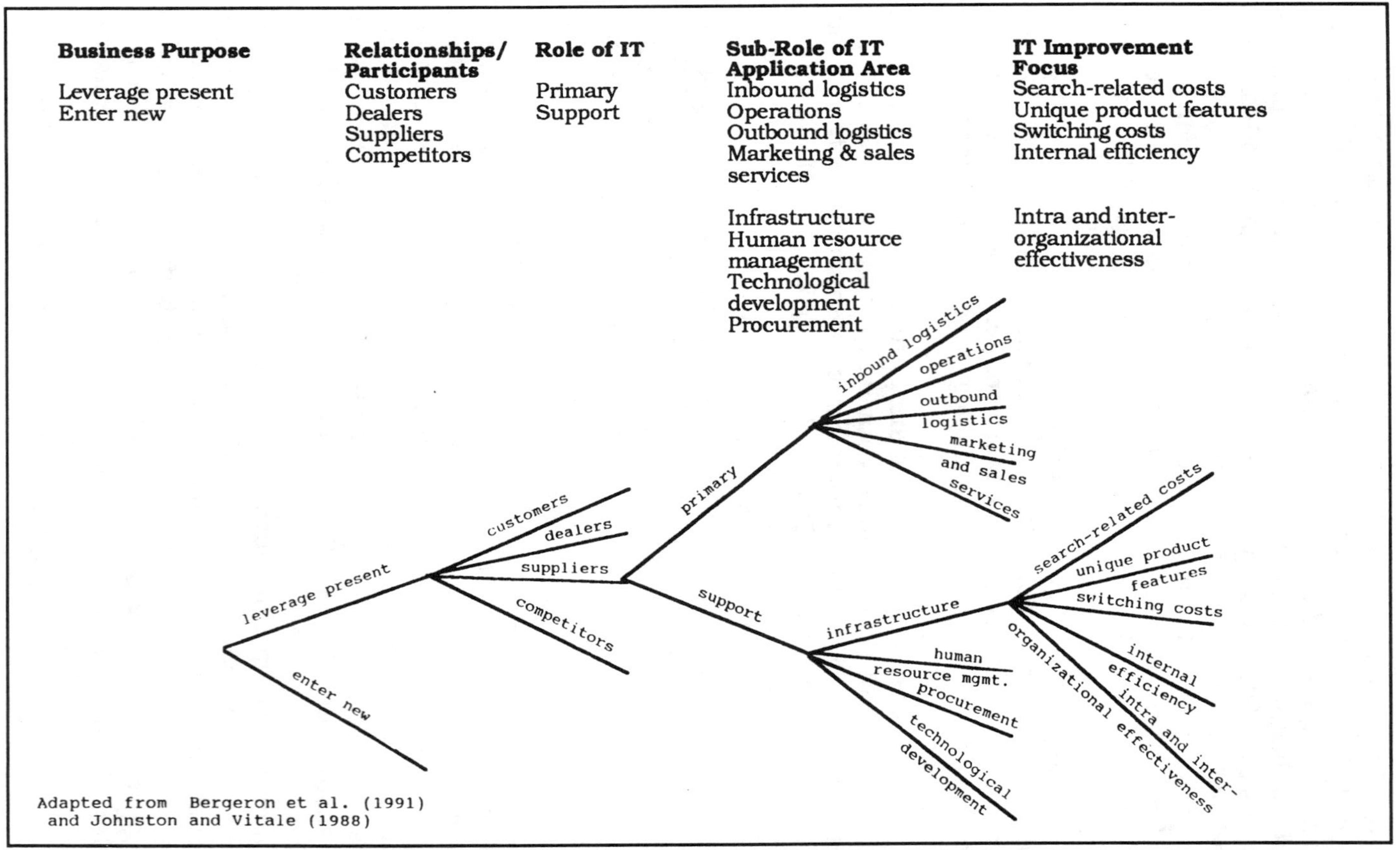

Figure 1: Decision Tree—Value Chain Search Process

search process to apply/discover creativity, synergy, and leveraging. As summarized in Figure 1, the search for exploiting creativity, synergy, and leveraging in the value chain encompasses examination of the business purpose, participants (and/or participant relationships), role of IT, sub-role of IT (application area), and analysis of the IT improvement focus.

Ives and Mason (1990) suggest use of SAST as a means of creatively analyzing the value chain to uncover synergies and leveraging. Their augmented service would use SAST to uncover new participants, roles of IT, and sub-roles of IT as depicted in Figure 1. Likewise, Ives and Mason employ SAST in their seven business practices, which are used to challenge assumptions about the firm's current bases of competing in the industry. The seven are: make to order or provide from stock, track or not track, profile or stereotype customer, deliver now or in the future, rent or sell, bill or cash, and negotiate or stipulate. These seven permit exploration of market/customer synergies and product/service/process synergies, both internal and external to the firm.

As used in the contingency model eight sector taxonomy (Table 5), the value chain descriptors range used is:

Maximum; internal		Minimum;
& external;	<————————	Internal;
Product & process		Process

Extent of change (alpha, beta, gamma). Macy and Petersen (1983) and Mohrman and Lawler (1984) proffer the taxonomy of organization change - alpha, beta, gamma, based on the work of Terborg, Howard, and Maxwell (1980) and Zmud and Armenakis (1978). Both the research of Terborg et.al., Zmud and Armenakis and that of Seashore, Lawler, Mirvis, and Cammann (1983) provide excellent treatment of methods, measures, and practices in measuring organization change. Gersick (1991) conceptualized extent of change using a different paradigm, punctuated equilibrium. Gersick examined six systems: adult, group, organization development, history of science, biological evolution, and physical science. For all six, Gersick identified periods of evolutionary change (corresponding to alpha, beta change), and revolutionary change (corresponding to gamma change). These revolutionary change periods may correspond with IT diffusion discontinuities, discussed in this chapter below.

Reported research pertaining to extent of organization change includes Mohrman and Novelli (1983), Bikson and Mankin (1983), Johnson (1983), and Collins, Hage, and Hull (1988). Mohrman and

Novelli (1983) found technology type linked to extent of change shifts, e.g., mediating technologies were associated with gamma change. Bikson and Mankin (1983) found the organization's orientation to change, as well as problem solving approach linked to IT implementation success. Johnson (1983) found alpha change linked to Roger's (1983) IT reinvention, change agent networks, and trialability. Collins, Hage, and Hull (1988) found mechanistic/organic organization characteristics linked to extent of change in manufacturing operations. Morhman and Lawler suggest that much IT research has remained focused on alpha changes[15], rather than researching extent of change associated with the acquisition and diffusion of IT.

As used in the contingency model eight sector framework (Table 5), the extent of change descriptors range used is:

Gamma; Effectiveness; Shift in Evaluation Criteria	<————————	Alpha; Efficiency; No shift in Evaluation Criteria

Patterns of IT investment.[16] The adoption and diffusion of innovations is typically described by an S-shaped cumulative probability density function (Rogers, 1983), (Makridakis and Wheelwright, 1983), describing rate of adoption of innovations.

Appendix C contains examples of three such distributions. Rate of adoption can be described using either number of adopters of the innovation over time, or percentage of adopters of the innovation over time. Rate of adoption also has been measured by IT expenditures (Lucas and Sutton, 1977), (Brancheau and Whetherbe, 1989), and (Gurbaxani and Mendelson, 1990). Gurbaxani and Mendelson (1990) suggest that a diffusion model is needed which integrates both diffusion effects and price effects in explaining IT/AD. Prior research, however, has largely ignored price effects of IT, in spite of the substantive improvement in price/performance characteristics of IT noted in the introduction to this chapter.

The research of Zmud (1982), Cooper and Zmud (1990), and Gurbaxani and Mendelson (1990) demonstrates that expenditure patterns in IT investment, at both the level of the individual firm and the aggregate, can be factored into two periods: an early transient period and a later steady state period. Learning dominates in the former, and price in the latter. During the early transient period, growth in IT expenditures is driven primarily by application of the technology to previously unconsidered areas in the business. In the steady state period, IT expenditures are driven primarily by the price effect of IT, i.e., the favorable price/performance ratio of IT makes it possible to automate increasing numbers and diversity of applications. Using the three separate growth curve models in Appendix C, Gurbaxani and Mendelson demonstrate that, for each model, an integrative price-adjusted learning curve model produces a better fit than simply the learning curve model alone.

Two additional factors are seen as mediators of the basic IT/AD S-shaped growth curve: technological discontinuities, and industry characteristics. Makridakis and Wheelwright (1983), Huber (1990), and Jarvenpaa and Ives (1990) identify technology discontinuities. Such discontinuities, or revolutionary periods, follow evolutionary diffusion periods. Huber (1990) identifies telephones, radio, and computers as examples of revolutionary shifts in IT; Makridakis and Wheelwright (1983) use the example of the technology shift between piston driven aircraft and jet aircraft. As examples of industry transitions in IT, Jarvenpaa and Ives (1990) cite the shift in the publishing industry with the advent of electronic publishing, and the shift in retailing associated with POS, scanning, and networks.

As used in the contingency model eight sector taxonomy (Table 5), the patterns of IT investment descriptors range used is:

Learning throughout; Maximum learning	<————————————	Price throughout; Minimal learning

IT performance measures. Appendix D summarizes prior research pertaining to IT investment measures. However, most of these studies did not examine linkages between IT investment and performance. The research of Zammuto (1982), Weill and Olson (1989), Dixon and John (1989), Maletz (1990), and McKeen and Smith (1991) indicates that given the complexity associated with organization diversity, no single criterion of IT performance is sufficient. Hence, multiple macrofinancial measures across multiple time periods are needed. Weill and Olson (1989) suggest such multiple measures take into account industry threshold investment levels; McKeen and Smith (1991) suggest industry characteristics be taken into account. With less organization diversity, traditional, singular measures such as ROE are adequate.

Weill and Olson (1989) further suggest classification of IT investment as strategic, informational, or transactional. This proposed taxonomy is related to the focus of the IT investment: strategic competitive advantage, improved management decision making, or reducing costs of doing business. IT performance measures suggested for the three categories are, respectively, revenue growth rates, return on assets, or indirect labor costs. In addition to customizing the IT performance measure to the focus of the IT investment, Weill and Olson also suggest that conversion effectiveness, the degree to which IT investment is converted to useful output, also be assessed. Conversion effectiveness is affected by organization characteristics, such as the political characteristics presented below.

As used in the contingency model eight sector taxonomy (Table 5), the IT performance measures descriptors range used is:

Multiple; Tailored; High conversion effectiveness	<————————	Single; Generic; Low conversion effectiveness

Technology type. Mason (1984) adapts Thompson's (1967) technological cores to posit four types of IT, as shown in the matrix display (Appendix E). The four technology types are: long-linked, intensive, extensive, and mediating. Long-linked technologies generally focus on efficiency, and are associated with minimal synergy and leverage. Synergies and leveraging generally increases as extensive and mediating technologies are used. Examples illustrating these four technology types can be found in Ives and Mason (1990), Lindsey, Cheney, Kasper, and Ives (1990), Copeland and McKinney (1988), and Wightman (1990).

As used in the contingency model eight sector framework (Table 5), the technology type descriptors range used is:

Extensive & mediating; Gestalt impact	<————————	Long-linked; Economic impact

The Political Perspective. Rogers (1983) researched diffusion of innovations in such disciplines as sociology, education, communication, and marketing. Viewing diffusion as a process embedded in a social network, Rogers' conceptualizations include the following: stages in the innovation process; adopter timings; attributes influencing innovation -relative advantage, incentives, compatibility with values and beliefs, technology clusters, trialability, opinion leaders, and change agents. Thus, diffusion occurs in a complex interdependency across varying levels of aggregation, including the individual, small group, organization unit, and the organization itself. Simply stated, IT is a part of a sociotechnical system — people, machines, systems, and organization. As such, the IT-organization context is a wicked problem (Mason and Mitroff, 1981)[17].

Markus and Robey (1988) utilize causal agency theory to adapt the work of Rogers (1983), as well as Pfeffer's (1982) analysis of action in organization, thus providing theoretical underpinnings for the political perspective of IT /AD. Markus and Robey (1988) identify an organization imperative which assumes organization choice over technological options. IT/AD is caused by the organization's information processing needs. The organization affects technology more than technology affects the organization (DeLisi, 1990).

Markus and Robey further identify an emergent perspective in which the uses and consequences of IT emerge unpredictably from complex social interactions, including such considerations as conflicting objectives, preferences and the operation of nonrational objectives and choice processes. This heuristic, interactive process between IT and the organization is also embodied in Mohrman and Lawler's (1984) Integrative/Disintegrative Model, Yates and Orlikowski's (1992) organization genres, and the research of Meyer and Goes (1988).

Five principle organization characteristics from the political forces identified as drivers of IT/AD have been identified and are utilized in IT/AD contingency model. The five, mentoring, gatekeepers, control, feedback, and dyadic linkages, are summarized in turn below.

Mentoring.[18] Earlier and retrospective research from McGill (1980) and Roche (1979) suggests a non-trivial density of mentoring relationships in management. The research of Rogers (1983), Evans (1984), Kerr and Slocum (1987), Noe (1988), Wilson and Elman (1990), and Gupta and Govindarajan (1991) identifies several mentor roles: transmitters of organization culture, identifying organization talent for fast tracking, and as role and behavioral models. Comparatively less research attention has been addressed to mentors' roles as linkages in information transmission networks (Evans, 1984), Wilson and Elman (1990). These informational roles could be as *gatekeepers* in a communication network, as filters of information (*control* of information flows), as change agents when transmitting innovations, as part of the formal/informal *feedback* processes when transmitting information bi-directionally , and as mentors in *vertical dyadic linkages* (VDLs) when promoting cadre relationships(Evans, 1984). Gatekeepers, control, feedback, and vertical dyadic linkages are discussed below.

Simulation modeling can be used to explore causal linkages associated with mentors functioning in a communication network, as evidenced by the research of Evans (1984), based on earlier work of Williamson (1971). Evans explored use of mentoring relationships and control loss. The empirical simulation results demonstrated the efficacy of mentoring in minimizing control loss under two conditions: large organization size and stable work force. Under conditions of either small organization size, or high turnover in work force, other control approaches, i.e., not involving mentoring, were found to be more effective.

As used in the contingency model eight sector taxonomy (Table 5), the mentoring descriptors range used is:

Highest Organization Levels; Empowerment	<————————————	Lower Organization Levels; No Empowerment

Gatekeepers. Delehanty, Sullo, and Wallace (1982) describe communication networks in terms of pairwise linkages among individuals, nodes and clusters, and special communicators, i.e., gatekeepers. The gatekeeper can be an individual or a team[19]. The gatekeeper receive(s) and processes both external and internal information and communicates it effectively to other network components.

Some gatekeepers may be more effective than others in receiving external information. Likewise, some gatekeepers may be more effective than others in transferring information within the network. Huff and Munro (1985) and Nelson (1990) suggest technology gatekeepers may provide special information regarding new IT from environmental scanning, or other applications of IT, because of awareness of such IT use elsewhere in the company.

Evans (1984) concludes that gatekeepers who are mentored, are better integrated into the organization's information network.

Gatekeepers: communication networks/information processing. Organization communication[20] consists of routing information flows between information sources and information sinks, i.e., recipients. With multi-source/multi-sink networks, system reliability is impacted by path length, as well as number of nodes connected and frequencies of contact with gatekeepers (Delehanty, Sullo, and Wallace, 1982). Nodes in the network may assume intermediary, translational, or amplificational roles. Gatekeepers are more effective than other types of nodes.

Zmud, Lind, and Young (1990) researched fourteen distinct organization communication channels[21] and six criteria for differentiating these channels, finding differences in lateral versus downward communication as related to both feedback characteristics and accessibility characteristics.

Huber (1982) examined two processes that increase system efficiency (message routing and message summarizing) and two processes that pertain to the organization's discretion in the way messages are handled (message delay and message modification). Huber's research relates information processing characteristics to organization characteristics. Huber's (1990) research distinguished between IT directed toward timeliness of intelligence and decision making versus IT that affects production of goods and services. Huber hypothesized that centralization/decentralization of decision making, number of organization levels, and number of nodes in the information transmission network will affect organization memory.

Nelson's (1989) empirical study examined relationships in a social network and intergroup conflict. Frequency of communication was measured by the number of communications in an average week. Nelson found low conflict situations to be associated with a higher number of intergroup communications.

Gatekeepers: message equivocality. Daft, Lengel, and Trevino's (1987) and Watson's (1990) research suggests that the gatekeeper's preference of communication medium is related to message equivocality and that communications high in equivocality should utilize information rich media. Digital Equipment (Kusekoski, 1989) provides an excellent example.[22]

In contrast, Daft and Macintosh (1981) and Kydd (1989) found that high equivocality in information did not automatically result in increased information processing. Daft, Lengel and Trevino (1987) further delineate that not all aspects of managerial communication high in equivocality are amenable to IT. Hence, high equivocality will not be associated isomorphically with high IT diffusion. Daft and Macintosh (1981) propose a contingency taxonomy classifying organization information processing in terms of task variety and equivocality of task information.

As used in the contingency model eight sector taxonomy (Table 5), the gatekeeper descriptors range used is:

Many; Teams; Across units	<————————————	Few; Individual; Within unit

Control. Selection theorists maintain that organization inertia precludes change in significant features of organizations, e.g., control (Alexander, 1991); transformation theorists maintain that organizations are capable of adapting to changing environmental conditions. In adopting the transformation theorists' viewpoint, Green and Welsh (1988) synthesize the usefulness of reframing control in terms of cybernetics and dependence. The cybernetic framework utilizes a self regulating control process related to the organization's goals.

Although classical management theory specified an isomorphic relationship between structure and control, Ouchi's (1977) research provided contradictory findings, leading to control being considered from a broader range of factors including economic and individual/ task characteristics (Evans, 1984), (Eisenhardt, 1985, 1989), (Gupta and Govindarajan, 1991), and (Ouchi, 1977, 1979).

Eisenhardt (1985, 1989) and Gupta and Govindarajan (1991) draw upon agency theory (Demski and Feltham, 1978); (Jensen and Meckling, 1976) which posits two control modalities: behavior and outcome. Behavior control is exercised through reliance on surveillance over the manager's decisions and actions; outcome control is exercised through reliance on the end results as the means for assessing a manager's performance. Both of these approaches reflect a cybernetic view of control. Eisenhardt (1989) further delineates that usually there is information asymmetry between principle and agent. Thus, control exercised through IT suggests that organization information systems may be used to increase both task programmability and outcome measurability, and used to decrease outcome uncertainty.

Ouchi (1977, 1979) and Eisenhardt (1985) further expand on control by positing control strategy to be a function of task characteristics. Whether control is exercised through behavior or outcome approaches is contingent upon the measurability of outcome and knowledge of the task transformation process[23], as shown in Appendix F.

As used in the contingency model eight sector taxonomy (Table 5), the control descriptors range used is:

Behavior; Few output measures <———————————— Outcome; Many output measures

Feedback characteristics. Mohrman and Lawler (1984) utilize Schoderbek, Schoderbek, and Kefalas'(1975) continuum of information feedback characteristics - first order, second order, and third order feedback. Mohrman and Lawler further identify increased multifunctionality of IT, increased flexibility in hardware systems, and increased accessibility/ flexibility of software as contributors to expansion of job tasks and organization roles. These three sources can present an increasing number of technological opportunities and choices to users at any level of the organization. The emergence of recent technologies such as networks and multimedia technologies, has allowed both the individual and the organization to use the increased multifunctionality of IT in formulating new interdependencies across organization functions and units. Over time, the locus of the feedback loop is seen as shifting from higher levels in the organization to the user level. Such a shift in the locus of the feedback loop concurrently brings with it generally increasing leverage and synergies in the application of IT.

Not all organizations respond isormorphically to such IT opportunities. The recursive, interactive dynamic between the IT characteristics and the organization characteristics will determine resultant information feedback characteristics.

User involvement in the transformational process, i.e., restructuring organization roles and redefining job tasks characterizes third-order feedback. Users discover new behaviors and goals, different from their original intent, when initiating use of the system. Third-order feedback enables creativity and changes in organization structures, practices. Information can be tailored to the requirements of a specific user. The Promise Card system and Tom Thumb Page supermarket examples (Ives and Mason, 1990) and TELCOT (Lindsey, Cheney, Kasper, and Ives, 1990) illustrate a third-order feedback.

Two examples of second-order feedback systems are provided in Ives and Mason (1990). The first is an expert system which selects the most appropriate lubricant based upon the temperature, chemical, and geological conditions. The second example, Missouri Book Services, utilizes software which combines multiple book orders from geographically dispersed areas according to predetermined rules. Thus, goal changing according to predetermined rules is part of the feedback process itself.

As used in the contingency model eight sector taxonomy (Table 5), the feedback characteristics descriptors range used is:

Third order; User level	<————————————	First order; Higher levels

Extent of dyadic linkages. Dansereau, Graen, and Hega (1975) and Evans (1984) researched VDLs. Managers do not employ a singular supervisory style when dealing with their subordinates. Rather, subordinates are divided into members of the cadre versus hired hands, who are not trusted and who are allowed little latitude. The superior/cadre relationship is an example of a strong dyadic linkage. Over time, each comes to understand the other, with the subordinate aware of and able to carry out the superior's goals. In contrast, the superior/hired hand relationship is an example of a weak dyadic linkage. Stevenson and Gilly (1991) found that informal relationships may be more effective VDLs for handling the type of ambiguous problems often faced by the more loosely-coupled, heterogeneous, innovative organizations.

Mentoring relationships are an example of cadre relationships. Further, gatekeepers (change agents) can be sponsored within the organization by mentors. Cadre VDLs enhance coordination both vertically and laterally. Thus, such cadre linkages between mentor(s) and gatekeeper(s) are important to both IT acquisition and IT diffusion. In contrast, hired hand, i.e., non-cadre relationships, diminish coordination and communication. Organizations with many such non-cadre VDLs are likely to be associated with low or minimal IT acquisition and IT diffusion.

Evans'(1984) research suggests overall control loss in the organization is directly proportional to the number of hierarchical levels in the organization and the extent of non-cadre VDLs at each level. The traditional pyramid shaped organization has many hierarchial levels, and thus greater opportunities for non-cadre VDLs and resultant control loss, as confirmed by Smith, Grimm, Gannon, and Chen (1991). In contrast, non-traditional organizations have fewer organization levels and thus less opportunities for non-cadre VDLs and their resultant control loss.

As used in the contingency model eight sector taxonomy (Table 5), the extent of dyadic linkages descriptors range used is:

Org. level low; Few non-cadre	<————————————	Org. level very high; Many non-cadre

THE IT/AD CONTINGENCY MODEL

Three primary arguments support the IT/AD contingency model and its accompanying explications as set forth in this chapter. First, prior research is fragmented, with a domain-oriented focus that has resulted in overly simplified IT/AD models in which a variety of organization and technology characteristics are posited to influence

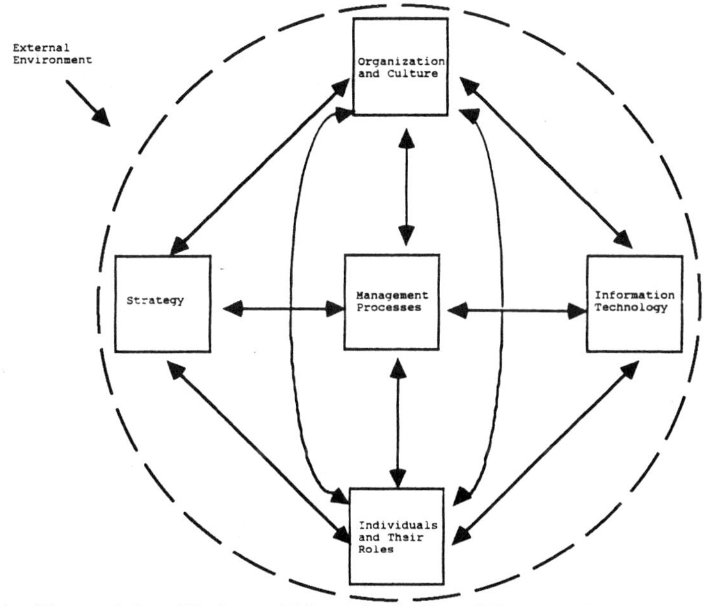

Reprinted by permission of Rockart and Morton, Implications of Changes in Information Technology for Corporate Strategy, *Interfaces*, 14(1), January-February 1984. Copyright 1984 the Operations Research Society of America and the Institute of Management Sciences, 290 Westminster Street, Providence, RI 02903 USA.

Figure 2: Rockart and Morton Model

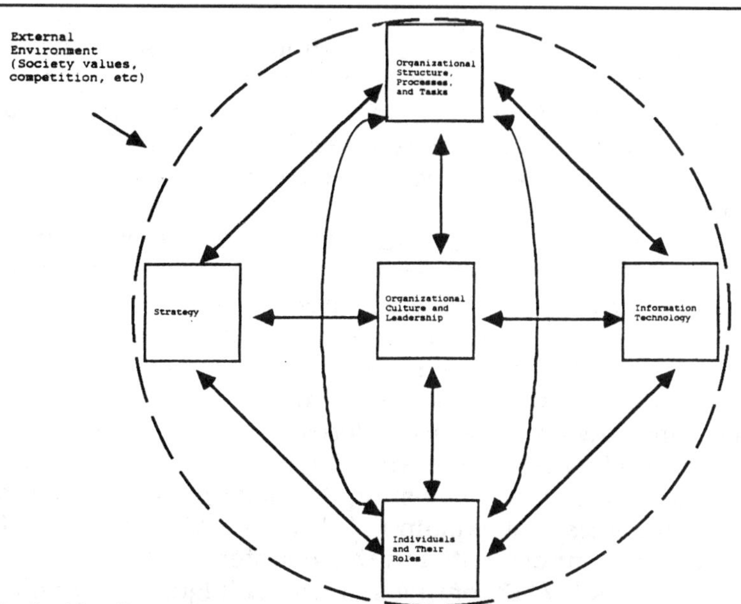

Reprinted from "Lessons from the Steel Axe: Culture, Technology and Organizational Change," *Sloan Management Review*, Fall 1990, pp. 84-92, by permission of publisher. copyright 1990 by the Sloan Management Review Association. All rights reserved.

Figure 3: DeLisi Model

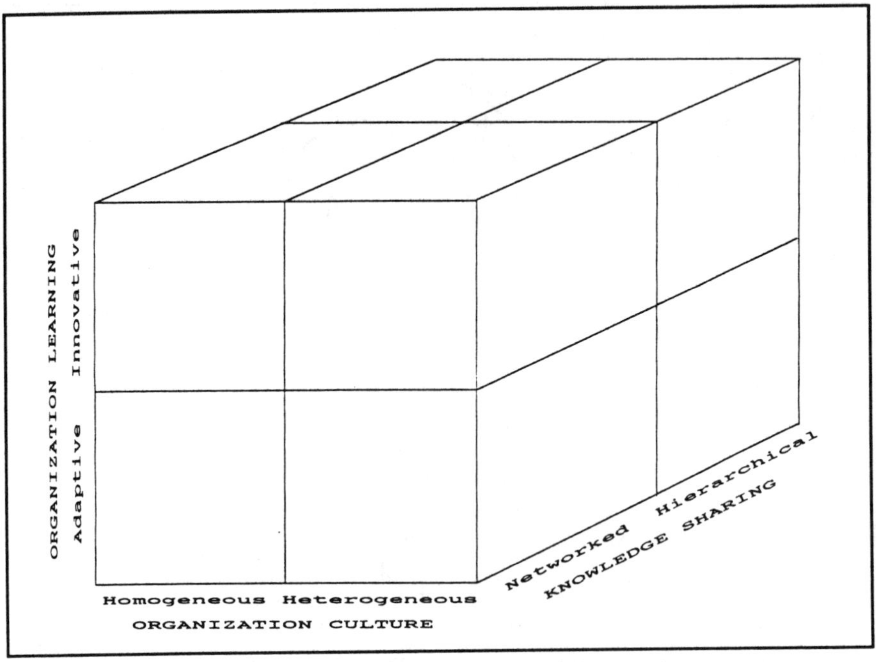

Figure 4: IT/AD Contingency Model

IT/AD. For example, IT/AD theories have emerged from diverse disciplines such as business administration - decision theory, organization behavior theory, policy and strategy, management science, marketing, information engineering, and communications. Further, each separate discipline is generally associated with dissimilar conceptual models, taxonomies, constructs, language, and measurement methodologies.

Second, prior research is normative. Two such examples are the normative conceptual paradigms explaining IT/AD. Figure 2 is from Rockart and Morton (1984), and Figure 3 from DeLisi (1990). In both, organization culture, organization processes, and individuals and their roles are depicted as forces driving IT/AD. However, the normative nature of these models does not easily translate into operational constructs for the practitioner, e.g., what operational constructs should be used to measure them.

Third, prior research fails to distinguish between primary forces and moderating forces that explain IT/AD and IT/AD patterns. In contrast, the paradigm presented in this chapter is a three dimensional parsimonious IT/AD contingency model (Figure 4), which is well grounded in theoretical underpinnings, as evidenced by their saliency in current IT/AD research and literature themes. Further, each dichotomous axis forms a mutually exclusive and collectively exhaustive set. From the contingent dynamic of the model emerges three significant qualities - creativity, synergy, and leverage. The emergence, or lack thereof, of these qualities distinguishes one organization from another.

Further Delineation of the Model - Eight Sector Taxonomy

The interactive, contingent nature of these driving IT / AD forces, is further explicated by its mapping onto the eight sector framework taxonomy (Table 5).

Each rational or political characteristic, represented by one row in the taxonomy, reflects the previous research:

- the rational perspective of IT/AD
- the political perspective of IT/AD

The taxonomy (Table 5) operationalizes the contingency model by providing ten measurement categories, or differentia that permit assignability, so that an organization can be "placed" on the taxonomy according to its closest fit.

Final Delineation of the Contingency Model - Identification of Moderating Variables

In order to develop further understanding, patterns of IT/AD must be examined. These patterns emerge as a result of moderating variables. Salient moderating IT/AD variables from the prior research are shown in Table 6. Major categories for these variables are then shown as part of Figure 5, the final delineation of the IT/AD contingency model.

APPLICATION OF THE CONTINGENCY MODEL/ FUTURE ACADEMIC RESEARCH

Application of the Contingency Model

The practitioner can utilize the IT/AD contingency model in several ways:

- as a diagnostic tool, to establish initial IT and organization reference points. Thus a summative, cross-sectional organization "actual" profile can be developed which represents an organization

	Heterogeneous Innovative Networked	Heterogeneous Innovative Hierarchical	Heterogeneous Adaptive Networked	Heterogeneous Adaptive Hierarchical	Homogeneous Innovative Networked	Homogeneous Innovative Hierarchical	Homogeneous Adaptive Networked	Homogeneous Adaptive Hierarchical
Rational								
Value chain	Maximum; internal & external Product & process	Internal & external Product	Internal & external Product	Internal & external Product	Internal & external Process	Internal Process	Internal Process	Minimum; Internal Process
Extent of change: alpha, beta, gamma	Gamma Effectiveness Ev. Cr. Shift	Beta Some gamma	Beta Some gamma	Beta Some gamma	Alpha Some beta	Alpha Some beta	Alpha Some beta	Alpha Efficiency No E.V. shift
Patterns of IT investment	Learning throughout Max. learning	Initial-learning Later-price	Initial-learning Later-price	Initial-learning Later-price	Price throughout Minimal learning	Price throughout Minimal learning	Price throughout Minimal learning	Price throughout Minimal learning
IT performance measures	Multiple, tailored, Hi conv. eff.	Multiple tailored, Hi conv. eff.	Multiple Med conv. eff.	Multiple tailored, Hi conv. eff.	Single Generic Moder. conv.eff.	Single Generic Moder. conv.eff.	Single Generic Low conv.eff.	Single Generic Low conv.eff.
Technology type	Extensive & mediating Gestalt	Extensive Some mediating	Extensive Some mediating	Extensive Some mediating	Intensive Minimal mediating	Intensive Minimal mediating	Intensive Minimal mediating	Long Linked Economic
Political								
Mentoring	Highest Org. Level;Empowerment	Middle to High	Middle to High	Middle	Middle	Middle	Low	Lower Org. Level No Empowerment
Gatekeeper characteristics	Many Teams (across units)	Many Teams (across some units)-some	Some Individual (w/i unit) Some team	Some Individual (w/i unit)	Some individual (w/i unit)	Some individual (w/i unit)	Few	Few individual (w/i unit)
Control	Behavior Few Output meas.	Behavior	Behavior	Behavior	Outcome	Outcome	Outcome	Outcome Many output meas.
Feedback characteristics	Third order User level	Third order	Second order Some third order	Second order Some third order	First order Some second order	First order Some second order	First order	First order Higher levels
Extent of dyadic linkages	Low Org. Level Few non-cadre	Low Few	Low Some	Low Some	Medium Several	Medium Several	High Many	V. High Org. Level Many non-cadre

Table 5: Contingency Model Eight Sector Taxonomy Rational/Political IT/AD Forces

Technology
- rate of change of the technology
- demand for/availability of technology
- benefit characteristics provided by technology
- importance of technology to strategy

Industry
- IT generations
- IT discontinuities
- rate of change of the technology
- aggregate demand for/availability of technology
- industry characteristics of IT

Organization
- position in organization life cycle
- size
- organization's competitive position within industry
- number and nature of previous experiences with IT migrations
- management familiarity with the technology
- early/late adopter of the technology

Potential Adopters
- demographics (age, education, etc.)
- perceptions (IT impacts on quality of work life, job enrichment, etc.)
- complexity/skill level requirements associated with technology

General Business Cycles

Table 6: IT A/D Moderating Variables

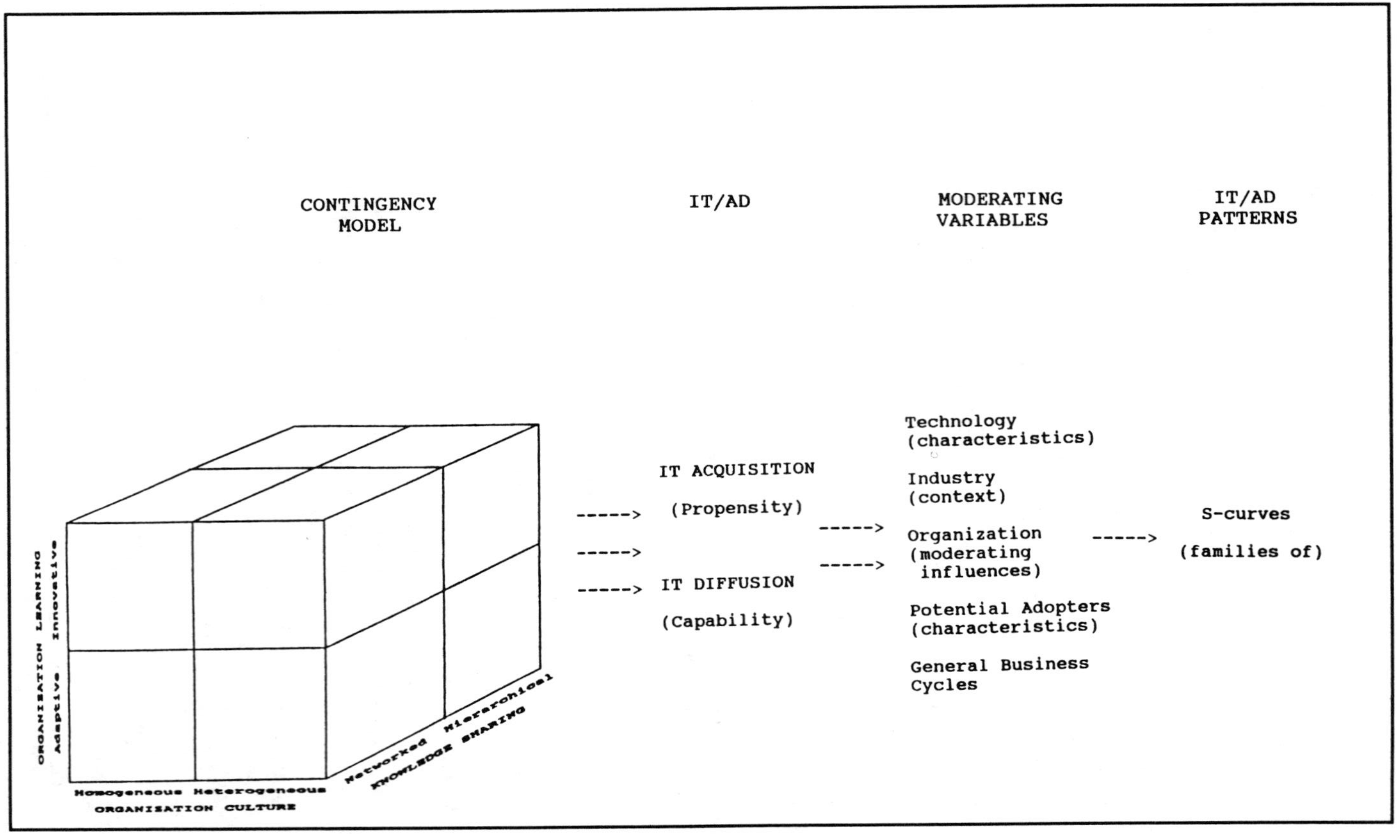

Figure 5: Contingency Model Delineation - Moderating Variables

consensus. Multiple alternative "target" states of the organization can be systematically explored.

- as a normative tool, to establish a "target" profile, representing a consensus of where the organization wishes to be. Actual and target profiles can be compared and resultant variances used as input to planning processes which explore alternative paths to the target profile.
- as a diagnostic tool, to permit systematic comparisons of the organization to one or more of its competitors. Intraorganization comparisons of both the rational and political characteristics utilized in the model can suggest future bases on which to compete and strategies for achieving targeted bases of competition.
- as a managerial tool, through the process of consensus building. Development of a shared actual reality as well as a negotiated target position may provide increased cohesion of the managerial team. In a similar way, intraorganization comparisons may assist conscious awareness of an organization's culture and its distinguishing culture characteristics viz-a-viz its competitors.

Specific analysis suggestions for each of the ten measurement categories used in the eight sector taxonomy (Table 5) are presented in Table 7.

Other Methodologies Used in Conjunction with the Model. Two forecasting techniques (Makridakis and Wheelwright, 1983), morphological analysis and cross-impact analysis, are offered as illustrative examples of the application of other models to the IT/AD domain.

Morphological Analysis. For example, if a new IT could potentially functionally interrelate with existing technologies in several markets and apply to several products, morphological analysis would systematically identify all permutations and combinations such IT configurations could take. A feasibility assessment process would then identify a reduced subset for further analysis.

Cross-Impact Analysis. The fundamental purpose of application of cross-impact is to better understand the diffusion process, in terms of events or trends, and their interrelatedness. Diffusion may be slowed or accelerated, by the conditional probability of one diffusion event needing to occur, before other diffusion events occur. Cross-impact simulation evaluates conditional probabilities, so that the model user can assess the interactive diffusion effects, thus enabling improvements in diffusion planning.

Organizational characteristics	Diagnosis/Intervention Applications
Rational	
Value-added chain	Diagnose both internal/external linkages. Assess impact of changes in linkages on organization learning and organization knowledge sharing.
Technology type	Examine linkage of IT planning processes with strategic planning processes. Assess current state of IT technology type. Utilize SAST (Ives and Mason, 1990) seven business practices to examine shift to different IT type(s).
Patterns of IT investment	Assess dominance of price vs. learning effects for existing IT(s). Diagnose/ assess extent and type(s) of required intervention (rational or political) necessary to effect structure(s) and process(es) change(s).
Extent of change	Assess/classify current state (alpha, beta, gamma). Explore feasibility of moving to different state.
IT performance measures	Assess appropriateness of existing performance measures. Explore rational/ political feasibility issues in adopting new performance measures.

Table 7: Contingency Model Diagnosis/Intervention Applications

Organizational characteristics	Diagnosis/Intervention Applications
Political	
Mentoring	Assess type (individual/organization) level in organization. Explore alternative characteristics and positioning.
Gatekeeper characteristics	Assess type (individual/organization) level in organization. Explore alternative characteristics and positioning.
Control modalities	Assess current state. Explore feasibility of shift to targeted new state(s).
Feedback characteristics	Assess current state. Explore extent/type(s) of organization interventions to move to targeted new state(s).
Dyadic linkages	Assess current state. Assess/classify/prioritize any resultant dysfunctional consequences. Explore extent/type(s) of organization intervention to move to targeted new state(s).

Table 7: Contingency Model Diagnosis/Intervention Applications Contd.

Future Academic Research

A broad program of research is proposed below, whose primary research foci include:

- Development of robust taxonomies/operational measures for each of the five rational and five political categories used in the eight sector taxonomy
- Type of research
- Level of analysis
- Attention to moderating variables

Development of robust taxonomies/operational measures. For each of the ten variable categories in Figure 5, robust taxonomies need to be developed, well grounded in prior research. Appropriate taxonomies require that the categories have clear differentia, be mutually exclusive, collectively exhaustive, and nonvacuous (Mason, 1984).

Future research pertaining to operational measures is also proposed. Operational measurement constructs used in future research should facilitate comparisons among researchers, and be well grounded in prior theory. Prior research pertaining to operational measures, as culled from the bibliography in this chapter, is shown in Appendix G.

A brief summary of proposed taxonomies and operational measures for each of the measurement categories in Table 5 is given in Appendix H.

Type of Research. The complexities of the IT/AD phenomenon suggests three broad venues for future research. Two of these venues utilize *in situ* research, consisting of both:

- Diachronic studies
- Synchronic studies

Both diachronic and synchronic approaches are commonly employed in theory building. Since the IT/AD process is dynamic, diachronic research is needed in order to explore the diffusion dynamic through the life cycle of the S-shaped diffusion curve. However, since the IT/AD process is highly contextual, synchronic research is also demanded in order to systematically explore the richness of such contextual variables. In particular, that richness is associated with the moderating (intervening) variables as set forth in Table 6.

A third venue, simulation modeling, is also recommended.

Simulation modeling affords both a systematic examination of causality through perturbations of the exogenous variables, as well as serving as a benchmark against which to test simulated relationships in the real world. Evans' (1984) research, in the earlier section *Mentoring*, is prototypical of the type of simulation research being suggested.

From the ten operational measurement categories used in the eight sector taxonomy, exemplars of categories which might be both useful and appropriate in future simulation research are mentoring, gatekeeper characteristics, control, dyadic linkages, and feedback characteristics.

Level of Analysis. The model would be applied at two levels:

- the level of the firm
- subunits within the firm

For purposes of exposition, the model has been conceptualized at an organization level. As already discussed, organization culture is not monolithic. Indeed, it is both efficacious as well as an appropriate research dynamic to test the model's tenets at suborganization levels, i.e., departments, units, work groups, etc. Since a given organization or organization unit may not perfectly fit a particular sector of the eight sector framework taxonomy, a closest fit would suffice.

Attention to moderating variables. Meaningful taxonomies should be developed for each category of variable shown in Table 6. Such taxonomies may unearth clusterings of similar patterns of IT/AD, related to characteristics of the moderating variable(s). IT/AD research needs to move beyond a monolithic diffusion curve, i.e., such as the ones in Appendix C, to families of diffusion curves, represented by intelligent clusters of moderating variables. Appropriate variable measurement constructs, consistent with each variable category, should be utilized.

CONCLUSION

This chapter has approached the diffusion of IT from the perspective that IT is a medium of human action. Individuals interact with IT, utilizing stocks of knowledge, resources, and norms that are the embodiment of the organization's characteristics. Thus IT/AD is the social product of subjective human action within specific cultural contexts. A sizeable body of prior theoretical and empirical research appears to support the primary, interactive influences of organization culture, organization learning and knowledge sharing on IT/AD. Unlike prior research, the conceptualization and reformulation of IT/AD presented herein suggests that earlier research results, often contradictory, can be explained by the holistic, integrative IT/AD model.

In addition, also unlike prior research, the eight sector taxonomy permits operationalization of the IT/AD diffusion model. The ten measurement categories of the taxonomy are well grounded in prior theory. Operationalizing the model with the taxonomy serves two audiences. First, academicians' research attention is directed toward the ten variable measurement categories, the moderating variables which impact the three primary driving IT/AD forces, and the search for meaningful patterns of IT/AD. Secondly, for the practitioner who must deal with the crucible of the real world, the taxonomy suggests management arenas deserving of the careful management attention, both for planning as well as control purposes.

The attention given to moderating variables should serve both to separate wheat from the chaff, as well as forming a basis for intelligent synthesis of future research results. Comparatively scant attention has been paid to IT/AD patterns. While other researchers have isolated specific moderating variables, e.g., industry, the larger picture of other moderating variables needs to be addressed, but within the context of the three integrative driving IT/AD forces.

Finally, the gestalt conceptualization presented in this chapter is but the prelude. It is hoped this conceptualization serves to stimulate thinking of other conceptualists. For the practitioner, perhaps the model can serve as the bridge between understanding of the macro forces at work and the management of specific organizational processes. It is this blend of macro understanding and well executed micro management that ultimately is the measure of IT/AD diffusion success.

APPENDIX A: PRIOR RESEARCH FINDINGS: LEVELS OF INVESTMENT IN IT

Researcher(s)	IT Investment Findings
Industry level	
Mason, 1984	In 1982, business devoted one-half of its capital spending to IT
Diebold Group, 1984; Strassman, 1985; Weill & Olson, 1989	Private sector IT investment commonly is 1.5-2% of revenues

Gurbaxani & Mendelson, 1990	Information intensive industries, e.g., banking and finance spend over 4% of revenue on IT
Harris & Katz, 1988; PIMS, 1984	High performing companies allocate a greater percent of revenues to IT than those with lower performance
Macro level	
Weill & Olson, 1989	The Office of Management and Budget reports 1982 IT expenditures of 1.2% of the federal budget, increasing to 1.6% in 1986
Gurbaxani & Mendelson, 1990	The data processing industry accounts for 2% of GNP. The stock of IT capital represents 7% of U. S. capital stock

APPENDIX B: PRIOR RESEARCH: PRIMACY OF ORGANIZATION CULTURE

Researcher	**Performance measure/impact causally linked to culture**
Smircich, 1983	Culture generates commitment; provides steady-state equilibrium
Duncan, 1989; Wilson & Elman, 1990	Strong culture impacts corporate success
Hofstede, Neuijen, Ohayv, & Sanders, 1990; Peters & Waterman, 1982	Strong cultures are more results-oriented than weak cultures
DeLisi, 1990; Duncan, 1989; Wilson & Elman, 1990	Culture is a major causal agent that drives IT /AD
Kedia & Bhagat, 1988	Culture constrains technology transfers across nations
Denison, 1990	Culture linked to organization effectiveness
Saffold, 1988	Culture linked to seven critical performance related processes

APPENDIX C:DIFFUSION S-CURVES: CUMULATIVE PROBABILITY DENSITY FUNCTIONS

S-curve	Formula	Researcher(s)
Gompertz curve	$\phi(T) = K \cdot A^{b^T}$	Lackman, 1977; Mahajan & Muller, 1979
Logistic curve	$\phi(T) = \frac{1}{K + A \cdot b^T}$	Blackman, 1974; Mahajan & Muller, 1979
Modified exponential curve	$\phi(T) = e^{a-b/T}$	Lucas & Sutton, 1977

APPENDIX D: PRIOR RESEARCH: IT INVESTMENT MEASURES

Researcher(s)	Measures used
Diebold Group, 1984	IT budget as % of revenues IT staff as % of total staff Ratio of hardware expenses to personnel costs
Bender, 1986	Ratio of IT investment to premium income
Strassman, 1985	Fraction of management costs devoted to IT
Cron & Sobal, 1983	Substitute measures: . ownership (own vs. lease) . number of standard application areas computerized . types of application areas computerized
Turner, 1985	Related DP expenditures (ratio of DP expenditures to total assets)

APPENDIX E: MATRIX DISPLAY OF MASON'S IT TYPES

		Distinctive outputs: One	Distinctive outputs: Many
Distinctive inputs	One	Long-link	Extensive
	Many	Intensive	Mediating

APPENDIX F: MATRIX DISPLAY OF OUCHI CONTROL PARADIGM

		Knowledge of task/transformation process: perfect	Knowledge of task/transformation process: imperfect
Availability of output measures	high	behavior or outcome	output
	low	behavior	ritual/selection

APPENDIX G: PRIOR RESEARCH: OPERATIONAL MEASURES USED

Framework characteristic	Researcher	Specific operational measures
Rational		
Value added chain	Bergeron, Buteau, & Raymond, 1991	Primary vs. support activities, Strategic thrust vs strategic target
	Carter, 1984	Multiple measures pertaining to the extent and type of computer applications
Extent of change	Mohrman & Novelli, 1983	Multidimensional effectiveness measures used to classify alpha, beta, gamma
	Van de Vliert, Huismans, & Stok, 1985	Correlations between shifts in a criterion and focal variable used to estimate the relative size of beta and alpha change
Patterns of IT investment	Gurbaxani & Mendelson, 1990	Aggregate computer user expenditures expressed in constant dollars
	Lucas & Sutton, 1977	Modified exponential IT growth curve applied to IS budgets
IT performance measures	Weill & Olson, 1989	Revenue growth rates, ROA, indirect labor (controlling for threshold investment, investment types, industry, and conversion effectiveness)
Technology type	---	---

APPENDIX G: CONTD.

Political		
Mentoring	Evans, 1984	Proportion of cadre relationships; number of individuals mentored by a superior; mentor levels above his/her protege
Gatekeeper: info processing/ communication networks	Stevenson & Gilly, 1991	Hospitals: near/far dichotomy reflecting distance from one professional node to another professional node; type of organizational relationship related to type of communication
	Gupta & Govindarajan, 1991	Density of communication (number of people in two units who interact with each other across organizational boundaries)
	Monge, Rothman, Eisenberg, Miller, & Kirste, 1985	Coded organizational proximity, used as measure of extent of communication
	Delehanty, Sullo, & Wallace, 1982	Gatekeeper - those individuals who were in the top fifth of their inter-departmental and extra-departmental communications frequency distribution.
	Zmud, Ling, & Young, 1990	Multidimensional scaling of fourteen communication channels
Gatekeeper: message equivocality	Daft, Lengel, & Trevino, 1987	Equivocality taxonomy for 60 critical incidents rated by panel of 30 judges

APPENDIX G: CONTD.

Control modalities	Alexander, 1991	Hospitals: five measures of dispersion of decision making authority
	Evans, 1984	Control given by subordinate; control received by superior
Feedback characteristics	Ang, Straub, Cummings, & Early, 1991	Feedback source: human or information technology Feedback delivery: face-to-face, computer mediated,computer generated
Dyadic linkages	Smith, Grimm, Gannon, & Chen, 1991	Airlines: number of departments and number of levels (controlling for size)
	Evans, 1984	Proportion of cadre members at each vertical level; control overlap between cadres/hired hands; span of control

APPENDIX H: PROPOSED TAXONOMIES/OPERATIONAL MEASURE(S)

Framework characteristic	Taxonomy/operational measure(s)
Value Chain	Taxonomy is shown in Figure 1, (Johnson and Vitale, 1988), and (Bergeron, Buteau, and Raymond, 1991). Operational measures include number of IT opportunities afforded, implementation costs, implementation duration.
Extent of Change	The taxonomy proposed is alpha, beta, gamma organization change (Mohrman and Lawler, 1984). Operational measures should be multi-dimensional; include effectiveness measures; and utilize appropriate discriminant procedures, as per Zmud and Armenakis (1978).
Patterns of IT Investment	The three growth curves as researched by Gurbaxani and Mendelson (1990) constitute the proposed taxonomy. IT expenditures should be expressed in constant dollars, and reflect price effects of technology. Both numbers of, as well as percentages of, should be used in cumulative probability distributions.
IT Performance Measures	The proposed taxonomy is based on the research of Weill and Olson (1989). IT expenditures should be tracked against a convenient base, i.e., revenues, total expenses, or management controlled costs (Strassman, 1985). All decentralized IT expenditures by functional department should be captured. IT industry threshold invest ment must be tracked and adjusted for. Conversion effectiveness indices must be developed.
Technology Type	The taxonomy proposed is Mason's (1984). An alternative taxonomy would utilize the business purpose framework (Weill and Olson, 1989). Technology clusters, e.g., by hardware/ software characteristics, would be developed for each category.
Mentoring	Examples of differentia taxonomies might include: mentor type (individual/team), placement in the organization level, extent of top management support, mentor process (formal/informal), and mentor/change agent relationship characteristics. Examples of operational measures include: number of individuals mentored, the proportion of cadre relationships to number of individuals within the span of control, placement of mentor (number of levels above his/her change agent), and duration/frequency of contact between mentor and change agent.
Gatekeeper Characteristics	Examples of differentia in such a taxonomy would include gatekeeper type (individual, team), formal versus informal, organization positioning, and type of communication channel.

	Examples of operational measures would include density of communication and message equivocality.
Control	The fundamental taxonomy dichotomizes behavior versus outcome control. Examples of operational measures include: locus of control, span of control, dispersion of decision making.
Feedback	The fundamental taxonomy would include differentia such as feedback source and method of feedback delivery. Examples of operational measures include: importance of feedback to decision making, flexibility of IT to provide revised feedback.
Dyadic Linkages	The fundamental taxonomy dichotomizes cadre versus non-cadre linkages. Examples of operational measures include: the proportion of cadre to non-cadre relationships, length of duration of the cadre relationship.

ACKNOWLEDGMENT

This chapter was developed from a paper co-authored with Julia A. Britt and published in the proceedings of the Information Resources Management Association International Conference, Charleston, SC, May 1992. The author gratefully acknowledges the work of Terry L. Mills, Pre-doctoral program, CSUDH, as research assistant, during the original development of the model. In addition to traditional research assistant duties, Terry contributed to the preliminary conceptualizations of the contingency model.

ENDNOTES

[1] See Hitt and Ireland (1987) for empirical research which critiques In Search of Excellence.

[2] The percentages in Appendix A are mirrored in business school IT budgets as well. A survey of AACSB-accredited business schools found IT budgets averaged 4.2% of total school budget (Frand and Britt, 1991).

[3] Mason (1984) noted underutilization of IT by U.S. manufacturing firms, i.e., a lower level of IT investment than would be maximum. The study cited by Mason applied log-linear regression analysis to a Cobb-Douglas model for U.S. manufacturing industries.

[4] Diffusion processes are characterized by a threshold process (acquisition), followed by a spreading process (diffusion). Von Bertallanffy's equation, $Y = e^{a-(b/t)}$ describes the diffusion process for the spread of a micro-organism in a host. The spread of a rumor can be described by applying Euler's Method, using the first derivative form of the equation $dy/dt = a(N-y)y$, where N = population and y the number who have heard of a particular piece of information.

[5] For simplification, organization culture is often treated as monolithic. Organization culture may not be monolithic. For example, Duncan (1989)

identified three subcultures, an enhancing, a counterculture, and an orthogonal culture, present within the firm's culture. The enhancing subculture embraces the dominant culture's views more than the dominant culture does. The orthogonal subculture takes its values from both the dominant and countercultures.

[6]These characteristics encompass both a functionalist view of organization culture [something the organization "has"], as well as the interpretive view of organization culture [something the organization "is"], (Riley, 1983).

[7]Two examples of the changeability of corporate culture are provided in: Shaw, J.B., Fisher, C.D., & Randolph, W.A. (1991). See also: Pressed by rivals, Proctor & Gamble is altering its ways. (1985, May 20). *The Wall Street Journal*, pp. 1; 22. Additional research also dealing with changeability of corporate culture includes Shaw, Fisher, and Randolph (1991), Gordon (1991), and Railing and Housel (1990)

[8]Kets de Vries and Miller (1986) identify a third category of culture, both destructive and unstable - a neurotic style corporate pathology.

[9]Heterogeneous: other classifier names used include organic, loosely structured, decentralized, complex. Homogeneous: other classifier names used include mechanistic, tightly structured, centralized, formalized.

[10] This reference provides an excellent overview of prior research concerning organization learning.

[11] The organization's strategic posture, structure, and internal as well as external environments are seen as influencing learning capacity, assimilation of new patterns and associations, the creative "tension" necessary for learning to occur.

[12] Rockart and Short (1989) highlight reasons for the appearance of networked knowledge sharing, including electronic communication, electronic brokerage, and electronic integration. Simon (1990) presents the view as to why nesting-block (hierarchical) knowledge sharing is used, rather than trying to design organizations where "everybody speaks to everybody". The limiting factor is the ability of people to absorb information, i.e., "bounded rationality".

[13] Knowledge sharing as used here is also embodied in Zuboff's (1988) "informatting" construct. Informatting refers to the ability to use information quickly and creatively, where and when it counts. An example is when skilled basketball players interact together (synergistically) to capitalize on "information" opportunities as they arise.

[14] The Proctor & Gamble "one page memo" is an extreme illustration of hierarchical knowledge sharing. See "Pressed by rivals, Proctor & Gamble

is altering its ways" (1985, May 20)

[15] Emery (1991) notes that traditional systems development methodologies and information engineering techniques foster minimal organizational change (alpha change), e.g., penalizing users for not getting system requirements definitions right the first time in the traditional system development life cycle. Such penalties constrain the user from new ways of thinking (gamma change) about how IT may better serve their needs. Emery proposes system development approaches that incorporate adaptive organizational learning.

[16] Methodological issues in measuring both IT investment and resultant performance arising from IT investment are set forth in Weill and Olson (1989).

[17] Various journal articles on this topic by these authors, jointly, singularly, or in collaboration with others can be found in *Management Science, Academy of Management Review, Academy of Management Executive.* See also Cosier and Schwink (1990) and Schweiger, Sandberg & Rechner (1989).

[18] Those with additional interest in the subject of mentoring are referred to a relatively recent journal, *International Mentoring,* published in Vancouver, British Columbia. Operationalization of a mentoring program in the firm is more fully treated in Kram (1985). A empirical study of 100 managers which examined mentored versus non-mentored managers is found in Zey (1984). The relationship of mentoring to career development is also explored in Kram and Isabella (1985). The subject of women and mentoring is treated in Noe (1988).

[19] Rockart and Short (1989), DeLisi (1990), Drucker (1988), and Applegate, Cash, Mills (1988) discuss the role(s) of teams. Maletz (1990) presents an excellent example of technology transfer teams at Xerox. Richardson, Jackson, and Dickson (1990) describe an IT/AD process at Texaco as having a tight gatekeeper linkages to the corporate planning process. Gatekeeper and mentoring activities are notable. The research of Cox and Blake (1991) provides insight into managing cultural diversity and the use of teams.

[20] Huber (1982) quotes John Kenneth Galbraith (1967) in *The New Industrial State*: "The real accomplishment of modern science and technology comes in taking ordinary men, informing them narrowly and deeply . . . and through appropriate organization, arranging to have their knowledge combined with that of other specialized but equally ordinary men." Thus communication becomes a matter of selecting and appropriately routing information.

[21] These channels included consultants: formal and informal); group: formal-meetings and informal-gatherings; written: handwritten notes, memos, printed reports, graphs, and computer reports; communication technologies: phone, voice conferencing, and facsimile; and computer mediated

technologies: electronic mail and voice messaging.

[22] Conventional IT made a corporate-wide view of Digital Equipment's business impossible. This decision task utilized ambiguous, conflicting information with cross-organizational and cross-geographical properties. A newer IT, videotext, provided the information richness, thus matching the message equivocality of the corporate-wide information being processed.

[23] However, positioning of an organization within this two dimensional control paradigm is based on, the assumption that organizations can adapt their control practices to accommodate major changes in their operating environments (Alexander, 1991). Further, institutionalized structures and practices (organizational norms, value, and culture), as well as reward/ punishment systems (Sitkin and Pablo, 1992), act as constraints on the organization's propensity to adapt control practices in response to the environment.

REFERENCES

Alexander, J.A. (1991). Adaptive change in corporate control practices. *Academy of Management Journal, 34*(1), 162-193.

Ang, S., Straub, D., Cummings, L., & Earley, P. (1991). Effects of information technology on feedback setting. In DeGross, J.I., Benbasat, I.., DeSanctis, G., & Beath, C.M. (Eds), *Proceedings of the Twelfth International Conference on Information Systems*, New York, (pp. 165-176).

Applegate, L., Cash, J., & Mills, D. (1988). Information technology and tomorrow's manager. *Harvard Business Review, 66*, 128-136.

Argyris, C. (1976). Organizational learning and effective management information systems: A prospectus for research (Working paper 76-4). Cambridge: Harvard University.

Argyris, C. & Schoen, D.A. (1978). *Organizational learning: A theory of action research.* Reading, MA: Addison-Wesley.

Argyris, C. & Schoen, D.A. (1982). *Theory in practice: Increasing professional effectiveness.* San Francisco: Jossey-Bass.

Barney, J.B. (1986). Organizational culture: Can it be a source of sustained competitive advantage? *Academy of Management Review, 11*(3), 656-665.

Bender, D. (1986). Financial impact of information processing. *Journal of MIS, 3*(2), 232-238.

Benjamin, R.I. & Scott Morton, M.S. (1988). Information technology, integration, and organizational change. *Interfaces, 18*(3), 86-98.

Bergeron, F., Buteau, C., & Raymond, L. (1991). Identification of strategic information systems opportunities: Applying and comparing two methodologies. *MIS Quarterly, 15*(1), 89-103.

Bikson, T.K. & Mankin, D. (1983). *Factors in successful implementation of computer-based office information systems: A review of the literature.* Unpublished manuscript, Rand Corporation.

Blackman, A.W. (1974). The market dynamics of technological substitutions. *Technological Forecasting and Social Change, 6*, 41-63.

Boynton, A.C. & Zmud, R.W. (1987). Information technology planning in the 1990s: Directions for practice and research. *MIS Quarterly, 11*(1), 59-72.

Brancheau, J.C. & Wetherbe, J.C. (1989). End-user computing and knowledge work: Managing the introduction of new information technology. *CIO Journal*, Spring.

Bullen, C.V. & Rockart, J.F. (1981). *A primer on critical success factors* (Working paper 69). Cambridge: Sloan School of Management, Massachusetts Institute of Technology.

Carter, N.M. (1984). Computerization as a predominate technology: Its influence on the structure of newspaper organizations. *Academy of Management Journal, 27*(2), 247-270.

Cash, J.I. & Konsynski, B.R. (1985). IS redraws competitive boundaries. *Harvard Business Review, 63*(2), 134-142.

Child, J. (1987). Information technology, organization and response to strategic challenge. *California Management Review, 30*, 33-50.

Collins, P.D., Hage, J., & Hull, F.M. (1988). Organizational and technological predictors of change in automaticity. *Academy of Management Journal, 31*(3), 512-543.

Cooper, R.B. & Zmud, R.W. (1990). Information technology implementation research: A technological diffusion approach. *Management Science, 36*(2), 123-139.

Copeland, D.G. & McKinney, J.L. (1988). Airline reservations systems: Lessons from history. MIS Quarterly, 12(3), 35-37.

Cosier, R.A. & Schwink, C.R. (1990). Agreement and thinking alike: Ingredients for poor management decisions. *Academy of Management Executive, 4*(1), 69-74.

Cox, Jr., T. & Blake, S. (1991). Managing cultural diversity: implications for organizational competitiveness. *Academy of Management Executive, 5*(3), 45-56.

Cron, W. & Sobel, M. (1983). The relationship between computerization and performance: A strategy for maximizing economic benefits of computerization. *Information and Management, 6*, 171-181.

Daft, R.L. & Lengel, R.H. (1986). Organizational information requirements, media richness, and structural design. *Management Science, 32*, 554-571.

Daft, R.L. & MacIntosh, N.B. (1981). A tentative exploration of the amount and equivocality of information processing. *Administrative Science Quarterly, 26*, 207-224.

Daft, R.L. & Weick, K.E. (1984). Toward a model of organizations as interpretation systems. *Academy of Management Review*, 9(2), 284-295.

Daft, R.L., Lengel, R.H., & Trevino, L.K. (1987). Message equivocality, media selection, and manager performance: Implications for information systems. *MIS Quarterly, 11*(3), 355-368.

Damanpour, F. (1991). Organizational innovation: A meta-analysis of effects of determinants and moderators. *Academy of Management Journal, 34*(3), 555-590.

Dansereau, F.G., Graen, G. and Haga, W.J. (1975). A vertical dyadic linkage approach to leadership within formal organizations: A longitudinal investigation of the role making process. *Organizational Behavior and Human Performance, 13*, 46-78.

Davamanirajan, P., Kriebel, C.H., & Mukhopadhyay, T. (1991). Information technology innovation and competition in the presence of switching costs. In DeGross, J.I., Benbasat, I., DeSanctis, G., & Beath, C.M. (Eds), *Proceedings of the Twelfth International Conference on Information Systems*, New York, (pp. 1-14).

Delehanty, T., Sullo, P., & Wallace, W.A. (1982). A method for prescriptive assessment of the flow of information within organizations. *Management Science, 28*(8), 910-924.

DeLisi, P.S. (1990). Lessons from the steel axe: Culture, technology, and organizational change. *Sloan Management Review, 32*, 83-93.

Demski, J. & Fletham, G. (1978). Economic incentives in budgetary control systems. *Accounting Review, 53*, 336-359.

Dean, J.W. & Snell, S.A. (1991). Integrated manufacturing and job design: Moderating effects of organizational inertia. *Academy of Management Journal, 34*(4), 776-804.

Denison, D.R. (1990). *Corporate Culture and Organizational Effectiveness.* New York: John Wiley & Son. Diebold Group. (1984). MIS/Telecommunications budgets and key indicators. New York: The Diebold Group.

Dixon, P.J. & John, D.A. (1989). Technology issues facing corporate management in the 1990s. *MIS Quarterly, 13*(3), 247-255.

Dos Santos, B.L. & Peffers, K. (1991). The effects of early adoption of information technology: An empirical study. In DeGross, J.I., Benbasat, I., DeSanctis, G., & Beath, C.M. (Eds), *Proceedings of the Twelfth International Conference on Information Systems,* New York, (pp. 127-140).

Douglas, M. & Wildavsky, A. (1982). *Risk and culture.* Berkeley: University of California Press.

Drucker, P.F. (1988). The coming of the new organization. *Harvard Business Review, 66,* 45-53.

Duncan, W.J. (1989). Organizational culture: 'Getting a fix' on an elusive concept. *Academy of Management Executive, 3*(3), 229-236.

Ein-Dor, P. & Segev, E. (1982). Organizational context and MIS structure: Some empirical evidence. MIS Quarterly, 6(3), 255-268. Eisenhardt, K.M. (1985). Control: Organizational and economic approaches. *Management Science, 31*(2), 134-149.

Eisenhardt, K. (1989). Agency theory: An assessment and review. The Academy of Management Review, 14(1), 57-74. Emery, J.C. (1991). Re-engineering the organization. *MIS Quarterly, 15*(1), iii-iv.

Evans, M.G. (1984). Reducing control loss in organizations: The implications of dual hierarchies, mentoring and strengthening vertical dyadic linkages. *Management Science, 30*(2), 156-168.

Fiol, C.M. & Lyles, M.A. (1985). Organizational learning. The *Academy of Management Review, 10*(4), 803-813.

Frand, J.L. & Britt, J.A. (1991). Eighth Annual UCLA Survey of Business School Computer Usage. Los Angeles: The John E. Anderson Graduate School of Management, UCLA.

Galbraith, J. (1973). *Designing complex organizations.* Reading, MA: Addison-Wesley.

Galbraith, J. (1974). Organizational design: An information processing view. *Interfaces, 4*(3), 23-36.

Galbraith, J. (1977). Organizational design. Reading, MA: Addison-Wesley. Galbraith, J.K. (1967). *The new industrial state.* London:Hamish Hamilton.

Gersick, J.G. (1991). Revolutionary change theories: A multilevel exploration of the punctuated equilibrium paradigm. *Academy of Management Review, 16*(1), 10-36.

Gordon, G.G. (1991). Industry determinants of organizational culture. *Academy of Management Review, 16*(2), 396-415.

Green, S.G. & Welsh, M.A. (1988). Cybernetics and dependence: Reframing the control concept. *Academy of Management Review, 13*(2), 287-301.

Gresov, C. (1984). Designing organizations to innovate and implement: Using two dilemmas to create a solution. *Columbia Journal of World Business, 19,* 63-67.

Gupta, A.K. & Govindarajan, V. (1991). Knowledge flows and the structure of control within multinational corporations. *Academy of Management Review, 16*(4), 768-792.

Gurbaxani, V. & Mendelson, H. (1990). An integrated model of information systems spending growth. *Information Systems Research, 1*(1), 23-46.

Hannan, M.T. & Freeman, J.H. (1977). The population ecology of organizations. *American Journal of Sociology, 82,* 929-964.

Harris, S.E. & Katz, J.L. (1988). Profitability and information technology capital intensity in the insurance industry. *Proceedings of the Twenty-First Hawaii International Conference on System Science, IV,* (pp. 124-130).

Henderson, J.C. & Sifonis, J.G. (1988). The value of strategic planning:

Understanding consistency, validity and IS markets. *MIS Quarterly, 12*(2), 187-200.

Hitt, M.A. & Ireland, R.D. (1987). Peters and Waterman revisited: The unended quest for excellence. *Academy of Management Executive, 1*(2), 91-98.

Hofstede, G., Neuijen, B., Ohayv, D.D. & Sanders, G. (1990). Measuring organizational cultures: A qualitative and quantitative study across twenty cases. *Administrative Science Quarterly, 35*, 286-316.

Huber, G. (1982). Organizational information systems: Determinants of their performance and behavior. *Management Science, 28*(2), 138-155.

Huber, G. (1984). The nature and design of post industrial organizations. *Management Science, 30*(8), 928-951.

Huber, G.P. (1990). A theory of the effects of advanced information technologies on organizational design, intelligence, and decision making. *The Academy of Management Review, 15*(1), 47-71.

Huber, G. (1991, December). We can do better: Integrating theories of novel organizations, new organizational forms, and information technology (a tutorial). In DeGross, J.I., Benbasat, I., DeSanctis, G., & Beath, C.M. (Eds), *Proceedings of the Twelfth International Conference on Information Systems*, New York.

Huff, S.L. & Munro, M.C. (1985). Information technology assessment and adoption: A field study. *MIS Quarterly, 10*(4), 327-339.

Ives, B. & Mason, R. (1990). Can information technology revitalize your customer service? *Academy of Management Executive, 4*(4), 52-69.

Jarvenpaa, S.L. & Ives, B. (1990). Information technology and corporate strategy: A view from the top. *Information Systems Research, 1*(4), 351-376.

Jelinek, M., Smircich, L. & Hirsch, P. (1983). Introduction: A code of many colors. *Administrative Science Quarterly, 28*, 331-338.

Jensen, M.C. & Meckling, W.H. (1976). Theory of the firm: Managerial behavior, agency costs, and ownership structure. *Journal of Financial Economics, 3*, 305-360.

Johnson, B.M. (1983). *Innovation in word processing*. A series of project reports, Institute for Communication Research and Policy Conference, Annapolis.

Johnston, H.R. & Carrico, S.R. (1988). Developing capabilities to use information strategically. *MIS Quarterly, 12(*1), 37-50.

Johnston, H.R. & Vitale, M.R. (1988). Creating competitive advantage with interorganizational information systems. *MIS Quarterly, 12*(2), 153-166.

Kedia, B.L. & Bhagat, R.S. (1988). Cultural constraints on transfer of technology across nations: Implications for research in international and comparative management. *Academy of Management Review, 13*(4), 559-571.

Kelley, D. & Amburgey, T.L. (1991). Organizational inertia and momentum: a dynamic model of strategic change. *Academy of Management Journal, 34*(3), 591-612.

Kerr, J. & Slocum, J.W., Jr. (1987). Managing corporate culture through reward system. *Academy of Management Executive, 1*(2), 99-108.

Kets de Vries, M.F.R. & Miller, D. (1986). Personality, culture, and organization. *The Academy of Management Review, 11*(2), 266-279.

Klempa, M.J. (1983). *Decision support systems: A field investigation integrating cognitive style, incongruity adaptation level, defense mechanism and organizational characteristics*. Unpublished doctoral dissertation, University of Southern California, 1983.

Klempa, M.J. & Britt, J.A. (1992). Managing information technology: An acquisition/diffusion contingency model integrating organization culture, organization learning, and knowledge sharing. In Khosrowpour, M. (Ed), *Proceedings of the 1992 Information Resources Management International Conference*, Charleston, (pp. 343-356).

Kram, K.E. (1985). *Mentoring at work: Developmental relationships in organizational life*. Glenview, IL: Scott Foresman.

Kram, K.E. & Isabella, L.A. (1985). Alternatives to mentoring: The role of peer relationships in career development. *Academy of Management Journal, 28*(1), 110-132.

Kusekoski, G. (1989). Corporate videotext: A strategic business information system. *MIS Quarterly, 13*(4), 447-456.

Kydd, C.T. (1989). Understanding the information content in MIS management tools. *MIS Quarterly, 13*(3), 277-290.

Lackman, C.L. (1977). Gompertz curve forecasting: A new product application. Journal of Marketing Research Society, 20(1), 45-47. Leavitt, H.J. & Whisler, T.L. (1958). Management in the 1980s. *Harvard Business Review, 36*, 41-48.

Lederer, A.L. & Sethi, V. (1988). The implementation of strategic information systems planning methodologies. *MIS Quarterly, 12*(3), 445-462.

Leifer, R. (1988). Matching computer-based information systems with organizational structures. *MIS Quarterly, 12*(1), 63-47.

Levsen, V.B. & Fry, L.W. (1987, April). Computer-based information systems: Implications for organizational design." Paper presented at the meeting of the Western Academy of Management, Seattle.

Lindsey, D., Cheney, P.H., Kasper, G.M., & Ives, B. (1990). TELCOT: An application of information technology for competitive advantage in the cotton industry. *MIS Quarterly, 14*(4), 347-357.

Lucas, H.C. & Sutton, J.A. (1977). The stage hypothesis S-curve: Some contradictory evidence. *Communications of the ACM, 20*, 254-259.

Macy, B.A. & Petersen, M.F. (1983). Evaluating attitudinal change in a longitudinal quality of work life intervention. In Seashore, S.E., Lawler, E.E., Mirvis, P.H., & Cammann, C. (Eds.) *Assessing organizational change: A guide to methods, measures, and practices.* New York: Wiley.

Mahajan, V. & Muller, E. (1979). Innovation diffusion and new-product growth models in marketing. *Journal of Marketing, 43*, 55-68.

Main, T.J. & Short, J.E. (1989). Managing the merger: Building partnership through IT planning at the new Baxter. *MIS Quarterly, 13*(4), 469-484.

Makridakis, S. & Wheelwright, S. C. (1983). *Forecasting: Methods and applications.* New York: Wiley/Hamilton.

Maletz, M.C. (1990). KBS circles: A technology transfer initiative that leverages Xerox's leadership through quality program. *MIS Quarterly, 14*(3), 323-329.

Markus, M.L. & Robey, D. (1988). Information technology and organizational change: Causal structure in theory research. *Management Science, 34*(5), 583-598.

Mason, R.O. (1984). Current research issues. In F. W. McFarlan (Ed.), *The information systems research challenge: Proceedings.* Boston: Harvard Business School Press, (pp. 279-304).

Mason, R.O. & Mitroff, I. (1981). *Challenging strategic planning assumptions.* New York: Wiley.

McFarlan, F.W. (Ed.). (1984). *The information systems research challenge: Proceedings.* Boston: Harvard Business School Press.

McGill, M.G. (1980). *Mentors and managers* (Working paper 80-103). Dallas: Cox School of Business, Southern Methodist University.

McKeen, J.D. & Smith, H.A. (1991). The value of information technology. In DeGross, J.I., Benbasat, I., DeSanctis, G., & Beath, C.M. (Eds), *Proceedings of the Twelfth International Conference on Information Systems*, New York, (pp. 41-52).

Meyer, A.D. & Goes, J.B. (1988). Organizational assimilation of innovations: A multilevel contextual analysis. *Academy of Management Journal, 31*(4), 897-923.

Mohrman, A.M. & Lawler, E.E. (1984). A review of theory and research. In F. W. McFarlan (Ed.) *The information systems research challenge: Proceedings.* Boston: Harvard Business School Press, (pp. 135-164).

Mohrman, A.M. & Novelli, L. (1983). *Three types of change in the automated office.* (Publication G 83-5). Los Angeles: Center for Effective Organizations, University of Southern California.

Monge, P.R., Rothman, L.W., Eisenberg, E.M., Miller, K.J., & Kirste, K.K. (1985). The dynamics of organizational proximity. *Management Science, 31*(9), 1129-1141.

Naisbitt, J. (1982). *Megatrends.* New York: Warner.

Nelson, D.L. (1990). Individual adjustment to information-driven technologies: A critical review. *MIS Quarterly, 14*(1), 79-98.

Nelson, R.E. (1989). The strength of strong ties: Social networks and intergroup conflict in organizations. *Academy of Management Journal, 32*(2), 377-401.

Neumann, Y. & Neumann, E. (In Press). Management strategy, president's cognitive style, and organizational growth/decline: A framework for understanding enrollment change in private colleges. *Journal of Educational Administration.*

Noe, R.A. (1988). Women and mentoring: A review and research agenda. *Academy of Management Review, 13*(1), 65-78.

Orlikowsky, W.J. & Baroudi, J.J. (1991). Studying information technology in organizations: Approaches and assumptions. *Information Systems Research, 2*(1), 1-28.

Orlikowsky, W.J. & Robey, D. (1991). Information technology and the structure of organizations. *Information Systems Research, 2*(2), 143-169.

Ouchi, W.G. (1977). The relationship between organizational structure and organizational control. *Administrative Science Quarterly*, 22, 95-111.

Ouchi, W.G. (1979). A conceptual framework for the design of organizational control mechanism. *Management Science, 23*(9), 833-848.

Peters, T.J. & Waterman, R. (1982). *In search of excellence.* New York: Harper.

Pfeffer, J. (1982). *Organizations and organization theory.* Boston: Pitman.

PIMS Program. (1984). *Management productivity and information technology.* Cambridge: The Strategic Planning Institute.

Porter, M.E. (1985). *Competitive Advantage.* New York: Free Press.

Porter, M.E. & Millar, V.E. (1985). How information gives you competitive advantage. *Harvard Business Review, 63*(4), 145-160.

Pressed by rivals, Proctor & Gamble is altering its ways. (1985, May 20). *The Wall Street Journal*, pp. 1, 22.

Raho, L.E., Belohlav, J.A., & Fiedler, K.D. (1987). Assimilating new technology into the organization: An assessment of McFarlan and McKenney's model. *MIS Quarterly, 11*(1), 47-58.

Railing, L. & Housel, T. (1990). A network infrastructure to contain costs and enable fast response: The TRW process. *MIS Quarterly, 14*(4), 405-419.

Richardson, G.L., Jackson, B.M., & Dickson, G.W. (1990). A principles-based architecture: Lessons from Texaco and Star Enterprises. *MIS Quarterly, 14*(4), 385-403.

Riley, P. (1983). A structurationist account of political culture. *Administrative Science Quarterly, 28*(3), 414-437.

Roche, G.R. (1979). Much ado about mentors. *Harvard Business Review, 57*(1), 14-28.

Rockart, J.F. & Scott Morton, M.S. (1984). Implications of changes in information technology for corporate strategy. *Interfaces, 14*(1), 84-95.

Rockart, J.F. & Short, J.E. (1989). I/T in the 1990s: Managing organization interdependence. *Sloan Management Review, 30*, 7-17.

Rogers, E. (1983). *Diffusion of innovations* (3rd ed.). New York: Free Press.

Rowe, A.J. & Mason, R.O. (1987). *Managing with style: A guide to understanding, assessing, and improving decision making.* San Francisco: Jossey-Bass.

Saffold, G.S., III. (1988). Culture traits, strength, and organizational performance: Moving beyond "strong" culture. *The Academy of Management Review, 13*(4), 546-558.

Schein, E.H. (1984). Coming to a new awareness of organizational culture. Sloan Management Review, 13(4), 3-16.

Schoderbek, C.G., Schoderbek, P.P., & Kefalas, A.G. (1975). *Management systems.* Dallas: Business Publications.

Schweiger, D.M., Sandberg, W.R., & Rechner, P.L. (1989). Experiential effects of dialectical inquiry, devil's advocacy, and consensus approaches to strategic decision making. *Academy of Management Journal, 32*(4), 745-772.

Seashore, S.E., Lawler, E.E., Mirvis, P.H., & Cammann, C. (Eds.) (1983). *Assessing organizational change: A guide to methods, measures, and practices.* New York: Wiley.

Shaw, J.B., Fisher, C.D., & Randolph, W.A. (1991). From materialism to accountability: The changing cultures of Ma Bell and Mother Russia. *Academy of Management Review, 5*(1), 7-20.

Simon, H.A. (1990). Information technologies and organizations. *The Accounting Review, 65*(3), 658-667.

Sitkin, S.B. & Pablo, A.L. (1992). Reconceptualizing the determinants of risk behavior. *Academy of Management Review, 17*(1), 9-38.

Smircich, L. (1983). Concepts of culture and organizational analysis. *Administrative Science Quarterly, 28*(3), 339-358.

Smith, K.G., Grimm, C.M., Gannon, M.J., & Chen, M.J. (1991). Organizational information processing, competitive responses, and performance in the U. S. domestic airline industry. *Academy of Management Journal, 34*(1), 60-85.

Stevenson, W.B. and Gilly, M.C. (1991). Information processing and problem solving: the migration of problems through formal positions and networks of ties. *Academy of Management Journal, 34*(4), 918-928.

Strassman, P. (1985). *Information payoff.* New York: Free Press.

Terborg, J.R., Howard, G.S., & Maxwell, S.E. (1980). Evaluating planned organizational change: A method for assessing alpha, beta, and gamma change. *Academy of Management Review, 5*(1), 109-121.

Thompson, J.D. (1967). *Organizations in action.* New York: McGraw-Hill.

Toffler, A. (1980). *The third wave.* New York: Morrow.

Trice, H.M. & Beyer, J.M. (1984). Studying organizational cultures through rites and ceremonies. *The Academy of Management Review, 9*(4), 653-669.

Turner, J. (1985). *Organizational performance, size, and the use of data processing resources* (Working Paper 58). New York: Center for Research in Information Systems, New York University.

van de Vliert, E., Huismans, S.E., & Stok, J.J.L. (1985). The criterion approach to unraveling beta and alpha change. *The Academy of Management Review, 10*(2), 269-275.

Walsh, J.P. & Ungson, G.R. (1991). Organizational memory. *Academy of Management Review, 16*(1), 57-91.

Watson, R.T. (1990). Influences on the IS manager's perceptions: Information scanning and the relationship with the CEO. *MIS Quarterly, 14*(2), 217-231.

Wetherbe, J.C. (1991). Executive information requirements: Getting it right. *MIS Quarterly, 15*(1), 51-65.

Weick, K.E. (1984). Theoretical assumptions and research methodology. In F. W. McFarlan, (Ed.) *The information systems research challenge: Proceedings.* Boston: Harvard Business School Press, (pp. 111-132).

Weill, P. & Olson, M.H. (1989). Managing investment in information technology: Mini case examples and implications. *MIS Quarterly, 13*(1), 3-17.

Wightman, K.R. (1990). The marriage of retail marketing and information systems technology: The Zellers Club Z Experience. *MIS Quarterly, 14*(4), 356-366.

Williamson, O.E. (1971). *Corporate control and business behavior: An inquiry into the effects of organization form on enterprise behavior.* Englewood Cliffs, NJ: Prentice-Hall.

Wilson, J.A. & Elman, N. (1990). Organizational benefits of mentoring. *Academy of Management Executive, 4*(4), 88-94.

Wiseman, C. (1985). *Strategy and computers: Information systems as competitive weapons.* Homewood, IL: Dow-Jones Irwin.

Yates, J. (1990). For the record: The embodiment of organizational memory, 1850-1920. *Business and Economic History* (2nd Series), 19, 1-11.

Yates, J. & Orlikowski, W. (1992). Genres of organizational communication: A structurational approach to studying communication and media. *Academy of Management Review, 17*(2), 299-326.

Zachman, J.A. (1982). Business systems planning and business information control study: A comparison. *IBM Systems Journal, 21*(1), 31-53.

Zammuto, R.F. (1982). Assessing organizational effectiveness: Systems change, adaption and strategy. Albany: State University of New York Press.

Zey, M.G. (1984). *The mentor connection.* Homewood, IL: Dow Jones-Irwin.

Zmud, R.W. (1982). Diffusion of modern software practices: Influence of centralization and formalization. *Management Science, 28*(12), 1421-1431.

Zmud, R.W. & Armenakis, A.A. (1978). Understanding the measurement of change. *Academy of Management Review, 3,* 661-669.

Zmud, R.W., Lind, M.R. & Young, F.W. (1990). An attribute space for organizational communication channels. *Information Systems Research, 1*(4), 440-457.

Zuboff, S. (1988). *In the age of smart machines.* New York: Basic Books.

Part IV

Emerging Technologies Decisions

CHAPTER 13

TECHNOLOGY CHOICE AND USER TRAINING: A TRADEOFF PERSPECTIVE

Nancy C. Weida
Bucknell University

The challenges involved in both choosing new technologies and in developing appropriate training programs for new and existing technologies are critical for organizational survival. The objectives of the chapter are to discuss general issues of technology choice and user training, and to present a tradeoff model to assist organizations in choosing appropriate levels of both. The model, because of its simplicity and intuitive appeal, can be applied to a wide range of decision choices.

Issues of process analysis, continuous improvement, the lure of new technologies and their inherent hidden costs, and the realities of user training are included in the chapter. The example of effective training in spreadsheet use, in particular in the context of the newly-available optimizers and solvers, is offered as an opportunity for organizations to improve information dissemination and decision making.

In preparing for both emerging technologies and the future "flat" organizational form, educators and industry must interact more effectively in preparing future managers for the changes ahead.

The primary mission of this book is to analyze the many facets of the issues, challenges, and trends of emerging information technologies facing organizations. This chapter considers the challenges involved in both choosing new technologies, and in developing appropriate training programs for new and existing technologies. The objectives of this chapter are thus to discuss general issues of technology choice and user training, present the importance of their interaction, and consider tradeoffs.

As new technologies continue to emerge, the issues of choosing the correct technologies and providing adequate and effective training will remain central. In making these important decisions, tradeoffs must be considered. In analyzing state-of-the-art technologies, organizations must realize that a thorough analysis of the underlying process to be automated or improved must be undertaken.

The chapter begins in the next section with a background of the topic from the point of view of the failure of new technologies to live up to their promise and promises. The reasons for such criticism will be discussed from a perspective of process analysis and continuous improvement. The section, *Technology Choices and Training*, contains the main thrust of the chapter, discussing the issues of technology choice and training by considering two main topics: (i) the lure of new technologies and their inherent hidden costs; and (ii) the realities of training and the temptation to undertrain. Solutions and recommendations are then offered for effective technology choice and training by introducing (i) a tradeoff model, (ii) success factors in technology choice and training, and (iii) the example of spreadsheet training, especially with respect to the use of newly-available optimizers or solvers. In the *Future Trends* section the implications of technology choice and training for the future "flat" organization is discussed. The chapter ends with conclusions and a plea for educators and industry to work together more effectively in preparing future managers.

BACKGROUND

Computer technology is frequently criticized for not living up to its promises and hype. Critics point to multimillion dollar installations that do not result in improved business practices. In many cases, the two major reasons for failure are: (1) technology choice; and (2) user training. An inappropriate choice of technology often occurs because poor planning and analysis of the system has taken place prior to the technology choice. Coupled with systems that may even be designed to perform the wrong tasks, incomplete or inappropriate user training exacerbates the problem.

In industry, there is concern that personal computers have not produced the payoff promised (Bowen, 1986, Plenert, 1987, Miller, 1989). Concern centers around the fact that anticipated productivity gains have not been realized. Of course, in order to use computer technology efficiently, it may be necessary to change work flows and processes, and to make sure that the computer is being used for appropriate tasks and in appropriate ways (Bowen, 1986). It is also necessary to ensure that the computer is actually being used, and not merely collecting dust in the corner of an office.

We must thus learn to judge the applications for which automation is most appropriate. We must also understand that processes must be changed before automation takes place. In so doing, it may even be the case that a simplified manual process is preferred to an automated, but more complex, one.

The hard lessons learned are that large payoffs come not from newer, fancier equipment, but from doing things differently. It is not cost-effective or smart merely to automate the old ways faster and faster with each new release of software and hardware. Success stories all involve *change* in the way of doing things, often in the basic aspects of the processes. Complete analysis of the system is performed first. It must be recognized that technology choice, installation, implementation, and training involve large commitments of money and time. Tradeoffs are involved in all phases of the process. Unfortunately, many organizations have had to learn the hard way that skimping on the training phase never pays off.

In this age of total quality management (TQM) and continuous improvement, organizations are becoming more aware of the importance of analyzing the process *before* the hardware and software are chosen. The idea is to avoid doing the wrong things *faster*! In so doing, the key is to "simplify, simplify, simplify" processes first. It may even be the case that simplification replaces automation.

Bowen (1986) describes how William D. Bradshaw of Northern Telecom approaches his clients' requests for new technology. He tries to limit the use of technology by improving the methods themselves. For example, in a job Bradshaw and his former supervisor William H. Murdaugh performed involving the shipment of telephone switching hardware, the hardware was boxed, sealed, and sent to quality control where inspectors had to open and eventually reseal the boxes. The clients were interested in an automated way of speeding the process, when it was the process itself that was in need of changing!

When managers fail to analyze the process before automating, painful lessons will be learned. This learning process can take a very long time, and frustrate all those involved. Often the learning curves are longer than anticipated. Much of the disappointment with technology can be alleviated by helping users develop more realistic expectations with respect to performance and startup time.

TECHNOLOGY CHOICE AND TRAINING

Issues, Controversies, Problems

The Lure of New Technologies: Hidden Costs. As computer and other technologies become more elegant and accessible, it is tempting to try to stay on the "leading edge" in terms of upgrades and new innovations. We must be careful, however, to understand the effects of such a strategy, and to realize that more technology does not automatically mean improved productivity and better decision making. The "leading edge" in business can be achieved only through the judicious use of emerging technologies.

New and emerging technologies are exciting, and important for us to consider! But many of us get caught up in an endless and costly spiral of constant upgrades of software and equipment because of the lure of the new. This is true, even when what we have currently is adequate for our needs.

While recognizing the excitement and implications of new technologies, we must cast a critical eye at how we use technology. We must be sure to prepare workers adequately to cope effectively with the emerging technologies of the twenty-first century. In addition, we must ensure that workers can be agents to change. Achievement of this goal does not necessarily require that every organization be equipped with the newest technologies on the market.

Ashworth (1986) has pointed out that personal computers in the workplace can lead to significant hidden costs as the trend of having novices use them for more complex applications continues. These costs arise from poorly built models leading to poor decisions. The costs are often hidden due to the fact that users may be overconfident of their abilities because they have mastered keystrokes, but not the modelling process itself. He suggests that companies can save money by using methodologies available to regulate the model development process. In particular, the phases of analysis, design, actual model construction, and testing must be emphasized and implemented in the training process.

Trauth and Cole (1992) discuss issues related to user support as end-user computing continues to grow. They use case studies to show how organizational support forms can overcome software interface limitations. The software interface will impact the user's ability to comprehend the modelling process.

Realities of Training: The Temptation to Undertrain. As discussed in Weida (1990), the emphasis in employee training appears to be on getting the computer to "work" correctly so that the task at hand can be completed as painlessly and as rapidly as possible. While it is important to train users to become efficient in the use of computer software, it is also essential to examine how users can be better trained to understand the analytical aspects of the software they are using. It is essential for users to understand that if software is used incorrectly, its output becomes the input to bad decision making by misleading the user into believing the computerized output is "right".

Training is clearly a key aspect of the use of any new technology. In fact, as many companies have learned, it may be the case that training will cost more than the software itself. Some companies have brought training in-house through the use of computer-aided-instruction (CAI). When CAI is used, however, the tendency to see the computer as "in charge" of the entire process must be avoided, and the modelling must come from the user. Over twenty-five years ago, Ackoff (1967) addressed the myth that users need only to *use* an information system as opposed to *understanding* it. In the modern-day scenario of microcomputers and more user-friendly interfaces this myth must still be addressed.

Unfortunately, conventional wisdom dictates that those familiar and comfortable with computers require minimal training, that somehow vague instructions and a user's manual can take the place of detailed instruction. While it is true that these more experienced users will not require extensive training concerning the use of the computer itself, much time must be spent on the issues of the uses, potential abuses and misinterpretations resulting from the models developed.

For example, as presented in Weida (1992b, 1992c, 1990), in the case of spreadsheet training, a disservice is being performed if the technical aspects of spreadsheets and personal computers are emphasized at the expense of a true understanding of the modelling process inherent in spreadsheet use, because by so doing the mistaken notion that the computer is doing all the "hard" work is reinforced in a trainee's mind. Spreadsheets, along with many other software applications for business, perform relatively simple calculations rapidly, and in an easy-to-use format. They do not, however, perform any of the analytical tasks necessary for good model-building, that is, the "hard" work. These analytical tasks must be performed by the user.

What are we trying to achieve in training? Technical competency, certainly, but there is a deeper and more lasting set of competencies that must be at the forefront of our thinking. These competencies include critical thinking and analytical skills, and an appreciation of the intricacies and varying types of data and information. This is because technologies will change, but the need for a well-honed set of analytical skills will become even more important as we enter the twenty-first century, and more technological innovations continue to be introduced. We must thus not give trainees the impression that technique and form is all that matters.

Thus we face a paradox: as more technologies emerge, workers need better-honed analytical skills to use and evaluate the effects of the new technologies effectively, but as we spend more time in training on analytical skills, we have less time available for teaching the new technologies. We thus need to weigh the tradeoffs very carefully, as we realize that we cannot do everything! We must be certain, however, that workers are not shortchanged in developing analytical and critical thinking skills, abilities that can grow throughout a lifetime. People deserve a chance to become lifelong learners.

Solutions and Recommendations: Effective Technology Choice and Training

Processes need to be re-evaluated to gain benefits from automation. As part of the continuous improvement analyses organizations conduct, automation must be examined in a new light. Also necessary are ways of increasing analytical skills of the users of technology, thereby improving decision making. Merely learning keystrokes during training is not enough. For example, when doing statistical analyses, it is critical to understand the assumptions made by the software in performing the desired computation. When using spreadsheet software, as discussed below, users must know that spreadsheets themselves are types of models.

A Tradeoff Model. In order to analyze tradeoff choice, consider a basic tradeoff model[1]. See Figure 1. The variable on the horizontal axis, x, is a variable under the control of the decision maker. When making a decision (i.e. choosing a value for the variable x), the decision maker explicitly or implicitly looks at the cost tradeoff between choosing larger versus smaller values of x. These costs in a particular scenario can represent dollars, or time, or another entity the decision maker prefers to have as low a value as possible. Some costs increase with x (the upward sloping curve in Figure 1), and some costs decrease with x (the downward sloping curve). The top curve represents total (expected) costs. In choosing x, the decision maker considers a "range of optimality" where the total costs (the top "U-shaped" curve) are low. If mathematical equations are available, the "optimal" (i.e. "best") value of x can be determined using elementary calculus, either performed by the user or by software such as Mathcad, Derive, or Mathematica. If empirical data are obtainable, simulations can be run to determine the range of optimality. But the important point is that numbers and equations are not required for this model to be useful for users of technology. Just by articulating the cost tradeoffs, and by viewing the general shape of the curves, an important decision aid is created. As described in Weida (1991), the use of computers in graphical analyses offers an excellent way of analyzing the uncertainties inherent in all managerial decision making, and of understanding the critical importance of sensitivity analysis.

The use of such a tradeoff graph is useful as a benchmark or first cut in the analysis of choosing a value of x. Other considerations can then be factored in, using the tradeoff graph as a base.

The variable x can represent any variable the decision maker can control. For example, if x represents the amount of initial training a typical employee is given when a new system is installed,

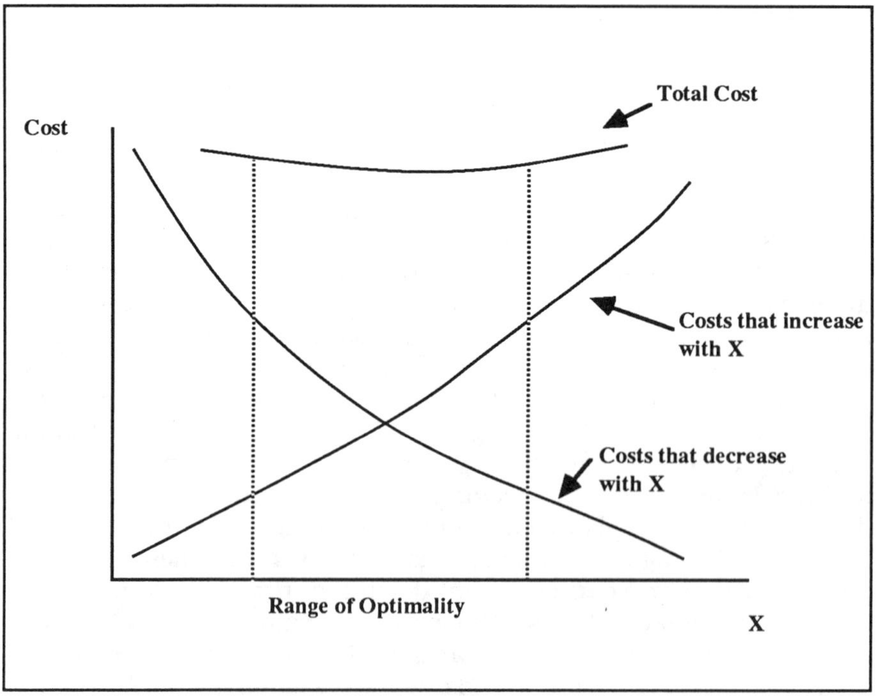

Figure 1

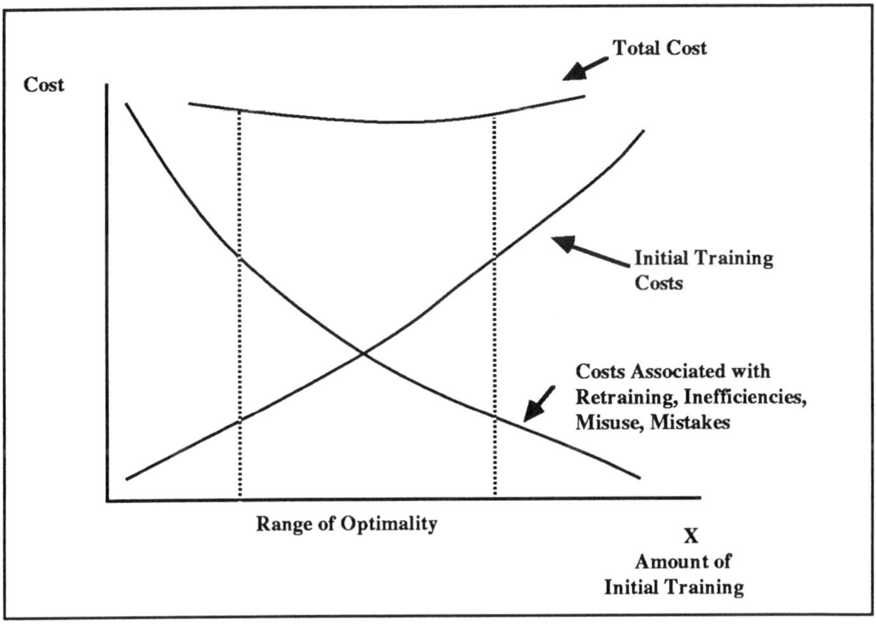

Figure 2

the costs that increase with x are those costs associated with the initial training itself, while the costs that decrease with x are those costs associated with not providing enough initial training, for example, retraining, inefficient use and misuse of the system, and mistakes. See Figure 2. In determining the "optimal" amount of initial training to provide, these costs must be traded off in such a way that the value of x chosen (i.e. the amount of initial training) minimizes total costs. Even if no data are available, this model is useful in helping the decision maker understand the tradeoffs involved.

As a second example, consider technology choice. Suppose three systems of unequal initial cost are under consideration. Suppose that as the initial cost of the system increases, the cost of upgrades and maintenance decreases. Let the variable x represent the system choice. The decision maker wishes to choose the system which best trades off the costs involved. Notice that x is discrete and finite, in that it can take on only one of three possible values (or four, if the decision option "buy no system" is allowed). Thus the mathematical optimum may not be physically possible. The tradeoff graph in Figure 3 is useful to illustrate the tradeoffs involved, and to show which choice is best (in a practical sense) from the point of view of the decision maker.

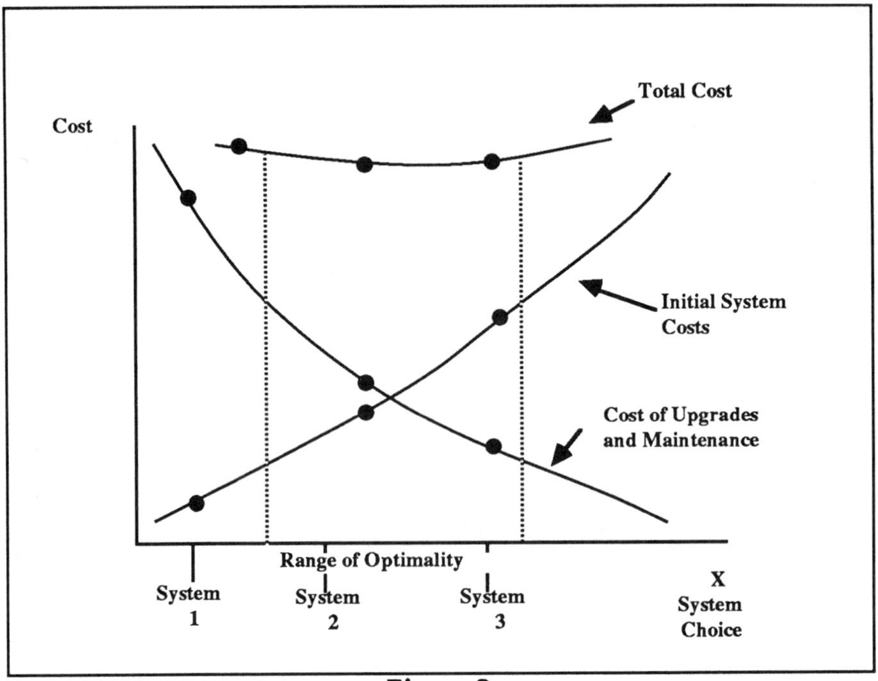

Figure 3

As a final example, consider the choice involved in choosing two-year maintenance contracts for a new system. Three choices are under consideration: (1) No external maintenance contract, thereby incurring no initial costs but high (potential) maintenance costs at a later date; (2) A modestly-priced maintenance contract, which provides coverage for "major" maintenance only, with day-to-day maintenance provided by the system owner; and (3) a high-priced contract which provides complete coverage. The range of optimality is shown in Figure 4.

As the reader can imagine, the use of the basic tradeoff model is wide-ranging, and can be modified to analyze any decision choice involving the trading off of costs. By using the tradeoff framework, other considerations can also be included. For example, the time value of money can be included by changing the shape of the curves.[2] The simple, yet realistic nature of the tradeoff graph allows it to be used, understood and trusted by people of all levels, and from diverse areas of a company. This is an illustration of the power of simplicity.

Successful Training. Currid (1992) recently polled successful managers regarding user training. Their suggestions for improving training involve the following: (1) Promote individuals' successes among competitive colleagues so as to make good computer skills

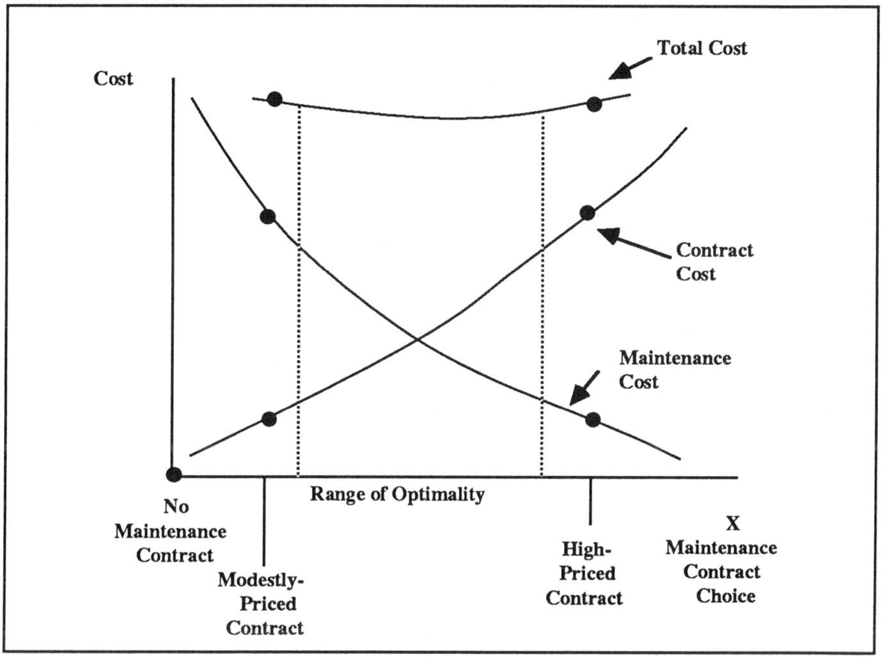

Figure 4

valued in the corporate culture; (2) Require computer training of everyone; (3) Encourage managers to enable employees to attend seminars, workshops, and other forms of training; (4) Recognize that training is a process, not a program; and (5) Make sure training is accessible for a long period of time.

Companies must be careful to cater to the varying learning styles of its employees. In addition, they must be sensitive to the timing of training. Training should ideally be done as systems are implemented, not before. In addition, care must be taken to avoid "information overload" on the part of employees bombarded with information in intense one-shot training programs. Thus, tradeoffs must be carefully considered.

More companies may resort to company-wide training in the future. Organizations are realizing that the relatively small amount of money (in comparison to the amount spent on hardware and software) spent in various training is money well spent. Since training is a process, not a program, companies can utilize continuous improvement in training as well as in their production and service processes. Companies also have learned that skills not used in day-to-day operations are quickly forgotten, thus requiring the need for training over extended periods of time. Thus, the tradeoffs involving the extra money and time spent on implementing and maintaining training programs are clearly tipped in the favor of improved training.

Example: The Case of Spreadsheet Training. Even though spreadsheets have been widely-available and widely-used for over a decade, their use and misuse may be costing companies millions each year. Much of this cost could be eliminated if proper effective training procedures were put in place.

Now that two of the most popular spreadsheets, Excel and Quattro Pro, have *optimizers* or *solvers* built-in, and Lotus 1-2-3's add-ins such as What's Best and What-if Solver are becoming better known, a new world of problem-solving capabilities is available on the popular spreadsheet platform. These features allow users to solve complex problems consisting of objectives (goals) and constraints (for example, restrictions with respect to resources and time), thereby solving linear programming and nonlinear programming problems. Because of these features' relative ease of use, it is imperative for users to understand the sophisticated underlying mathematical model for a particular situation.

As Weida (1992c) describes, in order for trainees to become qualified users of spreadsheet software, they must be trained to conceptualize spreadsheets as mathematical models. New users should also be encouraged to look for further applications of the model being developed, because in many cases a model will be modified for use in different decision making situations. This is due to the fact that the underlying mathematical model may be similar even though outward differences of the business decision making situations are evident. A good modeler looks for, appreciates, and takes advantage of these similarities.

As users begin to appreciate the nature of the modelling process, they will be better able to recognize that many problems can more easily be understood and solved using other than spreadsheet software. For example, in several instances it may be the case that database software is a more appropriate tool than spreadsheet software. A user trained to think in terms of models may be better able to make this distinction.

Some authors (e.g., Middleton (1986), Werner (1988)) have advocated the importance of getting new users working quickly on problems when first confronted with spreadsheet software. While it is important to make users feel comfortable with the technology, this approach has often been carried to an extreme, and to a point that is actually harmful. Kee and Mason (1988), for example, warn against the use of such a "quick and dirty" approach in solving problems using spreadsheets due to the fact that the results are usually undocumented, unstructured, error-prone, and difficult for others to use or understand. By increasing user understanding of the modelling process, better solutions to problems, regardless of the technology incorporated, should be the result.

A significant finding of the empirical work of Davies and Ikin (1987) is that so few users of spreadsheet software received any formal education in spreadsheet use beyond basic manipulation. The authors find this troubling because professional programmers receive in-depth training in computer languages and various aspects of program construction, documentation, debugging, and testing. The authors note that this lack of complete training may be the root cause of the multimillion dollars of mistakes many believe are made each year due to incorrect use of spreadsheets.

Before any user has complete access to a personal computer, formal education in documentation and model building must be completed. Levanthal (1985) has noted the importance of making sure trainees understand the benefits to be gained by using spreadsheet technology, before being trained in the specifics of its use. She points out the need for helping new users learn to identify which tasks are most important, and which can most usefully be improved using computer technology.

Even with better training it is critical to understand that different analysts may interpret the same data and spreadsheet differently, and offer alternate choices of action. Again, the idea that the computer is somehow "right" must be dispelled. Also, data inaccuracies become even more distorted when data manipulations are performed in a spreadsheet. Trainees must learn to have a healthy skepticism regarding the accuracy of data that are input into spreadsheet models. This is particularly critical when using the new optimizers and solvers.

Others have recently pointed out the importance of continuing to emphasize a problem-solving focus in teaching the uses of all forms of technology. For example, Kee and Mason (1988) have warned of potential difficulties resulting from novice users creating complex spreadsheets. This is due to the lack of controls. To combat this problem they recommend that the issue of internal controls to promote the reliability, efficiency, and security of spreadsheet software be studied.

FUTURE TRENDS

Vazsonyi (1991) discusses the future business environment in terms of the "information organization." He extends Peter Drucker's description of an orchestra as a metaphor of the non-bureaucratic, flat organizational structure of the future by describing top management in the coming information organization as the creator of the vision and composer of the musical score, who revises the score as the environment changes. The "orchestra" (i.e. the rest of the company) interprets the score and translates the vision of top management into reality. Thus, in the future, there will be fewer levels of sifting, filtering, interpretation, and distorting of the information top management requests, and receives.

Vazsonyi (1991) asserts that the managers of the future will thus be "knowledge workers." These knowledge workers will collect, manage, and disperse information. Ideally, they will possess a generalist's understanding of the broad objectives of the field, while at the same time being specialists in their fields.

The proper use of electronic mail will help create the future "flat" organization by increasing a manager's ability to communicate. This is achieved by making more people directly report to a particular individual, thereby creating fewer levels. The result is fewer top managers, with more people reporting to these top managers.

In the future "flat" organization, technology choice and training will remain critical issues. As more people have access to more information both internal and external to the organization, the tradeoff model can be easily utilized and shared by more people in making such choices. Because of its non-technical nature and utility, it can be of real value in decision making.

CONCLUSION

Organizations must be adequately prepared to cope effectively with the changing technologies and environments available for the workplace of the twenty-first century. The lure of new technologies in recent years has been tempered by both economic realities and unmet (and sometimes unrealistic) expectations. Especially in tight economic times, organizations must learn to be selective about the technologies they use by first carefully analyzing the processes to be automated. Then, effective training programs must be designed and implemented to trade off optimally the costs of providing training with the costs associated with undertrained employees.

And what about the training of future managers? As described in Weida (1992a), in today's economic climate, it is not unusual to find more students expressing a preference for skill-building and resume-enhancing, as opposed to deep and lasting intellectual development. We should not be surprised to find more students feeling this way, given the expense of higher education, and the stiff competition for jobs upon graduation. We must be sure, then, to give our students the necessary skills they want, need and deserve. At the same time we must plant the seeds of future intellectual enhancement and lifelong learning. This is not to imply that we should ignore technology. Nor should we take the attitude that "technology is not worth learning since it's all going to change anyway!" We all must be exposed to as much technology as is feasible, provided that analytical and critical thinking skills are not compromised.

Partnerships between industry and higher education need to be maintained and enhanced. More research studies need to be conducted to examine the interaction of technology use and learning. It is our obligation to see that emerging technologies in education and industry are used responsibly and effectively.

ENDNOTES

[1] The reader may recognize the structure of this model as that of the "Economic Order Quantity (EOQ)" Model.

[2] This is true provided that the upward sloping and downward sloping cost curves are increasing and decreasing, respectively, throughout the domain of interest, so that the resulting total cost curve remains convex (or "U-shaped").

REFERENCES

Ackoff, R. L. (1967). Management Misinformation Systems. *Management Science, 14*(4), B147-B156.

Ashworth, A. (1986, September 18). Between the (Spread)sheets: How to Build Model Models. *Computing Canada*, pp. 3-6.

Bowen, W. (1986, May 26). The Puny Payoff from Office Computers. *Fortune*, pp. 20-24. Currid, C. (1992, February 3).

Corporate Computer Literacy Can be Addressed by Simply Training Users. *Infoworld*, p. 52.

Davies, N., & Ikin, C. (1987, December). Auditing Spreadsheets. *Australian Accountant*, pp. 54-56.

Kee, R. C., & Mason, J. O., Jr. (1988, February). Preventing Errors in Spreadsheets. *Internal Auditor*, pp. 42-47.

Levanthal, N. (1985). Software Shuffle: Training for the Right Reasons. *Management World, 14*(6), 44-48.

Middleton, B. (1986). Getting Up to Speed on Spreadsheet Software. *Supervisory Management, 31*(4), 12-14.

Miller, M. M. (1989, September 18). PCs and Productivity: Where's the Payoff? *Infoworld*, pp. 59-62.

Plenert, G. (1987, November). The PC — A Time-Saving Necessity or a Fiasco?

Journal of Systems Management, pp. 30-32.

Trauth, E. M., & Cole, E. (1992). The Organizational Interface: A Method for Supporting End Users of Packaged Software. *MIS Quarterly, 16*(1), 35-53.

Vazsonyi, A. (1991, December/January). The Coming of the Information Organization. *Decision Line*, pp. 17-18.

Weida, N. C. (1990). Training Implications of Spreadsheet Modelling. *Proceedings of the 1990 Information Resources Management Association International Conference* (Executive Summary), 147.

Weida, N. C. (1991). The Importance of Teaching Students Interactive Graphical Decision Making on the Personal Computer. Proceedings of the 1991 International Business Schools Computer Users Group Annual North American Conference, 105-108.

Weida, N. C. (1992a). "Do We Have to Know This for the Exam?" Teaching Skill-Hungry and Grade-Oriented Students in Quantitatively-Oriented Courses. *Proceedings of the 1992 International Business Schools Computer Users Group Annual North American Conference*, 425-428.

Weida, N. C. (1992b). Let's Be Careful About Throwing Money and Technology at Pedagogical Problems. *Proceedings of the 1992 Information Resources Management Association International Conference*, 81-83.

Weida, N. C. (1992c). User Education in Spreadsheet Modelling. Discussion Paper, Bucknell University.

Werner, T. W. (1988). Microcomputers in the Workplace (Yes, but Have You Considered...?) *Professional Safety, 33*(12), 19-21.

CHAPTER 14

AN OVERVIEW OF THE OUTSOURCING DECISION

Karen Ketler and John Walstrom
Eastern Illinois University

Jennifer L. Wagner
Roosevelt University

Outsourcing is the process of contracting with an external vendor part or all of the activities of the information systems department. Some organizations elect to outsource the entire information systems department. Others only outsource a specific segment, such as network management. Still, other firms elect not to outsource. Factors in the outsourcing decision include (1) cost, (2) personnel, (3) control, (4) organizational characteristics, (5) vendor characteristics and (6) contract issues. This article develops a five-step decision methodology for determining whether a specific organizational information systems activity is a candidate for successful outsourcing. The analyses include: 1) the strengths and weaknesses of the information systems department; 2) characteristics of the data/segment; 3) characteristics of the organization; 4) vendors and 5) contract.

Outsourcing is the transferring of an internal activity of an organization to an external vendor. The outsourcing concept is not new. It has been applied to accounting and bookkeeping services for many years. Similarly, information systems (IS) activities have been outsourced since the dawn of business computing. However, there is a renewed interest in outsourcing in the 1990s.

The rate of growth of information technology is increasing, and is expected to continue to increase at an exponential rate. It is not surprising that many organizations are experiencing difficulty in keeping up with the technology changes. Outsourcing is one solution to this problem. It is a means of managing the emerging technologies in the 1990s.

Organizations can be grouped into three categories based on their IS outsourcing practices. The first category is complete outsourcing. These firms hire one or more vendors to oversee their entire information processing. In the past, this service was provided from an off-site centralized location; however, vendors have recently started offering this service from the customer's site(s).

Partial outsourcing, an option chosen by a second group of organizations, is the transferring to a vendor one or more IS segments from the firms' IS function. Facilities management, systems development and maintenance programming have been outsourced since the 1960s. In the 1990s, network management, telecommunications and systems integration are the fastest growing outsourced segments, averaging approximately 23% annually (McMullen, 1990).

The third category of organizations do not outsource. Eighty percent of the respondents in a recent survey indicated that they did not outsource any of their IS activities *and* had no plans to start outsourcing within the next five years (Radding, 1990b).

Most firms have spent countless hours of research before deciding on an outsourcing strategy. Once the research is completed, organizations often reach very different conclusions. Kinney Wall Coverings made the decision to follow a complete outsourcing strategy, while Southland Corporation opted for partial outsourcing of its computer operations segment. On the other hand, Avon Products totally rejected outsourcing and kept all IS segments in-house.

Kinney Wall Coverings

The IS staff at Kinney Wall Coverings of Oakland, California consists of two individuals: a director and his assistant. The rest of the IS department has been outsourced to OBS Companies in San Francisco. Rapid changes in computer technology and IS staffing problems were major reasons for reaching the outsourcing decision. Decisions concerning technology no longer the responsibility (and liability) of Kinney. During the time that Kinney has been outsourcing, OBS has made five changes in computer technology. Access to state-of-the-art equipment is one advantage of outsourcing. Another advantage is that risk associated with hardware upgrades and conversions is reduced (Radding, 1990b).

A third advantage of outsourcing for Kinney Wall Coverings is the elimination of IS staffing problems. Kinney now has access to highly trained IS professionals without having recruitment and retention concerns. When a user requires additional software, the two IS members at Kinney meet with the user. Together, they design the application. The design is then forwarded to OBS for a cost estimate. The user accepts or rejects the application based on the cost estimate provided by OBS (Radding, 1990b). This arrangement means that Kinney is no longer faced with the problem of hiring temporary programmers for short-term development projects.

Elimination of the risk of associated with technological changes, and personal problems were advantages of outsourcing for Kinney Wall Coverings. However, personnel issues were considered a disadvantage of outsourcing for Southland. They selected a partial outsourcing strategy to alleviate a financial crisis.

Southland

Southland Corporation, the parent company of 7-Eleven convenience stores, needed capital in order to offset the construction costs of a large building located near corporate headquarters. This 11-story building was unoccupied except for two floors which housed Southland's data center. They planned to lease the rest of the building, but the rental outlook in Dallas was poor (Williamson, 1991b).

Southland Corporation found itself in this tenuous situation as a result of a leveraged buyout and junk bonds. Affiliated Computer Systems (ACS), a budding outsourcing services provider, offered Southland a solution to its problems. ACS would lease the entire building and manage the data center for Southland. As a result of this outsourcing venture, Southland reduced its IS expenditures 18% over a two year period. ACS gained its first outsourcing client, and Southland had eased its monetary crisis with the leasing revenues and decreased IS expenditures.

However, the venture was not all positive. Outsourcing at Southland caused personnel problems. What would happen to the 297 individuals in the IS department at Southland? Only 33% of the original 297 members of the IS department would remain at Southland, primarily in the area of system development. ACS hired 70 individuals (24%) from Southland's staff. Unfortunately, 128 individuals (43%) were laid off or voluntarily left the company (Williamson, 1991b). While Southland found a solution to financial problems and Kinney found a solution to personnel problems in outsourcing, it is not a solution for every organization. Avon Products is an example of a firm that considered and rejected the outsourcing concept.

Avon Product

Avon Products, looking to reduce their IS expenditures by 15%, contacted four outsourcing vendors. All of the vendors recommended consolidation of numerous regional data centers. However, outsourcing vendors could only offer a 5% cost savings to Avon. Avon Products felt that the 5% savings was not attractive enough to offset the additional risk associated with the loss of control of their IS services (O'Leary, 1990). Avon rejected the outsourcing offers. They did elect to restructure and consolidate their data centers which resulted in an annual savings of $3 million (Mandell, 1991).

Avon Products has an IS department with an excellent performance record. Outsourcing vendors were unable to make major improvements in the well-run organization. Avon was also concerned with the risk associated with returning an IS segment back to the organization if the outsourcing venture proved unsuccessful. It is difficult to return an outsourced segment back to an organization as the IS staff and its technical expertise is greatly reduced as a result of the outsourcing contract.

In these three examples, one organization indicates that outsourcing solved its *personnel* problems. Yet, in another organization, outsourcing created personnel problems. Similarly, one organization liked the elimination of the risk of technology conversions associated with outsourcing; yet, Avon Products expressed concern over risk and the loss of *control* over the quality of IS services. Some organizations save up to 50% of their IS expenditures through outsourcing (Due, 1992; Huff, 1991); others have only nominal savings. This paradox makes it difficult to cite true advantages and disadvantages of outsourcing.

Objectives

Outsourcing success depends upon the organization. The focus of this chapter is to develop a decision methodology for determining whether a specific organizational IS segment and its associated data are candidates for successful outsourcing. In order to accomplish this task, the specific objectives are:

1. To review the literature on the importance of financial, personnel

and control issues on the outsourcing decision
2. To discuss the steps in the outsourcing decision
3. To establish criteria to determine if there is a problem/weakness in the IS area which can be solved by outsourcing
4. To analyze the characteristics of IS segments and data which can be successfully outsourced
5. To identify organizational traits which are keys to successful outsourcing
6. To analyze the attributes of the vendor which will contribute to a positive outsourcing partnership
7. To discuss the critical variables in the outsourcing contract

BACKGROUND

History of Outsourcing

In the 1960s, the data processing service bureau industry offered a solution to the high cost of computer hardware. Vendors provided outsourcing services in the form of operations management. Customers eliminated the expense of computer hardware. Cost was a primary factor in the outsourcing decision in the 1960s.

In the 1970s, computer hardware decreased in price. Data processing centers decentralized to provide better service to the users. As a result, there was an increase in the demand for software applications. Because the existing supply of IS specialists could not fulfill these requests, the outsourcing of systems development and contract programming increased in popularity. The inadequate supply of IS specialists and other issues related to personnel were the major factors in the outsourcing decision during the 1970s.

Emphasis in the 1980s was on the use of information for a competitive advantage. IS became a strategic weapon and a valued function of the firm. Organizations sought to control their IS services and questioned the risks associated with outsourcing. The outsourcing trend began to fade as IS investments grew in both technology and personnel.

In the 1990s, management is seeking options to increase the efficiency of IS departments and to show greater returns on the investment in information technology. Restructuring, in the form of downsizing, consolidating, and centralizing, is becoming popular. The 1990s are also characterized by the growth of international markets. Organizations are able to compete in the global marketplace due to improved telecommunications technology. However, staffing of the IS function is problematic due not only to the shortages of IS personnel but also to the wide variety of required skills resulting from rapid technological changes. Outsourcing solves both restructuring, and personnel problems.

However, the issue of the strategic value of information complicates the outsourcing decision. Additional analysis of what information can provide a competitive advantage is required. The simple answer is to determine what information is strategic and outsource the rest. However, with system integration, the line between strategic and non-strategic data may be difficult to locate.

Literature Review

Outsourcing in the 1990s is an issue that divides IS managers. The irony of this division is that both the proponents and opponents of outsourcing cite the same variables, but their perspective is different. The common threads that were seen not only in the three examples of organizations in the previous section, but also in the history of outsourcing are the variables of personnel, cost and control.

These same variables were cited as being both advantages and disadvantages of outsourcing in a 1991 survey, conducted by the market research firm of Ledgeway/Dataquest. Over 500 CIOs and IS directors of Fortune 1000, government and public sector organizations participated in the study. The most frequently cited advantages of outsourcing were in the personnel area. Sixty-eight percent of the respondents looked to outsourcing as an alternative to temporary staff increases for short-term projects. Increased knowledge and expertise of the staff was cited as an advantage by 53.6%. Outsourcing as a solution to the recruitment problems associated with the inadequate supply of IS professionals was mentioned by 39.1%. However, 36% cited loss of in-house expertise as a disadvantage of outsourcing (Schwartz, 1992).

Responses were also mixed relative to the cost variable. Approximately 20% of the CIOs cited cost reduction as an advantage of outsourcing. Improved financial performance was mentioned as a benefit by nearly 5%. However, higher than expected costs was cited as a drawback by nearly 40% (Schwartz, 1992).

Strategic implications were mentioned as an advantage by 12.8% of the CIOs. Outsourcing allows management to emphasize the primary business of the organization rather than spending time and effort on IS operations. Nearly six percent of the respondents cited sharing the risk associated with technology decisions as an advantage. However, 31% mentioned loss of control as a disadvantage of outsourcing (Schwartz, 1992).

An analysis of the impact of each of these three variables

(financial, personnel, and control) has been conducted by numerous authorities in the literature. A review of the literature that investigates the relationship of each of these variables to the outsourcing decision follows.

Financial Issues

Many authorities cite cost reduction as the primary issue for outsourcing (Huff, 1991; Radding, 1990b). The underlying reason bringing about these cost reductions is economies of scale. An outsourcing vendor is able to spread fixed IS costs over a broader base of customers. They can offer IS services to the customers at a lower cost and still show a profit. Poorly managed IS centers can expect to reduce their IS expenditures by as much as 50% by outsourcing (Due, 1992; Huff, 1991).

In addition, incremental increases in the power of computer hardware are available at a declining price structure. This allows service providers to purchase larger machines at a lower cost per processing unit. A data center with a computer system executing less than 50 millions instructions per second (MIPS) would benefit from economies of scale (Kelly, 1990).

Controversy does exist concerning how to evaluate the cost savings associated with outsourcing. Leibs (1990) believes that in-house IS expenses can be reduced from 4% to 5% through consolidation, improved price/performance ratio of hardware, and downsizing. Scheier (1990) states the cost of a well-run corporate data center should decrease between 10% and 15% annually due to falling hardware prices.

Due (1992) includes the decrease in personnel salaries as an advantage of outsourcing. He explains that outsourcing is one process whereby an employer can dismiss their less productive employees. He adds that fewer employees mean less investment in pension plans and other employee benefits. However, the dismissed (or transferred) employee may be entitled to a severance package. For example, after Kodak negotiated with Businessland, Inc. for personal computing outsourcing services, Kodak was liable for a $15,000 severance package for each employee who transferred to Businessland. This totaled $150,000 (Krass, 1990).

Huff (1991) cites the avoidance of capital expenditures as a benefit of outsourcing. With facilities management, the customer pays a service fee as opposed to the capital investment required for in-house computer hardware. Managers are generally able to obtain operating budget funding more easily than capital budget funding. However, this transfer may have a negative effect on the tax liability of the firm. Computer hardware can be depreciated; outsourcing fees cannot (Krass, 1990).

The reduced capital investment associated with outsourcing the facilities management segment can result in an increased return on equity (Wagner, 1992; Oltman, 1990b). However, outsourcing may have a negative effect on the gross profit margin (Wagner, 1992). Outsourcing fees increase expenditures and reduce profits.

Kaufman (1990) cites more clearly defined costs as an advantage of outsourcing. He points out that costs are explicitly stated in the contract. Powers (1990), and Schwartz (1992) disagree. Powers indicates that initial outsourcing billings are 20% higher than expected. He attributes this to: 1) poor forecasting of actual computer usage by the client; 2) low vendor estimates; and, 3) an honest misunderstanding of the contract. Good forecasting skills are essential in clearly defining costs because most contracts specify costs based on usage. But forecasting usage five to ten years in the future is difficult. Higher than expected costs was cited as a disadvantage of outsourcing by nearly 40% of the respondents in the Ledgeway/Dataquest survey (Schwartz, 1990).

Personnel Issues

Economies of scales and cost issues again enter into the outsourcing decision on the personnel side. O'Leary (1990) states that as information technology expands, it is difficult for small firms to have an expert in each area. Outsourcing offers these firms increased knowledge and expertise.

However, outsourcing costs the firm because it loses its in-house expertise (Schwartz, 1992). This loss can be expensive. As the in-house expertise decreases, there is a corresponding increase in the need to contact vendors more often with questions. Scheier (1990) wonders whether the vendors' answers reflect the interests of the client or the interests of the vendor.

Outsourcing is a solution to the problem caused by the need to temporarily increase IS staff due to a large systems development project. It eliminates, or at least reduces, the problems associated with recruitment and training of the IS staff. But, as previously pointed out, outsourcing can also create personnel problems.

Due (1992) states that once outsourcing rumors start within an organization, morale and productivity of the IS staff declines. The employees worry not only about layoffs and reduction in benefits, but also about being forced to learn a different skill or technology. Eventually, employees start to leave the firm. Unfortunately for the firm, the more qualified individuals leave first, sometimes even before the outsourcing decision is made (O'Leary, 1990). This makes the transition to outsourcing difficult for both the client and the vendor. To reduce the probability of losing valuable personnel, Due (1992) states that the vendor sometimes tries to win over the key employees by increasing benefits, travel and training.

Once an IS segment has been outsourced, the organization must decide what to do with its displaced workers. Quite possibly, if the outsourced segment was significant, the vendor may need to increase its IS staff. Hiring an individual already trained in the vendor's new applications would be ideal. But, transferring personnel from the client to the vendor is not always successful. Caldwell (1989) cites the difficulty of adjustment, and cultural changes which the employees encounter as reasons for unsuccessful transfers. Redditt and Lodahl (1990) believe that 20% to 30% of the transferred workers leave the vendor within the first year. Some employees will not even accept a transfer because they have had a previous relationship with the vendor (Due, 1992).

Redditt and Lodahl (1990) offer other options for displaced employees. The organization can move an IS employee to other internal units that need IS expertise. Another option is to place a key IS employee with a customer of the firm. The customer gains a knowledgeable employee, and the firm has increased the loyalty and communication with one of its customers. However, even with the previous options, there are still layoffs associated with outsourcing. To assist these employees, outsourcing vendors are now providing placement services (Caldwell, 1989).

Control

Control is another category of issues that proponents of outsourcing view as an advantage, while opponents see it as a disadvantage. O'Leary (1990) states that some vendors believe that the control issue is "a lot of smoke." Most vendors are reputable. Thus, there is little risk in giving up control. On the opposite side, Huff (1991) believes that the loss of control is the primary disadvantage of outsourcing.

To eliminate the risk associated with outsourcing, Wilder (1990b) recommends that the strategic areas of IS be determined. Huff (1991) points out that outsourcing can free IS managers from operational concerns so that they have more time available to focus on the strategic areas. Due (1992) also believes that core management activities and associated resources should not be outsourced. Kelly (1990) quotes vendors who believe that data are not strategic. Strategic issues involve the use of data, not the data themselves.

With systems integration, it is difficult to distinguish between strategic and non-strategic areas. O'Leary (1990) and Huff (1991) believe that facilities/operations management is not a strategic area of IS. O'Leary (1990) adds that the application area is strategic. This is especially true in the service industry if IS products are embedded in the services (Radding, 1990a). Radding (1990a) also advises against outsourcing in highly competitive industries.

The most frequently discussed control issue is disaster recovery. Kelly (1990) calls it the litmus test for vendors. Concerns include security, backup, and disaster recovery procedures. The client is seeking assurances that the vendor will spend an appropriate amount of time and effort on emergency problems. Clients need to know the answers to questions such as: 1) What plan does the vendor have if the data center is destroyed? and 2) Which client would be restored first?

The issues of savings, personnel and control are primary variables in the outsourcing decision. However, they do not adequately cover the complexity and variety of issues in the decision. The following section will attempt to discuss the complexity of the decision and identify a wide variety of variables which need to be researched before the outsourcing decision is made.

OUTSOURCING DECISION METHODOLOGY

Overview of the Outsourcing Decision Methodology

The outsourcing decision is complex. It generally takes 80% of the CIOs time over a three to six month period (Williamson, 1991b). It cannot adequately be depicted in a simple model. However, the major steps involved in the decision can be identified, and the critical variables in each step can be analyzed. The proposed five step model is shown in Figure 1.

The rectangles reflect the processes of analysis and research, and the diamonds identify the decision points. The model consists of five processes and four decisions. The first three processes are internal to the organization. The last two processes are external. The two external processes can be repeated numerous times until an agreement is reached or the negotiations are terminated. Decisions concerning whether or not to continue the analysis are made after completing: 1) the problem identification; 2) the internal processes; and, 3) each iteration of the external processes. A brief description of each process follows:

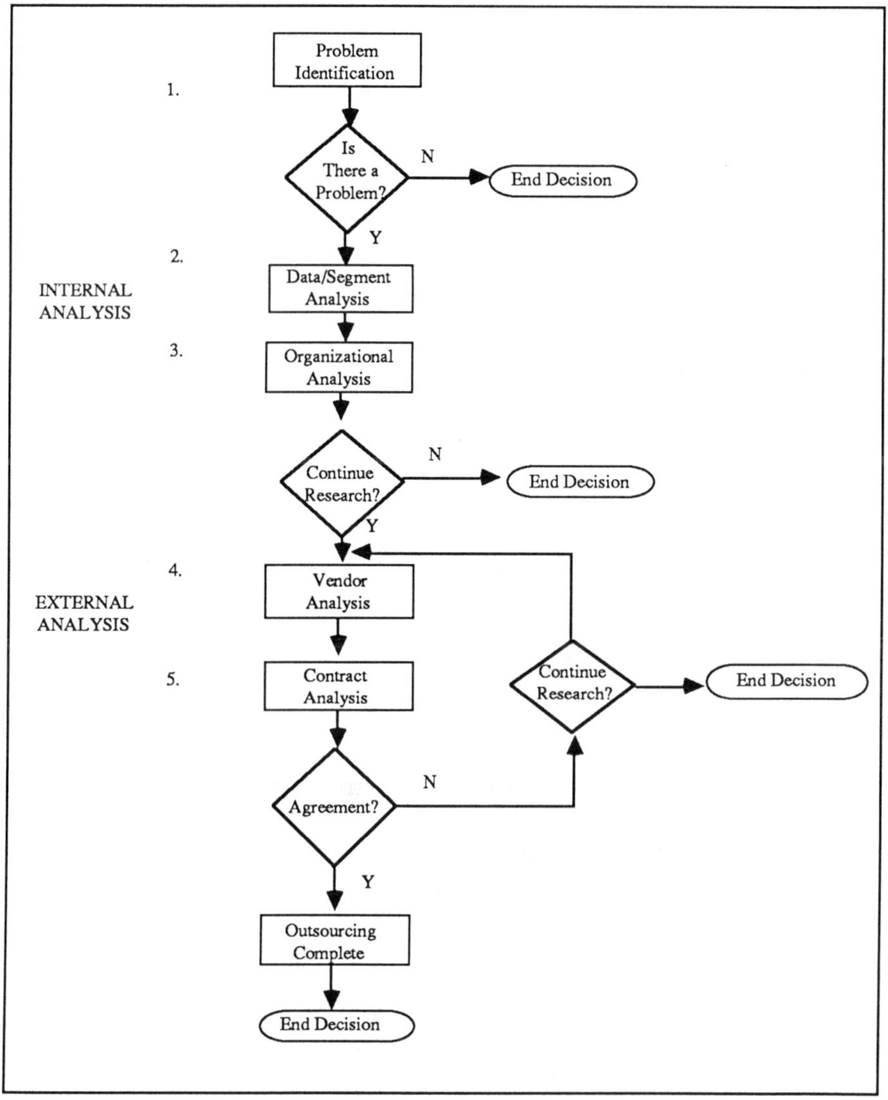

Figure 1: Model of the Outsourcing Decision

1. The problem identification process includes the analysis of the strengths and weaknesses of the IS department. Issues include economic, personnel and quality control topics. The first goal of this step is to determine if there is a problem which outsourcing might solve. The second goal is to determine the segment or segments involved with the problem. Then, should partial or complete outsourcing be considered?

2. The problem is further identified in the data/segment analysis. Does this data have strategic value? Other characteristics of the data/segment which might contribute to the success or failure of outsourcing are reviewed.
3. The last of the internal processes requires an objective view of organizational characteristics. Organizational culture, history, degree of vertical integration and other variables may influence the outsourcing decision.
4. Analysis of the vendor may be the most critical process. The goal of this step is to study vendor characteristics such as their outsourcing track record, long range planning, security, and knowledge of the client's industry.
5. The final process is the analysis of the contract terms. In this step, the organization is often at a decisive disadvantage. The outsourcing vendor is experienced in the desired contract language while the client is not.

Step 1: Problem Identification

The first step is a detailed analysis of the IS department in order to determine its strengths and its weaknesses. The goal of the problem identification step is seeking the answer to the following questions:

1. Is there a problem in the IS department which IS outsourcing might solve?
2. If yes, what is it? Should the organization consider partial or complete outsourcing? Is the problem centered on a particular segment or activity within the department?

Departmental reviews must be objective and comprehensive. Individuals who work in, or manage, the department are not objective. Neither are potential outsourcing vendors. But, it is not difficult to locate an unbiased reviewer. Although IS is very competitive within an industry, there is a camaraderie attitude across industries. User groups, professional organizations, such as the Data Processing Management Association (DPMA) or the Association for Computer Machinery (ACM), and educators are available. These contacts provide a source of competent, objective reviewers.

Howard Anderson of the Yankee Group created a quick quiz to assist an organization in determining whether or not it is a candidate for outsourcing (Anderson, 1990). The purpose of the quiz is to help managers realize what outsourcing can do for an organization. The quiz consists of 15 questions worth 10 points each. These questions probe IS expenditures, personnel issues, control topics and quality of IS services. The majority of the questions fall into one of three categories: 1) Hardware (cost/service activities); 2) Software (personnel intensive activities); and, 3) Strategic Issues (control).

However, the questions are stated so that responses are given in a format of "all" or "nothing". For example, "is the growth of CPU services greater than 10% per year?" If yes, the organization receives 10 points; if no, zero points are awarded. An organization with a high score is a likely candidate for outsourcing. However, in many instances, the cost, personnel and control factors do not fit an "all" or "nothing" response. In the real world, very few issues are "all" or "nothing". Therefore, the quiz was modified to acknowledge intermediate values. In addition, the original quiz does not attempt to isolate what the IS problem area might be. The modified quiz groups the questions into categories of hardware, software, and control. This grouping is done to attempt to more readily identify an IS segment for outsourcing. Figure 2 presents the quiz, in the modified format. Some questions are subjective, such as "what percent of divisional managers would rate divisional IS as excellent?". Therefore, several individuals in the organization should complete the quiz.

Decision 1: Are the Weaknesses of the MIS Department Suitable for Outsourcing? If the quiz indicates that an organization may be a candidate for outsourcing, then the organization should attempt to determine whether the IS problems are confined to one area or spread throughout the entire center. If the problem is centered in the hardware area, then facilities management, telecommunications, and network management are segments for outsourcing consideration. Software problems are centered in the systems development and maintenance segments. If points were gained in the control area of the quiz, then the risks associated with outsourcing are small. However, if the control area responses indicate a competitive industry, outsourcing should be carefully analyzed before any decisions are made.

If there is no problem, there is no need to fix anything or to give further consideration to outsourcing. "It is isn't broke, don't fix it." However, those organizations that score high in a problem area of the quiz, should continue with the internal analysis steps of the model in figure 1, specifically with an investigation of the data/segment characteristics.

Step 2: Characteristics of Data/Segment

This step in the model is a two-fold process. The first part involves an analysis of the traits of the data, and the second is an

Category: Hardware

Question	1	2	3	4	5	6	7	8	9	10
1. What is the growth of CPU services per year?	<0%	0%		5%		10%		15%		≥20%
2. At what percent are your hardware expenses decreasing?	<0%	0%			5%			10%		≥12%
3. What is the ratio between the growth of divisional IS expenditures to the growth of corporate revenue?	.5			.75			1			≥1.25
4. At what percent are your cost per CPU second decreasing?	<5%	6%			10%			14%		≥16%
5. What percent of your IS expenses are you able to bill back to the end users without complaint?	100%		90%		80%		70%		60%	≤55%
6. What percent of the price discounts for off-shift processing to you pass on to your end users?	100%		90%		80%		70%		60%	≤55%
7. What percent of time is service available on the batch network?	100%		99%		98%		97%		96%	<96%
8. What is the average percent of downtime of the on-line network during prime-time hours (8 AM - 8 PM)?	100%		99%		98%		97%		96%	<96%

Adapted from Anderson, 1990

Figure 2: Modified Quiz to Determine Outsourcing Candidacy

Question	1	2	3	4	5	6	7	8	9	10
Category: Software										
1. What is the annual rate of turnover in the IS department?	0%		3%		6%		9%		12%	>12%
2. At what yearly rate are your personnel costs increasing?	≤2%	2%		3%		4%		5%		≥6%
3. What is the ratio between the growth of divisional IS expenditures to the growth of corporate revenue?	.5			.75			1			≥1.25
4. What percent of your applications portfolio more than five years old?	≤10%		30%		50%		70%		90%	100%
Category: Control										
1. How many competitors' IS strategies do you know?	5		4		3		2		1	0
2. What percent of the division general managers would rate divisional IS as 'excellent'?	100%			75%			50%			≤25%
3. What percent of your senior non-IS management (COO, CFO, ...) explain your IS strategy?	100%			75%			50%			≥25%

The larger your point value, the more likely a candidate you are for outsourcing.

Figure 2: Modified Quiz to Determine Outsourcing Candidacy
(continued from previous page)

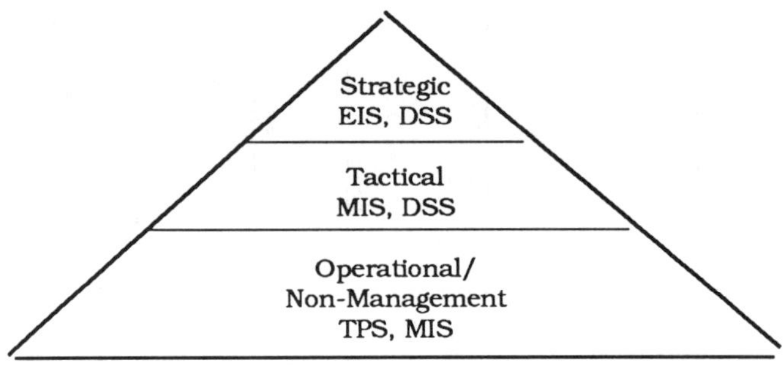

Figure 3: Hierarchical Analysis of IS

analysis of the characteristics of the segment. The major issue is one of control. If the data is not strategic, the risk of outsourcing is reduced. However, with integrated systems, it is difficult to locate the line between strategic and non-strategic data.

One method of deciding whether data is strategic is to determine who uses it. Upper level management generally uses strategic information in Executive Information Systems (EIS) or in Decision Support Systems (DSS). Lower level management and non-management employees generally use the non-strategic data associated with operational management and the transaction processing system (TPS). This hierarchy of information is reflected in Figure 3. Highly competitive service industries in which IS is part of the service are exceptions to this concept at the operational/non-management level. In these organizations, even TPS data can be strategic.

There are concerns about the segment being outsourced. These concerns can be grouped on the basis of whether the outsourced segment is primarily software or hardware. Software segments include system development and maintenance. Buck-Lew (1992) studied successfully outsourced system development projects. He found that these projects have the following characteristics:

1. Short duration (usually less than 1 year);
2. Small project team (generally less than 7 individuals);
3. Sponsored by top management; and,
4. No accounting interface.

Costs are easier to forecast with the smaller projects. Top management sponsorship provided easy funding for outsourcing. In addition, completion dates were generally critical in these projects.

The IS manager could reduce the risk associated with a missed completion date by outsourcing the project. Finally, not having an accounting interface was important to both the client and the vendor. Vendors felt increased liability, and clients felt increased risks when the project interfaced with the accounting system.

Buck-Lew (1992) found that projects with interfaces to the accounting systems could successfully be managed using hybrid teams consisting of personnel from both the client and the vendor. These hybrid teams also reduced the level of difficulty involved in the transition of systems from outsourcing development to in-house maintenance. The history of the development was preserved. In addition, the learning curve associated with maintaining a new project was reduced.

While some organizations outsource system development projects and perform routine maintenance in-house, other organizations do the reverse. Age of application is a crucial factor in the success of outsourcing system maintenance. Maintenance activities are high immediately after implementation. Forecasting time and expenditures would be difficult. However, maintenance activities are at a minimum two years after implementation. After this point, maintenance requests grow slowly (Lehner, 1990). Outsourcing system maintenance at this point is advantageous. The outsourcer can not only offer ideas to "rejuvenate" the application, but as time progresses, can offer input into the development of a replacement system.

The concept that software segments that are in the "control" and "stable" stage of growth are suitable for outsourcing can similarly be applied to computer hardware. Three of the stages that Nolan (1979) discusses in his stage growth model of IS management are: 1) initiation; 2) contagion; and, 3) control. Similar to the outsourcing of maintenance projects in the "stable" stage, Wagner (1992) recommends outsourcing for organizations whose IS are in the control stage. She states that the initiation stage, which is characterized by development of initial applications, is unsuitable for outsourcing because it requires intimate knowledge of both the technology and the organization. Similarly, contagion, which is characterized by the spread of applications, also requires knowledge of the organization. Consequently, the control stage is the least organization specific and is, therefore, the most suitable for outsourcing.

However, once IS has reached the control stage within the organization, new technology can be outsourced based on the level of in-house expertise. For example, telecommunications and network management are commonly outsourced segments. In such instances, typically, the amount of in-house expertise on these topics is limited (Buck-Lew, 1992). Sometimes, the newer technologies (in an older IS department) are likely candidates for outsourcing.

Step 3: Organizational Characteristics

This step in the model involves analyzing characteristics of the organization such as culture, structure, and vertical integration. Organizational culture contains variables that are important in the outsourcing decision. For example, some organizations require flexibility and spontaneity in order to respond to market opportunities. These organizations are classified as open/adaptive/organic (OAO). OAO organizations would not be strong candidates for outsourcing. Their orientation toward problem solving and their evolutionary process would make outsourcing difficult. However, at the other end of the spectrum are the close/stable/mechanistic (CSM) organizations. These organizations are somewhat suited for outsourcing as their procedures rarely change (Wagner, 1992). The question is whether the CSM organizations are flexible enough to accept the outsourcing concepts. Most organizations which elect to outsource are neither OAO or CSM. They fall somewhere in-between, but tend to be towards the CSM end of the spectrum.

There is also a relationship between end-user computing and the spontaneity of the organization. End-user computing and fourth generation languages were developed as a response to the *ad hoc*, less defined, changing applications in the user departments. Wagner (1992) questions whether an organization should outsource those systems with which the end-users interact. When such systems are outsourced, it must be transparent to the end-user. Organization structure includes the degree of vertical integration within the organization. Companies in the 1980s emphasized the control of the production process from raw materials until delivery of the finished product to the customer. They were increasing their control over the value chain. These organizations are now faced with the reverse decision: the breaking up of the value chain. It may be difficult for vertically integrated companies to relinquish control of the IS function.

Decision 2: Are Factors Internal to the Organization Suitable for Outsourcing? At this stage of the decision methodology, the firm has completed the analysis of the internal factors affecting the outsourcing decision and now must decide whether its application and organization are likely candidates for successful outsourcing. If the response is negative, alternative in-house solutions should be investigated. If the response is positive, the organization should continue with an external analysis of the vendors and the contracts. Figure 4 identifies the key issues, internal to the organization, in the

	Question	1	2	3	4	5	6	7	8	9	10
1.	How would you describe the data in the segment to be outsourced?	Non-strategic									Strategic
2.	Who uses the data	Clerical			Lower Management			Middle Management			Upper Management
3.	Degree of interface with the accounting system	Low									High
4.	Age of segment to be outsourced	Old									New
5.	Size of segment to be outsourced	Small				Medium					Large
6.	Age of IS in the organization	Old									New
7.	Degree of vertical integration in the organization	Low				Medium					Large
8.	Organizational structure	Changing/ Flexible									Stable/ Mechanistic
9.	Extent of end-user computing	Low									High

The lower the points, the higher the probability of successful outsourcing.

Figure 4: Organization and Data Analysis

outsourcing decision.

Step 4: Vendor Characteristics

The vendor is often the difference between a successful outsourcing relationship and a failure. Vendor selection is much more complex than simply accepting the lowest bid submitted for services. Williamson (1991e) recommends that a firm look beyond the economic incentives. The concept of "Let the Buyer Beware" is applicable. Both Williamson (1991e) and Oltman (1990a) have developed lists of desirable characteristics and questions relevant to vendor selection. The issues can be grouped into seven categories: 1) reputation, 2) financial stability, 3) technological planning, 4) personnel resources, 5) experience in the client's industry, 6) working relationships and 7) contract flexibility.

The vendor's reputation and track record in outsourcing is probably the most crucial element in reducing outsourcing risks. Oltman (1990a) predicts a "shake out" within the outsourcing industry. He believes that in a few years only a handful of the most reputable vendors will remain. This leads to the second issue in vendor selection, the ability of the vendor to remain in business throughout the contract duration. Thus, it is critical that the financial status of the firm under consideration be analyzed.

Evidence of long range planning by the vendor will ease the risks which the clients are undertaking. What plans does the vendor have for technology upgrades and conversions? Will the client have access to state-of-the-art equipment throughout the lifetime of the contract? (Williamson, 1991e). Is the vendor in the international marketplace? If not, how can the vendor assist clients in global competition?

Another reason IS managers look to outsourcing is for additional personnel resources. Can the vendor offer specialized personnel in each of the client's application areas? Does the vendor have a high turnover rate? Will the personnel be dedicated to one client or several?

Experience with the client's industry is another desirable trait in vendor selection. Many smaller service providers are located in a niche, such as banking. By concentrating their efforts to servicing a specific industry, smaller firms are able to compete with the larger vendors (Oltman, 1990a). However, this also increases the importance of vendor reputability. Serving several clients from the same industry can cause a conflict-of-interest.

A good working relationship between vendor and client is essential. It is complicated by the potential transfer of employees.

Are there similar working conditions, atmosphere, and ethics within the two organizations? Is there two-way communication between client and vendor? Higher than expected costs are cited as a common drawback of outsourcing (Schwartz, 1992). Open communication between vendor and client is required and can prevent the problem from adversely affecting the relationship. This category also includes a very subjective "gut feeling" of the client. Is this the right vendor?

The final category of vendor characteristics is contract issues such as flexibility of negotiations. Contract negotiation is a complex topic. The next section is dedicated to these issues.

Step 5: Contract Issues

The IS manager is at a decisive disadvantage in outsourcing negotiations with the vendors. While the vendor has conducted such discussions on numerous occasions, it is a new experience for the IS manager. He/she must do some research by talking with other companies which have outsourced IS activities. Corporate lawyers should also be utilized.

Williamson (1991a) states that the ideal outsourcing contract has terms for every contingency. But this is not realistic. What happens is that contract language turns out to be too rigid or too flexible. Consider the environment and culture of the organization when deciding how detailed the outsourcing contract should be.

Contracts that are too rigid result in additional time spent by both client and vendor in negotiating special projects. Also, vendor expenditures (and, therefore, the client's) increase as the contract rigidity increases. One vendor had to refuse a maintenance project in order to avoid a penalty for failure to meet a contractual condition on resource availability (Williamson, 1991d). A rigid contract may cause the vendor to have under-utilized technology and personnel, and this will be reflected in higher prices. In addition to increased costs, the client may also have problems with adding or deleting services. This means a customer may end up paying for a service which is no longer needed.

However, a contract written with vague language may force the client to accept whatever service is available. To illustrate, assume a contract clause requires a response time of three seconds or less for 98% of the applications (Williamson, 1991d). A vendor may fulfill this clause and still have dissatisfied customers. The user may have one critical application with an unsatisfactory response time.

Once the organization has determined the desired level of detail in the contract, the terms of the outsourcing contract should be investigated. Five categories of contract issues are: 1) price, 2) service, 3) personnel, 4) ownership, and 5) miscellaneous.

Price. It is not sufficient to merely cite prices for anticipated usage. The forecasted usage is often in error. Therefore, prices for various levels of usage need to be included in the contract. Procedures and prices for adding or deleting services need to be addressed. The party which is responsible for license fees also needs to be specified in the contract. Finally, dates of formal price reviews and limits to the price increases should be included in the contract. This eliminates the risk of a vendor rapidly increasing prices after a client has become "locked" with the vendor. The IS manager should watch for creative pricing techniques of vendors. Some vendors include cost-of-living increases in their price structures.

The IS manager should also be cautious not to assume price clauses in the contract is the true cost of outsourcing. Hidden costs such as increased tax liability and severance packages also need to be included.

Service. Price considerations will itemize what the client will do for the vendor, while the service clauses indicate what the vendor will do for the client. The services that the vendor delivers to the client, and the quality of these services are necessary terms of the outsourcing contract. What is acceptable response time for on-line transactions? Characteristics of the computer hardware on which the applications reside need to be included in the contact. Will the hardware be dedicated to the one client or be shared with other clients? If the hardware is dedicated, what can the vendor do with any excess capacity? Other issues include disaster recovery, security, and backups.

Personnel. The contract should also address issues related to the transfer or termination of the client's staff. If employees are to be transferred to the vendor, will similar benefits be offered? What will happen to the accumulated benefits? Will seniority be honored?

Ownership. The fourth category of contract issues center on ownership and control. How much, if any, input will the client have on technological decisions? Can a vendor change a client's applications? Formal lines of communication need to be established. Additional issues include the confidentiality of information and conflict-of-interest issues. Can the vendor enter into another outsourcing agreement with a competitor of the original client?

Miscellaneous. The customer should include clauses about satisfaction. What options are available to the client if outsourcing turns out to be unsatisfactory? A short term clause in the contract would permit the IS manager to "try out" the contract. An option for a longer contract would be enacted if the trial period proved successful. Procedures for entering and exiting the contract need to

Vendor Characteristics

	Item	1	2	3	4	5	6	7	8	9	10
1.	Track record	Successful			No record					Unsuccessful	
2.	Knowledge of client's industry	Much								Little	None
3.	Amount of long range planning	Much								Little	None
4.	Effectiveness in international marketplace	Much								Little	None
5.	Knowledge/Expertise/Support of Technical Personnel	Much								Little	None
6.	Communication/working Relationship Technical Personnel	Positive			Neutral					Negative	
7.	Financial Stability	Positive			Neutral					Negative	

Contract Issues

	Item	1	2	3	4	5	6	7	8	9	10
1.	Level of Detail	Comfortable			Neutral					Uncomfortable	
2.	Decreased costs passed to customer	15% or more						Zero		Increased Costs	
3.	Satisfaction with service levels	Much				Some				Little	None
4.	Satisfaction with ownership issues	Much				Some				Little	None
5.	Terms for entering/exiting contract; short term clause	Satisfactory			Neutral					Unsatisfactory	

The lower the point value, the more satisfactory the vendor and contract.

Figure 5: Vendor and Contract Checklist

be addressed. While procedures for entering outsourcing contracts are available, little is written on procedures to move a previously outsourced segment back in-house.

The contact can be used to reduce the risks of outsourcing. But it involves skills in which IS managers are not experienced. They need legal and practical advice from lawyers and other outsourcing clients.

Decision 3: Are the Vendor and Contract Terms Agreeable? After the contract offers and vendors have been studied, the organization must decide whether 1) to accept the offer, 2) continue negotiations with the same or different vendors or 3) keep the information systems function in-house. A sample checklist, that will assist an organization in deciding whether or not the vendor and contract terms are satisfactory, is provided in Figure 5. When the vendor and the contract issues are satisfactory to the organization, the outsourcing decision is complete.

Summary

This chapter focused on identifying the circumstances which increase the likelihood of successful outsourcing. It merely touches on the topics which need to be researched and does not provide an answer to all the issues of outsourcing.

A model of the outsourcing decision provides a framework for analysis. Before outsourcing any part of the IS activities, there must be an identifiable problem that the organization wishes to solve. The next two steps involve an internal investigation of the data/segment and the organizational characteristics. If the data are not strategic and the segment is in a stable stage, it is suitable for outsourcing.

Wagner (1992) summarizes:

> Characteristics of an ideal outsourcing situation. . .: The organization itself should not be very vertically integrated; it should be toward the closed/stable/mechanistic end of the corporate culture continuum. The specific application to be outsourced should be non-strategic, mature (under control), at the clerical or information reporting level and not directly involved with end-user computing.

Buck-Lew (1992) adds that the system development projects for outsourcing should be characterized by: short duration; small project team size; sponsored by top management; not interfaced with the accounting system; and low expertise within the company on the proposed technology.

If the internal investigation indicates that the data/segment and organization are candidates for outsourcing, then, the external investigation of vendors and contracts needs to be conducted. Vendor issues include 1) reputation and track record, 2) financial stability, 3) long range planning, 4) personnel resources, 5) experience in the client's industry, 6) working relationships and 7) contract flexibility. Contract terms include 1) price, 2) service, 3) personnel, 4) ownership, and 5) entering/exiting contract procedures.

The challenge to the organization is to determine the probability of a successful outsourcing relationship over a five or ten year period.

THE FUTURE

Outsourcing is a growing industry. McMullen (1990) predicts outsourcing will grow at more than a 10% annual rate for the period from 1988 to 1993. Revenues are expected to increase from 19.7 billion in 1988 to $32.5 billion in 1993. Due (1992) states that nearly 50% of the largest 100 U.S. firms are expected to outsource part or all of their IS activities by the end of 1992.

With this rapid growth of the outsourcing industry, basic principles at work in a competitive economy can be used to predict changes in the industry. First, the increased revenue in the industry will cause an increase in the number of firms which offer outsourcing services. This will result in increased competition. The outsourcing "service" will become refined. The quality of the service will increase, and the prices will decrease. The less efficient firms in the marketplace will not be able to survive and will leave the industry. Only a few, top quality firms will remain. These vendors will be reputable organizations with a quality product at a fair price.

This should be a warning to managers to seek out the reputable, financially sound vendors; otherwise, the vendor may not remain in business for the duration of the contract. However, after the competitive forces reduce the firms in the outsourcing industry, control issues will be reduced.

IS managers often lament about the fast rate of technological change. Realistically, however, the fact is that this rate will never be any slower than it is today and in all likelihood will continue to accelerate. How to keep up with this ever-increasing rate of technological change is a problem now that will even be greater in the future. Outsourcing is one solution to the problem, but it is not always the best solution.

Emerging technologies are more powerful today than in the past. However, in the wrong hands, the power can be dangerous. The power must be channelled into productive applications. This task belongs to management. The challenge to managers is to utilize outsourcing to the advantage of their organization. For some organizations, this will mean rejecting the concept and keeping all IS activities in-house. Other firms will select partial outsourcing and only outsource selected IS segments. A few, courageous organizations will select complete outsourcing and turn over their entire IS department to the vendor.

CONCLUSIONS

Organizational factors and perspective are the keys to the success or failure of outsourcing. The problem is that a factor in the outsourcing decision can be viewed as an advantage by some individuals and as a disadvantage by others. For example, one manager might be a proponent of outsourcing because it gives the organization access to additional personnel with increased knowledge and expertise. Another manager, an opponent of outsourcing, might cite the loss of in-house expertise as a disadvantage. Similarly, the proponents mention the sharing of the risk of technological decisions with the vendors as an advantage while the opponents cite loss of control as a disadvantage. It is an organizational decision. Checklists for 1) determining if there is a problem, and if so, identifying its central focus, 2) accessing the suitability of the problem and organization for outsourcing, and 3) evaluating the vendor and contract issues were discussed in this paper. These issues need to be addressed by an organizational steering committee. The outsourcing decision is a group decision. Various group decision support systems (GDSS), such as Expert Choice, are available to assist in quantifying the groups ideas.

But, the issues addressed by the steering committee may not end when the outsourcing decision is made. If the decision is positive, the implementation of outsourcing becomes the next major milestone which the committee must undertake.

REFERENCES

Ambrosio, J. (1991, March 25). Outsourcing at Southland: Best of Times, Worst of Times. *ComputerWorld.* p. 61.

Anderson, H. (1990, January 8). Could You Use Outside Assistance? *ComputerWorld.* p. 76.

Anthes, G. (1991, March 25). Outsourcing May be the Only Answer for Many. *ComputerWorld.* p. 51.

Bergstein, M.E. (1990, October 15). Standing Up to Scrutiny. *Computer Systems*

News. p. 21.

Buck-Lew, M. (1992). To Outsource or Not? *International Journal of Information Management. 12*(1). 3-20.

Caldwell, B. (1989, September 25). Is Outsourcing A Good Move? *InformationWEEK.* pp. 42-46.

Carlyle, R.E. (1989, July 1). The Selling of IS. *Datamation.* pp. 22-26.

Crowell, P. (1990). To Process or Not to Process. *Bankers Monthly. 107*(4). 56-57.

Digital Equipment, Eastman Kodak Sued Over 'Outsourcing'. (1992, March 23). *Wall Street Journal.*

Dorn, P. H. (1989, October 16). Selling One's Birthright. *InformationWEEK.* p. 52.

Due, R. T., (1992). The Real Costs of Outsourcing. *Information Systems Management. 9*(1). 78-81.

Franchi, M. (1990, August 1). Business is Good for Outside Service Vendors. *Datamation.* p. 101.

Friedberg, A. H. & Yarberry, W. A., Jr. (1991). Audit Rights in an Outsource Environment. *Internal Auditor. 48*(4). 53-57.

Greer, J. & Page, D. (1992, April/May). Chestnuts in the Fire #7: Outsourcing, the Public Admittance of Failure. *AICCP Newsletter.* p. 2.

Hammersmith, A. (1989, September 18). Slaying the IS dragon with outsourcery. *ComputerWorld.* p. 89.

Huff, S. (1991). Outsourcing of Information Services. *Business Quarterly. 55*(4). 62 - 65.

Kass, E. M. (1990a, January 15). Kodak DECs Its NETs. *InformationWEEK.* p. 22, 26.

Kass, E. M. (1990b, August 6). Slick Moves at Sun Oil. *InformationWEEK.* pp. 12-13.

Kaufman, D. (1990, November 12). The Top Ten Reasons To Outsource. *Computer Systems News.*

Kelleher, J. (1990, January 8). Interview: Sometimes a Great Notion. (Interview with Howard Anderson). *ComputerWorld.* p. 76.

Kelly, J. (1990, September 15). Outsourcing: Who Pulls the Strings? *Datamation.* pp. 103-106.

Ketler, K. & Walstrom, J. (1992, July). Outsourcing as a Managerial Decision. *Decision Line.* pp. 6-7.

King, J. L. & Nolan, R. L. (1991). The Nolan Stage Model: A Debate. *Twelfth International Conference on Information Systems.* December 16-18, 1991.

Krass, P. (1990, February 26). The Dollars and Sense of Outsourcing. *InformationWEEK.* pp. 26-31.

Lehner, F. (1990). Cost comparison for the development and maintenance of application systems in 3rd or 4th generation languages. *Information and Management. 18*(3). 131-141.

Leibs, S. (1990, December 17). IS Budgets: Cutting Costs, But Not Corners. *InformationWEEK.* pp. 34-42.

Mandell, M. (1991). Corporate Computer: How Necessary? *Across the Board. 28*(3). 51-54.

McCormick, J.J. (1990, September 10). Outsourcing Action. *InformationWEEK.* pp. 84, 88, 92.

McCusker, T. (1991, April 1). There is Life After Outsourcing. *Datamation.* pp. 62-65.

McMullen, J. (1990, March 1). New Allies: IS and Service Suppliers. *Datamation.* pp. 42-46.

Nolan, R. L. (1979). Managing the Crises in Data Processing. *Harvard Business*

Review. 57(2). 115-126.

O'Leary, M. (1990, June). The Mainframe Doesn't Work Here Anymore. *CIO.* pp. 27-35.

Oltman, J. R. (1990a, April 16). Check out Partners. *ComputerWorld.* p. 78.

Oltman, J. R. (1990b, April 16). 21st Century Outsourcing. *ComputerWorld.* pp. 77-78.

Powers, A. (1990). Negotiating a Service Bureau Contract Is a Lot Like Buying a Car. *Bank Management.* 67(2). 60-61.

Quinn, J. B, Doorley, T. L., & Paquette, P.C. (1990). Beyond Products: Services-Based Strategy. *Harvard Business Review.* 67(2). 58-67.

Radding, A. (1990a, May). Outsourcing. *Bank Management.* pp. 56 - 61.

Radding, A. (1990b, January 8). The Ride is No Bargain if You Can't Steer. *ComputerWorld.* pp. 67 - 72.

Redditt, K. L. & Lodahl, T. (1990, January 8). So, What Do You Do With the People. *ComputerWorld.* p. 73.

Rothfeder, J. (1989, June 19). More Companies Are Chucking Their Computers. *Business Week.* (Industrial/Technology Edition). pp. 72-74.

Scheier, R. L. (1990, February 19). Buyers Need to Weigh the Risks of 'Out-Sourcing'. *PC Week.* pp. 121, 125.

Schwartz, J. (1992, February). Ordering Out of IS. *CIO.* p. 18.

Scott, R. (1989, July 31). Kodak hands MIS to IBM, Businessland. *MIS Week.* pp. 1, 12.

Stevens, L. (1990, January 8). Knowing What's Outside Can Help, Even If You're Staying In. *ComputerWorld.* January 8, 1990, p. 75.

Teresko, J. (1990, July 16). Make or Buy? Now It's a Data-Processing Question, Too. *Industry Week.* pp. 54-55.

Up in Arms Over Outsourcing. (1992, February 10). *InformationWeek.* p. 10.

Use of Resources is At Issue in Decision to Outsource. (1992, February 12). *Bank Automation News.* pp 3-4.

Valovic, T., Wang, G., Mandels, A. & Clarke, C. (1990). Telecommunications trends: A Yankee Group Roundtable. *Telecommunications.* 24(4). 31-36.

Wagner, J. (1992). Issues in Outsourcing. *Proceedings of the 1992 Information Resources Management Association International Conference,* 1992. pp. 214-217.

Wilder, C. (1989, July 31). Kodak Hands Processing Over to IBM. *ComputerWorld.* p. 1.

Wilder, C. (1990a, January 1). Outsourcing: Fad or Fantastic?" *ComputerWorld.* p. 8.

Wilder, C. (1990b, June 11). Outsourcing: From Fad to Respectability. *ComputerWorld.* p. 1.

Williamson, M. (1991a, October 15). The Contract. *CIO.* p. 40.

Williamson, M. (1991b, October 15). The Decision. *CIO.* pp. 24-35.

Williamson, M. (1991c, October 15). The Pitfalls. *CIO.* p. 34.

Williamson, M. (1991d, October 15). The Shining Example. *CIO.* pp. 44-45.

Williamson, M. (1991e, October 15). The Vendors. *CIO.* pp. 38-40.

CHAPTER 15

IMPLEMENTING DECISION SUPPORT SYSTEMS: LESSONS LEARNED FROM IMPLEMENTING A DANISH REGIONAL COMPUTERIZED ECONOMIC-DEMOGRAPHIC MODEL

Kim V. Andersen
University of Copenhagen

Problems related to implementing a decision support system at local levels of government were investigated. Using an organizational perspective and relying on data gathered from a nationwide survey, this chapter shows that technical features, organizational attributes, environmental preconditions, and transfer policies affected the outcome of the implementation process of a Danish computerized regional economic-demographic model (considered to be a decision support system). Despite the problems encountered during the implementation process, the users and the administrative decision-makers at the local levels continue to believe that modeling is useful for planning purposes in their workplace.

One of the emerging challenges posed by new technologies is the implementation of decision support systems (DSS) in various public and private organizations. DSS were earlier mainly located on a central main-frame, but progress in computer technologies now allows various DSS to be stored and run on PCs.

In general, previous studies agree that the use of DSS leads to change on both individual and organizational levels (Silver, 1990). This has been discussed on local, state, federal, and international levels (Keen & Morton, 1978; King, 1983; Kraemer & King, 1988; Te'eni, 1990). The outcome of the implementation of DSS is critical not only for the producer, but also for organizations that buy DSS and the employees that use it.

This chapter reports the results of a recent Danish study on the implementation of the economic-demographic model RIMO[1] (considered a DSS) in the local governments and the regional labor market authorities. This chapter argues that the outcome of the implementation of the DSS is affected by the perceived role of the model; the environmental, the organizational, and technical factors; and the model transfer.

RIMO was developed by the Danish National Agency of Physical Planning (DNAPP) and implemented by the counties and the regional labor market authorities. RIMO was first used in the early 1980s by DNAPP and by a few counties. By the end of the 1980s, the regional labor market authorities also implemented the model.

During the late 1980s and the early 1990s, the developers of RIMO received primarily negative responses from the users of the model. There were both technical problems and inadequate application problems. A research project, whose results are reported in this article, was formulated to investigate what went wrong during the development and the implementation of the model and to suggest possible improvements for future development.

The study achieved both promising and disparaging results from DNAPP's point of view. On one hand, the study found that staff professionals and head managers at the local levels continue to believe that modeling is useful for solving planning problems. On the other hand, the study found that the model was not used extensively because technical factors, organizational features, environmental attributes, and transfer policies were violated during the implementation process. In addition, the users of the model did not perceive their colleagues to be interested in using the model. These results will be discussed in this chapter.

The chapter begins with a brief background on the key questions addressed. Thereafter the methodology used in the empirical study is outlined. The chapter then proceeds with describing the use of the model, the perceived interest in the model, and the implementation of the model in the local organizations.

Background

Over the past 30 years substantial changes have occurred in the societal context within which planning and decision-making take place. These changes have facilitated the use of more complex models (in the rest of this chapter, the term *models* will replace the more general term DSS) in various fields and administrative levels in the public sector as well as in the private sector (Dutton & Kraemer, 1985; Greenberger, Crenson, & Crissey, 1976; Madsen, 1991). During the 1960s and 1970s, regional modeling expanded in such areas as land-use planning, transportation, and local government finances (Dueker, 1982).

Organizational and political scientists have systematically studied the implementation of computerized economic models in only a few empirical cases[2]. Often such studies have focused on controversial models such as the Limits to Growth models as in Meadows and Robinson (1985), and not on the ongoing and often successful institutional use of models. This is surprising since economic modeling is utilized in a large part of the public and private sector. For example, citizens are frequently confronted with model-based calculations on the expected public deficit, their personal debts, or the predicted need for environmental regulations.

However, successful implementation may be thwarted by various barriers. These barriers can be technical in character or financial ones that interfere with the development and transfer of the model. In addition, they may be organizational or individual resistance. Implementation also create a range of effects within the organization such as: is modeling value neutral to the existing culture in the organization; are the actors' roles the same; and can new administrative procedures operate along with the existing organizational structure and culture? Since only a few sporadic answers are available to these questions, there is definitely a need to study the implementation and the use of models in real world settings.

Regional Modeling in Denmark[3]

While computers in general are used extensively at the regional and local levels in Denmark (King & Kraemer, 1984), computerized models for regional planning have been developed and used in only a few cases (Jeppesen, 1978; Madsen et al., 1989)[4]. The first demographic regional models in Denmark were developed during the 1950s and the 1960s. In the late 1960s the National Planning Agency (Landsplanudvalget) succeeded in constructing a regional demographic model to be used by the counties and by the largest cities. The largest cities also constructed models for their own regions. The first regional economic planning models were not developed until the early 1970s.

During the 1980s the National Agency for Physical Planning

developed the Regional Iterative Model (RIMO) to enable planners in a variety of fields to work with a computerized model. On the basis of population, employment, and economic data, the model can compute the course of development for population; supply of labor; employment; unemployment; educational background for the population, for the labor force, and for employment; domestic housing; and commercial/industrial construction. RIMO is a mainframe based demographic-economic model which consists of a labor-balancing system to match the estimated supply of and demand for labor (Andersen & Nielsen, 1991).

At the national level, using a predicted rate of development at the national level as the frame for the projections, the model focuses on the assessment of development in all county municipalities. At the county level, the model is designed to assess the development in the county and local commuting districts. Therefore, RIMO consists of two distinct models: one model (DAN) computes the development at the national and the regional level, the other (PLAN) provides information on the regional and local commuting district levels. The regional users are usually provided with only one PLAN-model and thus do not have the capability to compute for other counties.

Constructing a model for fourteen counties and splitting these into smaller regions (local labor markets) raise methodological and practical questions (Bolton, 1990; Madsen et al., 1989). One of such practical questions is that constructing a model with the same type of (selected) data available for each county might be useful for some counties, but not necessarily so for all counties. The model has been implemented in mainly two organizations: the counties and the regional labor market authorities. Both the counties and the labor market authorities use different information systems to analyze current developments at regional and local levels.

User Organizations: Counties and Labor Market Authorities

Counties. The model originated from the need for coordinating sectorial planning and assisting physical planning in the counties. Denmark's total area is approximately 43,000 square kilometers—equivalent to one-ninth of California. Five million Danes live in a country divided into fourteen county authorities[5], each with its own elected county council. The *counties* are, among other things, responsible for physical planning, providing guidelines for regional industrial development, and running most high schools and hospitals. Meeting these needs for statistical information were especially important during the 1970s.

Along with rapid developments in computing technology, regional imbalances and economic growth facilitated the building of models intended to assist in physical planning (Jeppesen, 1978). Other factors that affected the growth of the model include the municipal reform of the 1970s and the growing unemployment during both the 1970s and the 1980s.

The municipal reform involved rolling budget procedures that required forecasts about the development of populations, income, and etc. (Madsen et al., 1989). In addition, a planning law reform was carried through during the 1970s, constituting a framework of national planning at the state level, regional planning at the county level, and local planning at the municipal level. The National and Regional Planning Act (Act of the Parliament) states that each county shall make a regional plan containing guidelines for future urban growth. These guidelines include addressing the delimitation of urban zones, determining the size and location of major commercial centers and transportation facilities, and determining the areas reserved for agricultural purposes and recreational purposes.

Labor Market Authorities

Within the *labor market*, Denmark has established regional labor market authorities and boards. The regional labor market organizations deal with problems concerning matching the supply of and the demand for the labor force at local levels. The labor market authorities are administrative secretaries for the regional labor market boards that consist of members from the labor market organizations (employers and employees), the county, and certain municipalities. The boards are, in other words, local cooperative organizations aimed at achieving consensus on issues related to the labor market.

Implementation of the model, in both the counties and the labor market authorities, required five features: *First*, the model had to be useful in both DNAPP and the Regional Planning Boards where it had to be suitable for the computation of results regarding strategic structure variables. *Second*, it was an important objective to design the model to utilize data produced by the Statistical Bureau of Denmark which offered an easier and quicker accessibility to high-quality data. In addition, the local users would be able to obtain the most current information. *Third*, the model had to be applicable in areas smaller than counties. Accordingly a county had to be divided into several commuting districts, typically consisting of three to five municipalities. *Fourth*, the model had to be an information system for local users, thereby enabling them to collect and implement various assumptions about such topics as the unemployment level of the local districts. *Fifth*, the model-system had to be cost effective enough to be employed at all levels (Nielsen, 1985).

These five features were difficult to meet during the development of the model. The difficulties were not only due to technical and practical problems related to data and the analysis of the data, political and organizational factors also influenced the development of RIMO. To investigate the nature of the complex implementation process of RIMO, systematical empirical evidence was gathered through a nation-wide survey. Hence, a framework containing a range of independent and dependent variables was developed.

FRAMEWORK AND METHOD

Framework

The framework coincides with the (now broadly accepted) idea that the implementation and the use of information systems must be understood from technical, cultural, and political perspectives[7]. To identify the nature and the most important factors for the outcome of the implementation process, four groups of factors were used in the study: environmental preconditions (supply), attributes of the user (demand) and developer organizations (supply), features of the technology (supply factors), and transfer policies. The supply and demand factors reflect a market-based explanation because the variables were derived from the assumption that opportunities and constraints in the environment affect model use in institutional, policy or political sense (Bretschneider, 1989).

Policy use refers to uses where a transferred model is used for one or more of the following purposes: the development of policies or programs, the selection among policies or programs, or the evaluation of a policy's or a program's effectiveness. *Political use* refers to uses in which a model is actually used to delay decision-making, to give symbolic attention to a decision, to confuse or obfuscate decision-making, to defeat a specific policy by giving specific attention to only one side of the argument when the model could have been used to give both sides, to justify or legitimatize a decision already made without the model, or to add a sheen of technical sophistication to the reputation or position of the decision maker. The *institutionalization* of model use refers to the incorporation of specific models and of modeling as an ongoing part of the policy making process.

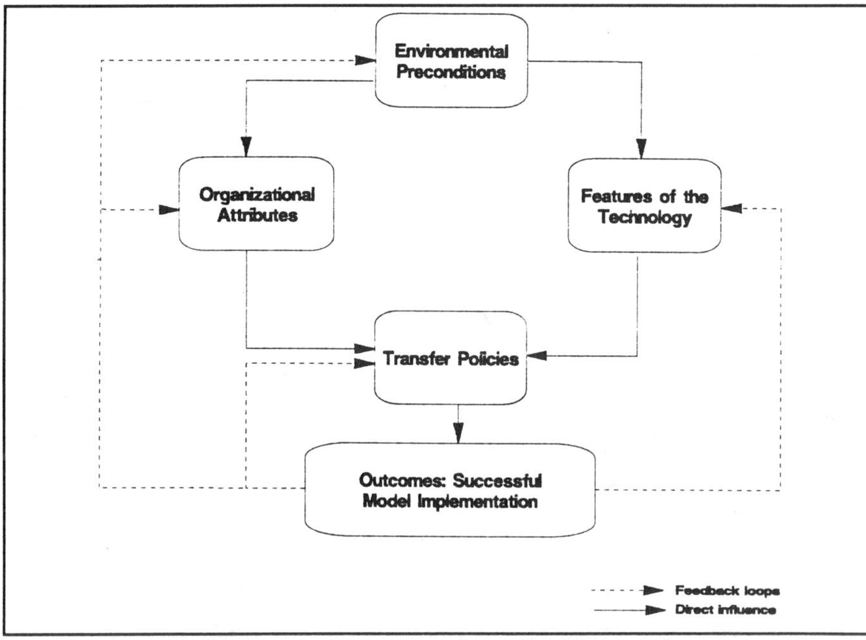

Figure 1: Framework of the Research

Method

The empirical evidence for the results derives from a nationwide survey conducted during 1990-1991, based on a mixture of both qualitative and quantitative methods.

The *qualitative analysis* consisted of reviewing the model documentation and interviewing the major actors involved in the implementation process. Such actors include model developers, model users, administrators, and planners. The *quantitative analysis* included a field survey (questionnaires) within the regional labor market authorities and the counties.

The implementation of the model in the regional labor market authorities was investigated by interviewing the directors and modelers, and by sending questionnaires to the modelers at the regional labor market authorities. The members of the regional labor market boards, which comprised the political dimension of the modeling process, were not interviewed (Andersen, 1991a).

To investigate the modeling activities in the counties, questionnaires were mailed to all counties and evaluated (Andersen, 1991b). In addition, interviews were conducted with department heads.

In total, 67 questionnaires were distributed to the employees in

Organizations	Survey Questionnaires[a]	Interviews
Counties:		
Fiscal planning	22 (9, 41%)	5
Education/industrial planning	22 (14, 64%)	4
Physical planning	23 (19, 83%)	8
Counties total	67 (42, 63%)	17
Regional labor market authorities	17 (17, 100%)	13

Note. [a] number of questionnaires. In parenthesis absolute and relative (rate of response) number of received questionnaires.

Table 1: Data Collection

the counties and 17 to the employees in the regional labor market authorities. The response rate varied from 41 percent to 100 percent, the lowest rate from fiscal planning in the counties, the highest from the labor market authorities. As shown in Table 1, the research findings are based on 59 questionnaires and 30 interviews, primarily with head managers. Questionnaires were distributed prior to the interviews in both the regional labor market authorities and the counties.

In the following sections we will outline the use of RIMO, the interest in the model, and the perceived role of the model. This part of the study was conducted to investigate whether there were a negative attitude towards modeling since it was hypothesized that a negative attitude could be critical for the outcome of the implementation process.

THE USE OF, INTEREST IN, AND PERCEIVED ROLE OF MODELING

The Use of Models

The models so far achieved neither widespread use in the counties or the regional labor market authorities, nor great impacts on decision-making at the local levels. Also, there were only a few cases of institutionalization of the model in the organizations.

Professional staff in the regional labor market authorities were asked to indicate whether models are used continually, ad hoc, seldom or never in their job correspondence. The respondents were asked to specify in regards to four types of job correspondence: 1) with the staff in their own office, 2) with the staff in other offices in the county, 3) with the staff in other private offices or public organizations, and 4) with politicians at any level.

The respondents primarily use the model within the office where they are employed, rather than in their job correspondence with other staff professionals in the county, other private/public relations, or politicians at any level. Hence, modeling activity takes place within the organization.

The Interest in and the Perceived Role of Modeling

The respondents in both the counties and the labor market authorities were asked to specify their perceived interest in using modeling in their job correspondence. The questions were not posed specifically to evaluate RIMO, rather they were purposed to identify the general interest in modeling. Table 3 provides the results from these questions[8]. Overall, the respondents perceived their job correspondence interest in modeling to be positive. Fifty eight percent of the respondents perceived that the politicians' interest in modeling is neutral, meaning that the politicians are either indifferent as to whether models are used or indifferent about the modeling process.

As shown in Table 3, the respondents perceived modeling as strengthening the decision-making process. However, the respondents do not use the model continually. The discrepancy between the trust in the effectiveness of modeling and the infrequent use of the available models forms an apparent paradox similar to that which was reported by a U.S. study conducted in the beginning of the 1980s on fiscal impact budget modeling (FIBS)[9]. In the Danish study, both head managers and professional staff were asked whether or not, "modeling strengthens the decision-making process" (see Table 4). No respondents strongly disagreed. In fact, the majority agreed that the use of model would strengthen the decision-making process. The relative number of department heads who believed in the success of modeling exceeded the number of staff professionals that agreed.

The responses listed in Table 4 show that there is a positive attitude towards the use of models and that both head managers and staff professionals perceive modeling as strengthening the decision-making process. In general, the head managers expressed a more positive interest towards modeling than the staff professionals. The numbers marked with (*) in Table 4 represent significant differences

Question: "Please indicate how often You use the model. Specify this in regard to a) staff in your own office, b) staff in other offices in the county, c) staff in other private or public organizations, and d) politicians at any level."	In Your relation with:			
	Other staff in the office %	Staff in other offices in the county %	Staff in other private offices or public organizations %	Politicians at any level %
Continually	48	8	11	30
Ad hoc	44	46	44	25
Seldom	8	31	22	25
Never	0	15	22	20
Total	100 (n=17)	100 (n=17)	99 (n=17)	100 (n=17)

Table 2: Frequency of Modeling in Four Different Job Relations of Professional Staff in the Regional Labor Market Agencies

Question; "Please, indicate whether you perceive the interest from your (job) relations to be positive, negative, or neutral in regard to use of models in connection to these job relations. Specify this in regard to 1) other staff in the office where you are employed, 2) staff in other offices within the county, 3) staff in other private offices and public organizations, and 4) politicians at any level."	The respondent's perception of the interest in the model by:			
	Other staff in the office %	Staff in other offices in the county %	Staff in other private offices and public organizations %	Politicians at any level %
Positive	84	65	56	42
Neutral	12	35	44	58
Negative	4	0	0	0
Total	100 (n=53)	100 (n=51)	100 (n=54)	100 (n=45)

Table 3: Perceived Interest in Use of Models in Four Different Job Relations

Statements:	Department Heads (Counties)				Staff Professionals (Regional Labor Market Authorities)			
	Agree	Neutral	Disagree	TOTAL (N=42)	Agree	Neutral	Disagree	TOTAL (N=17)
1. Models are adopted to analyze the consequences of different policies	71%	24%*	6%*	101%	69%	13%*	19%*	101%
2. Modeling strengthens the position of the staff	24	40*	37	101	35	29*	36	100
3. Modeling strengthens the decision-making process	92*	6*	3	101	73*	20*	7	100
4. Models are used to legitimate already made decisions	23	19*	58*	100	33	40*	27*	100
5. Politicians are against modeling, because modeling might highlight political conflicts	57	13	30*	100	57	21	21*	99

Note. * significant (.05 level) difference in attitude between staff professionals and department heads

Table 4: Attitude Toward Modeling of Department Heads and Staff Professionals

in attitude towards modeling between the head managers and the staff professionals. The staff professionals (the forecasters) that used the model were less positive towards modeling than the head managers that did not use models themselves (indirect users). Summing up, we found no evidence that there is in general a negative attitude towards modeling in the local user organizations. It must be other factors that influenced the nature of the implementation process.

THE NATURE OF THE IMPLEMENTATION PROCESS

To survey the importance of the factors influencing the implementation process, four groups of factors were defined in the study: environmental preconditions, organizational attributes, technical features, and transfer policies (see Figure 1). The factors marked (*) in Table 5 were significant at the 0.05 level. In the following sections, the significant factors in each of the four groups will be discussed.

Environmental preconditions

The eight factors measuring the importance of environmental preconditions surveyed were: substantive economic theory for the model, funding for model development and transfer, status of computing technology, availability and quality of data, predisposition to technique, competitiveness among organizations, flexibility in personnel practices, and saliency of policy issues.

Among these factors, the study on RIMO found that the outcome of the implementation process is perceived by the users to be significantly influenced by the funding of the model. Since developing and implementing the model require strong and steady support, the level of funding, sources of funds, and the flexible methods of support influence the success of the implementation process. Currently, the financial support for the model is based on both sales (products) and research funding.

During the development of RIMO there have been problems in achieving a steady level of funding resulting in a high flow of personnel resources employed by different institutions. However, the central model developers and students have continually been employed by DNAPP.

During the initiation of the model in the late 1970s, there was a positive attitude towards both the model and towards modeling in general. However, in DNAPP—that funded the development—there

Group of Factors	Factors
Environmental Preconditions	Substantive Theory
	Funding for Model Development and Transfer *
	Status of Computing Technology
	Availability and Quality of Data
	Predisposition to Technique
	Competitiveness Among Organizations
	Flexibility in Personnel Practices
	Saliency of Policy Issues
Organizational attributes	
a) User Organization	Agency's Need for Analysis *
	Fit of Model to Agency's Mission *
	Internal Resources Available for Modeling *
	User's Familiarity with Technique *
	Existence of Cooperative Arrangements for Model Implementation *
b) Modeler Organization	Modeler's Reputation *
	Modeler's Identification with a Model
	Modeler's Political Neutrality
	Organizational Type
	Division of Labor
Features of the Technology	Nature of Model Error *
	Characteristics of the Data *
	Maintainability of the Model *
	Accumulation of Knowledge
	Cost of Model Acquisition and Use
	Complexity of the Model *
	Intended Purpose of the Model: Product vs. Research
Transfer Policies	Model Packaging *
	Marketing Styles and Strategies
	Transfer Agent
	Pricing
	User Groups

Note. * factors significant at 0.05 level, n=59

Table 5: Factors Influencing Model Implementation. Users Perceptions

were different views on the allocation of resources. The different attitude also reflected differences in what physical planning should deal with and how it should be conducted. In an agency dominated by non-economists, the developers of RIMO succeeded in securing funding for RIMO. But the funding was limited and it has been a problem during the development that there were not stable or adequate funding to attract economists from such areas as the growing research departments at universities.

During 1989-1990, external funding was introduced to finance further developments of RIMO. The National Labour Market Authority (the main financial contributor to further development) wanted a useable model primarily for the regional labor market authorities.[12] The introduction of external funding implied that more resources were allocated to the project, allowing user manuals for the model to be published—almost ten years after the first version of the model was developed. Documentation on the data used in the model was published and the model became nationwide, meaning that all the local labor market districts (commuting districts) were covered by the model.

Organizational attributes

Organizational attributes include attributes both in the central model developer organization and the local model user organizations. It was expected that structural and behavioral attributes of the organization would influence the implementation of the model.

The attributes of the model *developer* organization include organizational type, internal division of labor, identification with the model, the reputation of the model developers, and the modelers' political neutrality. Among these factors, the respondents in the Danish survey found only the modeler's reputation to be of significant importance for the outcome of the implementation of the model.

To a large degree, the model users employed in the local organizations have to depend on the model developer organization to explain the model, to help to run it, and to interpret the results from the model. This is true during the introduction of the model to the user organizations as well as during the routinization phase. In other words, the reputation the model developers have on these factors is very important. The developers of RIMO did not realize the importance of trust and reliability until late in the introduction phase.

The outcome of the implementation process is also crucially related to attributes of the model users organization such as: the compatibility of the model to the agency's need for analysis, the compatibility of the model to the agency's mission, the internal resources available for modeling, the users' familiarity with the technique, and the existence of cooperative modeling arrangements among users. In the Danish study, all of these factors significantly affected the outcome of the implementation process.

Internal resources available for modeling—in particular users experienced with the appropriate modeling techniques from education or previous employment—were found important. In agencies that do not have experienced model users, the model developers have to teach the staff how the model operates, what information it can provide, how the model can be applied into policy analysis, and so on. Therefore, it is easier to implement the model at agencies whose staff has experience with the appropriate modeling techniques either from education or previous employment. Agencies that must rely on outside support to interpret results, tend to model sporadically and inefficiently. However, the reverse is also true. For example, modelers that tend to interpret sporadically and inefficiently and without control over the modeling process, tend to rely mainly on outside support in the modeling process.

Also, the existence of cooperative modeling arrangements between users is critical to implementation. Such arrangements at local or regional (county) levels can involve users and developers to benefit from local knowledge and expertise in modeling. There have been attempts to establish such arrangements between the regional labor market authorities and the modelers in the counties. Due to low frequency of use in both organizations (in particular in the counties) and due to different interests in the modeling process, such arrangements did not work out. The labor market authorities are primarily interested in making forecasts related to unemployment (supply), whereas the counties are primarily interested in making forecasts related to employment (demand).

The model is difficult to handle, thereby adding emphasis to the relevance of internal resources available and modeling experience. Only a few of the model users are familiar with economic modeling or with the appropriate computer technique to run the model. Most of the users were educated in the social sciences, but in general were not exposed to econometrics nor used models in their college education.

The users often did not know what was the intended purpose of the model, how the model runs theoretically, nor how to handle the results. For example, in the capital area of Denmark (Copenhagen), the users knew about econometrics, were familiar with the technique, and had experience with using computerized models. These users had years of experience with modeling in their own regions and did not find that RIMO expanded their knowledge. Also, they found too many errors and that the data did not meet the needs of their organizations.

What is also essential to explain why the implementation process did not succeed in the routinization phase is that the user organizations' need for the model was not very strong and the model did not coincide with the local organizations' mission. The RIMO model was originally developed for use in physical planning and hence, contained specific variables towards such planning and was intended for making long term forecasts, not short term ones. The regional labor market authorities adopted the model in the beginning of the 1990s. As a part of this introduction new features of the model were developed. However, basic features of the model have not been changed and even now, the model still does not adequately incorporate the organizations' mission. There is no doubt that the regional organizations can better utilize a model which fits their purpose well, however it is difficult to develop a model that suits the mission of all the local organizations.

Features of the technology

The seven features of the technology surveyed were: nature of the model error, characteristics of the data, maintainability of the model, accumulation of knowledge, cost of model acquisition and use, complexity of the model, and intended purpose of the model (product versus research purpose). Six of these features were found to significantly influence the outcome of the implementation of the model, cf. Table 5.

For implementation in the technical process of policy making, the data provided by the model must be not only of sufficient technical quality (representative and reliable) but also of high quality compared to other sources. In addition, the measurements used in the model have to be appropriate for the decision-making process. For the initial year, the data and the database provided by RIMO were of sufficient technical quality (representative and reliable)[13]. However, the model was not upgraded in time, meaning that the data was available in governmental statistical reports before the data was available for the model users.

While some users found that the model lacked details, others found that the model was too detailed and complicated. None of the users found the model user friendly, nor did anyone find that the available application programs sufficiently solved his problems.

By using RIMO it is possible to make predictions for the national level, even though it is not the main purpose of the model. Several local users find it interesting to compare the previous development and predictions on for example the employment in the local areas with expected development in employment on the national level. Using RIMO, the results on the predicted total employment in Denmark did not comply with the forecasts made by the ADAM-model, which is the "official" Danish model used by the Ministry of Finance[14]. This discrepancy makes the model unreliable and causes problems for the implementation process. For example, the head managers did not want to directly present the results derived from the model in their contact with the politicians, because they are concerned that the politicians will question the results, such as asking why RIMO's estimated number of unemployed does not match the numbers presented in national reports.

Although the technical problems occurring using RIMO, the agencies used the model. However, they tend to reduce their dependence on the model by examining other sources of information.

Transfer policies

Transfer policies are the decisions and practices that are intended to aid the transfer and the use of the models, including marketing styles and strategies, model packaging, transfer agents, pricing strategies, user groups, and ongoing management of the transfer process. Among these factors, only model packaging was found to significantly influence the outcome of the implementation process, cf. Table 5.

The model developers did not pay enough attention to establish a policy for model transfer. RIMO had no support software (model packaging) and the manuals were difficult to comprehend. Since the lack of application programs makes it even harder to use the results from modeling for further analysis, these disadvantages were especially unfavorable to users who were unfamiliar with modeling. As described above, the users were in general not familiar with modeling techniques and often did not know how to solve technical problems when such occurred during the modeling process.

The documentation of RIMO and the choice of methods used in the model have often been questioned by the potential users. In seminars held during the development phase of the model, potential users repeatedly complained about the lack of model packaging and requested changes. However, the developers of RIMO did not implement the suggestions made by the users. Instead, the model was expanded within a research framework, and not developed as a product for sale—with the needs of the end users in mind.

Hence, it is surprising that the developers of RIMO developed and marketed the model without surveying the users' needs for model packaging. Furthermore, they did not give the users a large role in the model development for a design capable of an expanded range of tasks and of running on personal computers. One explanation of the lack of incorporating the users' needs in the development of the model might be the lack of interaction between the different groups of people involved in the development and differences in organizational power. The programmers, the model developers, and the transfer agents did not interact frequently. This, combined with the fact that the programmers and developers were more interested in creating new features of the model rather than improving the existing parts, prevented the incorporation of the suggestions from the users.

Development, Adaptation, Routinization

Combining findings from questionnaires and interviews, the Danish study found that the factors varied in importance through three phases during the implementation process: development, adaptation, and routinization.

Adaptation refers to (1) the period during which a model is considered for adoption, which is based on some pilot testing of the model, and (2) the period during which broader support for the model is developed, plans are made for instructing and training relevant practitioners, the model begins to be used as widely as resources would permit, and the results of use are monitored. Adoption is thus included in adaptation.

Routinization refers to the period in which the model no longer appears as a new innovation per se, but becomes a part of the common activities of the organization. The notation (++, +, 0) used in Table 6 mark the relative importance of each of the factors in the three phases. Listed in Table 6, the findings indicate that the factors are most critical in the routine phase.

Table 6 lists the factors found significant among the users. Each factor was evaluated according to the importance to the three phases during the implementation process (development, adaptation, and routinization). Since the respondents were not asked to rank them, it is not possible to predict which phase is most important or which factor is most important.

As expected, the table shows that it is more difficult to get the model used routinely than to get the model adapted in the organizations. It was the national agency of the labor market that bought copies of the model from DNAPP and then introduced the model to the regional labor market authorities. Hence, the problems regarding the technical features etc. did not occur before the routinization phase since it is not until this phase that the users' needs will affect the success of the model. In other words, if we have measured the success of the model by the number of local organizations where it is adopted, the model would have been regarded as quite successful. Focusing on what determines the routinization use of the model, organizational attributes and technical attributes were especially critical.

Group of Factors:	Factors:	Implementation process		
		Development	Adaptation	Routinization
Environmental Preconditions	Funding	++	0	0
Organizational Attributes	Reputation[a]	0	+	++
	Need for the analysis	0	+	++
	Fit of model to agency's mission	0	+	++
	Internal resources available	+	+	++
	Familiarity with the technique	0	+	++
	Cooperative Arrangements	0	0	++
Features of the Technology	Characteristics of the data	++	++	++
	Nature of the model error	0	0	++
	Maintainability of the model	0	++	++
	Complexity of the model	0	++	++
Transfer of the Technology	Model Packaging	0	+	++

Note. [a] Model developer organization. 0 indicate the factor was not found important, + and ++ indicate the factor was important. ++ indicates a more important factor than +.

Table 6: Factors Influencing Model Implementation in Three Phases: Development, Adaptation, Routinization

DISCUSSION

The Danish study is important because not only it identifies which factors to strengthen in order to implement this model successfully, but also it addresses problems that will face other local, state, and federal governments and private organizations alike in the climate of increasing technology and computerization in the workplace. The problems faced in implementing RIMO can thus be expected to emerge in other contexts in the coming years as the use of DDS and MIS systems expand[16].

In a recent study on computer-aided regional planning, Roy and Snickars (1992) find that detailed knowledge of the future of specific parts of the regional system, which are generated by mathematical models, can contribute valuable input into the planning process. Dueker (1982) and Dutton and Kraemer (1985) achieved similar conclusions.

Other studies have emphasized that the use of models and DSS requires a more structured approach than either model developers, users, and funders have taken in the past (Lawless, 1987, p. 250). Similarly, the URBIS studies found that cities were experiencing the most payoffs from computerization in areas of fiscal control, cost avoidance, and increased interaction with the public. There was only a minimal level of payoffs observed in non-fiscal management control and planning decisions (Northrop et al., 1990, p. 512).

Lawless' study also emphasized that in the study on the use of the Patrol Car Model in Police Departments no single type of model meets the users' needs in all the nationwide organizations. For example, the needs of suburban police departments are quite different from the needs in urban and rural ones. Similarly, the study of RIMO found that the needs in the local organizations are different even though they administratively are subordinated to the same national agency. The trend in the public administration towards decentralization might increase these differences.

The Danish study found the framework and research design developed in a UC Irvine study conducted in the 1970s and 1980s useful and worth replicating (Kraemer et al., 1987). The Irvine study developed a set of 30 propositions (the four set of factors used in this study) about factors contributing to successful implementation of computer modeling in federal policy making in the U.S. Specifically, they surveyed the importance of these factors only in successful model implementations. Hence, the Irvine study was biased towards the success of models (Perrolle, 1988). In contrast, both the Danish study and the history of computer modeling—from the Limits to

Growth project of the 1970s to the Nuclear Winter Model in the 1980s—have taught us to be vary of such assumptions.

We pointed out that the Danish model did not achieve widespread use or had a great impact on decision-making processes, nor was it institutionalized in the local user organizations. The results from each of the surveyed factors explained why this did not occur.

The Danish study emphasized the importance of the interaction between the perceived roles of modeling in general (not just the use of RIMO); and environmental, technical, organizational factors, and transfer policies. The dominance of these factors varies during the implementation phases, and unfortunately it is not possible to determine which factor is the most important.

Although RIMO was introduced into the local user organizations, the Danish model was often considered to be technically inappropriate and thus, not incorporated routinely. However, the head managers and staff professionals perceive the model to strengthen the decision-making process. Despite the numbers of errors and failures, they continue to believe so.

This apparent paradox can be explained by an information-processing perspective which suggests that there is a positive bias for more information (Sproll, 1985). In other words, people prefer more information than less, and thus tend to overinvest in information (Feldman & March, 1981). This perspective might explain why it is important to have the model, but not important to use it.

The Danish study emphasizes several factors that need to be addressed to facilitate the incorporation of the model into the workplace. Although all of the four set of factors (see Table 5) were important, the study found that organizational attributes of the user organizations and technical features were especially important in the implementation process. The factors chosen to investigate the nature of the implementation process were useful in obtaining such insight. Unfortunately, the four sets of factors are interrelated, and it is not possible to determine the relative importance of each of these factors.

However, there are validity problems in the Danish study. The analyzed model so far has not been routinely integrated neither in the administrative routine nor in the political decision-making process. Also, the Danish study is a single year study and thus unable to identify long-term effects. As pointed out often, there is a serious need to pursue such long-term studies in order to identify the outcome of the implementation processes in the long run.

Summing up, one can ask why a model like RIMO could survive all the difficulties faced. One might also predict that its development cannot continue. However, the story of RIMO is also the story of institutional factors influencing the development, marketing, and introduction of the model in local organizations. Andersen and Madsen (in press) explained the development of RIMO from a technocratic perspective, and hypothesized that the model will not survive in the long run since it is likely that others and more adequate models will be marketed. Also, it is likely that the further development will be questioned within the institutional frame where RIMO so far has been developed and marketed.

In contrast, at least four factors might stimulate the survival of the model. First, the RIMO model is unique worldwide both because it is nationwide and it now has a history of more than ten years since the first version was tested in an user organization. Since expertise has been established within the developer organization, termination of RIMO will render this expertise. Second, DNAPP has recently discussed whether to privatize the model development and whether to continue to fund part of the further development of the model. This would solve some of the political problems the agency has because of its involvement in the project. Also, privatization would introduce the market mechanism which could increase the recognition of the users' needs in the further development of the model. Third, the developers have already begun the transition of the model to a PC-based version which could solve some of the problems identified in the survey.

Fourth, the Danish study found a positive attitude toward modeling, which is in contrast to findings in previous studies. For example, Roy and Snickars (1992) found that there is still considerable skepticism among planners concerning the value of sophisticated modeling systems in forecasting and scenario construction. Considerable skepticism arises particularly in cases where the planners and their political clients do not fully understand the market processes involved. In contrast, the study described in this chapter identifies a positive attitude towards modeling and hence, indicates the likelihood that modeling also in the coming years will be a part of the workplace for planners at the local levels of government, at least in Denmark.

Increased cooperation between users and model developers might be one of the ways to overcome problems in the future development and in the marketing of the analyzed model. The design of and the initiative to such cooperations could be generated and could be funded by the model developers. This chapter has not addressed in particular, why there are not already established informal or formal cooperative arrangements. One possible explanation is that there are different interests sought by users, users in different organizations, and developers in using the model. Finally, the model has to address problems (directly) relevant for the planning process at local levels before users will participate in such arrangements.

ENDNOTES

[1] Regional Iterative Model.

[2] Kraemer (1984; 1985) and Dutton and Kraemer (1985) provide the best case studies that I am aware of which describes the political environment of computerized fiscal-impact model systems (FIBS) intended for urban planning.

[3] Others and more advanced regional models have emerged in Denmark. In the mid-1970s the Local Governments Research Institute on Public Administration and Finance (AKF) conducted a survey on regional models. At that time, only a few of the models were main-frame based, while most were spread-sheet based (Bundgaard-Jørgensen, 1976). In the beginning of the 1980s, a regional model (SØREN) was developed for the southern part of Denmark, and later, IRIS for the capital area of Copenhagen. By the end of the 1980s, AKF developed EMIL based on the lessons learned from SØREN and IRIS. EMIL is a PC-based model that provides information about the regional economy and the labor market. Attempting to make a summary of accounts for each of the counties, EMIL uses traditional macro-economic parameters at the regional level. The output of the model consists of economic and demographic information related to the regional and local levels. From the start EMIL was developed as a product transferable to regional and local users. The computer technology and data available during the development of EMIL were more advanced than the conditions facing RIMO at the start of its project (since its development began nearly ten years earlier than EMIL). For one thing, this allowed the developers of EMIL to construct regional input-output tables and to build the model on that concept. The development of EMIL has been partly financed by DNAPP.

[4] In this context, computerized models for regional planning do not include spread-sheet based models.

[5] Exclusive of the capital area.

[6] Seventeen percent of the work force in Denmark is employed by the local governments. In contrast, only seven percent of the 1985 work force in the U.S. is employed by local governments. The local governments (municipalities and counties) in Denmark spend 44 percent of the GNP (1983) while the public sector in total spends 61 percent of the GNP (1982) (Bogason, 1987).

[7] The frame does not specifically incorporate possible social implications of the introduction, the adoption, and the adaptation of the models. To some extent such implications are included in organizational attributes. Danziger (1985) provides an overview of the knowledge of the social impacts of computerization. See also Dunlop and Kling's (1991) collection of papers on the social aspects of computerization.

[8] Table 3 does not distinguish whether the respondents are employed by the labor market authorities or the counties.

[9] The argument for the *apparent* paradox is that presuming that the local users perceive modeling to strengthen the decision-making process, respondents would have a preference for modeling and would thus use the model continually. The apparent paradox then is that the users do not use RIMO routinely.

[10] Significant means in this chapter at 0.05 level using a chi-quare test on the data.

[11] This factor reflects that the model developers choose which kind of computer technology is used in the model. It is thus assumed that the model developers do not influence the development of a particular computing technology. In other words, from the model developers' point of view, the computer technology is an environmental precondition.

[12] The rationale for external funding assumes that the potential users are willing to finance the development. Further, it is often argued that if they are not willing to do so, the development of the model will not be continued. This view on external funding of the model is contrasted with the arguments that the development of models takes a long time and thus "the market" cannot incorporate such projects. External funding of the project can also be analyzed in the context of the privatization and the modernization of the public sector. In the beginning of the 1980s, the Danish government introduced self-financing projects within existing governmental agencies. Making an externally funded RIMO would decrease the numbers of employees within the official statistics on public employment and support the privatization and modernization program.

[13] In RIMO data is available for the past two years.

[14] Political decision-making gets even more "confused" with the forecasts made by several governmental agencies and local governments because different prognoses produce conflicting results. Because of the relatively small size of Denmark and the relatively high degree of consensus on economic policies, different prognoses on national development do not seem necessarily vital in solving administrative problems.

[15] Model packing is here defined according to Danziger et al. (1982): technology (hardware, networks, software), people (technical experts, users, managers), and technique (organizational protocols, policies, and procedures).

[16] DSS are more targeted than MIS systems. DSS are tightly focused on a specific decision or a class of decisions, whereas MIS systems provide managers with a routine flow of data and assistance in general. This distinction between DSS and MIS is difficult to maintain in practice since MIS systems have adopted features from the DSS (Sprague & Carlson, 1982; Laudon & Laudon, 1991).

REFERENCES

Andersen, K. V. (1991a). *Hvad mener modelbrugerne?* [How Do the Model Users Think about Modeling?]. Copenhagen: National Agency of Physical Planning.

Andersen, K. V. (1991b). *Edb-modeller i amtskommunerne* [Computerized Models in the Danish Counties] (Working paper No. 10). Copenhagen: University of Copenhagen, Institute of Political Science.

Andersen, K. V. (1992a). Implementation, Use, and Perceived Role of Regional Computerized Planning Models: Experiences from Denmark. In M. Khowrowpour (Ed.), *Proceedings of the 3rd International Conference of the Information Resource Management Association* (pp. 13-22). Harrisburg, PA: Idea Group Publishing.

Andersen, K. V. (1992b). Planlægning, modeller og politik [Planning, Models, and Politics]. *Politica, 24*(2), 206-218.

Andersen, K. V. (1992, February). *Regional Modeling: Lessons from Denmark. In J. Huttman (Chair), Regional Analysis.* Symposium conducted at the Thirty-First Annual Meeting of the Western Regional Science Association. South Lake Tahoe, Nevada.

Andersen, K. V., and Madsen, P. K. (in press). Expelled from the Garden of Eden: Economic Modeling and Politics in Denmark. *Informatization and the Public Sector.*

Andersen, K. V., and Nielsen, H. (1991). RIMO - en regional strukturmodel [RIMO: A Regional Structural Model]. *Samfundsøkonomen, 9*(6), 40-43.

Bogason, P. (1987). Capacity for Welfare: Local Governments in Scandinavia and the United States. *Scandinavian Studies, 59*(2), 184-202.

Bolton, R. (1990). Regional Econometric Methods. In R. G. Bodkin, L. R. Klein, and K. Marwah (Eds.), *A History of Macroeconomic Model-Building* (pp. 451-481). Brookfield, VT: Edward Elgar.

Bretschneider, S. I. (1989). Political and Organizational Influences on the Accuracy of Forecasting State Government Revenues. *International Journal of Forecasting, 5*(5), 307-320.

Bundgaard-Jørgensen, U. (1976). *Economic Long-range Planning in Danish Municipalities.* Copenhagen: Economic Research in Local and Regional Government.

Danziger, J. N. (1985). Social Science and the Social Impacts of Computer Technology. *Social Science Quarterly, 66*(1-2), 3-21.

Danziger, J. N., Dutton, W. H., Kling, R., and Kraemer, K. L. (1982). *Computers and Politics: High Technology in American Local Governments.* New York: Columbia University Press.

Dueker, K. J. (1982). Urban Planning Uses of Computing. *Computers, Environment, Urban Systems, 7,* 59-64.

Dunlop, C., and Kling, R. (Eds.). (1991). *Computerization and Controversy: Value Conflicts and Social Choices.* New York: Academic Press, Inc.

Dutton, W. H., and Kraemer, K. L. (1985). *Modeling as Negotiating: The Political Dynamics of Computer Models in the Policy Process.* Norwood, NJ: Ablex Publishing.

Feldman, M., and March, J. G. (1981). Information as Signal and Symbol. *Administrative Science Quarterly, 26,* 171-186.

Greenberger, M., Crenson, M. A., and Crissey, B. L. (1976). *Models in the Policy Process: Public Decision Making in the Computer Era.* New York: Rusell Sage Foundation.

Jeppesen, J. (1978). Kaffegrums. *Problemer og metoder ved fremskrivning* [Tea Leaves: Problems and Methods in Forecasting]. Copenhagen: Local Governments Research Institute on Public Finance and Administration.

Keen, P. G. W., and Morton, M. S. S. (1978). *Decision Support Systems: An Organizational Perspective.* Reading, MA: Addison-Wesley.

King, J. (1983). Successful Implementation of Large Scale Decision Support Systems: Computerized Models in U.S. Economic Policy Making. *Systems, Objectives, Solutions* (November).

King, J. L., and Kraemer, K. L. (1984). National Policies for Local Government

Computing: an Assessment of Experiences in Ten OECD Countries. *International Review of Administration Science, L*(2), 133-147.

Kraemer, K. L. (1984). The Politics of Model Implementation. In J. Richardson (Ed.), *Models of Reality: Shaping Thought and Action* (pp. 131-160). Mt. Airy, MD: Lomond Books.

Kraemer, K. L. (1985). Modeling as Negotiating: The Political Dynamics of Computer Models in Policy Making. *Advances in Information Processing in Organizations, 2,* 275-307.

Kraemer, K. L., Dickhoven, S., Tierney, S. F., and King, J. L. (1987). *Datawars: The Politics of Modeling in Federal Policymaking.* New York: Columbia University Press.

Kraemer, K. L., and King, J. L. (1988). Computer-Based Systems for Cooperative Work and Group Decision Making. *ACM Computing Surveys* (June).

Laudon, K. C., and Laudon, J. P. (1991). *Management Information Systems* (2nd edition). New York: Macmillan.

Lawless, M. W. (1987). Institutionalization of a Management Science Innovation in Police Departments. *Management Science, 33*(2), 244-252.

Madsen, B. et al. (1989). *Regionaløkonomiske modeller i Danmark, Norge, Sverige, og Holland* [Regional Economic Models in Denmark, Norway, Sweden, and the Netherlands]. Copenhagen: Local Governments Research Institute on Public Finance and Administration.

Madsen, P. K. (1991). *The Politics of Economic Modeling: Use and Abuse of Economic Science in Policy-Making.* Copenhagen: University of Copenhagen, Institute of Political Science.

Meadows, D. H., and Robinson, J. M. (1985). *The Electronic Oracle: Computer Models and Social Decisions.* New York: John Wiley and Sons.

Nielsen, H. (1985). Application of a Model for the Labor Market as an Information System. Research Colloquium on *Spatial Information Systems and Their Role for Urban and Regional Research and Planning.* Vienna, Austria.

Northrop, A., Kraemer, K. L., Dunkle, D., and King, J. L. (1990). Payoffs From Computerization: Lessons Over Time. *Public Administration Review, 50*(5), 505-514.

Perrolle, J. A. (1988). The Social Impact of Computing: Ideological Themes and Research Issues. Social Science *Computer Review, 6*(4), 469-480.

Roy, G. G., and Snickars, F. (1992). Computer-aided Regional Planning. Applications for the Perth and Helsinki Regions. *The Annals of Regional Science, 26*(1), 79-96.

Silver, M. S. (1990). Decision Support Systems: Directed and Nondirected Change. *Information Systems Research, 1*(1), 47-70.

Sprague, R. H., and Carlson, E. D. (1982). *Building Effective Decision Support Systems.* Englewood Cliffs, NJ: Prentice-Hall.

Sproll, L. S. (1985). Comments on "Modeling as Negotiating: The Political Dynamics of Computers Models in Policy Making." [Review of *Modeling as Negotiating: The Political Dynamics of Computer Models in the Policy Process*]. *Advances in Information Processing in Organizations, 2,* 309-311.

Te'eni, D. (1990). Support Systems for High Level Policy Making: What Makes Them Special? *Information & Management, 19,* 41-50.

CHAPTER 16

CASE TOOLS AS WORK REDESIGN

Dwight A. Haworth and Leah R. Pietron
University of Nebraska at Omaha

The purpose of this research is to explore the degree to which Zuboff's observations about the introduction of computer technology into the workplace may be extended to computer programmer-analysts. Responses from a questionnaire were analyzed using the data analysis techniques of Q methodology. Three identifiable patterns of usage emerged from the data analysis (accounting for 54.7 percent of overall variance). The patterns of usage are interpreted as an informating mode of use, an automating mode of use, and a panoptic mode of use. The results support Zuboff's findings and extend her analysis by identifying the panoptic mode of use as separate from the automating mode of use. The relationship between informating and work redesign is discussed. The fact that a higher number of responses fall in the informating category implies that work redesign may be more of an issue than previously suspected. And as more advanced tools are introduced, work redesign issues will be more important in achieving a successful CASE tool introduction.

Software development has been rationalized and specialized into a series of discrete steps. These steps are clearly shown in the extant models of the software development process. The reduction of software development to a sequence of simplified steps recalls the approach of the scientific management movement in designing industrial jobs. Because this approach makes each worker responsible for a part of the process and makes no worker responsible for the overall product, in certain types of work this approach leads to declining product quality and suboptimum productivity. These same problems, low quality and low productivity, have been part of the impetus toward CASE technology.

One prescription for these problems is to recombine these discrete steps into one job with the worker responsible for the product (Hammer, 1990). In work redesign terms, this recombination is called job enlargement (Griffin, 1982; p. 21). Automation of one or more of the previously discrete functions usually makes enlargement possible. Integrated CASE tools provide automated support for enlargement of the software development job by making it possible for one programmer/analyst to analyze and define requirements, design the system components, and to automatically generate program code. In a manual development methodology, these functions would be separate steps and probably would be performed by different persons, but in a CASE environment one programmer/analyst can do all of them. The parallelism between work redesign and the introduction of CASE technology is clear.

The parallels do not stop at what is done; there are many similarities between the factors that influence success and failure. Reports appear daily describing the problems of organizational readiness when introducing CASE tools: management support, long term commitment, methodological compatibility, organization structure, organizational communication, and so on. These same problems appear in the literature on work redesign.

The parallels between CASE tool introduction and work redesign extend to the impacts on individual workers. Among the impacts common to CASE tool introduction and to work redesign are the need for training, the changes in on-the-job communication patterns, the increase in personal responsibility and accountability, and the changes in the skills applied on the job.

In their review of CASE, Chen, Nunamaker, and Weber (1989) summarize the influences that CASE tools may have on programmer-analysts. CASE tools rationalize and mechanize work that has heretofore been considered an art; consequently, CASE tools have psychological impacts on the programmer/analyst that extend beyond the discomfort arising from the requirement to learn a new way of doing the work. According to Chen, et al., when ignored these psychological effects may thwart a successful CASE tool introduction.

Chen, et al. (1989) then reached to the work redesign literature for answers. They state that in addition to automating the work of the programmer/analyst, management must have the goal of informating that work. The infinitive "to informate" is attributed to Zuboff (1988) and is defined as "to free people from cognitive overload so that they can concentrate on developing a more comprehensive, explicit, and abstract knowledge of their work" (Chen, Nunamaker, & Weber, 1989, p. 10). Zuboff (1988) observed production workers who were in transition from a manually-controlled system, in which workers used direct sensory input for decision making, to a computer monitored system in which they were required to substitute abstract data for direct sensory input (seeing, feeling, smelling, hearing). Zuboff (1988, pp. 75-76) labels the production workers' former skills as "action-centered" and describes the new realm in which the workers were required to operate as one of "intellective skills." To master their new work environment, the production workers were required to reskill, to acquire the intellective skills required by the altered nature of their work.

When compared with the job of a programmer/analyst, the intellectual content of the former job of the production workers was limited. Basically the tasks of the programmer/analyst are intellective before the introduction of CASE tools and little change in type of skill is needed. Because of the job differences between Zuboff's subjects and programmer/analysts, it is uncertain whether her findings apply to programmer/analysts being introduced to CASE tools. The purpose of this paper is to explore the degree to which Zuboff's conclusions may be extended to computer programmer/analysts using CASE tools in the systems development process.

BACKGROUND

Automating a process is to "rationalize [it] while decreasing the dependence on human skills" (Zuboff, 1988, p. 10). The human being is either eliminated from the process or becomes a data collection and input servant for a computerized process. Such deskilling of work, making labor subservient to machines, was an early key to mass production in smokestack industries. The more recent experiences of these industries suggest that simple automation is ineffective, that the worker's input is needed, and that quality depends on the worker's initiative. Answers to the problems of automation have been found in several movements, participatory management, quality circles, and work redesign, to name a few. An element common to these approaches is to provide the worker with additional information for use on the job.

Informating a process is the act of increasing the information content of the process (Zuboff (1988), p. 10). Zuboff (1991, p. 5) explains, "...'informating' occurs as processes, objects, behaviors, and events are translated into and made visible as explicit information." But informating also implies that the job be redesigned to require use of the new information (Zuboff, 1989). For the system development process, the redesign centers on the use of the computer to produce graphical representations of program designs, to store documentation in a central repository, and in some cases to generate code. Lower level tasks are automated, and the focus of concern is shifted to earlier in the life cycle. The programmer/analyst must concentrate on getting the requirements right and let the tool(s) do the menial work that was previously the art and craft of the job. The new process follows the system development methodology that is implicit in the CASE tool; the new information is that information required by and arising from the formalisms of the methodology.

Informating a process also increases the need for communication between the human operator and colleagues. The larger viewpoint available to the programmer/analyst creates an awareness of the need to coordinate design details and results in a work redesign described by Hammer (1990) as the linkage of parallel processes during the task. Often CASE tools automate that coordination through the facilities of data dictionaries and/or design repositories; data access is standardized and design consistency is checked. The early coordination of database design and process design becomes even more important because the results of early decisions, recorded in the tool's repository, will be enforced throughout subsequent activity. Zuboff (1988, p. 400) credits the higher level of abstraction present in the automated task as the impetus for increased communication.

In relating informating to simple automation, Zuboff (1988, p. 11) says "Informating derives from and builds upon automation. Automation is a necessary but not sufficient condition for informating." A diagramming tool may automate the production of data flow diagrams but include no features to check consistency among parts of the diagram; this is simple automation. To include the ability to check for consistency from one level of decomposition to another requires additional functionality be built into the system. This is an example of an informating function; it requires automation, but additional programming is required for it to occur.

In her study of reactions to the applications of computers to the workplace, Zuboff also examines the reactions of managers. She observes that perceptions of disturbed relationships, altered roles, and diminished authority sometimes emerge. Zuboff (1988, p. 323) describes the reactions of managers and the appeal that computer-based monitoring and control may hold. Zuboff (1988, pp. 319-336) develops the "information panopticon" as an extension of Jeremy Bentham's architectural panopticon. The architectural panopticon was conceived as a transparent multi-storied office building in which all workers could be observed and their activities monitored from a central office. Thus, panoptic power is that capability of information technology to support surveillance and control activities.

Zuboff fails to elaborate the differences between panoptic power and automation. She appears to regard them as almost synonymous in her description of management's use of technology as the means to control access to organizational information (Zuboff, 1988, p. 390). Although Orlikowski (1988) and Hoffnagle and Beregi (1985) state that automation establishes a degree of technical control, panoptic power is more than the constraints implicit in tool capabilities. Automation does not necessarily include functions that allow monitoring of worker performance or that restrict access to knowledge bases as described by Zuboff; these functions must be added to simple automation. Just as informating is an extension of automating, supporting panoptic power is also an extension of automating.

These work redesigns, informating and panoptic, are based on antithetical motivations and methods. On one side is an informated workplace, with technology providing new information to the worker and supporting heightened responsibilities for the worker. At the other extreme is a computer-based panopticon, with technology providing surveillance and control capabilities that exceed the dreams of the harshest autocrat. Between these two extremes lies a spectrum of possibilities blending various proportions of the attributes of each, all resting on a foundation of simple automation of tasks.

MAJOR ISSUES OF WORK REDESIGN

Issues, Controversies, Problems

The challenge of CASE is to introduce the technology and avoid counterproductive reactions. The extent to which informating, automating, and panoptic modes of work redesign apply to CASE tools may offer a key to successful introduction of CASE technology to the workplace. Often CASE tools are discussed and introduced to the workplace as if they were of no more significance than adding a spelling checker to a word processor; the prospect that the introduction of the CASE tool may be a significant work redesign is ignored.

If informating, automating, and panoptic modes of use tend to emerge in conjunction with the introduction of a CASE tool, that finding will make explicit the fact that such tools can be more than simple automation. Such a finding will make clear that managers must be more sensitive to effects that arise from work redesign, whether the redesign was intended or not. A finding that there are several potential modes of use may suggest clues to detect and correct undesirable trends before the benefits of the technology are undermined.

CASE tools contain various features. Some features simply automate the process of diagramming, others facilitate the design of screens and reports, and still others perform consistency checking. Some features support communication between programmers, and others provide project monitoring and progress reporting to management. Clearly, the quality of potential support depends on the nature of the features included in the CASE tool.

But beyond the potential quality of support, the quality of the realized support may vary considerably depending on the combination of features used and ignored. Among the influences on feature use are training, company policy, and resistance to change. Considering the possible interactions among these influences, it is uncertain that any consistent patterns of feature use will emerge. This uncertainty is central to the present study.

From Zuboff's descriptions of observed modes of computer application, the following research questions were formed:

1. Is there a pattern of usage that can be characterized as an informated mode of use?
2. Is there a pattern of usage that can be characterized as an automated mode of use?
3. Is there a pattern of usage that can be characterized as a panoptic mode of use?

Further, the high information content and intellective nature of the programmer/analyst's work suggests that the natural inclination of programmer/ analysts may be to pursue an informated mode of use. Therefore, if an informated mode of use can be identified, the following question will extend our understanding of work redesign for programmer/analysts:

4. Does the informated mode of use occur more frequently than would be expected by chance?

Confirmation of these modes of use may serve as a basis for improving success in CASE tool introduction. Lessons learned from automation and work redesign in other occupations may be extended to guide managers as CASE technology is implemented in the workplace. Information about the uses made of various features may be worthwhile in selecting tools and planning training.

Self-reports of feature usage are essentially subjective responses. Q methodology was developed to analyze subjective responses (Brown, 1980, p. 5). The methodology usually employs a characteristic data collection method called Q sorting, but the analytic method may be used on any type of responses that reflects relative preferences among a set of items (McKeown & Thomas, 1988, p. 34). The value of the method is that it allows subsets of respondents to be identified and evaluated as individuals or as groups. Because we are interested in individuals and groups who employ CASE tools similarly, the analytic method of Q methodology is appropriate for the present study.

A questionnaire was constructed that contained six items about computer environment, training, and first exposure to Excelerator. The questionnaire then asked the respondents to rate their use of the features of Excelerator on a 0 to 5 scale with 0 representing no use, 1 representing very low use, 2 representing low use, 3 representing medium use, 4 representing high use, and 5 representing very high use. The features included in the questionnaire were those identified in the documentation of version 1.8 of Excelerator. No attempt was made to gather information to evaluate the success or efficiency of the tool after it was introduced.

Subjects were members of an Excelerator XL Users Group. Questionnaires were mailed to 730 members of the group. Two hundred fifty responses were received representing 34.2 percent of the questionnaires. Of the 250 received, 206 were usable (28.2 percent of the total mailing).

The non-administrative features of Excelerator were evaluated using documentation and the experience of the researchers. Each feature was classified as to whether it supported an automating mode of use, an informating mode of use, or a panoptic mode of use. The reference criteria was that discussed above: An automating feature provides simple computer assistance for a manual process; an informating feature provides additional information about the process or supports communication of information among users; and a panoptic feature provides information on user performance. Several of the features may be interpreted as either informating or panoptic, depending on who uses the output of those features; these are identified as informating/panoptic in the classification. The classification is used to interpret the responses of the subjects.

To identify subsets of respondents, the responses were factor analyzed with a varimax rotation using techniques described by

Feature	Mode of Use
Data Flow Diagrams	Automating
Structure Charts	Automating
Data Modeling Diagrams	Automating
E-R Diagrams	Automating
Structure Diagrams	Automating
Presentation Graph	Informating
Records/Elements	Automating
Data	Automating
Process	Automating
Graphs	Automating
Screens/Reports	Informating/Panoptic
Other	Automating
Report Design	Automating
Screen Design	Automating
Screen Data Entry	Automating
Screen Data Reporting	Informating/Panoptic
Document Graph	Informating/Panoptic
Document Production	Informating/Panoptic
Word Processing	Automating
Project Management	Panoptic
Graph Analysis	Informating/Panoptic
Entity List	Informating/Panoptic
Report Writer	Informating/Panoptic
Extended Analysis	Informating/Panoptic
Export	Informating
Import	Informating
Lock	Informating
Export & Lock	Informating
Import & Lock	Informating

Table 1: Excelerator Features and Potential Use

Brown (1980). The varimax rotation produces a factor structure in which each factor is orthogonal (minimally correlated with) to every other factor. In the interest of parsimony, the number of factors is limited to those containing two or more subjects that load significantly on that factor and on no other factors. The standard error (S.E.) for a zero order loading is +/- 0.1857 (the reciprocal of the square root of the number of items (Brown, 1980, p. 43). For the purpose of identifying factors and of determining feature use in those factors, a respondent is considered to have a significant (P = 0.0001) factor loading if his/her loading on a factor exceeds +/- 0.7186 (3.87 x S.E.).

Using the criteria described above, three orthogonal factors were determined from the data. Twenty-eight respondents load significantly on Factor 1, ten respondents load significantly on Factor 2, and three respondents load significantly on Factor 3. All other factors have fewer than two respondents loading significantly on them. These three factors account for 54.7 percent of the total variance.

The three factors may be considered to be empirically derived patterns of use reflected in the responses of the subjects. To determine the meaning of the factors, factor scores for the courses are calculated. A factor score is determined from the responses of the subjects who load significantly on that factor. The calculation of the weight of a respondent on a factor is given by Brown (1980, p. 241) as $w = f / (1 - f^2)$ where w is the weight and f is the factor loading.

The relative magnitude of each respondent's weight is used in calculating the factor score, a composite answer set that represents a prototypical answer set for that factor. The relative magnitude is calculated by identifying the respondent with the largest weight on a factor and using that weight as the denominator in a ratio that determines the relative importance of each respondent's answer set. For example, the respondent with the largest weight on Factor 1 has a weight of 4.1590. Another of the respondents has a weight of only 1.8608 and, therefore, the answers of that respondent count 1.8608/ 4.1590 or 44.7 percent in determining the factor score. The answers of that respondent would be multiplied by .447 as they are added to the factor scores for Factor 1, whereas the answers of the respondent with the largest weight would be multiplied by 1.000 when they are added to the totals that make up the factor scores.

The factor score for each of the features is calculated. Because there are different numbers of respondents contributing to the factor scores for each factor, the results must be normalized for comparability. Table 2 shows the score for each of the features in Factor 1. The standard deviation of these scores is calculated and used to determine a normalized (z) score for each feature. Similarly calculated scores for Factor 2 and for Factor 3 are shown in Table 3 and Table 4 respectively.

For the purpose of comparing the scores and interpreting the meaning of the factors, the differences between the normalized scores of a feature on Factor 1, Factor 2, and Factor 3 are calculated (Table 5). Statistically significant differences may be identified by determining the standard error of the difference (SED) between the factors, given by Brown (1980, pp. 297-298) as

$$SED_{ab} = SQRT(SE_a^2 + SE_b^2)$$

Feature	Total	z
Data Flow Diagrams	658	1.2045
Structure Charts	401	-0.1270
Data Modeling Diagram	518	0.4792
Entity-Relationship Diagrams	457	0.1631
Structure Diagrams	220	-1.0648
Presentation Graph	390	-0.1840
Records/Elements	685	1.3444
Data	657	1.1993
Process	596	0.8833
Graphs	608	0.9454
Screens/Reports	271	-0.8006
Other	145	-1.4534
Report Design	230	-1.0130
Screen Design	229	-1.0182
Screen Data Entry	153	-1.4119
Screen Data Reporting	135	-1.5052
Document Graph	267	-0.8213
Document Production	267	-0.8213
Word Processing	200	-1.1684
Project Management	138	-1.4896
Graph Analysis	517	0.4740
Entity List	622	1.0180
Report Writer	594	0.8729
Extended Analysis	520	0.4895
Export	679	1.3133
Import	679	1.3133
Lock	514	0.4584
Export & Lock	495	0.3600
Import & Lock	495	0.3600
X bar	425.52	0.0000
s	193.01	1.0000

Table 2: Normalized Factor Scores for Factor 1

Feature	Total	z
Data Flow Diagrams	250	1.4907
Structure Charts	201	0.7867
Data Modeling Diagram	186	0.5712
Entity-Relationship Diagrams	191	0.6430
Structure Diagrams	178	0.4563
Presentation Graph	226	1.1459
Records/Elements	226	1.1459
Data	222	1.0884
Process	221	1.0740
Graphs	221	1.0740
Screens/Reports	226	1.1459
Other	90	-0.8080
Report Design	202	0.8011
Screen Design	219	1.0453
Screen Data Entry	169	0.3270
Screen Data Reporting	153	0.0971
Document Graph	106	-0.5781
Document Production	95	-0.7362
Word Processing	81	-0.9373
Project Management	61	-1.2246
Graph Analysis	114	-0.4632
Entity List	135	-0.1615
Report Writer	99	-0.6787
Extended Analysis	85	-0.8798
Export	104	-0.6069
Import	96	-0.7218
Lock	28	-1.6988
Export & Lock	28	-1.6988
Import & Lock	28	-1.6988
X bar	146.24	0.0000
s	69.60	1.0000

Table 3: Normalized Factor Scores for Factor 2

Feature	Total	z
Data Flow Diagrams	122	1.3954
Structure Charts	92	0.4644
Data Modeling Diagram	114	1.1471
Entity-Relationship Diagrams	122	1.3954
Structure Diagrams	84	0.2162
Presentation Graph	54	-0.7148
Records/Elements	94	0.5265
Data	104	0.8368
Process	104	0.8368
Graphs	84	0.2162
Screens/Reports	54	-0.7148
Other	74	-0.0942
Report Design	38	-1.2113
Screen Design	38	-1.2113
Screen Data Entry	38	-1.2113
Screen Data Reporting	38	-1.2113
Document Graph	94	0.5265
Document Production	94	0.5265
Word Processing	94	0.5265
Project Management	84	0.2162
Graph Analysis	120	1.3333
Entity List	110	1.0230
Report Writer	64	-0.4045
Extended Analysis	130	1.6436
Export	38	-1.2113
Import	38	-1.2113
Lock	38	-1.2113
Export & Lock	38	-1.2113
Import & Lock	38	-1.2113
X bar	77.03	0.0000
s	32.23	1.0000

Table 4: Normalized Factor Scores for Factor 3

where the standard error (SE) of the normalized factor score is

$$SE = 1.000 \text{ SQRT}(1 - r)$$

and

$$r = (N)(0.80) / ((1 + (N-1)(0.80))$$

and N is the number of subjects. The standard error of the difference can then be multiplied by the appropriate value from a table of percentage points of the normal distribution, such as given by Montgomery and Peck (1982, pp. 462-463), to find the value representing the desired level of significance.

Factor 1 is characterized by high scores for Records/Elements, Export, Import, Data Flow Diagrams, and Data (Table 2). Of these five features, only Export and Import are significantly ($p < .001$) different from their scores on the other factors. Our a priori classification of Export and Import was to the informating category; the other three features were placed in the automating category. At the opposite end of the factor scores are Screen Data Reporting, Project Management, Other, and Screen Data Entry. The lowest score, Screen Data Reporting, is classified as informating/panoptic; it is significantly lower ($p < .001$) than its score on Factor 2, but not different from its score on Factor 3. Project Management, classified as panoptic, scores significantly lower ($p < .001$) than on Factor 3. The remaining low scores, Other and Screen Data Entry, are classified as automating and are significantly lower ($p < .001$) than they appear on Factor 2. Considering these observations, the relatively high position of the informating features and the relatively low position of the panoptic feature, Factor 1 is judged to be an informating mode of use.

Factor 2 is characterized by low scores for both informating and panoptic features (Table 3). All of the communication-related features and the panoptic feature are ranked in the bottom half of the factor scores. All of the automating features except Other and Word Processing are ranked in the upper half of the factor scores. Because of this pattern of feature use, Factor 2 is judged to be to be an automating mode of use.

Factor 3 is characterized by a score for Project Management that is significantly higher ($p < .001$) than on any of the other factors (Table 5). Factor 3 differs from Factor 2 in that Document Graph, Graph Analysis, Entity List and Extended Analysis, all classified as informating/panoptic, have significantly higher scores on Factor 3.

Feature	Z1-Z2	Z1-Z3	Z2-Z3
Data Flow Diagrams	-0.2862	-0.1909	0.0953
Structure Charts	-0.9137	-0.5914	0.3223
Data Modeling Diagram	-0.0920	-0.6679	-0.5759
E-R Diagrams	-0.4799	-1.2323	-0.7524
Structure Diagrams	-1.5211	-1.2810	0.2401
Presentation Graph	-1.3299	0.5308	1.8607
Records/Elements	0.1985	0.8179	0.6194
Data	0.1109	0.3625	0.2516
Process	-0.1907	0.0465	0.2372
Graphs	-0.1286	0.7292	0.8578
Screens/Reports	-1.9465	-0.0858	1.8607
Other	-0.6454	-1.3592	-0.7138
Report Design	-1.8141	0.1983	2.0124
Screen Design	-2.0635	0.1931	2.2566
Screen Data Entry	-1.7389	-0.2006	1.5383
Screen Data Reporting	-1.6023	-0.2939	1.3084
Document Graph	-0.2432	-1.3478	-1.1046
Document Production	-0.0851	-1.3478	1.2627
Word Processing	-0.2311	-1.6949	1.4638
Project Management	-0.2650	-1.7058	-1.4408
Graph Analysis	0.9372	-0.8593	-1.7962
Entity List	1.1795	-0.0050	-1.1845
Report Writer	1.5515	1.2774	-0.2742
Extended Analysis	1.3693	-1.1541	-2.5234
Export	1.9202	2.5246	0.6044
Import	2.0351	2.5246	0.4895
Lock	2.1572	1.6697	-0.4875
Export & Lock	2.0588	1.5713	-0.4875
Import & Lock	2.0588	1.5713	-0.4875
SED	.1823	.2928	.3183
.01 significance level +/-	.4703	.7554	.8212
.001 significance level +/-	.5998	.9633	1.0472

Table 5: Differences Between Normalized Scores

In contrast, Presentation Graph, classified as informating, has a significantly lower score on Factor 3 than on Factor 2. Thus, when compared to Factor 2, Factor 3 has a higher score for the panoptic mode feature and a lower score for one informating mode feature. Further, Factor 3 has low scores for all of the communication-related features. Comparing Factor 3 with Factor 2 leads to the conclusion that Factor 3 represents a panoptic mode of use because the panoptic features score relatively high and the informating features score relatively low.

Examination of the differences between the Factor 1 scores and the Factor 3 scores yields distinctions between the informating mode and the panoptic mode of Excelerator use. The informating mode of use clearly has higher scores for the communication-related features and for the report writer feature. The importance of the communication features arises from the heighten need for communication in an informated environment, but the rationale for the significant score of the report writer feature is less obvious. The report writer feature is the only of the features that were rated a priori as informating/panoptic to have a significantly greater score on the informating mode of use. A reason is suggested by the *Excelerator Reference Guide* (Index Technology Corporation (1986), p. 6-39), "Use Report Writer when you need *detailed reporting* [italics added] on more than one entity type ...." The level of detail provided is appropriate for the detailed work of the system analyst but may exceed the needs of a manager.

Examination of the features that score higher on Factor 3 than on Factor 1 begins with Project Management. This feature has a significant level of use only on Factor 3 (Table 5) and is the basis for labeling Factor 3 as the panoptic mode of use. Of the analysis features (all characterized a priori as informating/panoptic), only Extended Analysis scores significantly higher on Factor 3 than on Factor 1. This arises from the fact that "Extended Analysis treats a project as a unified system." (Index Technology Corporation (1987), p.1) This system-wide viewpoint is much more consistent with the needs of management than is the detailed view offered by Report Writer. The two other analysis features, Graph Analysis and Entity List, do not show significant ($p < .001$) differences among their levels of use in Factor 1 and Factor 3.

Two other informating/panoptic features show significantly greater use in Factor 3 than in Factor 1. These are Document Graph and Document Production. These two features support organization and production of documentation for the project (Index Technology Corporation, 1986). This documentation is not user documentation or program documentation but rather documentation that supports management oversight and control. Thus, the significantly greater use of these features in Factor 3 is consistent with the characterization of Factor 3 as representing a panoptic mode of use.

Having identified Factor 1 as an informating mode of use allows consideration of whether more respondents load on Factor 1 than would be expected by chance. Considering the 41 respondents who were found to load significantly on one and only one of the three factors, are the 28 who load on Factor 1 a statistically greater number than would be expected by chance?

The null hypothesis for evaluating this question is

$$p <= p^*$$

where p^* is the probability that a respondent would load on Factor 1 by chance. In this case $p^* = 0.33$, three possible categories with an equal probability of each. The alternative hypothesis of interest is

$$p > p^*$$

The binomial test statistic for the null hypothesis is given by Conover (1980, p. 444) as

$$t = (n)(p^*) + (w)\ SQRT((n)(p^*)(1-p^*))$$

where n is the sample size, and w is the quantile of the standard normal distribution. For this study, a critical region of alpha = .001 is used; therefore, w = 3.0902. Consequently, the value of t = 22.993 or approximately 23. Because the number of respondents loading significantly on Factor 1 is 28, the null hypothesis is rejected, and we conclude that the number of respondents loading on Factor 1 is greater than chance at a significance level of .001.

To evaluate all of the respondents, each was classified according to the factor on which he/she had the highest factor loading. One hundred-eight (108) respondents fall in the informating category, 74 in the automating category, and 24 in the panoptic category. For a binomial test using the same criteria as above, but with n = 206, the critical value is 90. Because 108 is larger than 90, we conclude that, for all of the respondents, the number loading on Factor 1 is greater than chance at a significance level of .001.

Solutions and Recommendations

The discovery of an informating pattern of use and the finding that it occurs more frequently than chance would dictate argue for the concept that CASE tool usage tends toward redesigning the programmer/analyst's work, rather than simply automating some features of that work. This finding is especially significant in light of the fact that Excelerator 1.8 has only six informating features. It is far less rich in informating features than some other CASE tools, or even later versions of Excelerator. One may hypothesize that a CASE tool with more informating features would more dramatically alter the job of the programmer/analyst.

The evidence that the informating mode of use appears to be a natural inclination among the Excelerator users is consistent with theory underlying job enrichment. In their monograph on job enrichment, Christopher and Christopher (1979, p. 4), drawing on the theories of Maslow and Herzberg, state that workers will seek out the stimulating aspects of a job as a means to avoid boredom. However, they go on to point out survey evidence that not all workers respond to job enrichment (Christopher and Christopher, 1979, pp. 60-62). This, too, is consistent with the evidence from the present sample. The number who were classified as automated mode users (74) is not significant ($p = .21$) at the usual levels, but it is greater than the number expected by chance (69). Christopher and Christopher (1979, pp. 60-65) and Rozen (1983, pp. 197-204) describe various conditions that mitigate against job enrichment. These conditions fall into three categories:

1. worker resistance to change,
2. biases toward the quick fix, and
3. organizational resistance to job enrichment.

CASE tools have in them a trap. They promise to be the quick fix that is so attractive, but in fact they may contain significant elements of job redesign that may invoke both individual and organizational resistance to change in both process and authority implied by job enrichment. Organizational resistance has been identified by Brown (1991), Roberts (1992), and Yuen and Spurgeon(1992), among others, as a significant barrier to CASE tool success. Both the evidence and the theory suggest that introducing CASE tools is more complex than imagined previously.

The findings suggest that the natural inclination of programmer/analysts is to pursue an informated mode of use, that informating the work may not be a problem if informating features are available, but that management must realize that work redesign is involved. The introduction of CASE tools must be managed accordingly in order to avoid the kinds of counterproductive psychological effects forecast by Chen, et al. (1989). The first area to address is individual resistance to change. Because all workers are not ready for change in their jobs, are not prepared to learn new techniques, and do not derive achievement satisfactions from the job, across the board introductions of CASE technology may be unsuccessful (Reif & Luthans, 1972). Reports from the field (Gifford, 1991; Roberts, 1992) indicate that changes in job focus and skills arouse resistance in the staff. Each programmer/analyst must be evaluated to determine the degree to which he/she will adjust to the use of CASE tools and changes in his/her job design. Although there is evidence that higher levels of education are usually associated with positive response to enhanced jobs (Reif & Luthans, 1972), generalizing that evidence to any group of programmer/analysts is risky. Management must evaluate the individual readiness of the programmer/ analysts and determine their willingness adapt to the changes implicit in the CASE tool being implemented.

Beyond individual readiness, there must be organizational readiness for CASE tools, and the job changes that should accompany their introduction. Part of the readiness will be achieved through training, not just tool training, but training in interpersonal skills and in background disciplines for the mainline of the firm's business. A difficult part of the preparation will be to delegate authority to lower levels, to allow work group autonomy, in other words, to refrain from using the panoptic features that may be embedded in the tools. The most difficult part of the preparation will be in reconciling that authority structures in one part of the organization may be markedly different from those in other parts of the organization, that lateral (coordinating) relations may be substantially disturbed, and that these new and different structures and relations must be reconciled with all concerned.

The evidence that programmer/analysts are biased toward an informated mode of use makes the availability of informating features an important consideration when selecting a CASE tool. The fit between the types of features embedded in the tool, and the nature of the work redesign may significantly affect the success of the tool. Providing a tool with informating features without actual job redesign may frustrate programmer/ analysts because they will be aware of the context and ramifications of the task without being empowered to use that information. Redesigning the job without providing a tool with features that support the job will also generate frustration and failure, and informating when either the worker or the organization is not ready for the enriched job will be ineffective. Simple automation of some of the programmer/analyst's tasks may yield some initial productivity gains, but if the job is deskilled and previously valued arts are devalued, one may expect that boredom and dissatisfaction will set in. Introducing a tool that increases panoptic control may please managers but will arouse resentment in a workforce that is inclined toward enhanced, informated jobs. Panoptic capabilities will appear to programmer/analysts as more punitive than constructive, more restrictive than liberating, more self-serving than empowering, and dissatisfaction and resistance to change may arise. These potential interactions between the features of the CASE tool and the job reinforce the need to address the introduction of a CASE tool as an instance of work redesign.

FUTURE TRENDS

The brief history of CASE tools shows a tendency toward integration. There is no reason to suspect that this trend will not continue. The more features that are integrated into a CASE tool, the greater the impact on the task of the programmer/analyst. These integrated CASE tools will support a trend away from the skills that were previously valued, coding, design, and design documentation. This trend suggests that there will be resistance to change from older workers and managers who were trained to value the art and craft of design and coding.

CASE tools are usually integrated around a methodology. The more fully integrated the product, the more strongly it reflects an implicit methodology. Understanding that implicit methodology will be required to gain the full benefits of a particular tool. Today, many of the stand-alone tools can be used without adopting a methodology, or they can be adapted to one's current methodology. The methodology issue will become a much more important issue in the future because adoption of an integrated CASE tool will require adoption of the methodology underlying that tool.

The combination of added functionality and declining price of hardware will make CASE tools a very feasible technology. In the future, the real barrier to getting the tools into the workplace will rest increasingly on management and training issues. As these tools become more powerful and take over tasks that were previously regarded as crucial, skilled tasks, training will be required to prepare programmers for their new roles. Personnel selection, change management, and planning will overshadow the cost and functionality issues that frequently rule today.

The trend toward lower-cost, highly functional CASE tools also implies that education for programmer/analysts will shift away from the traditional curriculum and toward the background knowledge, methodologies, and interpersonal skills that will be the core of the emerging job. Likewise, CASE tool research will follow the tool; there will be a highly technical track devoted to rationalizing and automating functions and integrating those functions into tools, and there will be a behavioral track to devoted to identifying and overcoming the barriers to successful CASE tool use in organizations.

CONCLUSIONS

Integrated CASE tools constitute a substantial redesign of the programmer/analyst's job. The problems of implementing CASE tools parallel many of the problems reported in the redesign of other types of jobs. Because of these parallels, it is recommended that managers who are introducing CASE tools review the work redesign literature for both potential problems and potential solutions.

In examining the use of CASE tools, parallels with the automation of other jobs have been found. Three separate patterns of feature usage have been identified among the responses by Excelerator users. These patterns can be interpreted as an informating mode, an automating mode, and a panoptic mode of use. Moreover, because the informating mode of use occurs more frequently than chance would indicate, all research questions are answered affirmatively.

These findings extend Zuboff's conclusions about the informating characteristics of computer-based systems. They findings suggest that application of Excelerator to the programmer/analyst has characteristics similar to the applications of computer-based systems that Zuboff studied.

Second, the finding of three distinct patterns of use supports not only the concept of informating as an extension of automating but also the concept of the panoptic mode as a distinct extension of automating. Moreover, as orthogonal patterns of use, the informating mode and the panoptic mode are not mutually exclusive; if appropriate types of features are available, both modes of use may be implemented simultaneously.

Finally, the larger number of respondents loading on the informating mode of use suggests that this mode of use and its attendant changes in the work of programmer/analysts is the likely outcome of the introduction of informating CASE tools into the workplace. The implicit changes in job skills suggest that management institute a broad range of training and address work redesign issues to realize potential performance benefits.

Several serendipitous observations suggest questions for future research. First, the data analysis implies that some of the features that contribute to an informating mode may be corrupted to support a panoptic mode of use. Under what conditions does this misapplication of features occur? Second, Excelerator is not as feature-rich as some tools. Does a more feature-rich tool foster a greater amount of informating use, or is the mode of use a function of other factors, such as training or job description? Finally, although three distinct patterns of use emerge from the responses, no conclusions may be drawn about the effectiveness of these patterns of use. Are there productivity or quality improvements associated with these patterns? Clearly, this is the significant question for future research.

REFERENCES

Brown, M. (1991, Fall). Making CASE work: Practical CASE adoption tips. *CASE Trends*, pp. 24-27.

Brown, S. R. (1980). *Political Subjectivity*. New Haven, CT: Yale University Press.

Chen, M., Nunamaker, J. F., & Weber, E. S. (1989). Computer-aided software engineering: Present status and future directions. *DATA BASE, 20*(1), 7-13.

Christopher, R. G., & Christopher, E. E. (1979). *Job Enrichment: How Far Have We Come?* Washington, DC: University Press of America, Inc.

Gifford, R. (1991, September 16) CASE culture shock. *Computerworld*, pp. 103-104.

Griffin, R.W. (1982). *Task Analysis.* Glenview, IL: Scott, Foresman, and Company.

Hammer, M. (1990, July-August). Reengineering work: Don't automate, obliterate. *Harvard Business Review*, 104-114.

Hoffnagle, G. F., & Beregi, W. E. (1985). Automating the software development process. *IBM Systems Journal, 24*, 102-120.

Index Technology Corporation. (1986). *Excelerator Reference Guide.* Cambridge, MA: Author.

Index Technology Corporation. (1987). *Excelerator Extended Analysis.* Cambridge, MA: Author.

McKeown, B., & Thomas, D. (1988). *Q Methodology.* Sage University Paper series on Quantitative Applications in the Social Sciences, 07-066. Beverly Hills, CA: Sage Publications, Inc.

Montgomery, D. C., & Peck, E. A. (1982). *Introduction to Linear Regression Analysis.* New York, NY: John Wiley & Sons, Inc.

Orlikowski, W. J. (1988). CASE tools and the IS workplace: Some findings from empirical research. In E. M. Awad (Ed.), *Proceedings of the 1988 ACM SIGCPR Conference on the Management of Information Systems Personnel* (pp. 88-97). New York, NY: The Association for Computing Machinery, Inc.

Reif, W. E. & Luthans, F. (1972). Does job enrichment really pay off? *California Management Review, 15* (1), pp. 30-37.

Roberts, M. L. (1992, January). Surviving CASE culture shock. *Enterprise Systems Journal*, pp. 82-85.

Rozen, M. E. (1983). *The Economics of Work Reorganization.* New York, NY: Praeger Publishers.

Yuen, M. K. & Spurgeon, J. R. (1992, July). Why organizations aren't more successful with CASE. *CASE Trends*, pp. 24-31.

Zuboff, S. (1988). *In the Age of the Smart Machine.* New York, NY: Basic Books, Inc.

Zuboff, S. (1989, January). Smart machines, smart people. *INC.*, pp. 29-36.

Zuboff, S. (1991, Summer). Informate the enterprise. *National Forum*, pp. 3-7.

GLOSSARY

Agency Theory. Examines information and risk-bearing costs between principal and agent. Principal and agent have differing goals and risk preferences. Typically there is information asymmetry between principal and agent.

Artificial Intelligence (AI). The subfield of computer science that is concerned with the employment of human thought processes to computer technology.

Backward Chaining. A search technique employed in production systems that originates with the action clause of a rule and progresses "backward" through a chain of rules in search of a verifiable collection of condition clauses.

Business System Planning (BSP). A comprehensive methodology for company-wide requirements definition and planning of information resources.

Client-Server Networks. Computer networks in which some nodes (servers) are dedicated to performing certain tasks in behalf of the nodes (clients) accessed by the users.

Cognitive Style. The subjective manner through which individuals arrange and modify information during a decision-making task.

Cognitive Theory: Theories about how the human brain works and how humans think and learn.

Computer-aided Software Engineering (CASE). Automated step-by-step procedures for software and system development that uses tools such as graphic facilities, screen and report painters, program code generators, and documentation generators.

Consultation. The interface technique in which the inference engine works from the goal backward using the stored rules to determine the questions it must ask the operator to obtain all of the information needed to recommend a decision.

Conversion Effectiveness. The effectiveness with which IT investment is converted to useful output.

Critical success factors. A selected number of factors that top management consider critical to the success of the company. How well a company performs in these areas determine to what extent it attains its goals.

Cross-Impact Analysis. A quantitative probability modeling methodology. One estimates, for a set of events, the probability that each event will occur within some specified time period. Next, one estimates for each event, the probability that the occurrence of any one of the developments would have on the likelihood of occurrence of each of the others. Thus conditional probabilities, i.e., cross-impact effects, are explored.

Data Model. A conceptual framework to represent and simulate segments of the decision making process.

Decision Support System. A computer-based information system that combines data and models to provide a vehicle for solving semi-structured to unstructured problems.

End User. The individual that uses the computer for performing ones own functional job tasks.

Example. An example is the basic unit of information in an example-based information system. An example is an interrelated set of variables tracked over time in order to bracket and represent, in a holistic manner, a complex phenomenon of interest to the decision maker.

Example Base. An example base is store of past examples used to aid decision making under an example-based information system. The examples store expert knowledge and are marked and grouped according to criteria meaningful to the decision maker.

Example-based Database (E-bDB) . A example-based database is a system for storing, retrieving, updating, organizing and maintaining an example base.

Example-based Decision Making. Example-based (case-based) decision making is characterized by reasoning over complex examples rather than by the triggering of 'if-then' rules.

Example-based Information System (E-bIS). An example-based information system maintains information in the form of examples.

Executive Information System (EIS) An information system that provides strategic information tailored to needs of top management.

Expert decision making. Experts often utilize example-based (case-based) decision making. Because of their great experience, experts do not reason using rules of thumb. Instead they consider the situation as a whole. They are able to comprehend the complexities of the problem directly and usually consult other similar examples from the past as an aid in decision making.

Expert System. An artificial intelligence program whose performance is meant to emulate that of human experts and depends more on the explicit presence of a large set of knowledge than on the possession of ingenious computational procedures.

Expert System Shells. A tool designed to make it easier for end users (or developers) to develop their own expert systems.

Explanation Facility. The segment of an expert system that presents a justification for the systems conclusion and the process followed to reach the systems conclusions.

Feedback. Feedback is a message transmitted back to the source/sender to reinforce the originating communication.

First Order Feedback. Output modified by predetermined limits, i.e., a simple automatic goal-maintenance system. Output is adjusted based on goal oriented behavior.

Functionally Adjacent Expert System. Expert systems which could share knowledge.

Gatekeeper. In a communication network, "special communicators" who possess, or have access to, more information and better quality information than their co-workers. The gatekeeper can be an individual, several persons funcitoning informally, or a formal team.

Heuristics. Informal, judgmental knowledge of a functional area that are generally accepted as good rules for decision making.

Hypermedia. Documents that contain multiple forms of media, including text, graphics, video, and sound, which can be interactively searched like hypertext.

Hypertext. A methodology for the construction and interactive use of text material, in which a body of text in electronic form is indexed in a variety of ways so it can be quickly searched by a user.

Image Processing. A computer-based technology which allows end users to electronically capture, store, process, and retrieve images that may include numeric data, text, handwriting, graphics, documents, and photographs.

Inference Engine. The segment of an expert system that executes the reasoning function.

Information Technology (IT). Computer hardware, software, telecommunications, database management, and other information processing technologies used in information systems. Local-area network (LAN). A network that connects computer systems and devices within a close geographical area such as a building or a premises.

Integrative/Disintegrative Model. The organization utilizes differing modalities to integrate IT; each modality engenders disintegrative consequences.

Interface. A shared boundary. For example, the boundary between a computer and its user.

Interrater Reliability. The level of agreement (or disagreement) among experts.

Isomorphic. Something identical with, or similar to something else in form or stature..

Knowledge Acquisition. The extraction and formulation of knowledge.

Knowledge Dynamics. The frequency with which knowledge must be updated.

Knowledge Intensiveness . The amount of knowledge needed to produce an expert opinion on a specific task.

Knowledge Interconnectivity. The degree of knowledge that must be shared to produce an expert opinion on a specific task.

Knowledge Work. Working with information (abstractions).

Knowledge Workers. People whose primary work activities include creating, using, and distributing information.

Light Pen. A photoelectronic device that allows data to be entered or altered on the face of a video display terminal.

Long-linked Technology. Long-linked technologies represent processes whose input/output relationship is one-to-one, i.e., serial processes. Information technology is used to coordinate and smooth such sequential activity.

Management Information Systems (MIS). Information systems which support the planning, control, and accomplishment of business processes and operations.

Meaning sensitive indexing. Examples in an example based are indexed not by some formal criterion of an attribute, but by a criterion important to the decision maker.

Message. A message is the stimulus transmitted from the sender/source to the receiver.

Morphological Analysis. Morphological analysis aims to discover structural interrelationships among objects or phenomena. In a systematic manner (identification of permutations and combinations) a large set of alternatives can be explored for feasibility.

Mouse: A small device that is electronically connected to a computer and is moved by hand on a flat survace in order to move the cursor on a video screen i the same direction. Buttons on the mouse allow users to issue commands and make responses or selections.

Object. A data element that includes both data and the methods or processes that act on that data.

Object-Oriented Language. A language that develops programs and applications which create and use objects to perform information processing tasks.

Pointing Devices. Devices which allow end users to issue commands, make choices, and enter graphic or alphanumeric data directly into the computer system as an alternative to the use of the keyboard.

Rapid Prototyping . An initial version of an expert system that is developed quickly to evaluate the effectiveness of the knowledge representation and inference mechanism.

Rule. A formal method for expressing knowledge through the use of IF-THEN statements to represent premises and conclusions.

Rule-based decision making. The reasoning of non-experts is characterized by searching a set of rules, identifying the rules relevant to the problem at hand and following those rules to solve the problem.

SAST. Strategic Assumptions Surfacing and Testing. A phased process designed to reveal the underlying assumptions of a policy or plan, as well as a map for exploring them. The process is based on four principles: adversarial, participative, integrative, and managerial mind supporting. The five phases of SAST are: group formation, assumption surfacing and testing, debate, information requirements analysis, final synthesis.

Semistructured Decisions. Decisions made when either the decision criteria or the decision variables are unknown, but not both are unknown.

Socio-technical approach. An approach that interfaces technology with human factors to minimize conflicts between the two and enhance overall productivity.

Spreadsheet. An application program used a computerized tool for analysis, planning, and modeling that allows users to enter and manipulate explicit or virtual data into an electronic worksheet of rows and columns.

Structured Decisions. Decisions made when both the decision criteria and decision variables are known.

Tabular. A systematic arrangement of numerical data in a column and row format.

Text Data. Words, phrases, sentences, and paragraphs used in documents and other forms of communication.

Third Order Feedback. A reflective goal-changing system. A system with memory, able to initiate alternative courses of action in response to changed environmental conditions. In addition, the system can coose the best alterative for a particular set of conditions, coupled with the ability to reflect upon its past decision making.

Trackball. A rollerball set in a case used to move the cursor on a computer's display screen.

Unstructured Decisions. Decisions made based on many unknowns in the areas of decision criteria and the variables upon which the decisions are based.

User Interface. The segment of a computer system that permits communication between the user and the computer system.

Value Chain. A concept introduced by M. Porter to describe the activities which contribute to the total value a firm offers to its customers. The value chain begins with the inputs from the suppliers and continues to the final sale to the customer plus after-sales service.

AUTHOR BIOGRAPHIES

Kim V. Andersen is employed at the University of Copenhagen, Denmark researching various aspects of computerized economic modeling. The research includes evaluation on the technical features of the models, implementation of the models, and which implications modeling might have on decision-making processes. Currently, he is involved in a European network on development of GIS systems. His research also includes general impacts of information technology on puyblic service and work. The author has published a range of articles on these subjects. The author was affiliated with the Public Policy Research Organization at the University of California, Irvine in 1991-1992.

Ronald L. Berry is completing his doctorate in Management Information Systems at Mississippi State University. His current research interests include information technology and corporate strategy, application of group decision support systems to the strategic decision making process, and cross cultural information system issues in multinational corporations.

Enno Ebels received his Masters Degree in Computer Science from the University of Groningen. Within the field of Computer Science he specialized in Management Information Systems. The testing and evaluation of the GOSSIP system described in this paper were subject of his Masters Thesis. Currently he is working as European Director of Information Systems for American Power Conversion Europe in Paris, France.

Nancy Green Hall is an Associate Professor of Decision Sciences at Kennesaw State College in Marietta, Georgia. She holds a Ph.D. in Business Administration with a major in Decision Science from Georgia State University. She received the M.B.A. from Georgia State in International Business. her interests are in decision support systems for strategic planning, fuzzy expert systems, and management information systems.

Tor Guimaraes holds the J.E. Owen Chair of Excellence in IS at Tennessee Technological University. He has a Ph.D. in MIS from the University of Minnesota and an M.B.A. from California State University, Los Angeles. He was a Professor and Chairman of the MIS Department at St. Cloud State University, and before that, an

Assistant Professor and Director of the MIS Certificate Program at Case-Western Reserve University. He has spoken at numerous meetings sponsored by professional organizations including ACM, IEEE, ASM, DPMA, INFOMART, and Sales and Marketing Executives. He has consulted on several IS topics with many leading organizations including TRW, American Greetings, AT&T, IBM and the Department of Defense. He has published over fifty articles in leading journals such as *Information Systems Research, Communications of the ACM, MIS Quarterly, Decision Sciences, OMEGA, Computers and Operations Research, Information and Management,* and *Database.*

Dwight A. Haworth received his B.S. degree from the United States Air Force Academy, CO, in 1963. he received his Ph.D. in Management Information Systems from Texas Tech University in 1990. He retired from the U.S. Air Force in 1981. His research interests are software maintenance and programmer productivity.

Richard M. Kesner currently serves as Chief Information Officer for Babson College, Wellesley, Massachusetts,where he is responsible for all aspects of the College's use of information technologies. He is also President and Senior Consultant for RMK Associates, Inc., a management,strategic planning, and MIS consulting firm.

Prior to forming RMK Associates, Richard Kesner served asthe V.P. of Development and Systems for the ParkmanCompanies, a diversified real estate development andmanagement company. He also spent nearly four years asthe V.P. of General Services and MIS for MultibankFinancial Corporation, a $3 Billion bank headquartered inDedham Massachusetts.

Dr. Kesner holds a M.A. and Ph.D. from StanfordUniversity, and an A.B. and M.B. from Oberlin College. He has also completed post-doctoral training in finance andstrategic planning at the Wharton School, University of Pennsylvania. Dr. Kesner has spoken internationally before professional and business audiences, and has published seven books and numerous articles. He is currently at work on a book about information resource management within public sector institutions.

Karen Ketler holds a Ph.D. from Kent State University in Business Administration with a major in Management Information Systems. She is currently employed as an Assistant Professor of Computer Management at Eastern Illinois University. Previously, she was employed for twelve years in postions ranging from programmer/analyst to director of a data center. her current research interests are outsourcing and reengineering (maintenance) techniques.

Brenda L. Killingsworth is an Assistant Professor of Management Information Systems at East Carolina University. Her graduate degrees were earned from East Carolina University (MBA, 1981) and The University of South Carolina (Ph.D. in MIS, 1987). Her areas of research interests include organizational issues involved in system implementation with specific emphasis in the management of knowledge, process, and strategies. She currently serves as Network Facilitator for the World Class Strategies Network (whose role is to offer a forum for research and practical exchange in management and information practices in North Carolina) at East Carolina University. She has published in such outlets as the *Journal of Computer Information Systems, Journal of Management Science and Policy Analysis, and Human Factors in Information Systems: An Organizational Perspective.*

Mathew J. Klempa is Assistant Professor, Computer Information Systems Department, School of Management, California State University, Dominguez Hills and holds a B.S. in Mathematics/Economics from Allegheny College, M.S., M.B.A., and Ph.D. degrees from the University of Southern California in Business Administration. His doctoral majors were Decision Support Systems and Policy and Strategy. He was formerly a corporate planner for a major bank holding company. His professional affiliations include the Academy of Management, Institute of Management Sciences, Decision Sciences Institute, Information Resources Management Association, and DIGIT - Diffusion Interest Group in Information Technology. His research interests include cognitive and individual differences in DSS use, end-user computing/ applications prototyping, internationalization of the information systems curriculum, and organization impacts of information technology, including the interaction between information technology and organizational dimensions such as structures, control mechanisms, culture, work processes, and performance.

Michael E. McLeod is an Associate Professor of Management Information Systems at East Carolina University. His undergraduate and M.B.A. degrees were earned at Auburn University. His Ph. D. was earned at the University of Georgia in 1975. He holds the CDP certification from the Institute for Certification of Computer Professionals. He has served as an information systems consultant on several projects for governmental and for-profit organizations. He is actively engaged in field studies involving empowerment of information systems professionals. His current research projects include total quality management in information systems and expert systems development and implementation.

Mark Andrew Mitchell is completing his doctorate in Marketing at Mississippi State University. His current research interests include the formation of strategic corporate partnerships and alliances, and product elimination and the organizational decision making process.

Aaron Patula is a MIS doctoral candidate in the Fogelman College of Business and Economics at Memphis State University. His current research interests include case-based reasoning, decision support for commodities trading and MIS in the former Soviet Union.

Leah R. Pietron received her B.S. from Mayville State College, M.S. and Ph.D. from the University of North Dakota, and M.B.A. from Northwest Missouri State University. Her research interest are CASE,end-user computing, multi-media applications, and networking.

P. Mohan Rao is an Associate Professor of Information and Decision Sciences at Salisbury State University in Salisbury, Maryland. He holds a Ph.D. in Business Administration with a major in Management Science from the University of Alabama. He received a Masters degree in Management Sciences from the University of Waterloo, Canada, and the M.Tech. in Chemical Plant Engineering from Regional Engineering College, Wartangal, J.N.T. University. His interests are in management information systems, expert systems, and producitivy management.

Robert Stegwee studied at DePauw University and at the University of Amsterdam, from which he holds a Masters degree in Computer Science, with a specialization in Management Information Systems. Currently he is an assistant professor of MIS with the Faculty of Management and Organization at the University of Groningen, the Netherlands. He holds a doctoral degree in Management and Organization from the same University. His doctoral research has focused on the development of a decision support system for information architecture specification. In conjunction with his work at the University of Groningen he has (had) affiliations with Moret Ernst & Young management consultants in Utrecht, the Institute of Knowledge Systems in Groningen, and Information Management Consultancy in Glimmen, all in the Netherlands.

Edward J. Szewczak is Associate Professor of MIS at Canisius College in Buffalo, NY. he received his Ph.D. from the Graduate School of Business at the University of Pittsburgh. He had previously served on the faculties of Robert Morris college and the

Southern Illinois University at Carbondale. His information systems research has been published in *Data Base, European Journal of Operational Research, Information & Management, Information Resources Management Journal, Journal of Microcomputer Systems Management, Journal of MIS, Omega* and *Simulation & Games* as well as in scholarly books and national and regional conference proceedings. He has also published in the *Journal of Management Studies, Logique et Analyse, Long Range Planning,* and *Organizational Behavior Teaching Review* on subjects ranging from strategic management to philosophical ethics.

Gregory B. Turner is completing his doctorate in Marketing at Mississippi State University. His current research interests include the formation of strategic corporate partnerships and alliances, the utilization of information systems in strategic marketing decisions, and information systems' role in the delivery of superior customer service.

Godwin J. Udo is assistant professor of MIS at Tennessee Technological University. He teaches and researches in the areas of information systems and production management. His research works have been accepted by journals such as *International Journal of Information and Management, International Journal of Management, Journal of Industrial Management, and Production and Inventory Management Journal.* He is a member of IRMA, DSI, TIMS, and APICS.

Jerry A. Van Os is Professor of Accounting and Management Information Systems and Director of the MBA Program at Westminster College of Salt Lake City. Dr. Van Os received his B.S. and M.B.A. degrees from the University of Utah and Ph.D. from Brigham Young University. Professor Van Os is a CPA and CMA and a member of the American Institute of Certified Public Accountants, Institute of Management Accountants, Society of Information Management, and Information Resources Management Association.

Jennifer L. Wagner received a Ph.D. from Northwestern Unviersity. She is currently Associate Professor of Management and Information Systems at Roosevelt University in Chicago. She is also director of Roosevelt's Master of Science in Information Systems program. Her research interests focus on organization issues such as employee turnover and longevity, as well as outsourcing and reengineering.

John Walstrom is a Professor of Computer Management at Eastern Illinois University. He holds the CDP and received his Ph.D. from the University of Nebraska-Lincoln. He has many years teaching experience in the MIS area and served nine years as director of a university computer center. His major interest areas include management of information systems and database management.

Nancy C. Weida earned her Ph.D. in Operations Research from the University of Delaware. She is currently an Assistant Professor in the Department of Management of Bucknell University where she teaches management science, operations management, managerial statistics, and management information systems. Her research interests include the study of student learning using computers, and applications of incomplete information game theory and the economics of information to business decision making. She is an active member of IRMA, IBSCUG, DSI and ORSA/TIMS.

INDEX

A

analytic hierarchy process 24
animation 123
approximate reasoning 164
Arthur Young Planning Method 44
artificial intelligence technologies 263
attitudes analysis 78
automated information systems 252
automating 390

B

Business Systems Planning 6

C

CASE environment 387
CASE tools 402
chief information officer 228
competitive advantage 4, 83, 84, 273
computer graphics 103
conceptual knowledge 141
contingency model 262, 270
cost-benefit analysis 64, 77, 213, 214
cost/benefit method 23
Critical Factors Analysis 34
critical mental models 141
critical success factors 6, 78, 248, 66

D

database design 389
decentralized 214
decentralized approach 218
decision support system 103, 119, 159, 206, 188, 109, 346
decoding 134
desktop 116
desktop publishing 83
dialectic 270
domain viability 212

E

electronic mail 230, 238, 132
electronic networks 236
electronic-conferencing 238
emerging information technologies 31, 81, 316
encoding 134
end-user computing 213, 215, 319
ends-means analysis 34
environmental noise factor 134
environmental preconditions 371
ESTOR 181
Example-based databases 196
Example-based information systems 176
Example-based reasoning 180
Excelerator 392
executive decision making 104
executive information system 103, 119, 136, 137
expert system development projects 214

expert system domain environment 204
expert system strategy 219
expert system technology 204
expert systems 154, 182, 206
expert systems' potential 158

F

feedback 134
fiscal impact budget modeling 367
forecasting techniques 291
fuzzy expert system 159

G

gatekeepers 136, 279
global competition 175
Global information needs 231
Goal programming 66
Goal Programming Analysis 78
GOSSIP 49
Graphic Construction 112
Graphic Integrity 113
graphic user interfaces 103, 123, 186
Groningen On-line Simulation Support for Informati 49
group decision support systems 356, 136

H

Heideggerian concept 183
hierarchical knowledge sharing 271
human/technology interfaces 145
Hyptertext 121

I

Informal Analysis 78
informating 388
information architecture 31, 42, 43
Information model 36
information overload 113
information planning methods 33, 50
information planning process 33, 35
information policy formulation 32
information presentation 106
information resource management 231, 232
information services professional 232
information system 103, 105, 320
iInformation technologies 3, 32, 231
Information Technology (IT) communication 131
information technology acquisition/diffusion 264
institutional decision support system 16
Integrated CASE tools 387
integrated information services 229
integrated logistics management 254
Interactive computer graphics 117
IT absorption management 16
IT absorption problems 10
IT Limitations 138

J

Just in Time Education 248
Just-In-Time (JIT) 251

K

knowledge 211, 213, 177, 141
knowledge engineering 167
knowledge sharing 270
knowledge tools 234
knowledge worker 231, 235

L

labor market, 363
Labor Market Authorities 363
leveraging 273
linguistic variables 166
Live-action video 123
logistics management 251
Long-linked technologies 278

M

Management and Information Decision Support System 120
management information systems 119
managerial decisions 155
mentoring 279
methodology engineering 47
multiattribute analysis 64, 77
multimedia 122, 246
multimedia packages 136
Musical Instrument Device Interface

123

N

National and Regional Planning Act 363
normative analysis 34, 50

O

Object-Attribute-Value 177
object-oriented interface 116
office automation 263
organizational attributes 373
organizational bias 9
outsourcing 331, 340

P

performance variations 160
physical planning 363
Post-Implementation Audit 27
presentation graphics 104
price/performance ratio 337
probability density function 276
Problem Domain Structuredness 194
procedural knowledge 141
process analysis 34, 51
process control techniques 160
productivity evaluation 154, 158, 167
productivity measurement system 161
project management 9
project selection process 8

Q

qualitative analysis 365

R

redesign centers 389
Regional Iterative Model (RIMO) 362
regional labor market authorities 365
regional modeling 361
rule-based thinking 182

S

sharing information 217
signal 134
simulation 65, 77
simulation modeling 279
SIS implementation 86
skill-Knowledge Distinction 176
socio-technical approach 5, 8
software development 386
software Implementation 191
spatial representations 108
STRATASSIST 154, 162
strategic business alliances 250
strategic implications 336
strategic information system 81
strategic planning 163, 179
Strategy Set Transformation 34
subject-object relationship 182
Symbiotic Information Systems 252, 255
symbiotic Marketing 253
Systems development 3, 389
systems effectiveness 76

T

total quality management 318
tradeoff model 321
training support system 189
transactions processing systems 85
transfer policies 376

U

user interface 189
Utilization Analysis 78

V

value analysis 65, 23, 77
vertical dyadic linkages 279
visual programming 125, 126
VP-Expert 166

W

work redesign 387, 403